Component Software

ACM PRESS BOOKS

This book is published as part of ACM Press Books – a collaboration between the Association for Computing (ACM) and Addison Wesley Longman Limited. ACM is the oldest and largest educational and scientific society in the information technology field. Through its high-quality publications and services, ACM is a major force in advancing the skills and knowledge of IT professionals throughout the world. For further information about ACM, contact:

ACM Member Services
1515 Broadway, 17th Floor
New York, NY 10036-5701
Phone: 1-212-626-0500
Fax: 1-212-944-1318
Email: acmhelp@acm.org
URL: http://www.acm.org/

ACM European Service Center
108 Cowley Road
Oxford OX4 1JF
United Kingdom
Phone: +44-1865-382388
Fax: +44-1865-381388
Email: acm_europe@acm.org
URL: http://www.acm.org/

Selected ACM titles

The Object Advantage: Business Process Reengineering with Object Tecnology (2nd edn) *Ivar Jacobson, Maria Ericsson, Agneta Jacobson, Gunnar Magnusson*

Object-Oriented Software Engineering: A Use Case Driven Approach *Ivar Jacobson, Magnus Christerson, Patrik Jonnson, Gunnar Overgaard*

Software for Use: A Practical Guide to the Models and Methods of Usage Centered Design *Larry L. Constantine & Lucy A D Lockwood*

Bringing Design to Software: Expanding Software Development to Include Design *Terry Winograd, John Bennett, Laura de Young, Bradley Hartfield*

CORBA Distributed Objects: Using Orbix *Seán Baker*

Software Requirements and Specifications: A Lexicon of Software Practice, Principles and Prejudices *Michael Jackson*

Business Process Implementation: Building Workflow Systems *Michael Jackson & Graham Twaddle*

Interacting Processes: A Multiparty Approach to Coordinated Distributed Programming *Nissim Francez & Ira Forman*

The OPEN Process Specification *Ian Graham, Brian Henderson-Sellers, Houman Younessi*

Design Patterns for Object-Oriented Software Development *Wolfgang Pree*

Component Software

Beyond Object-Oriented Programming

CLEMENS SZYPERSKI

ACM Press
New York

ADDISON-WESLEY

Harlow, England ■ Reading, Massachusetts ■ Menlo Park, California ■ New York ■ Don Mills, Ontario ■ Amsterdam ■ Bonn ■ Sydney ■ Singapore ■ Tokyo ■ Milan ■ Madrid ■ San Juan ■ Mexico City ■ Seoul ■ Taipei

© Clemens Szyperski 1998

Pearson Education Limited
Edinburgh Gate
Harlow
Essex CM20 2JE
England

and Associated Companies throughout the World.

Cover designed by Designers & Partners, Oxford
Typeset by Prepress Projects, Perth, Scotland
Typeset in Galliard and Franklin Gothic
Printed and bound in the United States of America

First printed 1997. Reprinted 1998 (twice) and 1999

ISBN 0-201-17888-5

British Library Cataloguing-in-Publication Data
A catalogue record for this book is available from the British Library

Contents

Trademark notice

The following are trademarks or registered trademarks of their respective companies:
AppleScript; CyberDog; Hypercard; Macintosh; Mac OS; NeXT; OpenStep; QuickTime and SANE are trademarks of Apple Computer.
Tuxedo is a trademark of BEA Systems.
Delphi and C++ Builder are trademarks of Borland.
DSOM; CBToolkit; CBConnector; ComponentBroker; PowerPC; REXX; SOM and Visual Age are trademarks of IBM.
Newi is a trademark of Integrated Objects.
Orbix; Orbix/Desktop and Orbix/Web are trademarks of IONA.
Lego is a trademark of Lego.
Communicator and Navigator are trademarks of Netscape.
Authenticode; ActiveX; COM; COM+; DCOM; OLE; Excel; Internet Explorer; Microsoft Office; PowerPoint; Visual Basic; Visual C++; Visual J++; Windows NT; Windows 95 and Word are trademarks of Microsoft.
BlackBox; Component Pascal; Denia; Direct-to-COM; Portos and Safer OLE are trademarks of Oberon microsystems.
CORBA; IIOP and OMA are trademarks of the Object Management Group.
x/Open and OSF are trademarks of The Open Group.
R/3 is a trademark of SAP AG.
Java; JavaBeans; RMI and Solaris are trademarks of Sun Microsystems.
Texas Instruments Composer is a trademark of Texas Instruments.
Visibroker is a trademark of Visigenic.

Preface

Software components enable practical reuse of software 'parts' and amortization of investments over multiple applications. There are other units of reuse, such as source code libraries, designs, or architectures. Therefore, to be specific, *software components are binary units of independent production, acquisition, and deployment that interact to form a functioning system.* Insisting on independence and binary form is essential to allow for multiple independent vendors and robust integration.

Building new solutions by combining bought and made components improves quality and supports rapid development, leading to a shorter time to market. At the same time, nimble adaptation to changing requirements can be achieved by investing only in key changes of a component-based solution, rather than undertaking a major release change.

For these reasons, component technology is expected by many to be *the* cornerstone of software in the years to come. There exists at least one strong indicator: the number of articles and trivia published on these matters grows exponentially. Software component technology is one of the most sought-after and at the same time least understood topics in the software field. As early as 1968, Doug McIlroy predicted that mass-produced components would end the so-called software crisis (Naur and Randall, 1969). With component technology just on the verge of success in 1997, this is a 30-year suspense story.

Software components are clearly not just another fad – the use of components is a *law of nature* in any mature engineering discipline. It is sometimes claimed that software is *too flexible* to create components; this is not an argument but an indication of immaturity of the discipline. In the first place, component markets have yet to form and thus many components still need to be custom-made. Introduction of component software principles at such an early stage means preparing for future markets.

Even in a pre-market stage component software offers substantial software engineering benefits. Component software needs *modularity* of requirements, architectures, designs, and implementations. Component software thus encourages the move from the current huge monolithic systems to modular structures that offer the benefits of enhanced adaptability, scalability, and maintainability.

Once a system is modularized into components, there is much less need for major release changes and the resulting 'upgrade treadmill' of entire systems.

Once component markets form, component software promises another advantage: multiplication of investment and innovation. Naturally, this multiplier effect, caused by combining bought and custom-made components, can only take effect when a *critical mass* is reached, that is a viable market has formed. For components to be multipliers, there needs to be a competitive market that continually pushes the envelope, that is it continually improves cost–performance ratios. However, creating and sustaining a market is quite a separate problem from mastering component technology. It is this combination of technical and economic factors that is unique to components.

It is indeed the interplay of technology and market strategies that is finally helping components to reach their long-expected role. However, it would be unfair to say that technically this has been possible since the early days of objects. After all, objects have been around for a long time: Simula's objects, for example, date back to 1969. The second driving force behind the current component revolution is a series of technological breakthroughs. One of the earliest was the developments at Xerox PARC and at NeXT in the late 1980s. The first approach that successfully created a substantial market came in 1992 with Microsoft's Visual Basic and its components (VBXs). In the enterprise arena, OMG's CORBA 2.0 followed in mid-1995. The growing popularity of distribution and Internet led to very recent developments, including Microsoft's DCOM (distributed component object model) and ActiveX, Sun's Java and its JavaBeans, the Java component standard.

There is one *technical* issue that turned out to be a major stumbling block on the way to software component technology. The problem is the widespread misconception of what the competing key technologies have to offer and where exactly they differ. In the heat of the debate, few unbiased comparisons are made. It is a technical issue, because it is all about technology and its alleged potential. However, it is just as much a social or societal issue. In many cases, the problems start with a confusion of fundamental terminology. While distribution, objects, and components really are three *orthogonal* concepts, all combinations of these terms can be found in a confusing variety of usages. For example, distributed objects can be, but do not have to be, based on components – and components can, but do not have to, support objects or distribution.

The early acceptance of new technologies and adoption of 'standards' is often driven by non-technical issues or even 'self-fulfilling prophecies.' Proper standardization is one way to unify approaches and broaden the basis for component technology. However, standards need to be feasible and practical. As a *sanity check*, it is helpful if a standard can closely follow an actual and viable implementation of the component approach. What is needed is a demonstration of the workability of the promised component properties, including a demonstration of reasonable performance and resource demands. Also, there need to be at least a few independently developed components that indeed interoperate as promised.

For a good understanding of component software, the required level of detail combined with the required breadth of coverage can become overwhelming. However, important decisions need to be made – decisions that should rest firmly on a deep understanding of the nature of component software. This book is about component software and how it affects engineering, marketing, and deployment of software. It is about the underlying concepts, the currently materializing technologies, and the first stories of success and failure. Finally, it is about people and their involvement in component technology.

This book aims to present a comprehensive and detailed account of most aspects of component software: information that should help to make well-founded decisions; information that provides a starting point for those who then want to dig deeper. In places, the level of detail intentionally goes beyond most introductory texts. However, tiring feature enumerations of current approaches have been avoided. Where relevant, features of the various approaches are drawn together and directly put into perspective. The overall breadth of the material covered in this book reflects that of the topic area; less would be too little.

Today there are three major forces in the component software arena. The Object Management Group, with its CORBA-based standards, entered from a corporate enterprise perspective. Microsoft, with its COM-based standards, entered from a desktop perspective. Finally, Sun, with its Java-based standards, entered from an Internet perspective. Clearly, enterprise, desktop, and network solutions will have to converge. All three players try to embrace the other players' strongholds by expansion and by offering bridging solutions. As a result, all three players display 'weak spots' that today do not withstand the 'sanity check' of working and viable solutions. This book takes a strategic approach by comparing technical strengths and weaknesses of the approaches, their likely directions, and consequences for decision making.

Significant parts of this book are non-technical in nature. Again, this reflects the very nature of components – components develop their full potential only in a component market. The technical and non-technical issues are deeply intertwined and coverage of both is essential. To guide readers through the wide field of component software, this book follows an outside-in, inside-out approach. As a first step, the component market rationale is developed. Then, component technology is presented as a set of technical concepts. On the basis of this foundation, today's still evolving component approaches are put into perspective. Future directions are explained on the grounds of what is currently emerging. Finally, the market thread is picked up again, rounding off the discussions and pointing out likely future developments.

Who should read this book – and how: roadmaps

As wide as the spectrum of this book are the backgrounds and interests of its expected readers. To support a variety of readers, the book is written with browsing in mind. Most chapters are relatively self-contained and chapters can thus be read in any order, although sequential reading is preferable. Where other material is tightly linked, explicit cross-references are given. For selective 'fast forwards,' various references to later sections aid skipping to natural points of continuation. Forward references are always of advisory nature only and can be safely ignored by the 'sequential reader.'

Professionals responsible for a company's software strategy, for technology evaluation, or for software architectures will find the book in its entirety useful. Reading 'speed' may need to be adjusted according to pre-existing knowledge in the various areas covered in Parts Two and Three. The numerous discussions of relative advantages and disadvantages of methods and approaches are likely to be most useful.

Managers will find sufficiently general coverage to enable the formation of a solid intuition; they may want to skim over some of the more detailed technical material. In the end, decisions need to be based on many more factors than just the aspects of a particular technology. To this end, the book also helps to put component technology into perspective. A suggested path through this book is: Part One; Chapters 4, 8, and 11 of Part Two; Chapters 12 and 17 of Part Three; Part V.

Developers will appreciate the same intuition-building foundation, but will also find enough detail on which to base technical decisions. In addition, developers facing multiple platforms or multiple component approaches will find the many attempts at concept unification useful. Fair technical comparison of similarities and differences is essential to develop a good understanding of the various trade-offs involved; terminology wars are not. A suggested path through this book is: Parts Two, Three, and Four, supported by Parts One and Five if market orientation is required.

Academics and students of advanced courses will find the book a useful and rich source of material. However, although this book could serve as reference reading in various units, it is not a textbook. Units focusing on component technology would benefit the most, including coverage of specific component technologies such as Java or ActiveX. Units on software engineering will also benefit. Finally, units on advanced or comparative programming languages may expand to language issues in component technology. A suggested path through this book depends on the needs of the particular subject. Part Two, and in particular Chapter 4, forms a basis; Chapters 5, 6, and 7 can be included for more intensive courses or post-graduate studies. The remaining chapters of Part Two can be included selectively. Part Three offers a rich selection of detailed information on current technology. Part Four explores current developments. Parts One and Five may be of interest for courses with an organizational or market perspective.

Statement and timestamp

I completed this book in the first half of 1997. In a rapidly emerging and changing field, a certain part of the material is likely to be out of date soon. I tried to avoid too deep coverage of the obviously volatile and instead aimed at clear accounts of the underlying concepts and approaches. For concreteness, I nevertheless included many technical details. I am a co-founder of Oberon microsystems, Inc., Zurich (founded in 1993), one of the first companies to focus fully on component software. In addition to carefully introducing and comparing the main players, I frequently drew on Oberon microsystems' products for leading-edge examples and comparison. These include the programming language Component Pascal, the BlackBox component framework and builder, and the component-oriented real-time operating system Portos with its development system Denia. The choice of these examples clearly reflects my involvement in their development, as well as my active use of several of these tools in university courses. Despite this personal bias I aimed at a fair positioning of all covered approaches.

This book in its present form would not have been possible without the help of many who were willing to read early drafts and supported me with their scrutiny and richness of comments and ideas. In particular, I would like to thank Cuno Pfister, who reviewed the entire draft, some parts in several revisions, and provided numerous comments and suggestions. Daniel Duffy, Erich Gamma, Robert Griesemer, Stephan Murer, Tobias Murer, Wolfgang Pree, and Paul Roe also commented on the entire draft. Dominik Gruntz, Wolfgang Weck, and Alan Wills provided deep and important comments on selected chapters. Marc Brandis, Bert Fitié, John Gough, and Martin Odersky provided further important comments. Remaining mistakes and oversights are of course mine.

Clemens Szyperski
Brisbane, June 1997

About the author

Clemens Szyperski is presently Associate Professor in the Faculty of Information Technology at Queensland University of Technology (QUT), Brisbane, Australia. He joined the Faculty in 1994 and received tenure in 1997. Since 1995, he has been director of the Programming Languages and Systems research group at QUT.

From 1992 to 1993 he held a Postdoctoral Fellowship from the International Computer Science Institute (ICSI) at the University of California at Berkeley. At ICSI he worked in the groups of Professor Jerome Feldman (Sather language) and Professor Domenico Ferrari (Tenet communication suite with guaranteed Quality of Service).

In 1992, Clemens received his PhD in Computer Science from the Swiss Federal Institute of Technology (ETH), Zurich, Switzerland, where he designed and implemented the extensible operating system Ethos under supervision of Professor Niklaus Wirth and Professor Hanspeter Mössenböck. In 1987, he received a degree in Electrical Engineering/Computer Engineering from the Aachen University of Technology (RWTH), Germany. Since joining ETH in 1987 his work has been heavily influenced by the work of Professor Wirth and Professor Jürg Gutknecht on the Oberon language and system.

In 1993, he co-founded Oberon microsystems, Inc., of which he is Director of Research. Oberon microsystems developed BlackBox Component Builder, first marketed in 1994 and one of the first development environments and component frameworks designed specifically for component-oriented programming projects. In 1997, Oberon microsystems released the new component-oriented programming language Component Pascal. He was a key contributor to both BlackBox and Component Pascal.

He has published numerous papers and articles and frequently presents his work at national and international conferences and workshops.

Motivation: components and markets

Part One covers the motivations and fundamental non-technical underpinnings of component software technology in a market context. Chapter 1 explains what is meant by the terms 'software component' and 'component software.' The important benefits of component software are outlined and the peculiar nature of software is explored to compare component software with component approaches in other engineering disciplines. Finally, some early component success stories are analyzed briefly. Chapter 2 links component technology to markets and presents a series of forecasts as to how component technology is expected to develop over the coming years. Chapter 3 covers the notion of standards, which is all-important for any component approach.

CHAPTER ONE

Introduction

This chapter defines the term software component and summarizes the key arguments in favor ofe/omponent software. Components are well established in all other engineering disciplines, but until recently were unsuccessful in the world of software. The reasons behind this failure can be linked to the particular nature of software. The chapter concludes with a discussion of the nature of software, its consequences for component software, and lessons learned from successful and unsuccessful approaches.

1.1 Components are for composition

One thing can be stated with certainty: components are for composition. *Nomen est omen*. Composition enables prefabricated 'things' to be reused by rearranging them in ever new composites. Beyond this trivial observation, much is unclear. Are most current software abstractions not designed for composition as well? What about reusable parts of designs or architectures? Is *reuse* not the driving factor behind most of these compositional abstractions?

Reuse is a very broad term covering the general concept of a *reusable asset*. Such assets can be arbitrary *descriptions* capturing the results of a design effort. Descriptions themselves normally depend on other, more detailed and more specialized descriptions. To become a reusable asset, it is not enough to start with a monolithic design of a complete solution and then partition it into fragments. The likely benefits of doing so are minimal. Instead, descriptions have to be carefully generalized to allow for reuse in sufficiently many different contexts. Overgeneralization has to be avoided to keep the descriptions nimble and lightweight enough for actual reuse to remain practicable. Descriptions in this sense are sometimes called components (Sametinger, 1997).

This book is *not* about reuse in general, but about the reuse of software components. To be specific, software components are binary units of independent production, acquisition, and deployment that interact to form a functioning system. Composite systems composed of software components are called *component software*. The requirement for independence and binary form rules out many software abstractions, such as type declarations, C macros, C++ templates, or Smalltalk blocks. Other abstractions, such as procedures, classes, modules, or even entire applications, could form components, as long as they are in a 'binary' form that remains composable. Indeed, procedural libraries are the oldest example of software components. Insisting on independence and binary form is essential to allow for multiple independent vendors, for independent development, and for robust integration. These issues are therefore covered in great detail in this book.

What is the motive for producing, distributing, buying, or using software components? What are the benefits of component software? The simplest answer is: components are the way to go because all other engineering disciplines introduced components as they became mature – and still use them. Shortly after the term software crisis was coined, the solution to the often cited crisis was also envisioned: software integrated circuits (ICs) (McIlroy, 1968; Cox, 1990)! Since then, for 30 years, people have wondered why this intuitive idea never truly came to fruition.

1.2   Components: custom-made versus standard software

In the following discussions it is assumed that component software technology is available. The question addressed in this section is: what are the benefits of using components?

Traditional software development can broadly be divided into two camps. At the one extreme, a project is developed entirely from scratch, with the help of only programming tools and libraries. At the other extreme, everything is 'outsourced,' in other words standard software is bought and parametrized to provide a solution that is 'close enough' to what is needed. Full custom-made software has a significant advantage (when it works): it can be optimally adapted to the user's business model and can take advantage of any in-house proprietary knowledge or practices. Hence, custom-made software can be *the* competitive edge in the information age – if it works.

Custom-made software also has severe disadvantages, even if it does work. Production from scratch is a very expensive undertaking. Suboptimal solutions in all but the local areas of expertise are likely. Maintenance and 'chasing' of the state-of-the-art, such as incorporating Web access, can become a major burden. Interoperability requirements further the burden: with other in-house systems and, more critically, also with business partners and customers. As a result, most large projects fail partially or completely, leading to a substantial risk. Also, in a world of rapidly changing business requirements, custom-made software is often too late: too late to be productive before becoming obsolete.

With all these guaranteed disadvantages in mind, which are offset by only *potential* advantages, the major trend toward 'outsourcing' in the industry is understandable. Production of custom-made software is outsourced under fixed-price contracts to limit the financial risk. To cover the time-to-market risk, there is a strong trend toward using standard software: software that is only slightly adjusted to actual needs. The burden of maintenance, product evolution, and interoperability is left to the vendor of the standard package. What remains is to carry over parametrization and configuration detail when moving to the next release – still a substantial effort, but unavoidable in a world of change.

What then is wrong with standard software? Several things. First, standard software may necessitate a greater or lesser reorganization of the business processes affected. Although business process re-engineering can be a very worthwhile undertaking, it should be done for its own sake rather than to make the best of suboptimally fitting standard software. Secondly, standard software is a standard: competitors have it as well and no competitive edge can possibly be achieved by using it (except by using it extraordinarily well). In any case, this is acceptable only when tight regulations eliminate competitive advantages. Thirdly, as standard software is not under local control, it is not nimble enough to adapt quickly to changing needs.

Here is an example of standard software forcing its footprint onto a large and well-established organization. In 1996, Australia Post decided to use SAP's R/3 integrated solution. With R/3, Australia Post can keep track of each individual transaction, down to the sale of a single stamp. Australia Post is a large organization with a federated structure; each Australian state has its own head office reporting to the central head office.

Traditionally, state head offices reported on the basis of summaries and accounts 'in-the-large.' For example, detailed sales figures for each branch office were not passed on beyond the state head office. R/3, however, supports only a monotonic hierarchy of access authorizations. It is not possible to grant the national head office access to the accounts in-the-large without also granting access to every individual transaction. This was disturbing news for state head offices: their traditional relative autonomy in making local decisions was undermined. Indeed, the strictly hierarchical business model enforced by R/3 clashed with the concept of a federated organization that delegates much responsibility and authority to its members, in this case the state posts. SAP's comment, when asked whether this aspect of R/3 could be changed, was 'Our systems implement best practice – why would you want to deviate from that?' It is too early to predict the consequences in this case, but the key point is that a standard solution may force drastic changes in the culture and operation of an organization.

With only two poles available, custom-made software loses out to a great extent. Standard packages create a level playing field and competition has to come from other areas. Increasingly, for example, software services are seen as something that is necessary simply to survive. Clearly, this is far from ideal when information and information processing have a great effect on most businesses and even define many of the newer ones.

The concept of component software represents a middle path that could solve this problem. Although each bought component is a standardized product, with all the advantages that brings, the process of component assembly allows the opportunity for significant customization. It is likely that components of different quality (level of performance, resource efficiency, robustness, etc.) will be available at different prices. It is thus possible to set individual priorities when assembling based on a fixed budget. In addition, some individual components can be custom-made to suit specific requirements or to foster strategic advantages. Figure 1.1 illustrates some of the trade-offs brought about by the spectrum of possibilities opened up by component software.

The figure is in no way quantitative, and the actual shape of the two curves is somewhat arbitrary. Intuitively, however, it is clear that non-linear effects will be observed when approaching the extremes. For example, at the left end of the scale, when everything is custom-made, flexibility has no inherent limits but cost efficiency plummets.

Component software also puts an end to the age-old problem of massive upgrade cycles. Traditional fully integrated solutions required periodic upgrading, usually a painful process of migrating old databases, ensuring upwards compatibility, retraining staff, buying more powerful hardware, and so on. In a component-based solution, evolution replaces revolution, and individual upgrading of components as needed and 'out of phase' can allow for much smoother operations. Obviously, this requires a different way of managing services, but the potential gains are immense.

1.3   Inevitability of components

Developing excellent component technology does not suffice to establish a market. The discipline is full of examples of technically superior products that failed to capture sufficiently large markets. Besides technical superiority, a component approach needs *critical mass* to take off. A component approach gains critical mass if the offered components are of sufficient variety and quality, if there is an obvious benefit of using the components, and if the offering is backed by sufficiently strong sources or sufficiently many second sources. Once critical mass is reached in a market segment, use of components in that segment quickly becomes inevitable. A 'vortex' forms that pulls in traditional solutions in the area.

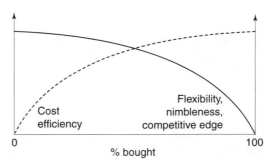

Figure 1.1   Spectrum between make-all and buy-all.

Not using available components requires reinvention of solutions. This can only be justified when the made solution is greatly superior to the buyable alternatives. Also, in a competitive market, components will improve in quality much faster than 'hand-crafted' solutions. The result is the above-mentioned vortex: it becomes increasingly difficult to escape from using components.

As long as all solutions to problems are created from scratch, growth can be at most linear. As components act as multipliers in a market, growth can become exponential. In other words, a product that utilizes components benefits from the combined productivity and innovation of all component vendors. The component vendors are focused, supply many different customers, and are thus able to perfect their components rapidly. Therefore, even where an organization manages to sustain its proprietary technology, its relative market share will quickly dwindle in a market rapidly dominated by component technology. Avoiding the proximity of a component vortex promises calm waters but also eliminates the impulse that can be gained from the mighty pull of the vortex.

Preparedness for an emerging component market can be the deciding success factor for a company approaching such a vortex. Insistence on proprietary approaches can be catastrophic. Part of being prepared is the adoption of software engineering approaches that are component friendly, that is they support modularity of requirements, architectures, designs, and implementations. Preparing for components thus leads to substantial advantages as a result of a better software engineering process, even if component markets are still seen as beyond the 'planning horizon.'

Out of preparedness a more proactive role can be developed. The first organization to create a convincing set of components for a certain market segment can set standards and shape the then emerging market to its own advantage. Instead of waiting for others or claiming that it is unlikely that in a particular domain a component market will ever form, stronger organizations may want to take the lead. An interesting example is the recent move by Sun to make its Solaris operating system 'modular' (Wirthman, 1997). Instead of offering a collection of specialized operating systems, Sun aims to produce modules that can be combined according to needs. This is a first step. If, in a next step, Sun releases important module interfaces, then this may well create a component market.

1.4   The nature of software and deployable entities

Software components were initially considered to be analogous to hardware components in general and to integrated circuits in particular. Thus, the term *software IC* became fashionable. Other related notions followed, such as *software bus* and *software backplane* (Figure 1.2).

Also popular is the analogy between software components and components of stereo equipment. More far fetched are analogies with the fields of mechanical and civil engineering: with gears, nuts, and bolts. However, comparisons did not stop at engineering disciplines and continued on into areas as extreme as the world

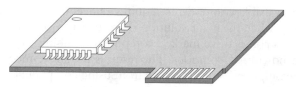

Figure 1.2   The software IC connected to a software bus.

of toys. The *Lego block* model of object technology was conceived but has also been strongly criticized. These analogies helped to sell the idea of software components by referring to other disciplines and areas in which component technology has been in use for some time and had begun to fulfill its promises.

All the analogies tend to give the impression that the whole world, with the one exception of software technology, is already component oriented! Thus, it ought to be possible – if not straightforward – to follow the analogies and introduce components to software as well. This did not happen for most of the industry, and for good reason. None of the analogies aids understanding of the true nature of software.

Software is different from products in all other engineering disciplines. Rather than delivering a final product, delivery of software means delivering the blueprints for products. Computers can be seen as fully automatic factories that accept such blueprints and instantiate them. Special measures must be taken to prevent repeated instantiation – the normal case is that a computer can instantiate delivered software as often as required. The term software IC and the associated analogy thus fails to capture one of the most distinctive aspects of software as a *metaproduct*. It is important to remember that it is these metaproducts that are actually deployed when acquiring software. The same holds true for software components.

It is as important to distinguish between software and its instances as it is to distinguish between blueprints and products, between plans and a building, or between beings and their genes (between phenotypes and genotypes). Whereas such lines are clearly drawn in other engineering disciplines, software seems 'soft' enough to tolerate a confusion of these matters.

There has been confusion about abstractions and instances since entity–relationship modeling (this was pointed out to the author by Alan Wills). To reintroduce a distinction that should have been in place from the beginning, phrases such as 'entity occurrence' and 'entity definition' are used. This confusion is even encouraged in the world of object technology. The corresponding distinction between class and object is frequently omitted, although there is occasional clarification of something as an 'object instance' or an 'object class.' The established practice of not distinguishing between objects and classes leads the way; as a result, the large number of nebulous publications on objects is not astonishing. To take an arbitrary example, consider the following astounding quotation (Cheung, 1996, p. 72):

'The port class has 1024 virtual-circuit classes.'

The article refers to an object model diagram as defined by the object modeling technique (OMT) (Rumbaugh *et al.*, 1991). A small excerpt of the diagram is shown in Figure 1.3.

What the author meant was: 'The port *object* has 1024 virtual-circuit *objects*.' There is nothing wrong with the cited article. The most likely explanation is that this 'glitch' was the result of an attempt by the editor to introduce sharpness of terms and *not* call everything an object. This sort of mistake is easy to make – OMT *object* model diagrams describe the static relations of *classes*, but when annotations refer to numbers of partners in a relation class instances (objects) are meant.

The confusion between objects and classes is closely related to the nature of software. For example, both the plan of a building and the building itself can be modeled as objects. At the same time, the plan is the 'class' of the building. There is nothing wrong with this, as long as the two kinds of objects are kept apart. In the world of logics, but also in database theory, this is called *stratification*, that is introduction and maintenance of strata or levels of organization. Construction (and breach) of such layers has to be based on deep understanding. Some might argue that this lighthearted way of dealing with object-oriented (OO) terminology had to be expected. After all, 'object' is one of the most indefinite and imprecise terms that people could possibly use to name a concept. It seems fairly objective to say that.

To understand why it is so important to differentiate between plans and instances, it is useful to take a brief look at some of the ramifications of delivering plans rather than instances. Plans can be parametrized, can be applied recursively, can be scaled, and can be instantiated any number of times. None of this is possible with actual instances. As, with software, it is the plans that are delivered, instances can be of different shapes by using different parametrizations of the plan. In other words, software is a generic metaproduct that can be used to create entire families of instances.

If analogies to components in other engineering disciplines break down, what about mathematics? Although defended by some, the purely mathematical approach fails exactly where the engineering analogies help – and vice versa. Mathematics and logic draw their strength from the isolation of aspects, their orthogonal treatment, and their static capturing. These are excellent tools to understand the

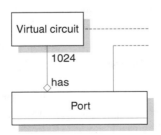

Figure 1.3 OMT object model with quantified 'has' relation.

software concepts of uniformity of resources, arbitrary copying, recursive nesting, parametrization, or configuration. However, mathematical modeling fails to capture the engineering and market aspects of component technology: the need to combine all facets, functional and non-functional, into one interacting whole, forming a viable product.

In conclusion, software technology is an engineering discipline in its own right and with its own principles and laws. Analogies with other engineering disciplines help us to understand certain requirements, such as those of proper interaction with markets and consideration of complex feature interactions. At the same time, these analogies break down quickly when going into technical detail. Deriving software component architectures by analogy with approaches in other disciplines is downright dangerous. The distinguishing properties of software are of a mathematical rather than a physical nature. However, placing emphasis solely on the mathematical underpinning is never enough to carry any engineering discipline. In particular, from a purely formal point of view, there is nothing that could be done with components that could not be done without them. The differences are concepts such as reuse, time to market, quality, and viability. All of these are of non-mathematical nature – and value. Mathematics is not goal driven, whereas engineering is: the goal is to create products.

1.5   Components are units of deployment

A software component is what is actually deployed – as an isolatable part of a system – in a component-based approach. Contrary to frequent claims, objects are almost never sold, bought, or deployed. The unit of deployment is something rather more static, such as a class or, more likely, a set or framework of classes. Objects that logically form parts of component 'instances' are instantiated as needed, based on the classes that have been deployed with a component. Although a component can be a single class, it is more likely to be a collection of classes, sometimes called a *module*. Components as a whole are thus not normally instantiated. Also, a component could just as well use some totally different implementation technology, such as pure functions or assembly language, and look not at all object oriented from the inside.

'Object orientation has failed but component software is succeeding.'
(Udell, 1994)

If classes are so similar to components, why did object technology not succeed in establishing significant component markets? The answers are manifold. First, the definition of objects is purely technical – briefly, encapsulation of state and behavior, polymorphism, and inheritance. The definition does not include notions of independence or late composition. Although such conditions can be added (Chapter 4, section 4.1), their lack has led to the current situation in which object technology is mostly used to construct monolithic applications.

Secondly, object technology tends largely to ignore the aspects of economies and markets and their technical consequences. Early proponents of object orientation predicted object markets, places that would offer catalogs full of objects or, more likely, classes, class libraries, and frameworks (Cox, 1990). The opposite has in fact occurred (Nierstrasz, 1991). Today we have only a small number of such sources. Most of them are driven by vendors that provide such semifinished software products to sell something else. Microsoft's Foundation Classes (MFC) is a good example. MFC primarily serves as a vehicle to simplify and unify programming for Microsoft's operating systems, component model, and application environments. There is no doubt that the vision of object markets did not happen. On the contrary, most of the few component success stories are not based on object-oriented approaches, although some are object based. (The relatively successful class libraries and frameworks are not software components in the strict sense used here.)

To some extent the misprediction of object markets is understandable. For a technologist, markets are too easily considered marginal, as something left for others to worry about once the technological problems have been solved. However, components are as much about the potential of technology as they are about technology. The additional investment required to produce components rather than fully specialized solutions can only be justified if the return on investment follows.

Typically, a component has to have sufficiently many uses and therefore clients for it to be viable. This is the central idea behind the notion of reuse. For clients to use a component instead of a specialized solution, the component needs to have substantial advantages. One advantage could be technological superiority, but other advantages are more likely to help: first solution of a known open problem, broad support base, brand name, and so on. Obviously, for larger organizations, 'markets' could be found in-house – interestingly, most large organizations are now organized into cost centres and selling to internal clients is not much simpler than to external clients.

1.6   Lessons learned

Where are the mentioned component success stories? The most popular is probably Microsoft's Visual Basic. However, the oldest are all modern operating systems. Applications are coarse-grained components executing in the environment provided by an operating system. Interoperability between such components is as old as the sharing of file systems and common file formats, or the use of pipe and filter composition. Other older component examples are relational database engines and transaction-processing monitors. More recent successes, using finer grained components, are plug-in architectures. These have been in widespread use since the introduction of Netscape's Navigator Web browsers. One of the first successful plug-in architectures was Apple's QuickTime. Plug-ins under the name of extensions have also been cultivated in the Mac OS, where they originated from 'inits,' patches to the system software in ROM that are loaded at boot time. DOS terminate-and-stay-resident applications (TSRs) are of comparable nature. What do all the above examples have in common? In all cases there is an infrastructure providing rich foundational functionality for the addressed domain. Components can be purchased from independent providers and can be deployed by clients. The components provide services that are substantial enough to make duplication of their development too difficult or not cost-effective. Multiple components from different sources can coexist in the same installation. None of the named systems really shines when it comes to arbitrary combinations of components. In all cases, such combinations can lead to misbehavior. Apparently, for a working component market, it is sufficient that composability is highly likely rather than absolutely guaranteed.

Besides all this, there is another aspect that is often overlooked: in all the successful examples, components exist on a level of abstraction where they directly mean something to the deploying client. With Visual Basic, this is obvious: a control has a direct visual representation, has displayable and editable properties, and has meaning that is closely attached to its appearance. With plug-ins, the client gains some explicable high-level feature and the plug-in itself is a user-installed and configured component.

Most objects have no meaning to clients that are not programmers. Class libraries and frameworks are typical developer tools and require highly trained and qualified programmers for their proper use. It is appropriate that *component construction* is left to persons of such standing. However, for components to be successful, composition and integration, that is *component assembly*, must not generally be confined to such a relatively small elite group. Today, there are many more authors of scripts than there are programmers. These customers are more interested in products that are obviously useful, easy to use, and can be safely mixed and matched – they are not in the least interested whether the products are object oriented.

Objects are rarely shaped to allow for mix-and-match composition by a third party, also known as 'plug and play.' Configuring and integrating an individual object into some given system is not normally possible; thus, objects cannot be sold independently . The larger units which are sold, frameworks, are even worse. Frameworks have traditionally been designed almost to exclude composition. Combining traditional object-oriented frameworks is difficult, to say the least.

Taligent's CommonPoint, the best-known approach aimed at the construction of many interoperating frameworks, failed to deliver on its promises (although other projects at Taligent did lead to the successful development of new technology). Above all, the approach was *overdesigned*, aiming for maximum flexibility everywhere: even the simplest things turned out to be complex. Individual developers were responsible for relatively small parts of the system and thus naturally aimed for *the* solution. The result was an extremely large system. [According to a 1995 Ovum report (Ring and Carnelly, 1995), CommonPoint provides over 100 frameworks covering about 2000 public classes, an equal number of non-public classes and 53 000 methods. For comparison, the Microsoft Windows API supports roughly 1500 calls.]

Dependencies in such a large system need to be managed carefully. However, the CommonPoint frameworks exposed far too many details and were only weakly layered. In other words, the overall architecture was underdeveloped. For the same reasons, other large industry projects have struggled before, including the major redevelopment effort at Mentor Graphics (Lakos, 1996). An interesting contributor to these fiascos was the chosen implementation language, C++.

C++ does not directly support a component concept, and management of dependencies thus becomes difficult. A fundamental mistake made at Taligent when designing CommonPoint was to assume that the C++ object model would be an appropriate component model, whereas in reality it is too fragile. Blackbox reuse, as introduced in later parts of the book, was neglected in preference for deep and entangled multiple inheritance hierarchies. Finally, overdesign and the C++ template facilities led to massive code bloat.

For components to be independently deployable, their granularity and mutual dependencies have to be carefully controlled from the outset. For large systems, it becomes clear that components are a major step forward from objects (classes). This is not to say that objects are not the right thing. On the contrary, object technology, if harnessed carefully, is probably one of the best ways to realize component technology. In particular, the modeling advantages of object technology are certainly of value when constructing a component. On the flip side, modeling of component-based systems is still a largely unresolved problem.

CHAPTER TWO

Market versus technology

Components are reusable assets. Compared with specific solutions to specific problems, components need to be carefully generalized to enable reuse in a variety of contexts. Solving a general problem rather than a specific one takes more work. In addition, because of the variety of deployment contexts, the creation of proper documentation, test suites, tutorials, online help texts, and so on is more demanding for components than for a specialized solution. This is especially so when components are to be sold as separate products.

Components are thus viable only if the investment in their creation is returned as a result of their deployment. If components are developed for in-house use, such a return on investment can be indirect via benefits of using components rather than monolithic solutions. Such benefits are typically a reduction in the time to market and increased manageability, maintainability, configurability, flexibility, and so on.

Of course, return on investment can also be sought by selling components. The direct sale of components to deploying customers is one way, but it is not the only one. Another way is the coupling of components and services: while the components may be cheap or free, their effective use may require significant expertise that is offered as a service. Yet another way drops components as a direct income source entirely, and instead leverages the vendor–customer relations built into a component market as a target for highly specific advertising. As with all mature markets, software component industries will eventually converge on a mixed income model.

Part Four, in particular Chapter 26, covers the aspects of component markets in much more detail. For now it is sufficient to say that software components, as all components in all areas, need to be understood in a market embedding. Components will exist only where component vendors and component clients join forces in sufficient numbers to reach a 'critical mass.' Of course, there are also substantial technical problems that need to be addressed and overcome, and Parts Two, Three, and Four cover these. However, the following simple observation may help to put things into perspective:

**Imperfect technology in a working market is sustainable;
perfect technology without any market will vanish.**

For the existence of software components, software component technology
needs to meet with proper software component markets. The market cannot exist
without, possibly primitive, technology; the technology cannot be sustained or
evolved without a sufficiently strong market. To address a common concern again:
for larger organizations or organizations with many similar products, 'markets'
could be found in-house. However, as stated before, most such organizations are
now organized into cost centers, and selling to internal clients is not much simpler than selling to external clients. Obviously, to escape from the vicious circle of
component technology and component markets, a techno-economic 'bootstrap'
is required.

Consider a simple example. (This and the following example follow a sugges-
tion by Alan Wills.) An engineering company, Souped-Up Software Inc., works
on a contract basis for many clients in a confined field, say tuning software for
engine control. Its clients have varied requirements, and traditionally each project
started from scratch. Then the company realized that most of its jobs had a lot in
common, and so it decided to extract and generalize a set of generic components.
This effort sat firmly on the experience obtained with the concrete specific projects
that it had run before. Thus, the new component set was slim and apt for its
purposes – the efficiency of the company increased substantially, quickly amortizing the initial investment in component development. In the meantime, the company opened a subsidiary selling the components to other engineering companies
in the same business but serving different regions.

Consider another example. The story of the above company's success reached
a start-up company, Daft Solutions Ltd. Its engineers knew everything about
componentware and decided to start by designing the ultimate component collection before even approaching a single first client. As first projects came in,
most of the generic facilities of the component set and even some of the components were not used at all. Also, the solutions it eventually delivered required
excessive amounts of processing power and resources. It turned out to be a fatal
mistake to generalize before solving some specific problems.

The two flip sides of the component market 'coin', markets versus technology,
are covered in more detail in the following sections.

2.1	**Creating a market**

How can markets be created? A full answer to this question is far beyond the
scope of this book. Clearly, markets thrive where supply and demand are in balance. A new product can only create a market if its arrival is already awaited;
otherwise, the cost of creating demand can be prohibitive.

An elegant way to *avoid* creating markets is to expand established markets carefully. This approach takes two steps. First, in a competitive environment, it is

necessary to improve offerings to retain the existing customer base and thus the existing market. Instead of aiming for revolutionary new products and therefore new markets, a succession of evolutionary refinements is used to 'migrate' the existing customer base to better technology. In the second step, this initial customer base helps to support the effort of attracting new customers for the improved product, that is it helps to expand the market. Microsoft's strategy from Visual Basic to the Internet is a good example. In a first step, Visual Basic controls (VBXs) were generalized to OLE controls (OCXs) – expanding the market from Visual Basic to all of OLE. In a second step, OLE controls were reshaped into ActiveX controls, which also work with Internet applications, expanding the market from the OLE-dominated desktop to the Internet.

Economy of scale and distribution are important aspects in the creation of component markets. Profit margins on inexpensive products are easily eroded by fixed costs, such as production, marketing, and distribution. As manufacturers of components can concentrate on their core competency, production of components should be cheaper than production of complete solutions. Regarding distribution costs, some components may not be able to command individually the prices that would make them viable. Bundling with related components can help. Streamlining the distribution process can also help – it is not clear why software has to come in shrink-wrapped boxes. For example, there are an increasing number of 'software kiosks' or 'component warehouses' that sell components across the Internet. Besides reducing the cost of distribution, the Internet may also become an affordable marketing platform.

Proper business models for software component industries are still in their infancy. Further discussion follows in Part Five, Chapter 28.

2.2   Fundamental properties of component technology

Establishing component markets rests on technological feasibility. Although many of the required key technologies are finally available, a solid overall understanding of component software is still lacking. There are a number of deep technical issues that need to be addressed before mission-critical systems can responsibly be built on component technology.

There is a single key aspect of component technology that causes most technical problems. Components come from independent sources and are integrated by third parties. In the absence of countermeasures, a component system is only as strong as its weakest component. Fault isolation is thus an essential theme, as is safety of individual components.

In traditional software engineering processes, module development and testing is followed by systems integration and testing. This approach leaves room for errors that are merely a result of composition and which are not apparent at the level of individual components, but which should be detected during systems integration and testing. With third-party integration, the situation becomes more difficult, as integration testing of modules from different sources needs to be addressed.

Part of the potential of software components – and a reason why the IC analogy fails – is the possibility of *late integration*. Java applets are an example of the extreme kind: not before a Web page is requested by a browser will the applet code be integrated into the requesting browser. When late integration is used, integration testing is no longer feasible. For most integration tests a negative result would come too late in the process: the components have already been acquired and deployed. Version checks are among the few tests that are useful and essential at the stage of late integration. A load-time complaint about incompatible versions of locally available components is a reasonable diagnosis.

Even if late sanity checks are performed, they can at most come to the rescue of the user, but cannot directly help to improve the quality of the components involved. A component vendor faces a combinatorial explosion of possible system configurations against which to test a component. In an open market of independent component developers, the set of possible combinations is not even known to any one of the involved parties. Furthermore, as components can be integrated as they become available, the number of combinations continues to grow even after deployment of a system.

Instead of full integration testing, testing against a few possible configurations is the best that can be done. More fundamentally, components need to be built in ways that allow for *modular checking*, that is the analysis of component properties based only on the component and the interfaces it builds on. Therefore, component vendors need to strengthen the per-component process. In many cases, this requires conservative engineering (defensive programming). The notion of component safety is important: even if a component fails to function, it must not violate system-wide rules. Safety is the foremost reason to discriminate among otherwise equal methods of component construction. One of the critical decisions to be made is the proper choice of programming languages and tools. If important safety properties are guaranteed by a language and its implementation, proof obligations can be taken off developers and costly safeguarding runtime measures can be eliminated (Chapter 6). Software development processes that do not depend on testing, such as Cleanroom (Dyer, 1992), naturally gain importance.

Once safety properties are in place, functionality and performance have to follow. Broad classes of safety requirements can be covered by the choice of methodology and tools. There is no such magic bullet to achieve functionality, and the effects of independent composition on overall functionality are not fully understood. Conservatism again seems to be the only advisable strategy. For example, OMG recommends mixing and matching its various object services, claiming orthogonality and interoperability. Although these services were designed with this goal in mind, recent studies show that actual mixing is not easy, and in some situations even impossible (Wallace and Wallnau, 1996).

Even where functionality and safety are firmly in place, performance remains a formidable problem. Performance of a component system is affected in non-trivial ways by the actual composition. Performance is primarily addressing the question: is it fast enough? However, problems of economical resource utilization are closely related, including demands for primary and secondary storage or network bandwidth.

2.3   Market forecasts

Market forecasts are about as reliable as weather forecasts – the reliability quickly decreases over the projected time. The situation does not get better merely because the majority of forecasters agree. However, if what is predicted is possible and the right people agree, then the prophecy may well fulfill itself. The following are a number of excerpts from forecasts made by some of the leading augurs between 1994 and 1996.

2.3.1   Gartner Group (1994–95)

The Gartner Group is interesting in that it quickly changed its mind over the course of a few months, as far as its success predictions for component technology were concerned. In its August 1994 report *Components Are Not Top of the Class*, it criticized components, meaning Microsoft COM-based ones, for not being full objects. In January 1995 (*A Plague on Objects*), it claimed that no component revolution will happen, because 'no single body or consortium would be strong enough to forge semantic contracts across a wide universe of discourse.' In February 1995, it predicted that components originally introduced for desktop applications would spread into other parts of organizations, as systems become more and more networked. In March 1995 (*Object Orientation for the Rest of Us*), it finally predicted the emergence of three new markets: components, component assembly tools, and custom applications developed using components.

2.3.2   Strategic Focus (January 1995)

The January 1995 Strategic Focus report indicates that, as early as January 1995, already one fourth (23.9%) of developers were using component technology. This is not as surprising as it may sound; technologies such as Visual Basic opened up the component market quite early. The report predicted an almost linear increase in the percentage of developers using component technology, reaching a coverage of 61.5% by the end of 1996. While no follow-up study was available to verify the accuracy of this prediction, it meshes well with the Forrester finding (see below) that by the end of 1996 38% of major corporations had already decided on company-wide component technology strategies and a further 28% were close to doing so.

2.3.3 Ovum (1995)

The 1995 Ovum report on distributed objects (King and Carnelly, 1995) predicted a substantial growth of the component software market. It presented a breakdown of the growth sectors into object request brokers (ORBs), component assembly tools ('builders'), component-based business applications, and component frameworks. Figure 2.1 summarizes the Ovum predictions of the individual growth of these market segments. The market for ORBs is not expected to reach substantial volume, as ORBs will become part of every platform, such as operating systems or Web browsers. Besides the expected success of business applications that use component technology, Ovum predicts substantial markets for component frameworks and component assembly tools.

2.3.4 IDC (May 1996)

The May 1996 IDC White Paper *Component Technology* (Steel, 1996) explains why software components are succeeding where objects so far have failed: objects are too fine-grained and their deployment requires too much understanding of an object's working. The report observes that the main component thrust developed out of Visual Basic custom controls and later ActiveX controls. It states that early 1996 Visual Basic was already used by three million programmers worldwide.

The report describes why it became impossible to escape from component approaches, once they took off. It is largely claimed that the cause of the rapid evolution of these technologies is what is called 'mass market innovation' (MMI):

> 'When simple technology is exposed to hundreds of thousands of technically-aware users around the world, the level of innovation is bound to be several orders of magnitude greater than that created in a single company's development shop.'

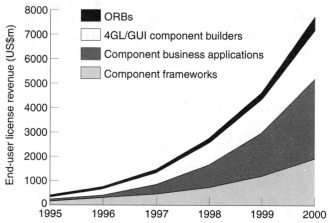

Figure 2.1 Annual global revenues based on end-user licenses in various component technology sectors.

However, turning MMI into profit-bearing products is a different matter. The report states that the dominating current component technology is that around Microsoft's standards. The substantial component offerings from Microsoft itself combine forces with MMI-produced share or freeware and offerings from independent software vendors. A problem with MMI is quality control.

In the report, IDC distinguishes five component types: first, 'middleware components,' including ORBs, transaction-processing monitors, and database management systems, take care of the wiring; secondly, 'logic components,' for example image-processing services, perform a specific non-visual service; thirdly, 'vertical components,' like mini-applications, serve a specific domain; fourthly, 'GUI components' enrich the toolset of user interface builders; and, fifthly, 'container components' provide visual embeddings and environments for visual components (controls).

2.3.5 Forrester Research (October 1996)

In its software strategy report *Objects on the Net* (DePalma *et al.*, 1996), Forrester analyzes the current directions of object technology, based on interviews with 50 of the Fortune 1000 companies in the United States and with several of the leading manufacturers of operating and database systems. These companies want to use object technology, but see substantial problems, including the need to retrain their staff. Many of these companies view component technology as the opportunity in this dilemma between old and new software technologies. Using the words of the report, there is a push from 'elitist objects' to 'populist components.'

The report claims that, by the end of 1996, 24% of the companies decided to base their component solutions on Microsoft's COM/OLE, 14% wanted to use OMG's CORBA, 28% were about to make a decision, and 36% were in the middle of the decision process.

Furthermore, the report predicts that by 1998 the various component models will stabilize and that components will then find their way from the desktop to the back-end, where component-based solutions will replace older architectures. Also, it predicts that by 1999 the current gaps between competing component worlds will have closed.

CHAPTER THREE

Standards

For component markets to develop, component standards must be in place. Standards are useful to agree on common models, enabling interoperation in principle. Standards can also be used to agree on concrete interface specifications, enabling effective composition. Finally, standards can be used to agree on overall architectures to assign components their place in a larger picture of composition and interoperation.

The following sections present a more detailed discussion of the need for standards, on the possible coexistence of multiple standards, and on the danger of overemphasizing universal 'wiring' or 'plumbing' standards. The chapter then concludes with a brief overview of current technical approaches to software components and some of the more general open problems.

3.1 The utmost importance of (quasi) standards

For a component to find any reasonable number of clients, it needs to have requirements that can be expected to be widely supported. It also needs to provide services that can be expected to be widely needed. How wide? The answer depends on the domain addressed by a component. A component needs to hold a significant portion of a market specific to its domain. If that market is truly large, a small portion of it may be enough for economic viability. If the market is only small, then even a total monopoly may not be enough to justify the investment. The size of a market depends on both the number of potential clients and the price that a client is willing to pay.

If a component viably addresses a market segment covering a small number of clients, the component vendor may exactly understand the individual client's needs and deployment environments. The vendor then makes sure that the component will function as required in these environments. Obviously, the extreme case is the development of components for just one purpose and for just one client. This extreme is normally called not component construction, but modular construction of fully client-specific solutions.

As the number of potential uses and potential clients grows, the chances that any component could possibly address all needs while being deployable in all environments decrease rapidly. The unavoidable middle ground that both clients and vendors need to seek is based on environment standards. It is totally irrelevant whether such a standard has been approved by a regular standardization body. The most successful standards have all been created where and when needed by those parties who needed them. Such so-called industry standards are not second class. On the contrary, it is a strange and ill-advised idea that standards are created by a committee, only to find out later whether they address the right problem.

Often the 'standard' is just the approach taken by the 'innovator,' the first successful vendor in a new market segment. With any workable standard in place, the growing number of clients is usually quickly paralleled by a growing number of vendors. The initially proprietary approach turns into an industry standard. Increasing pressure from customer groups further reduces the proprietary nature of the new standard by pushing for release of control to a neutral standards organization. The resulting competition raises the quality of the components, lowers prices, and attracts further clients. Until superseded by far superior approaches, that is new standards, the created market will continue to thrive.

A standard should specify *just* as much about the 'interfacing' of certain components as is needed to allow sufficiently many clients and vendors to work together. To draw from an analogy: the standards for parts such as screws specify not only a raster of diameters, lengths, etc., but also acceptable deviations, so-called tolerances. The cost of making a part increases dramatically with decreasing tolerances. The equivalent in the software world would be a standard specifying levels of detail that lead to 'friction' when combining different software parts.

For software components, the need for standards was recognized a long time ago. One approach is to build working markets first, followed by the formulation and publication of standards. In the software component world, Microsoft (COM, OLE, ActiveX, COM+) is the most prominent player following this approach. Another player is Sun Microsystems (Java, Java Beans). Another approach is to build standards first and then to build the markets. The prime player in this arena is a huge industry consortium: the Object Management Group (OMG). The various OMG standards are organized in the object management architecture (OMA). The most prominent part is the common object request broker architecture (CORBA). Other parts are the various standards for object services and facilities.

Where markets are created first, working products need to come before established standards. The result can be a technological suboptimality. Products using ad hoc solutions may be sold before a full understanding of all ramifications is reached. To upgrade to better solutions without losing the established base of customers, products need to be evolved carefully. Almost all successful standards, independent of the discipline area, emerged this way.

Where standards are created first, technologically optimal solutions can be prescribed *if* such optimality can be reached with the current level of understanding.

Whether such standards have possible *and viable* implementations is open until demonstrated by a conforming realization.

3.2 Wiring standards are not enough

The problems to be addressed by standards are enormous. In particular, the vast number of domain- and application-specific aspects threatens to interfere with the standard and the standardization process. It is tempting to concentrate on levels that are free from the semantic problems of such higher level areas. Good candidates are standards at the 'plumbing' or 'wiring' level. It is obvious that components need to be connected with each other to be useful. It is also obvious that such connections need to follow standards to make it at all likely that any two components have compatible 'connectors.'

Connection standards solve an important problem. At first, it would seem that it is necessary to agree on a single connection standard. At second glance, however, a look at the world as it is reveals that this may not be the case. Almost all countries in the world have their own standard for power outlets, voltage levels, frequencies, etc. Clearly, a common standard is desirable, but it does not seem essential as long as the remaining market per standard is large enough and bridging technology is available when needed.

On the drawing board, it would be trivial to design such common connection standards. What is more: it would be trivial to design compatible connectors to join totally incompatible services. Consider a system that used the same outlets and plugs for water and gas, or for power and telephone lines.

Clearly, wiring compatibility is an important area. Getting it right can have enormous economic benefits. However, if everything works except for the actual wiring, then people usually find a way around this problem – and call it an adapter.

Where an approach that starts with standards and proceeds on to products is adopted, it is natural that the first standards to arrive deal with the 'wiring' level. If nothing real exists that could be built upon, it is difficult to engage in domain- or application-specific standardization efforts. Thus, OMG released CORBA first: the common object request broker architecture. CORBA is a wiring standard that enables communication among objects that are programmed in different languages and supported by different operating systems. Initially, CORBA solved the connection problem only per CORBA implementation, quite similar to the above example of country-specific power outlets. This defect was fixed with CORBA 2.0.

In contrast, Microsoft first had OLE (then OLE 1) and Visual Basic, two directly marketable and successful high-level technologies. Only later did Microsoft introduce COM, generic OLE (initially OLE 2), ActiveX, Visual Basic for Applications, and other technologies to broaden and generalize its options. Only then did they start to release some of these as 'standards' to encourage other vendors to follow suit. These standards are now maintained by the Microsoft-dominated but non-profit organization Active Group, a part of the Open Group.

Current component standards have not risen much above the level of spreadsheets, word processors, graphing and presentation packages, and various interactive controls. The standardization of compound document applications and builders extends above simple 'wiring,' but is still not domain specific. Domain specifics are added by 'scripting' components, which is really programming rather than mere 'plug-and-play' composition (see Chapter 10). However, all current software component camps need to strengthen up on domain-specific standards. Some of the most capital-intensive markets are of the kind in which a smaller number of clients operate in a field of high specialization. Banking, medical services, factory automation, corporate management, and entertainment industries are some examples.

3.3   Too many competing standards are not useful

Who will win the standardization race in component technology? Interestingly, there is no need for a single winner. As long as market shares remain large enough, multiple standards can coexist and compete. Even in highly mature engineering disciplines, it is more the rule than the exception that there are a number of alternative standards for a given situation.

Thus, well-meaning attempts to get it right the first time, by standardizing an area that has yet to be populated by products, may be less than ideal. Nevertheless, it can be successful and lead to superior products that then gain large market shares. However, there are only few examples along these lines. Whether in the area of programming languages (for example Algol, Ada), operating systems (for example OSF/1), communication protocols (for example ISO OSI), or elsewhere: constructed rather than derived standards rarely took off.

An interesting exception to this rule is the IEEE floating point standard. This standard was forged out of thin air to overcome the useless variety and incompatibility across vendors found at the time. Several other contenders for standardization existed, all of which were backed by strong commercial players. However, that was exactly the problem. None of the vendors was willing to buy into a standard that had been defined (and already implemented!) by the competition.

All this would have led to a persisting number of incompatible standards. After all, we still live with ASCII and EBCDIC encodings of character sets. We still live with big and little endian encodings of integers. In all these cases, the conversion between the different representations is a nuisance and a technical inefficiency, but it is possible. In the case of floating point representations, the situation is different: in many cases, it is actually impossible to convert values from one floating-point format to another without loss of precision. Thus, the pressure for uniform international standardization had reached critical limits.

Today, all but a few supercomputers follow the IEEE floating point standard. For the purposes of data exchange, the level of agreement satisfies most demands. Apple Computer was probably the first company to take this standard very seriously. The Standard Apple Numerical Environment (SANE) implements the standard to painstaking detail – and has been available since the times of the Apple II machine!

3.4   Where is software component technology today?

Most standardization efforts in the component arena are either at the 'wiring' level or at the intra-component level. Examples of wiring standards have been mentioned above. Intra-component standards aim at the innards of a component, rather than at the aspects of component interoperation. Intra-component standards are the focus of traditional software engineering efforts. This is because traditional software engineering fully concentrates on the production of monolithic systems, with few provisions for interoperability.

Examples of intra-component standards are those concerned with programming languages or class and template libraries. Other examples are processes aimed at the production of monolithic software, such as the waterfall life cycle model, the concept of integration testing, and the idea of complete requirements. The obvious question has to be: if all these established and proven things do not help with component-oriented programming, that is programming beyond monoliths, what else would? The answer is less obvious and in many cases still subject to ongoing research. For some answers – and more problems, see Part Four.

It seems clear that domain-specific components will become the most profitable of all and that substantial markets will be created. However, domain-specific standards today raise the most questions. Should the standards come before the products and markets, or vice versa? There are already a few products in the direction of business objects (Sims, 1994). Also, there are standards-first attempts by the OMG's special interest groups, although not too much has resulted from these efforts so far. Neither the products nor the sketches of standards have reached a level of maturity or impact that would allow any predictions today. Some more detail can be found in Chapter 18, including an attempt to explain why these efforts have been of limited success so far.

3.5   What's next?

With a slowly developing maturity of software components comes a slow liberation from overtraditional objects. Nevertheless, much can be learned from object technology, and some of it can be generalized or transformed to serve components.

Particularly urgent matters revolve around architectural concepts in a component world. It is far too simplistic to assume that components are simply selected from catalogs, thrown together, and magic happens. In reality, the disciplined interplay of components is one of the hardest problems of software engineering today. Questions arise such as 'how can the abstract interaction of components be described?'; 'how can variety and flexibility be covered?'; 'how can critical system-wide properties be guaranteed in the presence of arbitrary third-party components?'; or 'how can performance be guaranteed?'

A particularly powerful approach is beginning to take shape – that of *component frameworks*. A related approach is part of the object technology repertoire: class or application frameworks (Deutsch, 1989; Lewis, 1995). Beyond the similar names, almost identical visions, and superficially similar construction principles, component frameworks are very different from class frameworks. Essentially, a component framework is a set of interfaces and rules of interaction that govern how components 'plugged into' the framework may interact. Typical component frameworks also provide an implementation that partially enforces these rules of interaction. The implementation of the component framework and those of the participating components remain separate.

Approaches to important component engineering problems are covered in Part Two. Component frameworks are briefly covered in Chapter 8, and discussed in detail in section 9.1.5. Part Four covers new approaches and case studies of first 'componentware,' including component architectures, programming, and assembly. Case studies of some early component frameworks are presented in Chapter 21.

Foundation

The first part opened the scene and provided a broad initial perspective. It is now time to consider sharper technical detail and concepts This part may prove to be difficult reading. As outlined in the preface, some readers may wish to read only some chapters of this part.

Chapter 4 picks up the vague definition of components from Chapter 1 and refines it to a more solid definition. Chapter 5 introduces the particular semantics problems that occur in interacting state-based systems. This is important, as all mainstream component software approaches introduce state. Together with Chapter 6, on polymorphism, the presented material helps to understand the role of object technology in the context of component software. Chapter 7 contrasts object and class composition, a distinction essential to the understanding of many of the current approaches to component software. Much space is granted to the discussion of various approaches of 'disciplined inheritance,' an issue of utmost relevance when using orthodox object technology to construct component software. Chapter 8 presents a list of criteria that can be used to partition a system design into components. Chapter 9 briefly explains the important concepts of reuse in software, including object-oriented patterns and frameworks, but also system architectures. Some understanding of these concepts helps to relate claims about component software to understood and established techniques. Chapter 10 explores the wide spectrum of programming tasks in component systems, ranging from simple scripting to distributed computing. Finally, Chapter 11 draws together a number of other definitions or remarks on component software as found in the literature.

CHAPTER FOUR

What a component is and is not

The terms 'component' and 'object' are often used interchangeably. In addition, constructions such as 'component object' are used. Objects are said to be instances of classes or clones of prototype objects. Objects and components are both making their services available through *interfaces*, and interfaces are of certain *types* or *categories*. As if that was not enough, object and component interactions are described using object and component *patterns* and prescribed using object and component *frameworks*. Both components and frameworks are said to be *whitebox* or *blackbox*, and some have even identified shades of *gray* and *glassboxes*. Language designers add further irritation by also talking about *namespaces*, *modules*, *packages*, and so on.

This plethora of terms and concepts needs to be either reduced by eliminating redundancies or unfolded, explained, and justified. The next section considers this universe of terms and concepts and provides brief explanations, relating the concepts to each other. The goal is to establish some degree of order and intuition as a basis for further discussions. Then, a refined definition of the term 'component' is presented and discussed. Finally, the linkages to standards for horizontal and vertical markets are summarized.

4.1   Terms and concepts

Some degree of familiarity with most of the terms covered in this section is assumed – and so is some degree of confusion about where one term ends and another starts. One way to capture the intuitive meaning of a term is to enumerate characteristic properties. The idea is as follows: something is an A if it has properties a1, a2, and a3. For example, according to Wegner's (1987) famous definition, a language is called object oriented if it supports objects, classes, and inheritance.

Unfortunately, the concepts relevant to component technology encompass many aspects. The massive overloading of the term object in recent years is the best example. Over time, the notions of module, class, and component have all become embraced by the term 'object.' Combining several terms into one can simplify things superficially, but not to good advantage beyond the simplest thoughts. As precision and richness of the vocabulary decrease, so does the richness of expressible and distinguishable thoughts. It is essential to strive for a balance, preserving conciseness and intuition. The following subsections thus present definitions of some key terms and relate them to each other.

4.1.1 Components

The characteristic properties of components are:

- ■ A component is a unit of independent deployment.
- ■ A component is a unit of third-party composition.
- ■ A component has no persistent state.

These properties have several implications. For a component to be independently deployable, the component needs to be well separated from its environment and from other components. A component therefore encapsulates its constituent features. Also, as it is a unit of deployment, a component will never be deployed partially. In this context, a third party is one that cannot be expected to have access to the construction details of all the components involved.

For a component to be composable with other components by such a third party, it needs to be sufficiently self-contained. Also, it needs to come with clear specifications of what it requires and provides. In other words, a component needs to encapsulate its implementation and interact with its environment through well-defined interfaces.

Finally, for a component not to have any persistent state, it is required that the component cannot be distinguished from copies of its own. Possible exceptions to this rule are attributes not contributing to the component's functionality, such as serial numbers used for accounting. Not having state, a component can be loaded into and activated in a particular system, but it makes little sense to have multiple copies. In other words, in any given process, there will be at most one copy of a particular component. Hence, although it is useful to ask whether or not a particular component is available, it is not meaningful to talk about the number of available copies of that component.

In many current approaches, components are heavyweight units with exactly one instance in a system. For example, a database server could be a component. If there is only one database maintained by this class of server, then it is easy to confuse the instance with the concept. For example, the database server together with the database might be seen as a module with global state. According to the above definition, this 'instance' of the database concept is not a component. Instead, the static database server program is, and it supports a single instance: the database 'object.' This separation of the immutable 'plan' from the mutable 'instances' is essential to avoid massive maintenance problems. If components were allowed to have mutable state, then no two installations of the 'same' component would have the same properties.

4.1.2 **Objects**

The notions of instantiation, identity, and encapsulation lead to the notion of objects. In contrast to the properties characterizing components, the characteristic properties of objects are:

- An object is a unit of instantiation; it has a unique identity.
- An object has state; this state can be a persistent state.
- An object encapsulates its state and behavior.

Again, a number of object properties directly follow. Because an object is a unit of instantiation, objects cannot be partially instantiated. Since an object has individual state, it also has a unique identity that suffices to identify the object despite state changes for its entire lifetime. Consider the apocryphal story about George Washington's axe, which had five new handles and four new axeheads – but was still George Washington's axe. This is a good example of a real-life object of which nothing but its abstract identity remained stable over time.

As objects get instantiated, there needs to be a construction plan that describes the state space, initial state, and behavior of a new object. Also, that plan needs to exist before the object can come into existence. Such a plan may be explicitly available and is then called a *class*. Alternatively, it may be implicitly available in the form of an object that already exists, that is sufficiently close to the object to be created, and that can be cloned. Such a pre-existing object is called a *prototype object* (Lieberman, 1986; Ungar and Smith, 1987; Blaschek, 1994).

Whether using classes or prototype objects, the newly instantiated object needs to be set to an initial state. The initial state needs to be a valid state of the constructed object, but it may also depend on parameters specified by the client asking for the new object. The code required to control object creation and initialization can be a static procedure, usually called a *constructor*. Alternatively, it can be an object of its own, usually called an *object factory*, or factory for short.

4.1.3 **Components and objects**

Obviously, a component is likely to come to life through objects and therefore would normally consist of one or more classes or immutable prototype objects. In addition, it might contain a set of immutable objects that capture default initial state and other component resources.

However, there is no need for a component to contain classes only, or even to contain classes at all. Instead, a component could contain traditional procedures and even have global (static) variables; or it may in its entirety be realized using a functional programming approach; or using assembly language, or any other approach. Objects created in a component, more precisely: references to such objects, can leave the component and become visible to the component's clients, usually other components. If only objects become visible to clients, there is no way to tell whether or not a component is 'all object oriented' inside.

A component may contain multiple classes, but a class is necessarily confined to be part of a single component. Partial deployment of a class would not normally make sense. Of course, just as classes can depend on other classes using inheritance, components can depend on other components: an *import* relation.

The superclasses of a class do not necessarily need to reside in the same component as the class itself. Where a class has a superclass in another component, the inheritance relation between these two classes crosses component boundaries. Whether or not inheritance across components is a 'good thing' is the focus of a heated debate between different schools of thought. The deeper theoretical reasoning behind this clash is interesting and close to the essence of component orientation. Further detail and arguments follow in Chapter 7.

4.1.4 Modules

From the discussions so far, it should be clear that components are rather close to modules, as introduced by modular languages in the early 1980s. The most popular modular languages are Modula-2 and Ada. In Ada, modules are called packages, but the concepts are almost identical. An important hallmark of truly modular approaches is the support of *separate compilation*, including the ability to type-check across module boundaries properly.

With the introduction of the language Eiffel, it was claimed that a class is a better module (Meyer, 1988). This seemed to be justified based on the early ideas that modules would each implement one abstract data type (ADT). After all, a class can be seen as implementing an ADT, with the additional properties of inheritance and polymorphism. However, modules can be used, and always have been used, to package multiple entities, such as ADTs, or indeed classes, into one unit. Also, modules do not have a concept of instantiation, whereas classes do. (In module-less languages, this leads to the construction of 'static' classes that essentially serve as simple modules.)

In recent language designs, such as Oberon, Modula-3, Component Pascal, and Java, the notions of modules (or packages) and classes are kept separate. In all cases a module can contain multiple classes. Where classes inherit from each other, they can do so across module boundaries. As an aside, it should be mentioned that in Smalltalk systems it was traditionally acceptable to *modify* existing classes to build an application. Attempts have been made to define 'module' systems for Smalltalk that capture components that cut through classes, for example Fresco (Wills, 1991). Composition of such modules from independent sources is not normally possible though, and this approach is therefore not further followed in this book.

Unlike classes, modules can indeed be seen as minimal components. Even modules that do not contain any classes can function as components. A good example is traditional maths libraries that can be packaged into modules and that are of functional rather than object-oriented nature. Nevertheless, one aspect of full-fledged components is not normally supported by module concepts. There are no persistent immutable resources that come with a module, beyond what has been hardwired as constants in the code. Resources parametrize a component. Replacing these resources allows the component to be configured without the need to rebuild it. For example, resource configuration can be used for localization. Note that configuration of resources is a very weak form of assigning mutable state to a component. As components are not supposed to modify their own resources, this distinction remains useful: resources fall into the same category as the compiled code that forms part of a component.

Modularity is not a new concept, and indeed is a prerequisite for component technology. Unfortunately, the vast majority of software solutions today are not even modular. For example, it is common practice for huge enterprise solutions to operate on a single data model, allowing any part of the system to depend on any part of the data model. Adopting component technology requires adoption of principles of independence and controlled explicit dependencies. Component technology unavoidably leads to modular solutions. The software engineering benefits can be sufficient to justify initial investment into component technology, even when component markets are not foreseen in the mid-term.

4.1.5 Whitebox versus blackbox abstractions and reuse

Blackbox and whitebox abstraction refer to the visibility of an implementation 'behind' its interface. In an ideal blackbox abstraction, no details beyond the interface and its specification are known to clients. In a whitebox abstraction, the interface may still enforce encapsulation and limit what clients can do, although implementation inheritance allows for substantial interference. However, the implementation of a whitebox is fully available and can thus be studied to enhance the understanding of what the abstraction does. (Some authors further distinguish between whiteboxes and glassboxes, with a whitebox allowing for manipulation of the implementation, whereas a glassbox merely allows study of the implementation.)

Grayboxes are those that reveal a controlled part of their implementation. This is a dubious notion, as a partially revealed implementation could be seen as part of the specification. A complete implementation would merely have to ensure that, as far as observable by clients, the complete implementation performs as the abstract partial one. This is the standard notion of *refinement* of a specification into an implementation. Indeed, statement specificatons can be seen as graybox specifications (Büchi and Weck, 1997).

Blackbox reuse refers to the concept of reusing implementations without relying on anything but their interfaces and specifications. For example, application programming interfaces (APIs) in most systems reveal nothing about the underlying implementation. Building on such an API is equivalent to blackbox reuse of the implementation of that API.

In contrast, *whitebox reuse* refers to using a software fragment, through its interfaces, while relying on the understanding gained from studying the actual implementation. Most class libraries and frameworks are delivered in source form, and application developers study the classes' implementation to understand what a subclass can or has to do.

The serious problems of whitebox reuse are analyzed in detail in Chapter 7. For now it suffices to say that whitebox reuse renders it unlikely that the reused software can be replaced by a new release. Such a replacement will probably break some of the reusing clients, as these depend on implementation details that may have changed in the new release.

A definition: software component

From the above characterization, the following definition can be formed:

> 'A software component is a unit of composition with contractually specified interfaces and explicit context dependencies only. A software component can be deployed independently and is subject to composition by third parties.'

This definition was first formulated at the 1996 European Conference on Object-Oriented Programming (ECOOP) as one outcome of the Workshop on Component-Oriented Programming (Szyperski and Pfister, 1997). The definition covers the characteristic properties of components discussed before. It has a technical part, with aspects such as independence, contractual interfaces, and composition. It also has a market-related part, with aspects such as third parties and deployment. It is a property unique to components, not only in the software world, to combine technical and market aspects. (An interpretation of this definition from a purely technical point of view is presented in Chapter 20.)

4.1.6 Interfaces

Part One has already introduced the basic market aspects of component technology. Chapters 5–7 cover the aspects of interfaces, contracts, semantics, and composition in detail. For the following, more market-oriented, discussion, it suffices to consider the interface of a component to define the component's access points. These points allow clients of a component, usually components themselves, to access the services provided by the component. Normally, a component will have multiple interfaces corresponding to different access points. Each access point may provide a different service, catering for different client needs. Emphasizing the contractual nature of the interface specifications is important: as the component and its clients are developed in mutual ignorance, it is the contract that forms a common ground for successful interaction.

What are the non-technical aspects that contractual interfaces have to obey to be successful?

First, as already mentioned in Part One, the economy of scale has to be kept in mind. A component can have multiple interfaces, each representing a service that the component offers. Some of the offered services may be less popular than others, but if none is popular and the particular combination of offered services is not popular either, the component has no market. In such a case, the overheads involved in casting the particular solutions into a component form may not be justified.

Notice, however, that individual adaptations of component systems may well lead to the development of components that themselves have no market. In this situation, extensions to the component system should build on what the system provides, and the easiest way of achieving this may well be the development of the extension in component form. In this case, the economic argument applies *indirectly:* although the extending component itself is not viable, the resulting combination with the extended component system is.

Secondly, undue fragmentation of the market has to be avoided, as it threatens the viability of components. Redundant introductions of similar interfaces have thus to be minimized. In a market economy, such a minimization is usually the result of either early standardization efforts among the main players in a market segment or fierce eliminating competition. In the former case, the danger is suboptimality due to 'committee design;' in the latter case, it is suboptimality due to the non-technical nature of market forces.

Thirdly, to maximize the reach of an interface specification, and of components implementing this interface, there need to be common media to publicize and advertise interfaces and components. If nothing else, this requires a small number of widely accepted unique naming schemes. Just as ISBN (International Standard Book Number) is a worldwide and unique naming scheme to identify any published book, a similar scheme is needed to refer abstractly to interfaces 'by name.' Just as with an ISBN, a component identifier is not required to carry any meaning. An ISBN consists of a country code, a publisher code, a publisher-assigned serial number, and a checking digit. Although it reveals the book's publisher, it does not code the book's contents. Meaning may be hinted at by the book title, but book titles are not guaranteed to be unique.

4.1.7 Explicit context dependencies

Besides the specification of provided interfaces, the above definition of components also requires components to specify their needs. In other words, the definition requires specification of what the deployment environment will need to provide, such that the components can function. These needs are called context dependencies, referring to the context of composition and deployment. If there were only one software component world, it would suffice to enumerate *required interfaces* of other components to specify all context dependencies (Olafsson and Bryan, 1997). For example, a mail merge component would specify that it needs a file system interface. Note that, with today's components, even this list of required interfaces is not normally available. The emphasis is usually just on provided interfaces.

In reality, there are several *component worlds* that partially coexist, partially compete, and partially conflict with each other. For example, today there are three major component worlds emerging, based on OMG's CORBA, Sun's Java, and Microsoft's COM. In addition, component worlds are themselves fragmented by the various computing and networking platforms that they support. This is not likely to change soon.

Just as the markets have so far tolerated a surprising multitude of operating systems, there will be room for multiple component worlds. In a situation in which multiple component worlds share markets, a component's specification of context dependencies must include its required interfaces *and* the component world (or worlds) that it has been prepared for. There will, of course, also be secondary markets for cross-component-world integration. By analogy, consider the thriving market for power plug adapters for portable electrical devices. Thus, chasms are mitigated by efforts to provide bridging solutions, such as OMG's *Interworking* standard (part of CORBA 2.0, July 1996 revision), which forms a bridge between Microsoft's COM and CORBA. Nevertheless, such bridging will always compromise where the bridged worlds are too different for the gap to be closed fully. When having a single universal standard offers overwhelming benefits, a 'shake-out' effect is likely to eliminate the number of competing standards, as happened with VCR standards.

4.1.8 Component 'weight'

Obviously, a component is most useful if it offers the 'right' set of interfaces and has no restricting context dependencies at all, in other words if it can perform in all component worlds and requires no interface beyond those whose availability is guaranteed by the different component worlds. However, only very few components, if any, would be able to perform under such weak environmental guarantees. Technically, a component could come with all required software bundled in, but that would clearly defeat the purpose of using components in the first place. Note that part of the environmental requirements is the *machine* that the component can execute on. In the case of a virtual machine, such as the Java VM, this is a straightforward part of the component world specification. On native code platforms, a mechanism such as Apple's 'Fat Binaries,' which packs multiple binaries into one file, would still allow a component to run 'everywhere.'

Instead of constructing a self-sufficient component with everything built in, a component designer may have opted for 'maximum reuse.' To avoid redundant implementations of secondary services within the component, the designer decided to 'outsource' everything but the prime functionality that the component offers itself. Object-oriented design has a tendency toward this end of the spectrum, and many object-oriented methodists advocate this maximization of reuse.

Although maximizing reuse has many oft-cited advantages, it has one substantial disadvantage: the explosion of context dependencies. If designs of components were, after release, frozen for all time, and if all deployment environments were the same, this would not pose a problem. However, as components evolve, and different environments provide different configurations and version mixes, it becomes a show stopper to have a large number of context dependencies. With each added context dependency it becomes less likely that a component will find clients that can satisfy the environmental requirements. To summarize:

Maximizing reuse minimizes use.

In practice, component designers have to strive for a balance. When faced with requirements that specify the interfaces that a component should at least provide, a component designer has a choice. Increasing the context dependencies usually leads to leaner components by means of reuse, but also to smaller markets. Additionally, higher vulnerability in the case of environmental evolution must be expected, such as changes introduced by new versions. Increasing the degree of self-containedness reduces context dependencies, increases the market, and makes the component more robust over time, but also leads to 'fatter' components. Figure 4.1 illustrates the optimization problem resulting from trading leanness against robustness.

The effective costs of making a component leaner, compared with making it more robust, need to be estimated to turn the qualitative diagram of Figure 4.1 into a quantitative optimization problem. There is no universal rule here. The actual costs depend on factors of the component-producing organization and of the target markets of the component. The markets determine the typical deployment environment and the client expectations, including component 'weight' and expected lifetime.

Note that it is not just coincidence that Figure 4.1 below and Figure 1.1 (p. 6) are so similar. The discussion in this section focused on the 'outsourcing' of parts of a component. In contrast, the discussion in Chapter 1 concentrated on the outsourcing of parts of a system, that is the outsourcing of components. The former is about reuse *across* components, whereas the latter is about reuse *of* components.

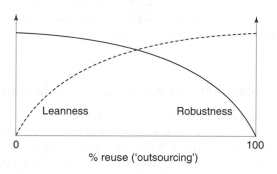

Figure 4.1 Opposing force fields of robustness (limited context dependence) and leanness (limited 'fat'), as controlled by the degree of reuse within a component.

4.2   Standardization and normalization

The 'sweet spot' of the optimization problem introduced above can be shifted toward leaner components by improving the degree of normalization and standardization of interface and component worlds. The more stable and widely supported a particular aspect is, the less risky it becomes to make it a specified requirement for a component. Context dependencies are harmless where their support is ubiquitous. For example, only 50 years ago it would have been a bad idea in many cases to form a business that depends on its customers having access to a telephone. Nowadays, in many areas of the world, this is clearly safe.

4.2.1 Horizontal versus vertical markets

When aiming for the formation of standards that cover all areas that represent sufficiently large markets, it is useful to distinguish standards for horizontal and vertical markets. A horizontal market sector cuts through all or many different market domains; it affects all or most clients and providers. A vertical market sector is specific to a particular domain and thus addresses a much smaller number of clients and providers. For example, the Internet and the World Wide Web standards are both addressing horizontal market sectors. In contrast, standards for the medical radiology sector address a narrow vertical market sector which, as in this case, nevertheless can have a substantial market volume.

Standardization is hard in horizontal market sectors. If a service is relevant to almost everyone, the length of the wish list tends to be excessive. Consider, as an example, the situation that standards committees for general-purpose programming languages have to face. At the same time, it is the horizontal market sectors in which a successful standard has the highest impact. The Web is one of the best examples.

Surprisingly, standardization in vertical sectors is just as difficult as it is in horizontal market sectors, but for different reasons. The number of players is smaller, so the likelihood of finding a compromise should be higher. However, the vertical sector considered for a standard has to be wide enough for a viable market. Also, with a smaller number of players, the mechanisms of market economies work less well and it is less likely that good, cost-effective solutions are found within a short time.

4.2.2 Standard component worlds and normalization

Component approaches are most successful where the basic component world and the most important interface contracts are standardized *and* these standards are sufficiently supported by the relevant industry. However, for standardization to help, it is important to keep the number of competing standards low. With a single strong international standardization body or a single dominating company or other organization behind a standard, this can work. However, more likely than not, standards will compete. A particularly dramatic explosion of 'mutually unaware' competitors can arise if vertical fragmentation leads to the reinvention of standards in allegedly different sectors when the same standard would suit multiple sectors. For example, it is conceivable that several image-processing standards in, say, medical radiology and radio astronomy could be shared.

The risk of having large numbers of competing standards, and thus small markets for many of them, can be reduced by means of *normalization*. By publishing and cataloging 'patterns' of common design, it is likely that otherwise mutually ignorant standardization bodies will discover mutual similarities in their target domains. It is, of course, a matter of scale whether discovery and exploitation of such similarities are worthwhile, that is cost-effective.

CHAPTER FIVE

Components,
interfaces, and re-entrance

Semantics: the actual meaning of things beyond their outer form or appearance. As component technologies are all about interoperation of mutually alien components, the *meaning* of the whole becomes a difficult issue. This chapter presents the subtleties and problems of software component semantics. Some current approaches are discussed, not ignoring that this area is still a focus of ongoing research.

This chapter and the next two are likely to be quite tough reading for many. It is safe to only skim over them at a first reading. However, the material presented is essential to an understanding of the rationales behind many contemporary approaches and technologies. Both chapters contain several hints for readers who wish to skip some of the material.

This chapter has two parts. The first introduces the important concept of contractual specifications of interfaces. The second part, starting with section 5.4, focuses on the specific problems of contractual specifications of interfaces in a component setting. In essence, it will become obvious that recursive and re-entrant calls across component boundaries introduce many of the complexities of concurrent programming. This second part is technical and subtle. It is safe to 'fast forward' to section 5.8. Many of the arguments in later sections and chapters build on the following discussions. It may thus be preferable to quickly read the following sections, concentrating on the examples, to improve understanding.

The material in this chapter is supported by examples developed in two programming languages: Java and Component Pascal. Appendix A presents a brief comparison of these two languages. Both languages have a familiar appearance, even for readers not versed in them. A precise understanding of these languages is not required to follow the examples. More subtle details are explained as they occur.

5.1 Components and interfaces

Interfaces are the means by which components connect. Technically, an interface is a set of named operations that can be invoked by clients. Each operation's semantics is specified, and this specification plays a dual role: it serves both providers implementing the interface and clients using the interface. As, in a component setting, providers and clients are ignorant of each other, the specification of the interface becomes the mediating middle that lets the two parties work together.

A component may either directly provide an interface or it may implement objects that, if made available to clients, provide interfaces. Interfaces directly provided by a component correspond to procedural interfaces of traditional libraries. There can be interfaces provided indirectly by objects that are made available by the component. Such indirectly implemented interfaces correspond to object interfaces.

5.1.1 Direct and indirect interfaces

Direct (procedural) and indirect (object) interfaces can be unified into a single concept. Essentially, the idea is to use static objects that can be part of a component. A procedural interface to a component is modeled as an object interface of a static object within the component. Most component implementations can be made to have their interfaces look like object interfaces. This is the traditional 'workaround' of pure object-oriented languages, including Java.

Modeling all component interfaces as object interfaces, in which a single component may provide multiple object interfaces, helps simplify the grounds for discussion of semantics. However, it is important to remember the consequences of using a true object interface rather than a procedural interface. Since the early years of computing, procedural libraries have been used to provide a service through an interface to many clients. However, different library implementations were never competing with each other within any one given configuration. Library implementations would only vary across platforms or across library versions. This is radically different with object interfaces.

An object interface introduces an *indirection* called method dispatch. For a given object, that object's class determines the implementation of the object's interface. At runtime, a method invocation is resolved by retrieving the target object's class and directing the call to the method implementation in that class. Method dispatch can lead to the involvement of a third party. In particular, it can involve a third party of which both the calling client and the interface-introducing component are unaware. This is the case when the object implementing an interface belongs to a component different from the component with which the client seems to interact through the interface. Traditional procedural interfaces are always direct: the definition of the procedural interface and its implementation belong to the same component. Of course, explicit procedural indirection is possible through procedure variables.

An example will make these things clearer. Consider a component TextServices that offers an interface GrammarChecker. TextServices also offers a mediator that can be used to select a default grammar checker. A default grammar checker is selected by passing an object that implements the GrammarChecker interface to the TextServices mediator. This installed third-party checker may then be used by other services implemented in TextServices, but also indirectly by clients of TextServices. Hence, a client that asks for a grammar checker might get one that is implemented outside TextServices. This is possible even though the client may only know about TextServices and TextServices itself may know nothing about the actual implementer of the grammar checker.

Figure 5.1 illustrates this scenario; the numbers indicate in which order objects are acquired. First, the grammar checker knows about the text service mediator. Secondly, the grammar checker registered itself as the default checker with the mediator – the mediator knows only about the abstract checker interface. Thirdly, the word processor knows about the mediator. Fourthly, the word processor acquires a reference to the current default checker from the mediator – just as the mediator, the word processor, knows only the abstract checker interface.

The effective coupling of two dynamically selected parties through a well-defined interface is a powerful concept called *late binding* and is right at the heart of object-oriented programming. In a component system, the situation is the same but the proper working of the resulting dynamic configurations is harder to control. With components, not only are the two connected parties unaware of each other, but it is likely that even the designers do not know each other. Thus, it is only the quality of the interface specification that holds things together.

5.1.2 Versions

In a component world, versions of components can be prolific. For example, many vendors may provide various 'upwards-compatible' enhanced versions of a successful component. Traditional version management, often based on the as-

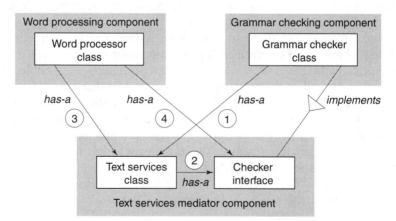

Figure 5.1 A word processing client calls on services of a grammar checker that it acquired indirectly from a component mediating between clients and providers of text services. The word processor, the mediator, and the checker reside in three separate components.

signment of major and minor version numbers, assumes that the versions of a component evolve at a single source. In a free market, the evolution of versions is more complex and management of version numbers can become a problem itself.

A subtle aspect of versioning arises when moving from direct to indirect interfaces, that is to object interfaces. With direct interfaces it suffices to check versions at bind time, that is when a service is first requested. As discussed above, indirect interfaces couple arbitrary third parties. In a versioned system, care must be taken to avoid indirect coupling of parties that are of incompatible versions. For example, a client originally requesting a service may be capable of working with version 1 of that service. Once it holds an object reference, it may pass the reference on to another component. However, the latter component might require version 2 of the service. Unless versions are checked in every place where an object reference crosses component boundaries, version checking is not sound.

Very few component infrastructures proposed so far address the component versioning problem properly. One possible approach is to insist on immutable interface specifications. Instead of trying to maintain the complex compatibility relation among various versions of interfaces, each interface, once published, is frozen and never changed again. Supporting multiple versions is then equivalent to supporting multiple interfaces. An outdated interface is simply no longer supported. Passing a reference of a particular interface version to other components is not a problem. The receiving component either accepts the reference because it can handle this particular interface or it expects a different version and thus a different interface – it will therefore not accept the reference. Using immutable interfaces is essentially the COM approach.

5.1.3 **Interfaces as contracts**

A useful way to view interface specifications is as contracts between a client of an interface and a provider of an implementation of the interface. The contract states what the client needs to do to use the interface. It also states what the provider has to implement to meet the services promised by the interface. (As pointed out by Wolfgang Weck, a contract binds two partners, in this case client and provider. Hence, the contractual specification of an interface really is just a contract template that is 'instantiated' at composition time of client and provider. In theory, the contract could be refined or renegotiated at that time.)

On the level of an individual operation of an interface, there is a particularly popular contractual specification method. The two sides of the contract can be captured by specifying pre- and postconditions for the operation. The client has to establish the precondition before calling the operation, and the provider can rely on the precondition being met whenever the operation is called. The provider has to establish the postcondition before returning to the client and the client can rely on the postcondition being met whenever the call to the operation returns. Pre- and postconditions are not the only way to form contracts, that is to add a specification to an interface. In addition, with pre- and postconditions not all aspects of an interface can be specified. Other forms of specifications are covered briefly further below.

Contracts are a simple idea but have subtle implications. Before delving into contracts for interacting objects, consider a simple procedural library, for example one that provides operations for text formatting. In addition, assume that the library's interface remains unchanged from one version to another but that its implementation is revised. What effect do such implementation changes have on clients of the library?

This question can only be answered in the context of a precise specification stating what the library, in the abstract, is supposed to do. A contract is an appropriate approach: pre- and postconditions are attached to every operation in the library. If the revised implementation is not to break any old clients, it must respect the (unchanged) contract, that is it can at most require less or provide more. (More technically, the implementation can weaken preconditions or strengthen postconditions. This will be explained in detail in Chapter 6.)

5.1.4 Contracts and non-functional requirements

As long as an implementation respects its contracts, revisions pass unnoticed by clients. Contracts and procedural or functional libraries fit together very well. It is worth noting that typical contemporary contracts often exclude precise performance requirements. However, even for simple procedural libraries, a new release adhering to the original contract but changing performance can break clients. Consider a math library that is used by an animation package. Next, the math library is improved to deliver more accurate results, but at lower average speed. This 'improvement' turns out to break the animation package, which now fails to deliver the required number of frames per second.

Take an example from the current practice that Swiss banks use when subcontracting a component to a third party. The contractual specification consists of the functional aspects – interface syntax and semantics with invariants, and pre- and postconditions – but also a so-called *service level*. The service level covers guarantees regarding availability, mean time between failures, mean time to repair, throughput, latency, data safety for persistent state, capacity, and so on. Service levels are monitored and used to pay on the basis of component use. Failure to fulfill the service level is treated on the same grounds as a wrong result: the component, that is the component vendor, broke its contract. It can be expected that this practice of including non-functional specifications into a contract *and* monitoring them strictly will become more widely popular in the future.

5.1.5 Undocumented 'features'

Note that it is always possible to 'observe' behavior of an implementation beyond its specification. For example, the precise reaction to certain parameter values can be explored. Knowledge about an implementation derived through such exploration can be used to make clients dependent on a provider's implementation. It is not even necessary to have access to the implementation's source code to create such dependencies. A most insidious way of exploring an implementation's unspecified 'features' is called *debugging*. While trying to fix problems, a debugger subtly reveals information that is not part of the contract. In practice, it is very difficult to avoid such non-contractual dependencies entirely. To minimize risks, a contract needs to maintain a balance between being precise and not being too restrictive.

5.2   What belongs to a contract?

The notion of contracts as interfaces annotated with pre- and postconditions, and perhaps invariants, is simple and practical. However, several important issues are not covered. For example, it is usually understood that an operation with a certain postcondition has to establish that postcondition before returning. However, it need not return at all! Simple pre- and postconditions on operations merely specify *partial correctness*; a partially correct operation either terminates correctly or does not terminate at all. The requirement that an operation should also eventually terminate leads to *total correctness*. This requirement can be added as a convention to all contracts. (The triple {precondition} operation {postcondition} is sometimes called a *Hoare triple* and is then indeed limited to partial correctness. A popular notation for totally correct conditions is Dijkstra's weakest preconditions for an operation and a given postcondition.)

5.2.1 Safety and progress

The concept that something guaranteed by a precondition will *lead to* something guaranteed by a postcondition can be generalized. By separating pre- and postconditions from concrete operations, they can be made self-standing requirements of a contract. A common notation is the *leads-to* operator used to express *progress conditions* in a contract. For example, the clause 'model update *leads-to* notifier calls' could be part of a contract between models and views. Progress conditions often rely on some form of temporal logic – providing logical operators such as leads-to (Chandy and Misra, 1988). They complement the *safety conditions* that can be expressed using invariants.

    The notion of contracts can thus be formalized to capture safety and progress conditions, although still neglecting performance and resource consumption. Contracts of this style have been introduced by Helm *et al.* (1990) and taken further by Holland (1992). A different approach to expressing progress are *statement specifications*, which use abstract non-deterministic statement sequences to specify safety and progress implicitly as abstract programs (Morgan, 1990). A brief discussion follows in section 5.10.

Object- and component-oriented practice still have to take advantage of such refined contract approaches on a regular basis. Pre- and postconditions, on the other hand, are widely accepted and usually combined with informal clauses to form complete contracts. The drawback of such semiformal approaches is the exclusion of formal verification.

5.2.2 Non-functional requirements

The specification techniques looked at so far (conditions, contracts, histories, statement specifications) are restricted to functional aspects. Contracts based on such techniques state what is done under which provisions. They do not state how long it would take or what other resources, besides time, would be consumed.

It is obvious that in most practical examples a violation of *non-functional requirements* can break clients just as easily as a violation of functional requirements. If a provider is exceedingly slow in performing a function, the client itself will be slow in performing its duty. The effect can cause an avalanche, the result of which is that the entire system fails to perform satisfactorily. Unless performance is regulated by contracts, it can be difficult or impossible to pinpoint the underperforming components.

Besides time, a provider also has to respect other resource limitations. If a provider uses, say, excessive heap storage, then this can affect the entire system. Just as with underperformance, this can lead to aggregate effects causing the entire system to fail. Again, unless regulated by contracts, it is not easily possible to determine the components that misbehaved, as there would not be any specified limits on resource usage.

5.2.3 Specifying time and space requirements

Ideally, a contract should cover all essential functional and non-functional aspects. It is not yet clear how this can best be achieved, leaving room for ongoing and future research. However, first examples do exist. The C++ Standard Template Library (Musser and Saini, 1996) bounds the execution time that legal implementations of a given abstract template function can take. Execution time is not specified in seconds, as that would be totally platform dependent. Instead, only the *time complexity* of legal implementations is bounded.

Specifying complexity bounds is an interesting compromise. For example, a contract might require a sort function to take no more than the order of $n \log n$ steps to sort n elements. This requirement rules out the use of most 'bad' sorting algorithms, but it still does not refer to a particular platform's performance. Likewise, a contract could require the same sort function to take at most $\log n$ additional storage cells to perform the sort.

Assume that the complexity bounds of a provider are given by the contract. It is then often possible to determine absolute time and space bounds for a given provider on a given platform. To do so, usually a small number of *measurements* suffice. The reason is that, ideally, the various possible providers, constrained by the same bound, can at most differ by constant factors. If someone managed to implement a sort that takes just n steps, then the single measurement would not be enough. Fortunately, it is not possible to sort n arbitrary elements in fewer than $n \log n$ time using just $\log n$ space overhead.

For example, one sort function on a given platform might take 1 μs $n \log n$, whereas another on the same platform might require 2 μs $n \log n$. With a single measurement of a sufficiently large sorting task (large enough to avoid startup anomalies and so on), the constants (1 μs versus 2 μs) can be measured.

The gap between complexity bounds in a contract and absolute bounds (in seconds or bytes) on a specific platform needs to be bridged. An engineer performing component composition would need to know. Fortunately, at composition time, the selection of concrete providers would be known. Thus, if providing components came with the additional characteristics required, the composing engineer, or an automated composer, could compute absolute bounds for a given platform. For example, a sorting component could certify that it indeed sorts in $n \log n$ time. It might even list characteristic performance figures for various platforms or announce performance relative to a well-known component.

Note that the specification of worst-case bounds may not be the best choice. Instead, specification of average-case bounds may be preferable in many cases. For example, Quicksort, the fastest average-case sorting algorithm, has a worst-case time complexity of n^2 and can thus not be used with a contract requiring $n \log n$ time in the worst case. However, Quicksort has $n \log n$ time complexity in the average case and is more than twice as fast as the fastest known sorting algorithm with worst-case $n \log n$ time bound (Heapsort). Unfortunately, average case bounds have a drawback: the constants of implementations cannot be simply measured and depend on platform and average input, for example average distributions in the sorting case.

In summary, the specification of time and space complexity bounds in a contract, for both the average and the worst case, could significantly add to the practical value of that contract. By avoiding reference to platform-specific bounds (in seconds and bytes), the contract remains sufficiently universal. To fill the gap, components that provide a service under such a contract should come with the additional information required to determine absolute bounds. To become common practice, non-functional specification techniques still have some way to go.

5.3 Dresscode: formal or informal?

The above discussion suggests that interface contracts should be as formal as possible to derive all necessary information and to enable formal verification. Given the complexity of formal specifications, it is not surprising that they are rarely used in practice. Pre- and postconditions as shown before are used, but represent a semiformal style only. Just consider the numerous plain English 'predicates' used where a formal predicate would first require the introduction of a much more precise formal model. However, it is worth noting that different parts of a system can be specified using different degrees of formality – the preciseness of the specification (and the *cost* incurred by it) have to be balanced against the criticality of the target part (and the *risk* incurred by using it).

The analogy that led to the name 'contract' is, of course, a real-world contract. Such a contract, to be valid, has to stay within the rules prescribed by the relevant legislation. However, none of the real-world laws are formal. New 'interpretations' are found every day and tested in court. This could well be the future for contracts between components, or rather between providers of different components and their users.

It is clearly desirable to stay away from court resolution of cases wherever possible. Hence, formalizing contracts, where possible and agreeable, is a good idea. However, attempting to formalize everything can easily lead to totally unapproachable and therefore unsaleable situations. It is important that a contract does not overspecify a situation. As in the real world, the enforcement of unnecessary requirements causes costs to increase dramatically and feasibility to diminish. The art of keeping contracts as simple as possible, but no simpler, has yet to develop in the young field of software components.

This concludes the first part of this chapter. The second part focuses on the specific problems of contractual specifications of interfaces in a component setting.

5.4   Callbacks and contracts

Contracts and procedural or functional libraries fit together very well. Unfortunately, the situation changes when introducing callback mechanisms to a library. A *callback* is a procedure that is passed to a library at one point; the callback is said to be *registered* with the library. At some later point, the callback is then called by the library. Figure 5.2 illustrates the call graph as it occurs in a system using callbacks. In a layered architecture, normal calls always originate in higher, more abstract, layers and then stay in their layer or move downwards. A callback usually reverses the direction of the flow of control: a lower layer calls a procedure in a higher layer. For this reason, callback invocations are sometimes called *up-calls* (Clark, 1985). The following detailed discussion of callbacks helps to build solid foundations for later discussion of the more involved issues raised by objects.

Callbacks are a common feature in procedural libraries that have to handle asynchronous events. For example, some windowing libraries use a callback to notify a particular window's client code when the window was resized by the user. Alternatively, the client could poll the library for events continuously, a model that is also quite common.

What is so special about callback procedures? In a strict procedural library model, it is always the client calling the library. The library's operations always run to completion before returning control. Thus, the client never observes any

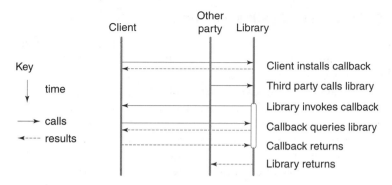

Figure 5.2 Call sequence between library and client in the presence of callbacks.

intermediate states that the library might go through. The only relevant library states, as far as the client is concerned, are those just before and just after a call to the library. While the library procedure proceeds, the client's state does not change. As the client has full control over its own state when calling a library procedure, the library call can be understood simply from the client's state just before the call and the library procedure's pre- and postconditions.

In the presence of callbacks, the situation changes. The intermediate library state at the point of calling the callback may be revealed to clients. A library thus has to be careful to establish a 'valid' state, as far as observable by the client, before invoking any callbacks. Furthermore, a callback may cause the library's state to change through direct or indirect calls to the library. Hence, the observable state of the library has to remain 'valid' for as long as any callbacks are active. In Figure 5.2, this critical region in the library has been marked. Validity of the library state is again specified as part of a contract. The callback interface is defined by the library. Hence, the contract comes with the library and specifies what a callback can expect and, to a lesser extent, what it has to do.

Procedural code can generally observe state and state changes. A library can make part of its state observable by exporting variables or inspection functions. A library's client can thus observe the relative order in which callbacks are performed and in which observable library state is changed. However, such ordering is not specified by normal pre- and postconditions, is not part of a normal procedural contract, and is therefore implementation dependent.

A simple way out would be to say that, as dependency on observable ordering is not part of the contract, a valid client must not depend on it. However, this is too rigid and would render callbacks quite useless. A callback procedure's role is all about state and state change. Most non-empty callbacks query the library and the client for further information, that is observe more state, before taking appropriate action.

5.5   Examples of callbacks and contracts

Some examples will help to clarify these ideas. This section presents and discusses in much detail an example that relies on callbacks. The example is developed in several stages, simulating a natural progression in the development and evolution of actual software. The objective is to show that callbacks indeed introduce subtle dependencies that even for simple examples lead to unexpected complexities and error-prone situations. This section can be skipped or skimmed over on a first reading. The thorough reader is invited to work through the examples – and asked to predict the problems that are pointed out as the examples develop.

It is common practice to demonstrate pre- and postconditions by using examples that are effectively flat abstract data types (ADTs). Thus, stacks and queues are used, instead of examples relying on callbacks or even webs of interacting objects. Although the raw concept of pre- and postconditions carries through, major points are missed by using trivial examples. The following examples thus start with a non-trivial scenario with callbacks. After examining these examples, the discussion continues with the closely related but more complex problems caused by cyclic object references.

5.5.1 A directory service

Consider a system that provides a basic directory service as part of a simple file system. The directory service supports callbacks to notify clients of changes in the managed directory. Such a notification service is useful, for instance, to keep a visual representation of the directory up to date.

Although this is only an example, it already represents an advance on the status quo of most current systems. The notification mechanism is exactly what would be needed to implement a file-and-folder metaphor on top of a file system in a reasonable way. Most current file systems do not support notification, and available 'desktop' implementations are therefore forced to poll the file system to discover changes. Surprisingly, this is even the case with the Mac OS, although there never was any other user interface to the file system.

The example is sketched in Component Pascal notation, which should be readily accessible to most readers. Component Pascal would allow for an object-oriented formulation, but again, for this example, this was intentionally not done as the objective at this stage is to study direct rather than indirect interfaces.

```
DEFINITION Directory;
   IMPORT Files;   (* details of no importance for this example *)
   TYPE
     Name = ARRAY OF CHAR;
     Notifier = PROCEDURE (IN name: Name);   (* callback *)
   PROCEDURE ThisFile (n: Name): Files.File;
       (* pre  n ≠ "" *)
       (* post  result = file named n  or  (result = NIL and no such file) *)
```

```
PROCEDURE AddEntry (n: Name; f: Files.File);
   (* pre  n ≠ "" and f ≠ NIL *)
   (* post  ThisFile(n) = f *)
PROCEDURE RemoveEntry (n: Name);
   (* pre  n ≠ "" *)
   (* post  ThisFile(n) = NIL *)
PROCEDURE RegisterNotifier (n: Notifier);
   (* pre  n ≠ NIL *)
   (* post  n registered, will be called on AddEntry and RemoveEntry *)
PROCEDURE UnregisterNotifier (n: Notifier);
   (* pre  n ≠ NIL *)
   (* post  n unregistered, will no longer be called *)
END Directory.
```

The simple directory service interface is grouped into two parts. The first part supports file lookup and addition or removal of named files, modeling a single flat directory for the sake of simplicity. The second part supports registration and unregistration of callbacks. Registered callbacks are invoked on addition or removal of a name. Each operation of the interface is specified using simple pre- and postconditions. State that is observable through an interface but which is not mentioned in a postcondition is guaranteed to remain unchanged.

5.5.2 A client of the directory service

Now consider a simple client that uses directory callbacks to maintain some visual display of the directory contents.

```
MODULE DirectoryDisplay;   (* most details deleted *)
  IMPORT Directory;
  PROCEDURE Notifier (IN n: Directory.Name);
  BEGIN
    IF Directory.ThisFile(n) = NIL THEN
      (* entry under name n has been removed – delete n in display *)
    ELSE
      (* entry has been added under name n – include n in display *)
    END
  END Notifier;
BEGIN
  Directory.RegisterNotifier(Notifier)
END DirectoryDisplay.
```

The client's callback procedure proceeds by first checking with the directory service to find out what change happened to the entry under the given name. Obviously, the notifier callback could get another parameter to pass this information directly. However, there is always a limit to what can be passed. It is thus highly realistic, as argued before, that a callback recursively invokes operations on the calling service.

There are several points left unclear in the Directory contract. For example, on redefinition of an entry, is the notifier called at all, called once, or called twice? Not calling the notifier would be justified because the list of registered names did not change. One call would reflect the fact that the binding of the name has changed. Two calls would correspond to the implicit removal of the old entry followed by the addition of the new entry. Such detail would need to be specified, but although possible this is difficult to achieve using only pre- and postconditions. Instead, a plain English by-clause is more likely to be used in practice – if such details are specified at all.

An even more difficult decision is whether to call the notifier before or after the directory itself has been updated. The design of the notifier with just the name as a parameter forces any useful callback to inquire the directory about further information. Hence, the only sensible thing to do is to call the notifier in implementations of AddEntry and RemoveEntry just before returning. Although in a sense obvious, this really ought to be added to the contract. Again, it is likely that such a clause would form part of the informal conditions in a contract.

5.5.3 Same client, next release

In a next stage, consider a variation of DirectoryDisplay that on screen uses a pseudo-name 'Untitled.' This name is used for anonymous files that have not been registered with the directory, but have been announced to the display service. The assumption is that no registered file will ever be called 'Untitled.' Obviously, users would be confused if the directory ever contained an entry for a file named 'Untitled.' Assume that the implementer of DirectoryDisplay had a brilliant idea: why not remove such an entry from the directory again, as soon as the notification call arrives? Said and done:

```
MODULE DirectoryDisplay;   (* Version 1.0.1 *)
  IMPORT Directory;
  PROCEDURE Notifier (IN n: Directory.Name);
  BEGIN
    IF Directory.ThisFile(n) = NIL THEN
      (* entry under name n has been removed—delete n in display *)
    ELSE
      IF n = "Untitled" THEN
        (* oops—you shouldn't do that ...*)
        Directory.RemoveEntry(n)   (* ... gotcha! *)
      ELSE
        (* entry has been added under name n—include n in display *)
      END
    END
  END Notifier;
```

```
BEGIN
  Directory.Register(Notifier)
END DirectoryDisplay.
```

Is this not a clever hack? Of course, none of us would do such a thing. How-ever, assume for a moment that someone did. Why would it be so bad? To make things clearer, consider the sketch given below of a possible implementation of Directory. The implementation is intentionally procedural and self-contained, that is it does not rely on any collection library or similar.

```
MODULE Directory;
  IMPORT Files, Strings;
  TYPE
    Name* = ARRAY OF CHAR;   (* trailing * exports definition *)
    Notifier* = PROCEDURE (IN name: Name);
    EntryList = POINTER TO RECORD   (* linked list of entries *)
      next: EntryList;
      name: POINTER TO Name; file: Files.File
      (* an entry is a pair of a name and a file *)
    END;
    NotifierList = POINTER TO RECORD   (* linked list of notifiers *)
      next: NotifierList;
      notify: Notifier
    END;
  VAR
    entries: EntryList;   (* list of registered entries *)
    notifiers: NotifierList;   (* list of registered notifiers *)
  PROCEDURE AddEntry* (n: Name; f: Files.File);
    VAR e: EntryList; u: NotifierList;
  BEGIN
    ASSERT(n # ""); ASSERT(f # NIL);
    e := entries;  (* search for entry under name n *)
    WHILE (e # NIL) & (e.name # n) DO e := e.next END;
    IF e = NIL THEN   (* not found: prepend new entry *)
      NEW(e); e.name := Strings.NewFromString(n);   (* create new entry *)
      e.next := entries; entries := e   (* prepend new entry to list *)
    END;
    e.file := f;   (* fill in file—replaces old binding if entry already existed *)
    u := notifiers;   (* invoke all registered notifiers *)
    WHILE u # NIL DO u.notify(n); u := u.next END
  END AddEntry;
  (* other procedures not shown *)
END Directory.
```

Unlike a contract, an implementation answers all questions about the what, when, and where – obviously, this assumes a sound and known semantics of the programming language used. The implementation details help to make the discussed problems concrete. Of course, this is only one of many possible implementations. It is therefore not appropriate to rely on implementation details when designing or implementing a new client.

Figure 5.3 shows the flow of control in detail as it occurs when a client tries to insert a file named 'Untitled' into a directory – an attempt undercut by the display notifier. The notifier is actually called recursively as a consequence of removing the entry from within the first notifier call. It is likely that this subtle interaction asked for some serious debugging. For example, a first attempt (version 1.0.1-alpha) might have been to catch and delete 'Untitled' first thing in the notifier, that is even before checking that the entry has actually been added rather than removed. Version 1.0.1-alpha terminated abnormally, reporting a stack overflow during a test insertion of an entry 'Untitled.'

5.5.4 A broken contract

Now recall the contract pertaining to AddEntry:

PROCEDURE **AddEntry** (IN n: Name; f: Files.File);
(* **pre** n ≠ "" **and** f ≠ NIL *)
(* **post** ThisFile(n) = f *)

The implementation of AddEntry in combination with the 'hacked' Notifier procedure *breaks this contract*. If AddEntry("Untitled", someFile) is called, the newly added entry is immediately removed by the notifier. Thus, the postcondition ThisFile("Untitled") = someFile does not hold on return from AddEntry. A client

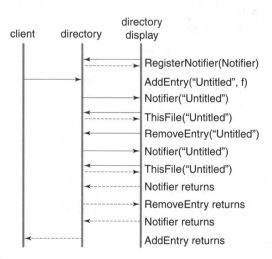

Figure 5.3 Call sequence between a client, the directory, and the directory display – version 1.0.1.

relying on this postcondition would thus break. Unfortunately, the notifier is 'out of the loop' then and the search for the culprit of the broken contract would naturally point to the Directory implementation. Note that both the client and the Directory implementation could have been deployed long before the component that installed the ill-behaved notifier was added.

5.5.5 Prevention is better than cure

How can a scenario of the kind analyzed above be regulated using contracts? What is missing is a contract between Directory and notifier implementations. Such a contract is difficult to capture, or at least the aspects that led to the above problems are difficult to capture. It is useful to think of callbacks as mechanisms that asynchronously observe and effect state changes. Asynchronously observable state, such as state observable by means of callbacks, allows contracts based on pre- and postconditions to fit less well. Asynchrony is more naturally dealt with by approaches developed to handle concurrency, such as process models. For example, histories of possible state changes could be used to specify the behavior of asynchronous systems (see section 5.9). Unfortunately, the resulting contracts are far less manageable than simple pre- and postconditions.

One aspect of the contract between Directory and notifier that can be captured is the requirement that a Directory instance has to notify all observers whenever the directory is changed. To specify this requirement, observers are abstractly modeled as holding an exact copy of their observed directory state and having the notifier as their only operation. A postcondition on all directory operations is then that these copies are again equivalent to the observable directory state. The only way the directory implementation can keep its part of the contract is to notify all observers after any change to the observable directory state. Another way to specify that directory operations call the notifiers is to incorporate abstract statement specifications into postconditions. For example, Fusion uses the notation [[call1; call2]] to specify that call2 always occurs after call1 (Coleman *et al.*, 1993).

What is not captured by this contract is the condition that a notified observer must not change the notifying observed object. This is difficult to capture in a formal contract but could be specified in plain text. The problem is that such a restriction is of *transitive* nature. A notifier may invoke any other operation that internally, for whatever reason, uses the service that originally notified. The restriction imposed on the notifier needs to be applied also to such indirect invocations. It is difficult to capture such a global dynamic restriction using a strictly local and modular descriptive contract. For example, the simple rule that a notifier may not call any state-updating operations cannot be adopted, as the very purpose of a notifier is to update the state of the notified entity.

An elegant middle ground is to equip a library using callbacks with state test functions. These tell whether or not a particular operation is currently available, without revealing too much of the library's internal state. Then all library operations can include references to such test functions in their preconditions. Correct callback implementations may thus be dynamically restricted to the manipulation of only a part of the otherwise accessible state. If done carefully, this allows a callback to perform only its function without depending on particular library implementations.

5.5.6 Proofing the directory service

In the Directory example, the addition of a test function InNotifier and its proper use in the preconditions of AddEntry and RemoveEntry would solve this particular problem. Version 1.0.1 of DirectoryDisplay would have to be rejected during conformance verification. The Directory interface refined below shows this use of test function InNotifier. Note that a missing postcondition, as in the case of Notifier, is equivalent to postcondition 'true.' An operation with such a trivial postcondition does not have any useful effect within the context of the contract.

```
DEFINITION Directory;   (* refined *)
    ...   (* unaffected parts omitted *)
    TYPE
        Notifier = PROCEDURE (IN name: Name);   (* callback *)
            (* pre  InNotifier() *)
    PROCEDURE InNotifier (): BOOLEAN;
        (* pre  true *)
        (* post  a notifier call is in progress *)
    PROCEDURE AddEntry (IN n: Name; f: Files.File);
        (* pre  (not InNotifier()) and n ≠ "" and f ≠ NIL *)
        (* post  ThisFile(n) = f *)
    PROCEDURE RemoveEntry (IN n: Name);
        (* pre  not InNotifier() *)
        (* post  ThisFile(n) = NIL *)
    END Directory.
```

As stated, test functions are a mixed blessing. It would be preferable to resort to a more declarative form in the contract, rather than relying on an executable function that inspects state. However, test functions can be invoked by any client of a service and thus solve the problem of transitive restrictions. In the example, **not** InNotifier() is part of the precondition of AddEntry and RemoveEntry and thus binds *any* client of these procedures. As the precondition can be checked at runtime, clients can be implemented to behave correctly, even if dynamically, under a transitive restriction imposed by some other notified component.

5.5.7 Test functions in action

Test functions in interfaces are certainly not commonplace today – dynamic restrictions are often just stated informally. For example, operations such as AddEntry may have an informal clause stating that they are not to be called directly *or indirectly* from a notifier. Such a clause in a contract is 'binding.' However, it violates the principle that a client should be able to perform the same guarding tests that a provider would use to safeguard itself against ill-formed calls.

Test functions are nevertheless used sometimes, even if not made available to clients. A prominent example is the Java security manager: an object that protects critical services from being called by untrusted code. The situation is similar to that of the notifier example above. The security manager needs to prevent direct *and indirect* calls to critical code from within untrusted methods. To do so, the implementation inspects the runtime stack to determine whether there is an untrusted method's frame on the stack. The security manager may need to obtain further information, depending on the particular operation to be guarded. Thus, it may need to call some code outside the security manager's class. To avoid problems resulting from recursive invocations to the security manager, the security manager itself has a test function, getInCheck, that returns true if the security manager is currently performing a security check.

This concludes the journey into the world of callbacks. The indirect recursion across abstractions caused by callbacks is a good basis from which to understand the similar difficulties introduced by webs of interacting objects.

5.6 From callbacks to objects

Object references seem to be simple and elegant. In reality, they are not simple, and some doubt their elegance. In any case, object references introduce linkage across arbitrary abstraction domains. Proper layering of system architectures thus lies somewhere between the challenging and the impossible – it is certainly not as natural as with procedural abstractions.

Understanding the implications of object references across a system is crucial. For example, the same object reference can be used at one time in a layer above that of the referenced object and at another time in a layer below that of the referenced object. A method invocation in the former case would correspond to a regular call; one in the latter case to an up-call. With object reference there is thus no need for explicit callback constructs: every method invocation is potentially an up-call, every method potentially a callback.

This is again a good point at which to resort to an example. As with the example 'session' on callbacks, it is safe to skip the rest of this section and the following section. A summary section after that will help to 'resynchronize.' However, again, studying the following examples carefully is recommended – the discussed problems *do occur* in practice and a good understanding is crucial for the full understanding of component technology.

Consider an interface for text processing. The interface is called TextModel because it supports only text manipulation, and not text display or a direct manipulation user interface. This time, for a change, the notation used is Java. As with Component Pascal, most readers will find the Java notation intuitive enough, even if they are not Java programmers. (Where the syntax of Component Pascal resembles that of Pascal or Oberon, the syntax of Java resembles that of C or C++.)

```
interface TextModel {
  int max ();
    // pre  true
    // post  result = maximum length this text instance can have
  int length ();
    // pre  true
    // post  0 ≤ result ≤ this.max() and result = length of text
  char read (int pos);
    // pre  0 ≤ pos < this.length()
    // post  result = character at position pos
  void write (int pos, char ch);
    // [ len: int; txt: array of char •
    //   pre  len := this.length(); (all i: 0 ≤ i < len: txt[i] := this.read(i)) :
    //        len < this.max() and 0 ≤ pos ≤ len
    //   post  thls.length() = len + 1
    //      and (all i: 0 ≤ i < pos: this.read(i) = txt[i])
    //      and this.read(pos) = ch
    //      and (all i: pos < i < this.length(): this.read(i) = txt[i - 1])
    // ]
  void delete (int pos);
    // [ len: int; txt: array of char •
    //   pre  len := this.length(); (all i: 0 ≤ i < len: txt[i] := this.read(i)) :
    //           0 ≤ pos < len
    //   post  this.length() = len - 1
    //      and (all i: 0 ≤ i < pos: this.read(i) = txt[i])
    //      and (all i: pos ≤ i < this.length(): this.read(i) = txt[i + 1])
    // ]
  void register (TextObserver x);
  void unregister (TextObserver x);
}
```

Note that, by convention, the notation x' in an operation's postcondition refers to the value of variable x before entering the operation. For values returned by methods of objects, this notation becomes less sharp. To avoid this problem, the above preconditions of write and delete contain explicit assignments to capture state that the corresponding postcondition can then refer to. In particular, these preconditions capture the initial length and contents of the text. The 'local variables' used to capture the state form part of the specification, not an actual implementation.

A text model is a sequence of characters with random access to read, insert, or delete characters at arbitrary positions. At any one time, a text has a defined length, which can be zero. It also has an upper bound on its length. (The condition this.length() ≤ this.max() really is an *invariant* of the text model. Invariants are conditions that constantly hold with respect to a given program fragment. In the context of interfaces, invariants are conditions over state exposed by the interface. In cases where all state is only accessible by explicit operation invocations, such as with Java interfaces, invariants in interfaces can always be folded into pre- and postconditions. It may still be more readable to express invariants separately.)

A text model supports registration and unregistration of objects of type TextObserver. This is similar to the concept of registration and unregistration of notifiers, as explained in section 5.1. Whenever a text model is modified, that is a character is inserted or deleted, the model notifies all registered observers. The observer interface is defined as:

```
interface TextObserver {
    void insertNotification (int pos);
        // pre character at position pos has just been inserted
    void deleteNotification (int pos);
        // pre character that was at position pos has been deleted
}
```

Any object implementing this interface can be registered. The implementations of insertNotification and deleteNotification can then take appropriate action to react to the models change.

The following interface, TextView, complements TextModel by facilitating the display and editing of text. The separation into model and view is a classic (p. 137). The traditional model view controller (MVC) separation has a third abstraction, controllers, to handle user interaction. For the sake of simplicity, some controller functionality is kept in the view and an explicit controller is left unspecified. Also, the detail of how a view acquires screen estate and how it draws to the screen has been left open.

```
interface TextView extends TextObserver {
    TextModel text ();
        // pre true
        // post result ≠ null
    int caretPos ();
        // pre true
        // post 0 ≤ result ≤ this.text().length()
    void setCaret (int pos);
        // pre 0 ≤ pos ≤ this.text().length()
        // post this.caretPos() = pos
    int posToXCoord (int pos);
        // pre 0 ≤ pos ≤ this.text().length()
        // post result = x-coordinate corresponding to text position pos
    int posToYCoord (int pos);
        // pre 0 ≤ pos ≤ this.text().length()
```

```
    // post result = y-coordinate corresponding to text position pos
int posFromCoord (int x, int y);
    // pre (x, y) is valid screen coordinate
    // post this.posToXCoord(result) = x and this.posToYCoord(result) = y
void type (char ch);
    // [ caret: int •
    //   pre  caret := this.CaretPos() : this.text().length() < this.text().max()
    //   equiv  this.text().write(caret, ch)
    //   post  this.caretPos() = caret + 1
    // ]
void rubout ();
    // [ caret: int •
    //   pre  caret := this.CaretPos() : caret > 0
    //   equiv  this.text().delete(caret - 1)
    //   post  this.caretPos() = caret - 1
    // ]
void insertNotification (int pos);
    //   inherited from TextObserver
    //   repeated here for strengthened postcondition
    // pre  character at position pos has just been inserted
    // post  display updated  and  this.caretPos() = pos + 1
void deleteNotification (int pos);
    //   inherited from TextObserver
    //   repeated here for strengthened postcondition
    // pre  character that was at position pos has been deleted
    // post  display updated  and  this.caretPos() = pos
}
```

Note that the notation **equiv** *statement* is used to indicate that the postcondition is the conjunction of the one of the equivalent statement and the one explicitly stated.

The view casts its text into lines and renders them on some unspecified display. The view also maintains a caret position: a marked position in the text, used for type and rub-out commands from the user. The caret is also pictured on the display, say as a vertical bar just before the character its position indicates. The mapping of character and caret positions to screen coordinates (and back) is also supported. This mapping can be used by some user interface object to interpret, for example, mouse pointer positions.

Note that a text view interface is declared to *extend* the text observer interface introduced above. The concept of extending interfaces, also called subtyping, is explained in detail in Chapter 6. With its extended observer interface, a text view can thus be used to observe a text model. Many, possibly different, text observers can be connected to a single text model. For example, there could be a text view and a text statistics view, where the latter displays the number of words in the text.

Consider as a first scenario the interaction between a text model and a text view. Some program fragment gets hold of a reference to the text model and inserts a character at some position. The model then notifies its observers, including the text view. The text view removes the caret mark from the display, updates the text display, repositions the caret, and redisplays the caret in its new position. The view's notifier method then returns. Finally, the model returns control to the original client. This process is illustrated in Figure 5.4.

Everything seems to be straightforward. Note how simply ordering objects, as indicated by the vertical lines in the diagram, causes the illusion of some well-layered activity. The flow of control seems to be as simple as that known from procedural libraries layered on top of each other.

However, at a second glance, things are less simple. The transfer of control from the model to the view occurs through an installed notifier – although the notifier is a method of an object in this case. It is thus a strictly non-hierarchical transfer. Recall that a text view depends on a text model's state and not vice versa. Therefore, an ordering that better reflects dependencies is that shown in Figure 5.5.

Why does this rearrangement matter? It more faithfully reflects the actual hierarchy – and, when going into more detail – leads to fewer surprises. To see why, consider what a text view needs to do to perform its display updating functions. At the point where the old caret mark is removed, the display still shows the text as it was before the change. Hence, the caret needs to be removed using the *old* text position to screen coordinate mapping. This is important, because the mapping of text positions to screen coordinates depends on the actual text, for example line-separating characters in the text force line breaks, characters may be of proportional width, the width of spaces varies in justied text, and so on.

Once the text display has been updated, it is time to redisplay the caret at its new position. This time the *new* (that is updated) mapping of text positions to

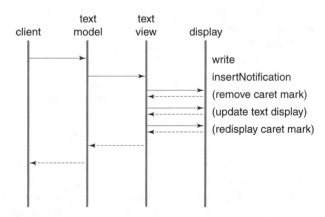

Figure 5.4 Message sequence occurring upon insertion of a character into a text model that is displayed by a text view.

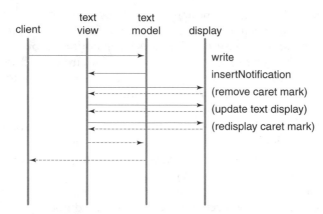

Figure 5.5 The same message sequence as in Figure 5.4, but with the ordering of objects reflecting primary dependencies.

screen coordinates has to be used. If the text view, under certain circumstances, uses the *wrong* mapping, user irritation and display clutter are likely to result. As an aside, almost all commercial applications, including the most prominent ones, produce such screen rubble at times. This may serve as evidence that the series of examples presented here, and their problems, are far from being contrived.

To summarize, here are the steps a text view needs to take to react to a notifier call:

(1) remove caret mark from outdated text display
    (a) map caret position to screen coordinates using mapping based on text *before* change
    (b) invert caret mark at computed display position;
(2) re-cast text and update text display;
(3) update caret position;
(4) redisplay caret mark in updated text display
    (a) map caret position to screen coordinates using mapping based on text *after* change
    (b) invert caret mark at computed display position.

The text has already changed when the view is notified. Therefore, step 1a relies on a *cached* mapping. The text view has to keep the coordinates of the caret on the screen. For all other purposes, caching is not necessary: the coordinates can be recomputed whenever necessary, based on the text and the algorithm used to cast the text into display lines.

Whether indirectly, through a cache, or directly, through a computed mapping, steps 1a, 2, and 4a depend on the text model and, at least logically, access it in its present or previous state. Figure 5.6 presents a refined part of the message sequence chart, showing how these three steps interact with the model.

And yet it would appear that the use of the correct mapping is simply a matter of using a correct text view implementation. However, remember that the text

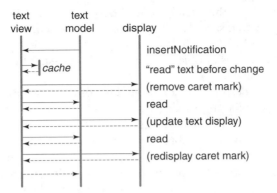

Figure 5.6   Message sequence in detail: interaction of text view and text model during update required by a change to the model.

view makes its mappings between text positions and screen coordinates publicly available. The methods posToXCoord, posToYCoord, and posFromCoord use these mappings to perform their function. The text view cannot perform its display-updating duties without calling other objects. Hence, other objects take control while the view is still performing its update functions.

In any case, other objects may call one of the mapping methods before or during the view update. In this case, which mapping should the text view present to the outside – the one that reflects the status of the text or the one that reflects the status of the display? If the mapping that is made available is inconsistent with the display, then user interface events, such as mouse clicks, can be mismapped. If the mapping is inconsistent with the text, then positions in the text are calculated wrongly, potentially leading to wrong or even illegal modification attempts.

Perhaps the view should make two sets of mappings available? If the view can tell that the two are inconsistent, it could also refuse to perform the mapping, for example by raising an exception. Whatever the choice, the flow of control against the layers of abstraction (up-call) clearly exposes inconsistencies to arbitrary other objects, a circumstance that should be reflected in the interfaces of text models and views but usually is not. For a discussion of how this could be done, see section 5.10.

5.7   From inter-object consistency to object re-entrance

This section builds on the example developed in the previous section. Readers who skipped the previous section are thus advised to skip this section as well.

The model view scenario developed in the previous section shows how multiple objects can be subject to consistency constraints. Objects could be arranged in strict layers, with messages being sent only from objects located in higher layers to objects located in lower layers. Doing so would eliminate the problems of observable inconsistency, as everything 'below' is consistent and everything 'above' is not observable. This is the main benefit of traditional layered architectures. For object systems, however, strict layering is rarely performed. Passing object references 'down' and abstractly dealing with upper objects in lower layers is one of the most powerful aspects of object orientation. Harnessing this potential, however, is a major challenge.

Recall the text model and view example. One of the problems with view consistency, affecting display and model, was that other objects may call one of the view's mapping methods before or during the view update. On closer inspection, things are even worse – multiple observers could be registered with the text model. If another observer was notified before the text view, other objects could gain control before the text view became aware that the underlying text had changed. This might even lead to another text model change *before* the text view learned of the first change. This issue of ordering in event-based systems is discussed in detail in section 10.7.

The real problem is *observation* of an object undergoing a state transition, with inconsistent intermediate states becoming visible. As objects encapsulate state, such observation is limited to what the object reveals. In other words, inconsistencies can only be observed by *entering* an object's method. (In some languages, objects can directly make some of their attributes accessible. Obviously, this can always be replaced by accessor methods in which observable inconsistencies become an issue.)

The situation is most intricate when considering object *re-entrance*, that is the situation in which an object's method is invoked while another method is still executing. It is, if anything, the right of an object's own method to cause a state transition for that object. If, while in progress and before reaching consistency again, the intermediate state is observed – by means of re-entrance – maintaining correctness becomes difficult.

As an example, consider the method type of a text view, as introduced above (interface on p. 59). This method is called by some user interface component when receiving, say, a key-press event. The text view reacts by inserting the character at the current caret position into the view's text model. From there on, the activities unfold as described before. Figure 5.7 shows the message sequence.

The view is now re-entered by the model notification while it is still processing the type message. Recall the specification of method type (from interface TextView):

```
void type (char ch);
    // [ caret: int •
    //   pre   caret := this.caretPos() : this.text().length() < this.text().max()
    //   equiv  this.text().write(caret, ch)
    //   post   this.caretPos() = caret + 1
    // ]
```

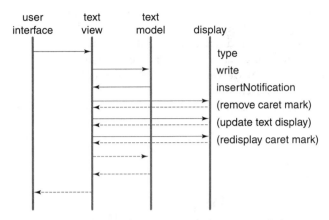

Figure 5.7 Message sequence caused by a request to insert a typed character.

Therefore, in addition to inserting the typed character into the text, the method is also supposed to update the caret position. Luckily, the desired update is already done by the notifier. Recall its specification as well:

void **insertNotification** (int pos);
// **pre** *character has been inserted at position pos*
// **post** *display updated* **and** this.caretPos() = pos + 1

The type method therefore performs all of its duties simply by calling the write method of its text model, which calls the insertion notifier. This is a rather subtle consequence of the specifications and the actual interplay of the text view methods involved.

Now consider the case where the notifier's specification is relaxed to maintain the caret position wherever possible. In particular, the caret should not move if it is located before the position of insertion. Also, it should be adjusted by adding 1 to its current position if it is located at or behind the position of insertion. The aim is that programmed text changes should not interfere with the caret, a user interface element.

Here is the changed insertion notifier specification:

void **insertNotification** (int pos);
// [caret: int •
//   **pre** caret := this.caretPos() :
//   *character has been inserted at position pos*
//   **post** *display updated*
//   **and** caret < pos ⇒ this.caretPos() = caret
//   **and** caret ≥ pos ⇒ this.caretPos() = caret + 1
//]

Now a programmed text change no longer interferes with the caret position. Of course, a program could still call the view's setCaret method. However, the type method also needs a modification. As type is supposed to reflect a user event, it still should update the caret position. As the notifier no longer does this, the type method has to change the caret itself. A first difficulty at this point is that the type method needs to be changed at all, but things get worse.

By now, the example has developed into a full-fledged re-entrance scenario. Consider the following implementation of the type method:

```
void type (char ch) {
    int pos = caretPos();
    setCaret(pos + 1);
    text().write(pos, ch);
}
```

Innocent as it seems, this implementation breaks its contract. It is wrong. The reason is that, in an attempt to keep the caret at a consistent position, the notifier called indirectly by text().write may still change the caret. However, it assumes that the caret is still positioned where it was before the insertion took place. Assume that the caret sits at position 3 when a character is typed in. The type method sets the caret to position 4 and then inserts the character at position 3. If the notifier left the caret alone, everything would be fine. However, the notifier detects that the caret is at or behind the position of insertion (it is actually behind that position). Therefore, the notifier does its duty and increments the caret position, leaving it at position 5.

For a programmer seeing all detail, the solution is obvious. The order of actions in the type method needs to be reversed:

```
void type (char ch) {
    int pos = caretPos();
    text().write(pos, ch);
    setCaret(pos + 1);
}
```

Deriving this necessity from an inspection of all presented specifications would be possible, but is quite involved. The type method could be further simplified by deleting the call to setCaret entirely, provided the postcondition of insertNotification remains as it is. As the position of insertion is invariably that of the caret, this postcondition guarantees advancement of the caret position by 1. Some might still prefer the redundant call to setCaret, as it makes the type method more robust under evolution of the other method specifications. Obviously, a trade-off between robustness and performance would be required if setCaret was an expensive operation. As can be seen, object re-entrance poses difficult problems even in this relatively simple example.

5.8 Self-interference and object re-entrance: a summary

Re-entrance of methods can pose problems, as objects normally have state and thus are not automatically re-entrant. A simple solution would be to require all invariants of an object to be established before calling any method. In other words, all state needs to be made consistent before calling a method. However, this is not possible where a state transformation requires a sequence of method calls. Unfortunately, this is commonly the case. At least self-recursive method calls, that is calls to the current object, should thus be possible even if not all invariants hold.

In addition, there are examples where objects are in a cyclic dependency. Desired invariants covering multiple objects in such a cycle cannot always be maintained. Such conditions can only be invariants for clients that cannot observe the transitory inconsistencies. Unfortunately, the observation of intermediate state can be difficult to prevent, as became apparent in the previous examples.

One way to address re-entrance problems caused by self-recursion or cyclic dependencies is to weaken invariants conditionally and make the conditions available to clients through test functions. Such conditions then allow for transitory violations of the original 'invariant,' leaving room for its re-establishment in cases in which multiple objects are involved. Note how such conditions are equivalent to the construction of test functions introduced for callback patterns (p. 55).

For example, in the model view or the observer design pattern, as used in the examples above, there is an 'invariant' stating that the view presents part of what is represented by the model. However, when the model is modified, it first has to notify its views of the change. Upon receipt of the notification, a view updates itself accordingly.

Clearly, the simple invariant 'a view presents the contents of its model' cannot be upheld and needs to be refined. A possible solution is to add a *time stamp* to the model, recording the most recent change to the model. The view also gets a time stamp, recording the version of the model that it currently reflects. The invariant then becomes 'a view that has the same timestamp as its model presents the contents of its model.'

Now consider a refinement of the view. In addition to the representation of part of its model's contents, the view also displays some sort of marks. A caret mark was used above; selection marks would be another example. The precise position on the display depends on the marked model contents. If the model changes, the marks potentially have to be moved or removed. Upon receipt of a notification that the model has changed, a view cannot rely on the model to compute the location of the old marks. Thus, it either has to cache all required information or the marks have to be removed before a model can be changed. The former way was taken in the above examples. Both approaches can be found in contemporary frameworks.

Such a subtle aspect is easily missed in the design of a complex object system unless all contracts are refined to ensure that they properly cover re-entrance conditions. A significant number of design and implementation errors – often hard to find and correct – go back to unexpected recursive re-entrance of objects. The recursion leading to such re-entrances is obscured either by subtle interactions of classes in an inheritance hierarchy or by subtle interactions of objects.

Contracts based on pre- and postconditions can capture the conditions to allow for safe interactions even in the presence of recursive re-entrance. The above time stamping used to weaken an invariant can also be applied to pre- and postconditions. However, such conditions are missing in almost all published interface specifications, pointing at a severe problem yet to be addressed in practice.

By now it should be clear that dealing with recursion and re-entrance is difficult enough in situations where the recursion is explicit and part of the design. However, self-recursion within a single object can be almost arbitrarily affected by class inheritance and thus leads to recursive re-entrance patterns that are neither explicitly specified nor necessarily expected. This thread is picked up again in Chapter 7.

Recursion and re-entrance become an even more pressing problem when crossing the boundaries of components. Recall that the problem in the type method (p. 64) was solved after stepping back and inspecting the overall situation. With components, this can be impossible to do as a component system, by definition, does not have a final form. The specification problems encountered in recursive re-entrant systems need to be solved in a modular way to cater for components. In other words, each component must be independently verifiable based on the contractual specifications of the interfaces it requires and those it provides.

5.9   Processes and multithreading

The problems of recursive re-entrance of objects and of concurrent interaction of processes are similar – and even identical in the case of objects interacting across process boundaries. The idea can be taken to the extreme, by assigning full process semantics to every object. 'Actors,' as proposed by Hewitt and refined by Agha (Agha and Hewitt, 1987), go even further and turn every object invocation into a separate process! However, the current consensus is that doing so is not efficient. Instead, objects and processes are kept separate and processes are quite often populated by multiple threads.

It would seem that making an object system *thread-safe*, that is protecting it against unwanted interferences from concurrent activities, would also solve the re-entrance problems. This turns out not to be the case. It must be possible for a thread to re-enter areas that it itself has locked. Otherwise, self-recursion and re-entrance patterns would simply lead to *deadlocks* – sometimes called self-inflicted deadlocks (Cardelli, 1994).

Assume that a thread had locked an object and, under self-recursion or indirect recursion, tries to re-enter that object. There are really only two possibilities. First, the thread can be treated as any other thread and has to wait for the locked object to be released. Of course, the locked object will never be released as the lock is held by just that thread that now waits. Therefore, the thread deadlocks and all objects that it locked remain locked indefinitely. This is not acceptable, as re-entrance in the presence of abstraction cannot be prevented.

Alternatively, a thread may be granted access to locked objects if the lock is held by just that thread. This rule avoids deadlocks and is indeed found in many concurrent object-oriented languages, including Java. Unfortunately, relaxing the locking rules to allow re-entrance by the same thread also reintroduces all the problems of re-entrance. Understanding and properly addressing the issues of re-entrance in object systems does not become any simpler by introducing processes or threads.

5.10 Histories

Another approach to capture the legal interactions among objects is the specification of *permissible histories*. This approach has its origin in *algebraic specifications* of abstract data types (ADTs). Histories in the technical sense are traces of states of a variable or a set of variables. Valid state transitions can then be specified by restricting the set of permissible traces. In other words, the specification *is* a formally captured set of permissible traces. For example, to specify that a variable's value can only stay the same or be increased, the specification could state that, in any permissible history of that variable, the recorded values are non-decreasing. By recording pairs of values in a trace, a history constraint can specify invariant relations among two variables, and so on.

In most history-based specification techniques, permissible traces or histories are specified indirectly. In addition to a specification of valid initial states, a set of transformations is given. Each transformation takes any permissible trace, transforms it, and yields another, usually longer, permissible trace. This transformational approach led to the name algebraic specification.

For example, suppose it is intended that it is always permissible to increment a certain variable by 1. In this case, a transformation would take any non-empty trace of that variable. This transformation would return a trace that is identical to the one taken, with the most recent value incremented by 1 and appended to the end of the trace.

When considering substitutability (Chapter 6), some further complications arise. In terms of traces, an object is substitutable for another if all traces of the new object, projected to the states and operations of the old object, are explicable in terms of the old object. This is similar to the notion of behavioral subtyping (Liskov and Wing, 1994) and ensures that a client expecting the old object cannot observe that the new object is used. More generally, if traces are used to specify an interface, then any class implementing this interface would have to satisfy the substitutability criterion. For example, if an interface specification states that some event A will always be followed by an event B, then all implementations of that interface have to ensure that this is observed.

The idea of trace-based specifications can be incorporated into type systems such that substitutability can be verified automatically. Obviously, where such types would require equivalence of computed results, the type system would no longer be decidable. Unfortunately, even when concentrating only on permissible sequences of operations, the resulting system is undecidable as the number of legal states is, in general, unbounded (Hüttel, 1991). By introducing type systems that merely specify approximate bounds on traces, decidable type systems that help to check substitutability conservatively can indeed be found (for example Nierstrasz, 1993). As with all practical type systems, these systems rule out some correct substitutions, but never permit incorrect ones. Specifications and type systems for objects are still an area of much ongoing work.

5.11 Statement specifications

In the example of TextModels above (section 5.6), it suffices to specify *when* notifiers will be called and *what* a notifier is allowed to do. In particular, all notifiers are called *after* completion of a text-modifying operation and notifiers are not themselves allowed to modify their notifying text. These conditions can be captured neatly by using a specification that takes imperative but high-level and non-deterministic form. Such specifications are sometimes called statement specifications as their form is somewhat similar to that of statement-oriented imperative languages. Statement specifications can be refined into correct implementations ('refinement calculus'; Morgan, 1990).

A specification of TextModels (attributable to Emil Sekerinski and Wolfgang Weck; Büchi and Weck, 1997) is given below. Readers who are not interested in formal specifications may safely skip the remainder of this chapter.

The specification largely follows Morgan's notation (Morgan, 1990), with the addition of a few intuitive constructs: class, keep, invariant over several classes, for ... do ... od. The class construct is similar to Morgan's module construct.

```
class TextModel;
  var text: seq char; observers: set Observer; max: N •
  procedure Max (result m: N) =
    m: [true, m ≥ max]; max := m;
  procedure Length (result l: N) =
    l := #text;
  procedure Read (pos: N; result ch: char) =
    ch := text[pos];
  procedure Write (pos: N; ch: char) =
    {max > #text} ;
    text := text[0 ... pos - 1] + <ch> + text[pos ... #text - 1];
    for o ∈ observers do o.InsertNotification(pos) od;
  procedure Delete (pos: N) =
    text := text[0...pos -1] + text[pos + 1...#text - 1];
```

```
    for o ∈ observers do o.DeleteNotification(pos) od;
    procedure Register (obs: Observer) =
      observers := observers + { obs} ;
    procedure Unregister (obs: Observer) =
      observers := observers - { obs} ;
    initially text = <>; observers = { } ; max = 0
  end
  class Observer;
    var text: TextModel •
    procedure InsertNotification (pos: N) =
      keep text^ ;
    procedure DeleteNotification (pos: N) =
      keep text^
  end
  invariant
    o: Observer; t: TextModel • o ∈ t.observers ⇔ o.text = t
```

Here are a few notes on the notation used:

> The selector operations on sequences s[i] and s[i...j] imply the pre-condition $0 \le i \le j < \#s$.
> The condition keep text^ means that none of the observable state according to the specification of text must be changed during this operation.

The specification of Max indicating the specific TextModels capacity is completely non-deterministic but specifies that the values returned by Max are non-decreasing. Variable Max is used for the sole reason of enforcing this constraint. This is important for Max to be used in the precondition of Write at all but has been left unspecified in the more informal specifications presented earlier in this chapter.

The specification of notifiers exhibits the problem mentioned earlier. It prohibits the notifier from modifying its notifying text. However, this precludes invocation of operations for which confined analysis, that is analysis over a confined context, cannot establish that the notifier does not indirectly modify this text. Global analysis solves this but is in conflict with components and independent extensibility.

CHAPTER SIX

Polymorphism

Polymorphism: the ability of something to appear in multiple forms, depending on context; the ability of different things to appear the same in a certain context. These are the two flip sides of the polymorphic coin. A refinement occurs once it is accepted that something does not have to be only what it appears to be. Then, dynamic exploration of what is behind the static appearance becomes possible.

This chapter sheds some light on the consequences of the above, somewhat philosophical, statements. In particular, the notion of substitutability is explained and related to the concepts of types and subtypes. Types lead to the notion of interfaces and their important role for components. As components are independently deployed, it is of utmost importance that the deployment environment accepts components that independently extend this environment. The important paradigm of independent extensibility is introduced to capture this requirement. The discussion of independent extensibility naturally leads to questions of security, safety, and trust. The chapter concludes with a discussion of different dimensions of independent extensibility, aspects of software evolution, and a short summary of some other forms of polymorphism not previously discussed in this chapter.

6.1 Substitutability – using one for another

Self-standing contractually specified interfaces decouple clients and providers. The same interface may be used by large numbers of different clients but also be supported by a large number of different providers. To avoid reducing the spectrum of possible clients and providers unnecessarily, an interface must be specified carefully. It should require too much neither from its clients nor from its providers. However, if it requires too little from clients or providers, the interface is just as useless.

If an interface requires too little from clients, for example no non-trivial preconditions, it can overburden providers. In particular, such an interface can be hard or even impossible to implement. Also, it can be impossible to implement it efficiently. On the flip side, if an interface requires too little from providers, for example no non-trivial postconditions, it is of no use to clients.

A carefully crafted interface requires no more than is essential for the service to be provided. Such interfaces usually leave significant headroom for clients and providers. In particular, clients and providers are always free to overfulfill their contract. A client may establish more than is required by the precondition or expect less than is guaranteed by the postcondition. Likewise, a provider may require less than is guaranteed by the precondition or establish more than is required by the postcondition.

Pre- and postconditions are usually specified using predicates. The notion of expecting less than is guaranteed takes the form of a logical implication: guarantees imply expectations. Likewise, an implication can be used to express that more might be provided than is required: the provided implies the required. Using the common symbol for implication ($\Rightarrow$), the above can be summarized as:

> established by certain client
> $\Rightarrow$ demanded by interface (precondition)
> $\Rightarrow$ required by certain provider

> established by certain provider
> $\Rightarrow$ guaranteed by interface (postcondition)
> $\Rightarrow$ expected by certain client

Here is an example: consider the interface TextModel as introduced in Chapter 5 (p. 58). The relevant section of the interface is repeated below.

```
interface TextModel {
    int max ();  // maximum length this text can have
    int length ();  // current length
    char read (int pos);  // character at position pos
    void write (int pos, char ch);  // insert character ch at position pos
    // [ len: int; txt: array of char •
    // pre  len := this.length(); (all i: 0 ≤ i < len: txt[i] := this.read(i)) :
    //        len < this.max() and 0 ≤ pos ≤ len
    // post  this.length() = len + 1
    //      and (all i: 0 ≤ i < pos: this.read(i) = txt[i])
    //      and this.read(pos) = ch
    //      and (all i: pos < i < this.length(): this.read(i) = txt[i - 1])
    // ]
    ...
}
```

Notice how the interface requires callers of operation write to make sure that the character to be written is inserted within the current range of the text. An implementation GreatTextModel may relax this by allowing insertions to happen past the end of the current text, by padding with blanks where necessary. Thus, a provider's implementation of write may have the following weakened precondition and strengthened postcondition; the changes are emphasized.

```
class GreatTextModel implements TextModel {
    ...
    void write (int pos, char ch) {
    // [ len: int; txt: array of char •
    //   pre  len := this.length(); (all i: 0 ≤ i < len: txt[i] := this.read(i));
    //          len < this.max() and  0 ≤ pos < this.max()
    //   post  this.length() = max(len, pos) + 1
    //      and  (all i: 0 ≤ i < min(pos, len): this.read(i) = txt[i])
    //      and  this.read(pos) = ch
    //      and  (all i: pos < i ≤ len: this.read(i) = txt[i - 1])
    //      and  (all i: len < i < pos: this.read(i) = " ")
    // ]
        ...
    }
    ...
}
```

The precondition of the interface TextModel.write does indeed imply that of the implementation GreatTextModel.write:

     this.length() < this.max() **and** 0 ≤ pos ≤ this.length()

⇒

     this.length() < this.max() **and** 0 ≤ pos < this.max()

The postcondition of the implementation GreatTextModel.write does indeed imply that of the interface TextModel.write, *provided* the stronger precondition of the interface held. If it did not, the interface makes no statement at all about possible postconditions:

    (from precondition:
      len := this.length(); max := this.max();
      (**all** i: 0 ≤ i < len: char[i] := this.read(i))
)
    len < max **and** 0 ≤ pos ≤ max
and
    this.length() = max(len, pos) + 1
    and (**all** i: 0 ≤ i < min(pos, len): this.read(i) = char[i])
    and this.read(pos) = ch
    and (**all** i: pos < i ≤ len: this.read(i) = char[i - 1])
    and (**all** i: len < i < pos: this.read(i) = " ")

⇒

    this.length() = len + 1
    and (**all** i: 0 ≤ i < pos: this.read(i) = char[i])
    and this.read(pos) = ch
    and (**all** i: pos < i < this.length(): this.read(i) = char[i - 1])

In both cases, the verification of these implications is straightforward and left as an exercise to the reader so inclined. Readers preferring not to go into this level of detail may safely skip this exercise.

There are surprisingly many further possibilities for providers to interpret the interface contract. For example, a provider may accept arbitrary positions, including negative ones, in all operations, simply by first clipping the specified position to the currently valid range. Or a provider may decide to grow a text dynamically, making max return a non-constant value. Or a provider may decide to create the illusion of an infinitely long text, preinitialized with all blanks.

Obviously, clients based on the interface contract will not be able to benefit from any of the above implementation refinements. However, the same implementations could also support another interface contract that reveals more general capabilities.

On the client's end of an interface, the same sort of relaxation is possible. A client may guarantee more than is required and expect less than is provided. For example, a client of TextModel.write may use the operation only to append to a text:

```
{ TextModel text; int pos; char ch;
  ...
  if text.length() < text.max() {
    text.write(text.length(), ch);
    // expect  text.read(text.length() - 1) = ch
  }
  ...
}
```

Notice how pre- and postconditions make it fairly difficult to express conditions such as: 'if text.length() < text.max() at one time, then this will continue to hold for as long as text.length() does not change.' Such a condition is vitally important to avoid a 'race condition' with precondition checks; the example above, for instance, depends on it. Owing to its notions of abstract time and sequencing, a history or statement-based specification technique as introduced in Chapter 5 can naturally cover such detail.

As is again easily verified, the client-established condition, together with the TextModel.length postcondition, implies the TextModel.write precondition. Also, the TextModel.write postcondition, together with the client's guarantees, implies the client's expectation:

$$\text{text.length()} \geq 0$$
and
$$\text{text.length()} < \text{text.max()} \;\textbf{and}\; \text{pos} = \text{text.length()}$$
$$\Rightarrow$$
$$\text{text.length()} < \text{text.max()} \;\textbf{and}\; 0 \leq \text{pos} \leq \text{text.length()}$$

(from precondition:
  len := this.length(); max := this.max();
  (**all** i: 0 ≤ i < len: char[i] := this.read(i))
)
pos = len
and
  text.length() = len + 1
  and (**all** i: 0 ≤ i < pos: text.read(i) = char[i])
  and text.read(pos) = ch
  and (**all** i: pos < i < text.length(): text.read(i) = char[i - 1])
⇒
  text.read(text.length() - 1) = ch

Understanding the flexibility introduced by requiring only implications, instead of equivalences, becomes very important when considering interactions of multiple providers and clients. Figure 6.1 illustrates the pivotal role of the interface contract when considering multiple clients and multiple providers of the services advertised by an interface.

Libraries always supported the concept of a service provider catering for many clients. However, in any one given configuration there is only one implementation of a library interface and the only concern on the provider's side is versioning. As explained above, the situation has changed dramatically with the introduction of self-standing interfaces and dynamic dispatch (late binding).

When is it legal to substitute one service provider for another? An unknown number of clients may rely on the service simply by relying on what is contractually promised by the service interface. Therefore, another service provider can come in if it satisfies the same contract. If a provider satisfies the same contract as another, the former is said to be substitutable for the latter.

6.2   Types, subtypes, and type checking

Ideally, all conditions of a contract would be stated explicitly and formally as part of an interface specification. In addition, it would be highly desirable to have a compiler or other automatic tool check clients and providers against the contract

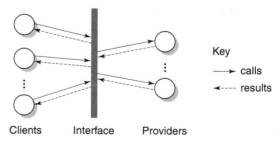

Figure 6.1 Pivotal role of interface contracts, coupling many clients with many providers.

and reject incorrect ones. In practice, this ideal is quite far from attainable. Fully formalizing the interface contracts is a first major obstacle. Doing so is difficult and often considered too expensive.

However, even where a formal contract is available, automatic checking remains a major challenge of ongoing research. It is known that an efficient general-purpose verifier is not feasible. Therefore, research concentrates on tools that use heuristics to automate most of the manual proof process. Such tools are called theorem provers. Theorem proving will be too expensive to be done in a production compiler for years to come, and it requires manual assistance by an expert.

Most conditions in a contract cannot be checked by today's compilers. Some cannot even be checked efficiently at runtime. However, it is worthwhile aiming for the earliest possible error checking to rule out potentially catastrophic faults. Hence, compiler-time checking is better than load-time checking, load-time checking is better than runtime checking, and runtime checking is better than no checking. However, sometimes later checking is the only possibility. For example, version conflicts among independently provided components can only be checked at configuration or load time. Likewise, index range errors can in the general case only be detected at runtime.

A class of errors that can lead to particularly disastrous results is memory errors. A memory error occurs when a program reads a memory cell based on a wrong assumption of what the cell contains. The program may expect, say, an object reference, whereas the cell really contains either something different, for example a floating point number, or has not been initialized at all. Memory errors are among the worst because they can affect entirely unrelated parts of a program, are notoriously hard to track down, and can be arbitrarily destructive.

Fortunately, there is a way to deal automatically with those conditions that need to be verified to eliminate memory errors. The idea is to group all values of related semantics, for example all integers, into sets. Such sets are called *types*. A type system ensures that all memory accesses are type compatible. By combining a type system with automatic memory management and certain runtime checks, a language implementation can fully eliminate memory errors – and some other error classes as well. Many modern languages, including Smalltalk, Java, Oberon, and Component Pascal, fall into this category. However, many others, including Object Pascal, Modula-2, C, and C++, do not.

Basic types, such as INTEGER or REAL, can be understood as sets of values. In the context of objects and interfaces, a type is best understood as a set of objects implementing a certain interface.

A type names all operations of an interface and the number and type of parameters and the type of returned values of each of the operations. The types of input and in–out parameters form a part of an operation's preconditions. The types of output and in–out parameters plus the type of returned values form a part of an operation's postconditions. However, other pre- and postconditions that are likely to be part of the underlying contract are not part of a type. Thus, a type is an interface with a simplified contract.

As a type is a simplified contract, it is possible that a program that passes type checking still violates some contracts. This is an important point and it is discussed below in section 6.5.

An object may implement more than the interface required in a certain context. It may implement additional interfaces, or a version of the required interface extended with additional operations, or both. For instance, the interfaces View, TextView, and GraphicsView below are in such an extension relation. TextView and GraphicsView are both interfaces that implement all operations in View, but also add operations specific to text and graphics viewing respectively. A more complete set of TextView operations has already been presented in Chapter 5 (p. 59).

```
interface View {
    void close ();
    void restore (int left, int top, int right, int bottom);
}
interface TextView extends View {
    int caretPos ();
    void setCaretPos (int pos);
}
interface GraphicsView extends View {
    int cursorX ();
    int cursorY ();
    void setCursorXY (int x, int y);
}
```

Under what circumstances can an object implementing one type be used in a context expecting another type? The answer follows directly from the above discussion of contracts. A client expecting a certain type really expects an object fulfilling a contract. Thus, all objects fulfilling the contract could be used. On the level of types, this includes all extended types as long as the understanding is that objects of an extended type respect the base contract.

Obviously, a TextView object or a GraphicsView object can be used wherever a View object is expected. As the set of text views is a proper subset of the set of views, TextView is called a *subtype* of View. Likewise, GraphicsView is a subtype of View.

The view examples show the formation of a subtype by defining a new interface and naming a base interface that is to be extended by the new interface. This is called *interface inheritance* and is the most common way to form subtypes. Another way is *structural subtyping*, in which no base interface is named. Instead, operations are repeated and a subtype is said to be formed if a subset of the operations coincides with operations defined for another type.

A variable of type View can refer to objects of type View, TextView, GraphicsView, or other subtypes. This is called *polymorphism*, and the variable is said to be of polymorphic type. As there are several different forms of polymorphism, this particular one is also called *subtype* or *inclusion polymorphism*. The latter name refers to the inclusion of subsets in their base set.

As far as the type system is concerned, objects of a subtype are substitutable for objects of a base type. However, again a warning: just as types simplify contracts, so does subtype polymorphism simplify substitutability. The fact that an object is in a proper subtype relation does not guarantee that the object's implementation respects the base contract, or, for that matter, any contract. On the other hand, it is fair to say that many of the outright 'dangerous' violations of contracts can be statically prevented by types and subtyping rules.

6.3 More on subtypes

The types of the parameters and the return value of an interface's operations form part of the pre- and postconditions of that operation. Discussion on 'overfulfilling a contract' by a service provider helps to understand what legal modifications to the types of an operation a subtype interface may apply. (It would be logical to talk about subcontracts when referring to the contracts associated with subtypes. Unfortunately, subcontract has an entirely different and well-established meaning.)

Note that this section mostly presents straightforward consequences of what has been discussed above, but is quite technical in nature. It can be safely skipped, especially on a first read.

Types of output parameters and return values form part of an operation's postconditions. A provider may establish more than is required by a contract. Hence, a subtype interface can replace the types of output parameters and return values by something more specific, that is by subtypes. In other words, the types of output parameters and return values may be varied from types to subtypes when moving from an interface of a certain type to an interface of a subtype of that type. As the types of output parameters and return values can thus be varied in the same direction as the types of the containing interfaces, this is called *covariance*.

Types of input parameters form part of an operation's preconditions. A provider may expect less than is guaranteed by a contract. Hence, a subtype interface could replace the types of input parameters by something more general, that is by supertypes. In other words, the types of input parameters may be varied from types to supertypes when going from an interface of a certain type to an interface of a subtype of that type. As the types of input parameters can thus be varied in the opposite direction of the types of the containing interfaces, this is called *contravariance*.

The requirements of co- and contravariance can be illustrated graphically by showing how a function could be substituted for another if it covers the same or a larger domain and if it has the same or a smaller range. Figure 6.2 illustrates this: in terms of domain and range, function g in the figure could be used in places where function f was expected.

Finally, types of in–out parameters simultaneously form part of an operation's pre- and postcondition. From a combination of the arguments for types in pre- and postconditions developed above, it follows that types of in–out parameters cannot be varied at all in a subtype interface. This phenomenon is sometimes called *invariance* of in–out parameter types. If, in addition to operations, an interface is also allowed to contain modifiable attributes, these also have invariant types.

Here is an example. Consider adding an operation getModel to interface View. In the case of a text view the model is of type TextModel, and this could be reflected by covariantly redefining getModel in TextView. The same can be done for getModel in GraphicsView.

```
interface View {
    ... // as above
    Model getModel ();
}
interface TextView extends View {
    ... // as above
    TextModel getModel ();
}
interface GraphicsView extends View {
    ... // as above
    GraphicsModel getModel ();
}
```

This is obviously useful. Clients that care only about View will get a generic Model when they ask for the views model. However, clients that know that they are dealing with a TextView object will get a TextModel.

Next, consider an operation setModel used to connect a view to a certain model. If part of View, setModel would have to take an object of type Model.

```
interface View {
    ... // as above
    void setModel (Model m);  // is this a good idea?
}
```

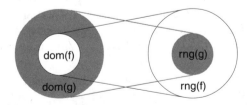

Figure 6.2 Contravariance of the domain and covariance of the range of a function g that could, in terms of domain and range, be substituted for a function f.

However, a TextView object needs a TextModel object as its model and a GraphicsView needs a GraphicsModel. If covariant change of input parameters was safe, setModel could be changed in TextView to accept a TextModel and in GraphicsView to accept a GraphicsModel.

Using a subtype interface allows substitution of a subtype object for a base type object. Thus, a text view would have to expect to be used in a context that knows only about interface View. Within that context the precondition of setModel simply requires, as far as types are concerned, a Model object. Thus, even if TextView was (incorrectly) allowed to modify covariantly the type of setModels input parameter, it would not help. The best that could happen is a dynamically caught type violation error.

Some type systems allow the introduction of typings that are coupled to the interface inheritance hierarchy. In other words, part of the precondition of the base operation is that subtype operations may covariantly modify certain parts that normally would fall under the contravariance restriction. Such type systems have to introduce other restrictions to remain sound, that is to continue to allow claims about absence of certain errors in well-typed programs.

For example, for static checking, the original Eiffel type system (Meyer, 1990) required a conservative global analysis of entire programs including all libraries used. Such a global analysis was called system-level type checking, and it clearly defeats the ideas of modular checking (p. 68). A library may type check on its own and thus be delivered to clients. Then, the combination of client and library code may lead to type errors *in the library*. Such type errors are indirectly caused by the addition of the client code, but are hard to explain. Modular checking requires monotonicity: if one module is determined to be internally type correct, then the addition of other modules cannot affect this result.

Type matching (Bruce *et al.*, 1997) and the recently revised Eiffel type system (Meyer, 1996) both allow for modular type checking of individual operations but require a more specific typing of variables. In particular, type matching requires that covariant changes in contravariant positions can occur only where the typed variable is declared to be monomorphic, that is cannot refer to an object of a subtype. Similarly, revised Eiffel requires that such covariant changes can only occur where the typed variable can be conservatively determined to be monomorphic. Sather is another object-oriented language that requires variables to be declared as either monomorphic or polymorphic (Szyperski *et al.*, 1994).

6.4 Object languages and types

Some languages, such as Smalltalk, do not have an explicit type system. In some of these cases, types can still be derived by a compiler by inspection of strictly local program fragments, such as in the Smalltalk dialect StrongTalk (Bracha and Griswold, 1993). In such languages, avoidance of explicit typing is a matter of convenience – there is less to write. The compiler can still check a program's typing and static type safety is preserved. Adding explicit typing is still useful, as it makes important architectural and design decisions explicit.

In other cases, including original Smalltalk, type inference is not possible without relying on global analysis of the entire code body (Palsberg and Schwartzbach, 1991). Type checking in Smalltalk and similar languages is thus deferred to runtime. For example, a Smalltalk expression 'x insert: 4 at: 3' requires that variable x refers at runtime to an object that understands the message *insert:at:*. However, in the general case, this cannot be verified statically. As a result, x may refer at runtime to an object that does not understand the message *insert:at:*. At least, this is checked dynamically and a 'message not understood' exception is raised at runtime in such a case.

More modern languages, such as Java and Component Pascal, use an explicit type system and statically check programs at compile time. In addition, they check narrowing type casts at runtime. (A narrowing cast is a cast in which the programmer asserts that a variable of a certain type really refers to an object of a subtype of that type. The cast narrows a set to a subset.)

For readers who followed the co-/contravariance story above, it is interesting that few of the mainstream languages support any changes in types of operations when forming subtypes. In C++, covariant return types were introduced only in early 1994 (Ellis and Soustrup, 1994, p. 421). Java still does not support any type changes. (The Java 1.0 beta specification allowed for covariant return values, while neither the alpha specification nor the final 1.0 or 1.1 specification does.) Like C++, Component Pascal supports covariant change of return values, but no other co- or contravariant changes.

6.5   Types, interfaces, and components

Some programming languages do not require the programmer to specify types and instead infer the most general types that still allow a program fragment to be type correct. Of course, this approach is impossible where interfaces are self-standing. At the time of creation of such an interface there may be no implementations available. Indeed, clients may be programmed before the first provider implementing the interface becomes available. To keep clients and providers independent, a self-standing interface has to be fully and explicitly typed to benefit from type checking.

Other programming languages establish subtype compatibility between two types structurally. Assume that an interface of one type happens to contain all operations contained by another type – and the operations in the two interfaces themselves are appropriately typed. In this case, the former type is inferred to be a subtype of the latter. As, in this case, subtyping is based on type structures, this is sometimes called *structural subtyping* in contrast to *declared subtyping*. Obviously, in situations in which all types are inferred, types do not have names and subtyping has to be based on structural compatibility.

When viewing types as simplified contracts, it becomes clear that structural subtyping is dangerous. The structure of a type covers only part of a contract – the part that can be expressed in the used type system. A *named* type refers to the full contract. If another type is then considered to be a subtype of this type, it has to respect the contract of its base type, in addition to its own contract. As the full contracts are only referred to, proper subtype relations cannot be infered automatically. Thus, a programmer should explicitly declare whether or not a type should be considered a legal subtype of another type. If so declared, the programmer accepts the obligation to verify that the subtype relation is indeed justified.

Many articles(for example Magnusson, 1991) describe the apocryphral tale of a graphics editor that accepted all objects that happened to have a method *draw*. Unfortunately, the user program failed horribly after accidentally inserting a cowboy object into the graphics editor, which then caused the editor to redraw all objects ...

It is sometimes argued that accidental structural subtyping is not likely in practice. The argument is that, for this to happen, all operations of the base type, including all of their parameter numbers and types and their return types, accidentally need to agree. For substantial interfaces this is indeed unlikely. Indeed, even for the *draw* example above, it is not likely that a graphics objects draw method would do without any parameters – as is likely to be the case for a cowboy object's draw method.

For small interfaces, and these are typical at the roots of subtype hierarchies, the situation is different. Quite often, root types have no or only a few very basic operations. Additionally, root types tend to be designed by following common design patterns. Thus, it is indeed possible and likely that accidentally derived subtypes lead to objects in positions where they, unknowingly, break their contracts.

For example, base types for interfaces such as Event and Property are likely to be empty. Or they may contain an operation to get some 'owner' object: the event source or the object having the property. Thus, the structure of base types, say Event and Property, may coincide. Deriving a subtype relation from that is unacceptable, of course: an event is not a property and vice versa.

Another aspect of components is their potential support of multiple interfaces. it is sometimes necessary to specify a required set of interfaces and then accept any component that provides at least these required interfaces. Such interface sets are sometimes called *categories*. For example, Microsoft's COM IDL has recently been extended to support such categories. This can be used to support one-stop tests, for example to check that a component implements all interfaces required to make it an ActiveX control.

In Java, even objects can implement multiple interfaces and interfaces can extend multiple interfaces. An example would be the merger of the two TextView examples presented above (pp. 59 and 78): a TextView interface would have to extend both the TextObserver and the View interface. In Java, this is possible.

However, Java has no concept of categories and an object's implementation of a set of interfaces must therefore be tested one by one.

6.6   The paradigm of independent extensibility

The principal function of component orientations is to support independent extensibility.

A system is independently extensible if it is extensible and if independently developed extensions can be combined (Szyperski, 1996). For example, all operating systems are one-level independently extensible by loading applications. However, recently, many applications themselves turned into independently extensible systems. Extensions to applications are usually called *plug-ins*. Applications, such as Netscape's Navigator, slowly turn into client-side operating systems by supporting an increasing number of increasingly complex plug-ins. The first examples of plug-ins supporting 'sub-plug-ins' have already arrived. On such example is Gazelle, a browser plug-in that supports downloading of Component Pascal 'applets' that execute in a local blackbox component framework (Paznesh, 1997). Java is by now a firm part of most browsers; otherwise, Java plug ins would be another example.

As applications are fragmented and turned into extensible architectures, operating systems do not stand still either. A radical design reduces the operating system itself to a minimal kernel, called a *micro-kernel*, and farms out almost all OS functionality to application-level servers. Micro-kernels were originally driven by research operating systems such as Mach (Accetta *et al.*, 1986) that by themselves never really made it into the markets. However, the micro-kernel design also influenced industrial-strength operating system designs, including Microsoft's Windows NT (Cutler, 1993).

Combining the 'dekernelization' efforts of operating system architects and the modularization efforts of application architects leads to a new vision for overall system architectures: components everywhere! However, it is not only about being able to construct the equivalent of the traditional operating system combined with a handful of applications. It is all about forming a system architecture that is independently extensible on all levels. It is about independent extensibility as a recursive construction principle applied uniformly. Such systems have been explored in research projects (for example the Ethos system; Szyperski, 1992a) and recently also in industrial projects. One of the most ambitious, the Taligent approach, failed. To understand why, it is helpful to return first to the early attempts to develop micro-kernel designs for operating systems.

Partitioning of systems into smallest components (to maximize reuse) conflicts with efficiency, but also with robustness when facing evolution and configurational variety. This was discussed in detail in Chapter 4. An argument similar to that for robustness can be made for performance. A micro-kernel architecture enforces total isolation of application-level processes to establish system safety and support security mechanisms. However, isolation comes at a price, and frequent crossing of protection domain boundaries can severely affect performance. [There are memory management units that separate address space management from protection domains, for example the ARM MMU (Furber, 1996). However, hardware support for many lightweight protection domains has yet to make it into the mainstream. Software alternatives exist (Wahbe et *al.*, 1993), but have yet to gain the degree of trust that a hardware protection mechanism commands.] In the end, for an operating system to be viable, its architects have to strive for a balance between flexibility on the one hand and performance and robustness on the other.

After initial waves of euphoria, many operating system experts now agree that extreme 'micro-kernelism' is not the optimal design for an operating system. After all, flexibility and configurability are only one side of an operating system's characteristics. The other side, and at least as important, is delivery of overall system performance. It is the latter requirement that directly conflicts with extreme micro-kernel designs. For example, Microsoft recently (NT 4.0) moved significant parts of the display driver code into the NT kernel to improve substantially the performance of graphics-intense applications.

How can component technology and independent extensibility as a recursive system design concept ever be viable if performance is so severely affected? The answer to this question would seem extremely important for the future of component technology. In reality, however, it turns out to be the wrong question.

The true question to be answered is: why is performance so severely affected? The obvious answer is 'because it is expensive to perform cross-context calls.' Whenever an invocation crosses contexts (processes and so on), the operating system has to ensure several things. It has to make sure that security policies are respected, that is check whether the call happens under proper authorization. Further, it has to adjust the hardware protection mechanisms, that is switch from caller to callee context. Finally, it has to make sure that the call parameters are transferred from the caller to the callee context. Once the called function returns, the process has to be reverted. In addition to the unavoidable basic costs, the switch also affects the processor caches. On some machines the caches even have to be flushed for security reasons.

All this is expensive: a cross-context call on well-tuned operating systems is still easily a hundred times more expensive than a local in-process call. This is not the operating system's fault. Most architectures rely on hardware-supported process isolation to guarantee safety, for example to protect a process in the presence of another out-of-control process that is trying to write to arbitrary memory addresses. Given a properly 'sealed' operating system and proper set-up of authorizations, even a maliciously ill-formed program written directly in the machine's assembly language cannot harm other programs executing on the same machine.

The cost of hardware protection is high but can be tolerated if the switching can be limited to, for example, a few hundred switches per second. This is the case under normal time-sharing operations of traditional operating systems. In this case, inter-process communication (IPC) is usually based on pipelining data streams that decouple source and destination and reduce the frequency of context-switching. Clearly, for tightly interacting components, 'inter-component communication' happens at much higher frequencies and is much more synchronous: the source component often has to wait for the result before it can continue.

On machines built for interactive use and made from cheap commodity items, called personal computers, this has long led to the utilization of rather different operating systems. Neither the Mac OS nor MS-DOS had a true process model. Hardware protection was mostly ignored. A malicious program could easily 'crash' the entire system. This was and often still is considered acceptable, as these machines typically serve a single user who is in charge and who can avoid the crash simply by avoiding the use of unreliable applications.

At the same time, these machines and operating systems perform very well when it comes to typical interactive use. System extensions or plug-ins are called directly, with no context switches involved. Component architectures in specialized areas have been in mainstream use for some time. For example, Apple's QuickTime included plug-in modules from the start, even although QuickTime's multimedia services are among the most performance-critical a system can offer.

Is it possible have your cake and eat it too? Could there be a third way, with efficient component composition that yet offers the sort of safety already demanded in section 2.2? One way is to choose carefully the granularity of components – if most interactions stay within a component's boundaries, the cost incurred when crossing component boundaries may be tolerable. Chapter 8 follows on with a discussion of various aspects governing component granularity. Another way is to guarantee statically that a component will be safe. This is discussed further in the next section.

6.7   Safety by construction: viability of components

The discussion on type safety points in the right direction. After all, hardware protection 'just' eliminates memory errors: it prevents one part of a system from accessing (reading, writing, or executing) any other part of the system for which it has no authorization. In a totally type-safe system, the equivalent reading is: no part can access any other part to which it has not been given a reference or which is not in its static scope of visibility.

Here is an example. The Java class files (Java's portable compiled format) and the Java virtual machine have been crafted to interact in a way that prevents type-unsafe applets from being executed in a non-local environment. Java is a type-safe language. It provides automatic memory management using garbage collection. Finally, it performs runtime checks on all operations that are 'dangerous' but cannot be statically checked, such as array bounds checks. Together, these techniques guarantee that memory errors cannot occur. As class files, produced by the Java compiler, could be tampered with, the virtual machine rechecks them when loading one coming from a non-local site, for example across the Internet.

Component Pascal is another example. The language offers similarly strong guarantees. Here the execution environment receives an intermediate portable form produced by the compiler that is based on an entirely different approach. This form is also rechecked, but then compiled into a local cache of binaries; future references to the same component directly use the cached binary. Like Java, Component Pascal is also fully garbage collected. Unlike Java, Component Pascal neither has nor needs an interpreter or a virtual machine.

6.7.1 Module safety

However, type safety and elimination of memory errors are not enough, although it is assumed that the language respects object encapsulation. Without any additional measures, it would still be possible for a program to call arbitrary services present in or loadable into the system. This would be all that is required to acquire references to arbitrary objects in the system and thus 'legally' (as far as the type system is concerned) to perform arbitrary manipulations. For example, there are ActiveX controls that shut down Windows.

The one additional requirement, also met by Java and Component Pascal, is *module safety* (Szyperski and Gough, 1995). A component has to specify explicitly which services, from the system or from other components, it needs to access. This is done in the form of module (or package) import lists. The language does not allow access to any non-imported module. Hence, if that list contains only permissible modules, then it is safe to load and execute the new component. This is like access control in file systems, but on a per-module (or per-class) basis, rather than a per-object basis. Objects are too dynamic to be identified explicitly for purposes of static access control.

With module safety in place, abstractions of entire multiobject services can be formed. Unlike classes, modules can enforce invariants across tightly interacting objects (Szyperski, 1992a). In a language not supporting any higher granularity of packaging than classes, access protection would have to be per-class, offering class safety instead of module safety.

Module safety is not quite as simple as it sounds. In component systems it is important that other components (and services) can be retrieved by name. The name itself may be made available to a component after that component has been compiled, checked, and loaded, that is at runtime. A clean and popular way to support component retrieval by name is a reflection service. Both Java and Component Pascal offer such services.

6.7.2 Module safety and metaprogramming

It should be impossible for a component to retrieve references to other components to which it has not been granted access. For example, in Java, a special security manager object is used to inspect whether the caller of a critical function has proper authorization. To do so, the call stack is traversed and checked for any untrusted activation record. If there is none, the call can proceed, as it cannot serve any untrusted component. The call to the security manager is performed by the critical operation itself, to protect itself against unwanted calls. The security manager throws a security exception if it does not authorize access for the direct or one of the indirect callers.

As admitted in the JavaBean's standard document (JavaSoft, 1996, p. 6.7.2), this approach can be undermined by a carelessly programmed but trusted service that performs asynchronous requests on behalf of clients (a so-called event adapter). In such a case, the true client will not be active at the time of the safety-critical call; only the trusted service will be. Another loophole would be if a critical object was registered in an unprotected registry. In this case, anyone guessing the access key or name, or, if it were supported, anyone enumerating all registered objects, could retrieve the critical object under a generic supertype, say Object. It would then be simply a matter of type test and cast to regain access to the critical object.

Even if a component legally accesses some module, it must not gain any access to the private (non-exported) parts of that module. For direct access, this is guaranteed by the language semantics. However, where meta-programming interfaces exist, these need to be explicitly restricted such that these services do not break encapsulation. This is contrary to some of the typical usages of meta-programming, such as debugging or data structure serialization services. Indeed, a system may offer two metaprogramming interfaces: one that is module safe and open for general use and another that is module unsafe and restricted to trusted components.

The BlackBox Component Framework (used with Component Pascal) is a currently unique example of a system offering a dual metaprogramming service. The type and module-safe service is open for general use, whereas the module-unsafe service is used by trusted components, for example by the BlackBox portable debugger. The Java JDK 1.1 includes metaprogramming facilities that are normally module safe (package safe). Some limited module-unsafe operations are available to trusted callers – subject to security manager validation.

6.7.3 Safety in a multi-language environment

Component technology allows the selection of different programming languages for the implementation of different components. Mutual protection of components in the same hardware protection domain thus requires type and module safety properties that are common to all languages used in such a configuration. This problem can be solved by sufficiently strong interface definition languages (IDLs). It is therefore unnecessary to restrict a system to a single programming language approach simply to benefit from language-level type and module safety. However, the strength of the overall approach will depend on the strength of its weakest part, that is the weakest of the languages used, including the IDL.

6.8 Safety, security, trust

Type safety, module safety, absence of memory errors: what makes this language–semantics-based approach trustworthy? The answer depends on the circumstances. If the target is a set of components, installed locally, interacting on a personal computer, then this approach may already be close to satisfactory. If the target is of highest security level, then this approach would be totally unacceptable. If the target is a low- to medium-security system that moves components across the Internet, this approach is probably at its limits.

What is wrong? First and above all, this approach fully relies on the tight semantics of the programming language used. To be fully trustworthy, a formal semantics of the language together with formal proofs of the claimed safety properties would be required. And, of course, the formal method itself needs to be trusted, including the tools that may be used to construct lengthy proofs semi-automatically. Very few programming languages satisfy this requirement; none of them is a mainstream object-oriented language.

Even if a language fully satisfies this criterion, its implementation could still break any proved property. Hence, to go all the way, the language processors and the language runtime systems again need to be formally specified and verified. This is quite a feat to achieve. Consider that language processing includes tools such as a compiler, an interpreter, or a byte code verifier. The language runtime includes mechanisms such as a virtual machine, a garbage collector, or a security manager. Obviously, this may lead to a bootstrap problem where the tools used to build the used tools again need to be formally verified, and so on. None of the widely available language implementations satisfies these criteria, not even in cases where the implemented language itself satisfies its safety criterion.

In the end, trust is a matter of reducing the unknown to the known and trusted, and doing so in a trusted way. This is obviously primarily a sociological process. For example, the way the Unix security mechanism was introduced played a major role in it being trusted. The designers of the mechanism published its details in full and encouraged everyone to try to break it. After years, the mechanism gained (or, better, earned) the trust it currently receives. This trust can be justified probabilistically. It is highly unlikely that a loophole remains undiscovered under the uncoordinated (stochastic) evaluation by many over an extended period of time.

The Java designers also publicized their security strategies early on and encouraged serious research groups (McGraw and Felten, 1997) to challenge the approach. In this way, known loopholes are published and fixed (See 'Frequently asked questions – applet security,' http://www.javasoft.com/sfaq/.) After years of steadily decreasing reports of found problems, people will increasingly trust the approach. Today, limitation of trust is appropriate, whatever the proponents claim, and even if they are right.

6.9   Dimensions of independent extensibility

In traditional class frameworks, extension happens through specialization: classes of the framework are subclassed to add the required behavior. If the framework does not offer the right abstractions, such a specialization may not be possible. However, the notion of implementation inheritance, as interpreted in most object-oriented languages, allows for quite radical changes to the classes introduced by the framework. Quite often, the required functionality can be forced upon the framework.

Traditional class frameworks are specialized at application construction time and thereafter disappear as no longer separable parts of the generated application. The only conflict resulting from 'forced' specialization is that migration of the application to the next release of the independently evolved framework may be difficult or impossible.

The situation is very different for independently extensible systems. Extensions from independent sources may be combined by using the same component framework. Forcing specialization would endanger the interoperability of independent extensions. Thus, even more so than for class frameworks, independently extensible systems require a clear statement of *what* can be extended. Each particular feature of an independently extensible system that is open for separate extension is called a *dimension of (independent) extensibility* (for example Weck, 1997).

Note that dimensions of extensibility are not necessarily orthogonal: the same effect may be achieved by extending along one of several possible dimensions. This is not normally desirable, as it offers designers of extensions an unwanted choice. Perfect orthogonality of dimensions is difficult to achieve and a total exclusion of possible overlaps may excessively restrict individual dimensions. The result would be a system that is orthogonal but not complete. As a result, important extensions become impossible. The theoretical ideal would be to form orthogonal dimensions of independent extensibility that together form an extension space that is complete with respect to extensibility requirements.

In practice, extensible systems rarely have orthogonal dimensions of extensibility. For example, the same system may support extensible abstractions for object serialization and object persistence. Although not identical, these two services certainly overlap. Multiple dimensions of extensibility form a *product space*, that is the set of all combinations of extensions along the individual dimensions. Where the dimensions are orthogonal, the resulting space is a *Cartesian product*. (A Cartesian product, also called cross-product, of n sets is the set of n-tuples containing all possible permutations of the elements of the n sets. The number of effectively different permutations is reduced if the original sets overlap, that is the corresponding dimensions are non-orthogonal.)

6.9.1 **Bottleneck interfaces**

If a system was independently extensible 'from scratch,' that is no fixed infrastructure would exist, then independent extensions could not interoperate at all. There would not be any common ground for them to interact. A common ground *after the fact* could not generally be provided as the extensions come from independent and mutually unaware sources. Component frameworks provide the required shared understanding that couples extensions. A component framework *opens* a number of dimensions for extending components. Also, a component framework may enforce some of the rules of interactions between extensions.

Interfaces introduced to allow the interoperation between independently extended abstractions are sometimes called *bottleneck interfaces* (for example Szyperski, 1992b). A bottleneck interface is a self-standing contract. As a bottleneck interface couples independent extension families, it cannot itself be extended. This is one of the arguments behind the claim that such an interface, once published, can only be withdrawn or replaced but not extended. Bottleneck interfaces, once published, are immutable (see also the next section). Obviously, components may be mutually aware of their extensions and engage in more special interaction. In poorly designed component frameworks, such mutual awareness is sometimes required for two components to interact properly. In other words, such component frameworks require seemingly independent components to enter in a 'conspiracy.'

6.9.2 **Singleton configurations**

A component framework may open dimensions of extensibility but require a *singleton configuration* for some of the dimensions. A configuration is a singleton configuration, regarding a specific compulsory dimension, if it provides *exactly one* component that extends that dimension. For optional dimensions, a singleton configuration provides at *most one* component. For example, a system may allow for the installation of a security manager but may insist on having at most one such manager in a configuration at any one time.

6.9.3 **Parallel, orthogonal, and recursive extensions**

Normally, for most or even all of its dimensions, a component framework would not require singleton configuration. Thus, a configuration can contain many components that all extend along the same dimension. This is called *parallel extension* (Weck, 1997). The main problem of systems allowing for parallel extension is peaceful coexistence. Two components extending along the same dimension are in danger of asking for the same resources. A component framework allowing for parallel extension has to define rules and provide means for arbitration. An example is a set of multiple controls embedded into the same container of a compound document architecture. Necessarily unique resources, like the current focus for keyboard input, need to be arbitrated when requests from multiple controls collide.

Separate extending components may also address orthogonal dimensions of a component framework. This is called *orthogonal extension* (Weck, 1997). The main problem with orthogonal extension is the provision of proper bottleneck interfaces to allow interaction between the orthogonal extensions. Again using the example of controls and containers in a compound document, controls and containers are addressing orthogonal dimensions. A single component may address both dimensions simultaneously, for example be control and container at the same time. A component framework for compound documents has to define and support the bottleneck interfaces that allow arbitrary controls to talk to arbitrary containers, and vice versa. A typical such interface is used by controls and containers to negotiate for screen space.

Both parallel and orthogonal extension are *flat*, that is extending components are mutually independent. *Recursive extensions* are also possible. A component can itself introduce a component framework. Components extending this new framework obviously depend on the framework-introducing component or at least the abstractions introduced by this component. Note that recursive extensions do not necessarily create a well-layered architecture. It is possible that a component simultaneously extends dimensions introduced by recursive extensions at different levels. For example, a system might have a component framework for distributed resource management. One of the components extending this framework may itself be a framework for compound documents. It is possible that, say, a container component extends dimensions of both the resource management and the compound document framework.

6.10   Evolution versus immutability of interfaces and contracts

A contract, that is an interface together with its specification, mediates between independently evolving clients and providers of the services the interface makes accessible. As soon as a contract has been published to the world, it (the interface and its specification) can no longer be changed. This holds for clients and providers bound by a specific contract.

A provider can always stop providing a particular interface. It will then potentially lose part of its client base – the part that has not yet been migrated to some newer interface. However, a provider can never change the specification of an existing contract, as that would break clients without any obvious indication. Also, a client cannot change its understanding of the contract without risking to break some existing providers.

The cornerstone of even arguing about contracts and changing contracts is a way to name uniquely the contracts that clients and providers refer to. As a contract, with all its informal bylaws, is itself quite difficult to capture, the name of the associated interface is commonly used.

6.10.1 Syntactic versus semantic contract changes

Changes to a contract can take two forms. Either the interface or the specification is changed. If the interface is changed, this is referred to as a *syntactic* change. If the specification is changed, this is called a *semantic* change. As providers are often 'in charge' of a contract, and typical providers in object-oriented settings are classes, the problem caused by contract change is sometimes referred to as the *fragile base class* problem. The syntactic and semantic variations of the fragile base class problem are discussed in detail in section 7.4.

A simple way to avoid these problems is to refrain from changing contracts, *once they have been published*. Of course, there is no problem with changing contracts (syntactically or semantically), as long as all bound providers and clients are under control. Thus, evolution of contracts within a tight organization is usually not an issue. However, by releasing clients or providers to the open market, the contracts involved become uncontrollable. Then change has to stop and the contracts have to be frozen, that is made *immutable*.

It is again helpful to consider the analogy of traditional contracts. No clause in a contract, once signed, can be changed *without agreement* of all involved parties. Of course, once there is an uncontrollable number of parties, getting agreement can become difficult or impossible. Examples are contracts between all employers and employees covered by some tariff union. However, such contracts do have mechanisms that allow for change. The two fundamental mechanisms are: acknowledging existence of overriding law and instances and statement of a termination time. (Thanks to Wolfgang Weck for pointing out this analogy.)

It is noteworthy that today only Microsoft's COM declares all *published* interfaces to be immutable. Even Microsoft itself adheres to the principle and introduces new interfaces, instead of modifying existing ones that almost fit. Support for the older interfaces is upheld for a while to maintain backwards compatibility, but eventually such older interfaces can and should go. IBM's SOM does something different. By explicitly supporting a *release order*, clients of different releases (versions) of an interface can coexist. Essentially, the explicit release order guarantees for every method a fixed index into a look-up table. For this to work, a new release can only add to an interface, it cannot take functionality away. A more detailed discussion of the two approaches can be found in Chapter 13 (SOM) and Chapter 14 (COM).

6.10.2 Contract expiry

Some of the current component infrastructures offer licensing services, and it is a natural property of licenses that they expire after a preset date. Hence it would seem straightforward to couple service provision under certain contracts with license agreements and their expiry date. The result would allow for a controlled evolution, in which clients and providers can blindly trust the *validity and existence* of a service under a certain contract until the expiration date is reached. Thereafter, manufacturers of clients and providers would have to renegotiate: a contract's lifetime could be extended or the contract could be replaced or refined.

Using contracts with 'use-by dates' has effects on users. Software systems can no longer be used indefinitely – or at least for as long as that outdated PC can be kept alive. However, there is also an advantage. Instead of supporting legacy contracts forever, adding more and more baggage to providers and clients, there is a clean way to cut off the past. As noted above, it is always possible to stop support for an aged contract. However, without mutually agreed expiry dates, this will always come as a surprise to some users.

6.10.3 Overriding law

What about the other mechanisms in traditional contracts, overriding law? In acts of self-justice, this principle is commonly applied by companies or organizations that dominate a market. Overriding law in this sense can mean the depreciation of clients or providers conforming to the old interpretation of a contract. A more moral way to achieve the same is interception by an accepted independent organization. Typical examples are the International Standards Organization (ISO), the American National Standards Institute (ANSI), the British Standards Institution (BSI), the German institute for industrial standards (DIN), and so on.

6.11   Other forms of polymorphism

There are other forms of polymorphism besides the subtype (or inclusion) polymorphism introduced above (section 6.2). These other forms are discussed briefly below. For a thorough coverage, see Abadi and Cardelli (1996).

Although subtype polymorphism is a dynamic scheme, the other forms are static and resolvable by a compiler. There are higher order type systems, where some of these other forms may also require dynamic resolution. Such type systems have not yet reached mainstream languages. Overloading, as supported by languages such as C++ and Java, is a form of polymorphism that groups otherwise unrelated operations under the same name. Overloading is sometimes called *ad-hoc polymorphism*, because it establishes only a superficial similarity that is based neither on typing nor on shared implementation.

The third form of polymorphism focuses on using the same implementation to serve a variety of types. For example, a list implementation can be parametrized with the type of the list elements. Any one instance of the list will serve one specific type, but the list implementation itself is generic and provided only once. This is called *parametric polymorphism* and is similar to generics in Ada. Properly implemented, parametric polymorphism does not lead to an explosion of generated code. A particularly lightweight variant that always produces exactly one copy of code has been proposed for Oberon (Roe and Szyperski, 1997) and may in the near future be supported by Component Pascal. Note that parametric polymorphism is also similar to C++ templates. However, C++ templates lead to code explosion, as a template is necessarily compiled to different code for each instantiation. Also, templates cannot be statically type checked: type checking cannot occur before parameters are supplied.

It is sometimes useful to specify constraints on type parameters. Parametric polymorphism does not allow this: any type can be used to parametrize a parametric abstraction. For example, a parametric list can be used to form lists over arbitrary types. For lists, that is fine. Consider a parametric container component: it accepts controls of a certain type, determined by the type parameter. However, whatever the type parameter will be, it has to be a subtype of Control, that is only control types are acceptable.

A stronger polymorphic form that accepts bounds in the form of minimal supertypes is called *bounded polymorphism*. Bounded polymorphism combines subtype and parametric polymorphism. For example, using subtype polymorphism, a list of control objects can be constructed, but the same list implementation cannot be further constrained to contain only text controls. Using parametric polymorphism, the latter can be achieved, but the list could also be parametrized to contain only models (or any other type of objects) – the subtyping property that each element is at least a control is lost.

In the control container example, control-specific operations need to be applied to all list elements. For such operations to be statically safe, a combination of subtype and parametric polymorphism would be required and bounded polymorphism could be used. The list would be parametrized with a type that has to be a subtype of the control type. The control type is a bound on acceptable parameter types.

CHAPTER SEVEN

Object versus class composition, or how to avoid inheritance

Before entering any discussion of inheritance, some definitions are necessary. Inheritance would seem, from the literature for and against it, to be one of the most sacrosanct terms in the object-oriented language vocabulary. Several different mechanisms are embraced within the term inheritance; any discussion that does not begin by clarifying precisely which mechanisms are referred to is guaranteed to be misleading.

This chapter begins by discussing the various aspects of inheritance and their manifestation in different object models and object-oriented languages. A detailed discussion of the problems introduced by some of these aspects follows. In particular, the facets of the fragile base class problem are covered in detail. Some of the problems can be avoided by adopting a highly disciplined approach to inheritance – and a number of such 'disciplines' are introduced in this chapter. A more radical way to solve these problems is to avoid (implementation) inheritance altogether and use object instead of class composition. This possibility and its ramifications are discussed in detail. The chapter concludes with a brief review.

7.1   Inheritance – the soup of the day?

If Simula 67 (Dahl and Nygaard, 1970) is taken as the origin of the concept, then inheritance combines three aspects: inheritance of implementation, inheritance of interfaces, and establishment of substitutability. However, if Smalltalk 80 (Goldberg and Robson, 1983) is considered the origin, then inheritance only combines inheritance of implementation and inheritance of interfaces, while substitutability is not required (although recommended). This may come as a surprise, but even the original Smalltalk 80 class library contains several well-known examples in which a class defines objects that are not substitutable for those of its superclass.

It is important to distinguish the Simula and Smalltalk interpretations of subclassing (inheritance). As explained before (p. 83), neither a language nor a compiler can enforce substitutability. However, a mechanism like inheritance may be *intended* to be used to imply substitutability, or not. In Simula – and also in

C++, Java, and Component Pascal – a subclass is supposed to guarantee substitutability and, in theory, a proof liability for the programmer follows.

The story becomes even more complex when considering further interpretations of inheritance. For example, in Eiffel it is possible to *undefine* inherited interface features. A class may thus not even be interface compatible with its superclass, ruling out substitutability completely. Furthermore, in languages such as Sather or Java, interface inheritance and implementation inheritance have been separated. In this case, it is possible to inherit a pure interface with no implementation (coded behavior) at all. And, finally, OMG IDL is a pure interface definition language ouside the realm of any implementations. Thus, it supports only interface inheritance (subtyping).

To summarize, there are three cardinal facets of inheritance:

(1) subclassing, that is inheritance of implementation fragments/code, usually called *implementation inheritance*;
(2) subtyping, that is inheritance of contract fragments/interfaces, usually called *interface inheritance*; and
(3) promise of substitutability.

It is surprising that the three facets are usually omitted or at least not clearly distinguished when starting heated discussions on the pros and cons. Part of an explanation might be the irrational discussion between 'objectionists' and 'hybridists.' Or is it fundamentalists/purists against technocrats/pragmatists? The former usually refer to the prime directive that object models shall support inheritance (although which of the inheritance facets they insist on is often left open). The latter argue that nothing is impossible and everything may have its place.

Subtyping, contracts, and substitutability have been covered in Chapters 5 and 6. Some of this material will be considered in more depth in this chapter. The 'how to avoid inheritance' promise refers solely to implementation inheritance, sometimes also referred to as code inheritance or subclassing. Also, despite the provocative chapter title, there is no intention of banning implementation inheritance outright. Rather, it seems appropriate to analyze carefully what implementation inheritance gives, what it costs, and where the trade-offs are. The deeper implications of implementation inheritance on components rather than objects need to be worked out clearly.

7.2 More flavors to the soup

As if the above splitting into often unmentioned facets were not enough, even implementation inheritance comes in many flavors. (An early object system for Common Lisp was even called Flavors; Moon, 1986.) For the following discussion it is not necessary to explore fully the endless list of variations. However, a few essential notions need to be covered to create a common basis for later comparisons.

7.2.1 Multiple inheritance

In principle, there is no reason why a class should have only one superclass. Why not mix and match by inheriting from a number of classes? The idea seems promising. There are two principal reasons for supporting multiple inheritance. The first is to allow interfaces from different sources to be merged, aiming for simultaneous substitutability with objects defined in mutually unaware contexts. The second is to merge implementations from different sources. (Multiple interface inheritance is sometimes called *multiple subtyping*. However, this is really a misnomer as every type can have multiple subtypes: *multiple supertyping* would be more appropriate. Likewise, *multiple subclassing* is a misnomer and *multiple superclassing* should be used.)

Establishing compatibility with multiple independent contexts is important. Multiple interface inheritance is one way to achieve this, although it is not the only one. OMG IDL and Java are examples of approaches that explicitly support multiple interface inheritance. In C++, multiple inheritance of abstract classes can be used. Microsoft COM does not support multiple interface inheritance (and does not support true single interface inheritance either), but allows a component to support multiple interfaces simultaneously, to much the same effect. A detailed discussion of these approaches follows in Part Three. For now, it suffices to state that multiple interface inheritance does not introduce any major technical problems beyond those already introduced by single interface inheritance (which is covered in detail further below).

Mixing implementation fragments by means of multiple implementation inheritance is a different story entirely. If the superclasses all come from totally disjoint inheritance graphs, and name clashes are properly resolved, the new class merely concatenates the inherited implementations. However, the superclasses are usually not guaranteed to be disjoint, with tricky semantic problems as a result. As illustrated in Figure 7.1, two superclasses may inherit code from a shared superclass. In general, superclasses may directly or indirectly share any number of classes further up the inheritance graph.

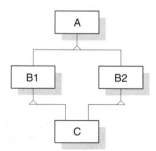

Figure 7.1 Diamond inheritance structure caused by a class (C) inheriting from classes (B1 and B2) that themselves inherit from a common class (A).

Figure 7.1 uses the OMT (object modeling technique) notation (Rumbaugh *et al.*, 1991; Rumbaugh, 1994) to depict inheritance relations among classes. In the figure, class C inherits from classes B1 and B2, both of which inherit from class A. The diamond shape of the inheritance graph in Figure 7.1 gives rise to the name the 'diamond inheritance problem.' This problem has long been documented in the object-oriented literature, and numerous 'solutions' have been proposed. The problem is really twofold, centered around both state and behavior.

For state, the basic question is: do both superclasses B1 and B2 get their own copy of the state defined by the shared superclass A? The two superclasses may operate independently on this state. If the state is shared, the two classes are coupled: one observes state changes caused by the other. Obviously, this breaks encapsulation. If the state is not shared, that is if each inheriting class gets its own copy, then consistency of a joined subclass C is in danger: which copy does it see? Would it need both superclasses to share some of the inherited state but not all? Generally, the client class C cannot fix the problem without fully understanding the *implementation* of the two superclasses.

Some approaches grant a class designer limited control over the sharing of inherited state. For example, in C++ a superclass can be made 'virtual.' This indicates that the superclass state should be shared with other subclasses that inherit from the same superclass and declare it 'virtual.' However, it is very difficult to decide whether or not a superclass should be made 'virtual' without fully understanding its implementation. (Also, at least in C++, there is a price to be paid: a method of a virtual superclass cannot recover the original object identity, that is has its own 'this.')

The behavior of the shared class A, that is its method implementations, adds another dimension to the problem. If B1 or B2 or both override some of A's methods, what behavior should then make it to C? Assume that B1 overrides a method that B2 left unchanged. Should a call to that method in the implementation inherited from B2 into C call the overriding code in B1? As for inherited state, the correct answer might even be different from method to method.

In some approaches, following the early example of Common Lisp Object System (CLOS) (DeMichiel and Gabriel, 1987), the multiple implementation inheritance is disciplined by prescribing a linear order of inheritance. The order artificially arranges classes such as B1 and B2 such that one takes precedence over the other. Such an ordering scheme allows programmers to predict precisely what the effects of multiple implementation inheritance will be, *provided* the inherited code is known and understood. Abstraction and encapsulation suffer.

Approaches to the semantics of multiple inheritance usually stay close to the implementation strategy chosen. For example, the scheme used for C++ (Stroustrup, 1987; Ellis and Stroustrup, 1994) is based on an earlier proposal for Simula (Krogdahl, 1984). This proposal aims at maintaining the integrity of 'subobjects:' the pieces of the state space inherited from the various superclasses. This concept has recently been formalized (Rossi and Friedman, 1995) to remove direct implementation dependency but still remains mostly at the level of explaining effects of 'feature interactions' rather than forming abstractions.

The designers of Java came up with an interesting solution: Java supports multiple interface inheritance but is limited to single implementation inheritance. The diamond inheritance problem is thus elegantly solved by avoidance without giving up on the possibility of inheriting multiple interfaces. The OMG IDL and COM do not support single or multiple implementation inheritance. The only major object model that does is SOM, IBM's system object model. SOM also supports multiple implementation inheritance (and thus has to address the diamond inheritance problem).

7.2.2 Mixins

Multiple inheritance can be used in a particular style called mixin inheritance (Bracha and Cook, 1990). The idea is that a class inherits interfaces from one superclass and implementations from several superclasses, each focusing on distinct parts of the inherited interface. The latter classes are called *mixins*, as they are used to mix implementation fragments into a class. The following example shows how an interface Window introduces three separate 'protocols' (sets of methods). The first protocol is used to handle a window as a whole, the second to handle its borders (title bar, scroll bars, and so on), and the third to handle its contents.

```
interface Window {
  // whole window:
  void drawWindow ();
  // window borders:
  void drawBorders ();
  void handleMouse (Event ev);
  // window contents:
  void drawContents ();
  Rect getVisibleSection ();
  Rect getContentsBox ();
  void scrollTo (Rect newVisible);
}
```

Each of the three protocols is now separately implemented by a mixin class:

```
abstract class StdWindowShell implements Window {
  void drawWindow () {
    drawBorders; drawContents;
  }
}
abstract class MotifWindowBorders implements Window {
  void drawBorders () {
    ...  // draw title bar
    Rect visible = getVisibleSection();
    Rect total = getContentsBox();
```

```
        ...  // draw scroll bars (compute thumbs using visible and total boxes)
    }
    void handleMouse (Event ev) {
        ...
        if (scroll bar thumb moved) {
            ...  // compute new visible region
            scrollTo(newVisible);
        }
        ...
    }
}
abstract class TextWindowContents implements Window {
    void drawContents () { ... }
    Rect getVisibleSection () { ... }
    Rect getContentsBox () { ... }
    void scrollTo (Rect newVisible) { ... }
}
```

Each of the three mixin classes implements one of the protocols in one particular way. Alternative mixins would implement the same protocols differently. For example, a mixin Win95WindowBorders would implement those for Windows 95 instead of Motif.

The mixin classes are all abstract: they implement only one of the protocols but use any of the other protocols as well. To form a concrete class, a mixin is selected for each protocol and a new class is written that inherits from each of the selected mixins. The following class MotifTextWindow combines the three mixins sketched above; note that this is pseudo-Java, as Java does not support multiple implementation inheritance:

```
class MotifTextWindow   // pseudo Java
    extends StdWindowShell, MotifWindowBorders, TextWindowContents {
}
```

In this example, there is nothing left to do: the composition of the complete set of three mixins fully implements a window that displays text and has the look and feel of a Motif window.

As mixins address independent implementation aspects, their combination by means of multiple inheritance is supposed to be straightforward. However, unless programming languages and object models start enforcing the independence of mixins, this is left as a convention for programmers to follow. Also, it is not clear whether insisting on total independence of mixins is acceptable, as this would rule out a mixin that itself inherits from some standard library's class. (Other mixins might inherit from the same library class.)

7.3　Back to basic ingredients

The above exploration of some of the ramifications of multiple implementation inheritance should suffice to understand that an apparently simple and useful generalization can have subtle and possibly unexpected consequences. For the purposes of describing the further problems with inheritance of interfaces and code, the single inheritance case suffices. The underlying structure is thus simplified from an abstract inheritance graph – a directed acyclic graph or heterarchy – to a much simpler inheritance or class *hierarchy*.

To go further, two additional aspects need to be considered: how to get classes right and how to make them robust. Getting a class right is a static issue: how can a class be implemented to ensure its correctness? Getting it robust is a dynamic issue: how can a class be implemented to tolerate evolution and versioning of its superclasses and subclasses? The discussion of both of these issues led to the formulation of the so-called fragile base class problem.

7.4　The fragile base class problem

Fundamentally, the question is whether a base class can evolve, that is appear in new releases, without breaking independently developed subclasses. Considering the scenario in which the base class forms part of an operating system's interface, the importance of this question becomes clear. In the example, if independent release changes are not possible, a separation of operating system and applications fails. This potentially tight dependency of independently developed subclasses on their base class is called the fragile base class problem.

To confuse things, different positions have been taken based on two different interpretations of the problem: a syntactic and a semantic interpretation. Consider the following two quotations:

> 'The problem is that the "contract" between components in an implementation hierarchy is not clearly defined. When the parent or child component changes its behavior unexpectedly, the behavior of related components may become undefined.'
>
> Sara Williams *et al.*, Microsoft (1995)

> 'By completely encapsulating the implementation of an object, SOM overcomes what Microsoft refers to as the "fragile base class problem," i.e., the inability to modify a class without recompiling clients and derived classes dependent upon that class.'
>
> F. R. Campagnoni, IBM (1995)

The first quotation refers to a problem of *semantics* of inheritance under release changes of the involved classes. The second quotation refers to a problem of binary interface compatibility or *syntactic* stability across release changes. It is obvious that a semantic problem cannot be solved by requiring or not requiring mere recompilation. In the following, the two interpretations of the fragile base class problem are looked at and their relations to inheritance are established.

7.4.1 The syntactic fragile base class problem

The syntactic fragile base class problem (syntactic FBC) is about binary compatibilty of compiled classes with new binary releases of superclasses. This is sometimes referred to as *release-to-release binary compatibility*. It has nothing to do with the semantics of inherited code.

The idea is that a class should not need recompilation, just because purely 'syntactic' changes to its superclasses' interfaces have occurred, or because new releases of superclasses have been installed. For example, methods may move up in the class hierarchy. However, as long as they remain on the inheritance path and retain a compatible list of parameters and return types, a subclass should not care and thus should not require recompilation. Likewise, new intermediate classes may be inserted or new methods added.

By initializing method dispatch tables at loading time, the syntactic FBC can be solved. IBM's SOM is doing just that and offers release-to-release binary compatibility of classes even under quite radical restructuring or extension of their superclasses.

It is interesting to see that a 1994 SOM White Paper (IBM, 1994) thereby declared the FBC problem solved, whereas SOM really only addresses the syntactic FBC problem. Binary compatibility is an important problem, and addressing it in full generality is certainly a major achievement of SOM's designers (Forman *et al.*, 1995). However, the semantic FBC problem goes much deeper and ironically seems to be best addressed by avoiding some of the mechanisms that initially led to the syntactic FBC problem.

7.4.2 The semantic fragile base class problem

The essence of the semantic FBC problem is: how can a subclass remain valid in the presence of different versions and evolution of the *implementation* of its superclasses? (If the interface also changes, then the syntactic and semantic FBC problems occur in combination.) To answer this question, the very nature of implementation inheritance needs to be understood first.

The remainder of this and the following sections take a long detour to explain the semantics of implementation inheritance. For many, this is probably diffcult reading, and skipping this material is safe. However, the material is required for a serious discussion of some of the deepest differences that occur between currently proposed object and component models.

The FBC problem is that a compiled class should remain stable in the presence of certain transformations of the inherited interfaces and implementations. Separating the syntactic from the semantic FBC problem allows elegant technical solutions (to the syntactic FBC problem) but is nevertheless questionable. The separate treatment and the infrastructural complexity required to solve the syntactic facet alone is costly and must be fully justified. The cost is only justified if, in practice, it is found to be common to rearrange interfaces or replace superclass releases *without* observably changing superclass behavior. If a superclass changed semantics from one release to the next, this would probably break subclasses. On the other hand, there remain many possible changes of 'syntactic' nature that cannot be addressed by a SOM-like scheme. Examples are: splitting a method into two, joining two methods into one, or changing the parameter list of a method.

For immature class libraries, the point can probably be made that solving the syntactic FBC problem by itself eases library evolution. However, it is less likely that longer-term evolution of more mature libraries follows the same pattern. Minor syntactic changes, by themselves, such as refactoring of superclass chains, are less of an issue for more mature libraries – that is what maturity is all about. Further evolution, once required, can be expected to require changes to the syntax as well as to the semantics of the library. This is where the semantic FBC problem comes in.

Before analyzing the additional intricacies contributed by implementation inheritance, recall the situation with traditional libraries, callbacks, and object webs as discussed in Chapter 5. As argued there, things become tricky as soon as the transition from simple 'down-call only' libraries to libraries with callbacks or up-calls is made. In conjunction with observable state, this leads to re-entrance semantics close to that of concurrent systems. Arbitrary call graphs formed by interacting webs of objects abolish the classical layering and make re-entrance the norm. As discussed in Chapter 5, this leads to quite complex semantics and substantial subtleties in contracts.

7.5   Inheritance: more knots than meet the eye

Implementation inheritance is usually combined with selective overriding of inherited methods: some of the inherited methods are replaced by new implementations. The new implementations themselves may or may not call the overridden code. A special case is the overriding of abstract methods: there is no overridden code that could be called. Another example is methods that are, by interface declaration, empty.

The separation of models and views, as used in the previous examples, can be overkill in cases where complexity is low enough and where exactly one view per model is required anyway. Simple controls fall into this category. Consider a class Text that combines the roles of text models and text views as described in Chapter 5. Text is an abstract class; the actual text rendering and the display of the caret mark are left to subclasses. Here is a partial sketch of the implementation of class Text. (The notation used is again Java and should be readily accessible to the reader.)

```
abstract class Text {
   private char[] text = new char[1000];
   private int used = 0;
   private int caret = 0;
   int max () {   // maximum length of text
      return text.length;
   }
   int length () {   // current length of text
      return used;
   }
   char read (int pos) {   // read character at position pos
      return text[pos];
   }
   void write (int pos, char ch) {   // insert or append ch at position pos
      for (int i = used; i > pos; i--) { text[i] = text[i - 1]; }   // shift trailing
                                                                    // characters right
      used++;
      if (caretPos() >= pos) setCaret(caret + 1);
      text[pos] = ch;
   }
   void delete (int pos) {   // delete character at position pos
      used--;
      for (int i = pos; i < used; i++) { text[i] = text[i + 1]; }   // shift trailing
                                                                    // characters left
      if (caretPos() >= pos) setCaret(caret - 1);
   }
   int caretPos () {   // current caret position
      return caret;
   }
   void setCaret (int pos) {   // set caret position
      caret = pos;
   }
   abstract int posToXCoord (int pos);   // map position to x coordinate
   abstract int posToYCoord (int pos);   // map position to y coordinate
   abstract int posFromCoord (int x, int y);   // map coordinates to position
   void type (char ch) {   // insert character ch at current caret position
      int pos = caretPos();
      write(pos, ch); setCaret(pos + 1);
   }
   void rubout () {   // rubout character before current caret position
      int pos = caretPos();
      delete(pos - 1); setCaret(pos - 1);
   }
}
```

Class Text is a merger of the relevant methods from the TextModel and TextView interfaces (pp. 58 and 59), enriched by partial implementations. Methods marked *abstract* have no implementation. An abstract method may be called by another, non-abstract, method of the same class. The abstract method is then called a *hook method*. For brevity, the pre- and postconditions have been left out; they are similar to the ones attached to the TextModel and TextView interfaces. (Proper Java programming style would be to introduce checked exceptions thrown on violation of most of the preconditions. Declaration, checking, and throwing are relatively verbose in Java. Thus, again for brevity, precondition checking is not included in this example.)

Obviously, class Text has most of the subtle interactions discussed earlier for separate text models and views. In particular, the setting of the caret in the methods write and type interacts in exactly the same way. However, as all interactions are now kept within one class, one could argue that the situation is less severe. This is indeed the case as long as no subclasses are formed, that is as no other class inherits parts of Text's implementation.

Next, consider a subclass SimpleText that inherits from Text, implements all abstract methods, and refines some of the concrete methods. The following section of code fully glosses over details such as partial visibility or scrolling, but it does show how the concrete method setCaret is refined to adjust the visual caret mark. (Note how a guard in method setCaret shortcuts this operation in the case where the caret is set to the position it already is at. This is done mainly to show how screen flicker and overheads can be controlled without demanding avoidance of redundant calls to methods despite their idempotency.)

```java
class SimpleText extends Text {
    private int cacheX = 0; private int cacheY = 0;  // cached coordinate of
                                                      // caret mark
    void setCaret (int pos) {
        int old = caretPos();
        if (old != pos) {   // if caret position does indeed change
            hideCaret();  // remove caret mark at old caret position
            super.setCaret(pos);  // update caret position
            showCaret();  // redisplay caret mark at new caret position
        }
    }
    int posToXCoord (int pos) {
        ... // compute x coordinate of anchor point of rendered
            // character stored at position pos
    }
    int posToYCoord (int pos) {
        ... // compute y coordinate of anchor point of rendered
            // character stored at position pos
    }
```

```
int posFromCoord (int x, int y) {
    ... // compute text position of the character whose bounding
        // box contains point (x, y)
}
void hideCaret () {    // remove caret mark—asumes caret
                       // is visible
    int x = cacheX; int y = cacheY;
    ... // draw caret mark in invert mode at point (x, y)
}
void showCaret () {    // displays caret mark—assumes caret
                       // is invisible
    int pos = caretPos();
    cacheX = posToXCoord(pos);
    cacheY = posToYCoord(pos);
    int x = cacheX; int y = cacheY;
    ... // draw caret mark in invert mode at point (x, y)
}
}
```

Figure 7.2 shows the complex message sequence occurring between Text and SimpleText as a result of a call to method type. For the sake of clarity, the message sequence caused by a showCaret call has been factored into a separate diagram (Figure 7.3). A hideCaret call relies on the cached coordinates of the preceding showCaret call and is thus simpler (and not shown).

When comparing with Figure 5.7 (p. 65), it should become obvious that invocation of an overridden method from within a class is very similar to invoking a callback from within a library. Call recursion freely spans class and subclass in both directions. The reader will no doubt be able to detect many critical subtle-

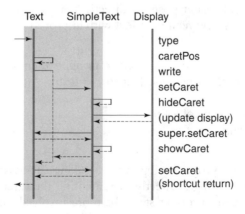

Figure 7.2 Callback-like message sequence between class and subclass in the presence of overridden inherited methods.

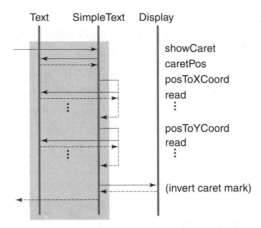

Figure 7.3   Message sequence subchart of *showCaret* in Figure 7.2.

ties, based on the discussions of callbacks. One recurring example is the need to cache display coordinates in the presence of model changes.

Where does the class scenario differ from that using callbacks? In a class, *every* method can potentially call any other method. In combination with subclasses and overriding, literally any method can become a callback operation for any other method. Obviously, there is no problem if the superclass of a class is fully abstract, that is it has abstract methods only. The method interaction is then fully and solely defined by the subclass. For example, Java interfaces are restricted to the introduction of constants and fully abstract methods. Thus, a Java interface is a fully abstract class. (Java also has abstract classes, but these need not be fully abstract. This confusing aspect of the Java language is discussed in Chapter 14.)

With the examples developed above, it is possible to see consequences of the semantic fragile base class problem (section 7.4.2). Class SimpleText overrides method setCaret to update also the display of the caret. This relies on class Text never manipulating the caret position directly, that is without calling setCaret. For example, assume a new version of Text with improved performance of method write:

```
void write (int pos, char ch) {    // insert or append ch at position pos
   for (int i = used; i > pos; i--) {  text[i] = text[i - 1]; }
   used++;
   if (caret >= pos) caret++;
   text[pos] = ch;
}
```

Of course, this is a programming error breaking subclasses. In the example, this error is obvious enough: directly incrementing the caret variable leaves the visual caret mark in an incorrect state. In more involved interactions between classes and subclasses, such errors are much harder to spot and avoid. The real question is: *why* is the above improvement of write illegal? The requirement that write ought to call setCaret is not easily expressed using postconditions. What is needed is a specification for the specialization interface, that is the interface of a class to its subclasses.

The following section looks at the slow but steady research progress made in this direction. While reading on, it should be remembered that, even in systems using implementation inheritance, there will always be more than one object. Hence, the two facets of the re-entrance problem, through inter-object and through intra-object recursion, really appear in combination. All approaches looked at in the following section address only the specialization interface of a single class.

7.6 Approaches to disciplined inheritance

The problems of implementation inheritance illustrated in the previous section have been known for quite a while. As early as 1986 Alan Snyder noted that *inheritance breaks encapsulation* (Snyder, 1986). The problems spotted at the time mostly pointed at weaknesses of programming languages, all of which have been addressed in the meantime. However, the general claim still holds: a subclass can interfere with the implementation of its superclasses in a way that breaks the superclasses. Likewise, an evolutionary change of a superclass can break some of its existing subclasses.

This section covers a number of attempts to discipline the implementation inheritance mechanisms. Obviously, many think that this powerful mechanism should not be given up on, but that it should be augmented with rules or conventions that help to reduce the risk of using this mechanism. This section is lengthy, and it is safe to skip or to just skim over it. However, it is strongly recommended that the reader continues with the next section, on object versus class composition, rather than the next chapter.

7.6.1 The specialization interface

In 1992, Gregor Kiczales and John Lamping described the problem in more detail and they pointed out its importance in the context of *extensible* software systems (Kiczales and Lamping, 1992). They named the special interface between a class and its subclasses the *specialization interface* of that class. Distinguishing between the client and the specialization interface is important for approaches supporting implementation inheritance.

C++ and Java, for example, support the notion of *protected* features of a class (Ellis and Stroustruup, 1994; Gosling *et al.*, 1996). A protected feature is accessible only to subclasses, not to regular clients of the class that only see the *public* features. The specialization interface of a C++ or Java class is the combination of the public and the protected interface. The client interface consists of only the public (non-protected) interface. In addition, the class can keep parts of its interface *private*. Private features can be used to solve the problems pointed out by Snyder.

In C++ and Java, a private feature is private to a class, not an object. Therefore, both languages maintain classes as the unit of encapsulation, not objects. Smalltalk is different in that it encapsulates at the object level: access to fields of another object, even of the same class, has to occur through method calls. Java and Component Pascal also support the important notion of *package-private* (or *module-private*) interfaces. These allow encapsulation of certain aspects on the level of packages (or modules), allowing direct access between multiple classes located in the same package (or module). The same can be achieved in C++ in a less structured way using *friend* declarations.

7.6.2 Typing the specialization interface

Given the specialization interface of a class, what are the legal modifications a subclass can apply? As described in some length in the sections above, overriding of methods needs to be done carefully to ensure correct interactions between a class and its subclasses. However, the introduction of protected interfaces merely excludes non-subclass code from using such interfaces. It does nothing to control the usage by subclasses.

In 1993, John Lamping proposed a type system approach to improve the control over specialization interfaces (Lamping, 1993). The idea is to declare statically which other methods of the same class a given method might depend on. Where dependencies form acyclic graphs, methods can be arranged in layers. Where dependencies form cycles, all the methods in a cycle together form a group.

If a method needs to call another method, it either has to be a member of the called method's group or it has to be a member of a higher layer's group. In such an approach, a subclass has to override methods group by group. Either all methods of a group are overridden or none are. A subclass can redefine dependencies for overridden or new methods as it offers a fresh specialization interface to its subclasses. However, a subclass has to propagate unmodified parts of the specialization interface where inherited methods are used.

Grouping and layering of methods, as captured by Lamping's dependency declarations, is seen as a design activity. The designer of a class specifies the permissible call dependencies between the methods of a class. Below is an example of a specialization interface, based on the class Text (p. 105). For clarity, the return types and signatures (parameter lists and types) have been left out. For each method that depends on other methods, the set of those methods is written immediately after the dependent method. In addition, two 'state abstractions' (caretRep and textRep) are used to refer abstractly to the state of class Text.

```
specialization interface Text {
    state caretRep
    state textRep
```

```
    abstract posToXCoord
    abstract posToYCoord
    abstract posFromCoord
    concrete caretPos   { caretRep }
    concrete setCaret   { caretRep }
    concrete max   { textRep }
    concrete length   { textRep }
    concrete read   { textRep }
    concrete write   { textRep, caretPos, setCaret }
    concrete delete   { textRep, caretPos, setCaret }
    concrete type   { write, caretPos, setCaret }
    concrete rubout   { delete, caretPos, setCaret }
}
```

In this example, the entire dependency graph is acyclic and therefore every method forms its own group. Several methods are affected only where representations are changed (textRep or caretRep). The dependencies specify the relative layering of the methods. The above interface is topologically sorted: a dependent method always follows the methods it depends on. Note how the abstract caret mapping methods have no declared dependencies. A subclass might decide to add dependencies when implementing an abstract method. For example, the caret mapping methods might then depend on method read. As no method in Text depends on these mapping methods, such a change would be legal in a subclass implementing the caret mapping.

Obviously, Lamping's simple system can be based on static declarations and conformance can be statically checked. (A set of methods *is* the structure of a simple interface type.) That is why Lamping calls it a typing of the specialization interface. Despite its simplicity, today no language directly supports Lamping's specialization interface typing. However, corresponding conventions have been proposed as a recommendation for C++ programmers (Taligent, 1994).

An approach quite similar to Lamping's was proposed by Franz Hauck, also in 1993 and at the same conference (Hauck, 1993). Like Lamping, Hauck concentrates on typing *self*, that is the type of the self-recursive structure of a class.

7.6.3 Behavioral specification of the specialization interface

Although Lamping's proposal improves the information available to subclass designers, it does not address semantic issues of implementation inheritance. After all, the approach aims at type system support, and type systems rarely address semantic issues. As described earlier, most semantic problems specific to implementation inheritance are related to problems of re-entrance caused by self-recursion. Recall that the problems of re-entrance do not occur in simple layered procedure libraries. The reason is that, in such a layered system, calls can only be made within (a part of) a layer or to a lower layer, but not upwards to a higher layer. In other words, a layered system performs no up-calls.

In 1995, Raymie Stata and John Guttag presented an approach to the behavioral (semantic) aspects of implementation inheritance (Stata and Guttag, 1995). They observed that the key requirement to be satisfied by any disciplined use of implementation inheritance would be the preservation of *modular reasoning*. It should be possible to establish properties of a class formally without a need to inspect any of the subclasses. Modular reasoning is of paramount importance for extensible systems, in which the set of subclasses of a given class is open. Any reasoning based on global inter-class analysis necessarily fails in extensible systems. It is interesting that layered systems are particularly well suited to modular reasoning.

Stata and Guttag propose to view a class as a combined definition of interacting part objects. In their paper, they name such part objects *divisions of labor* or *method groups*. Essentially, each such division owns part of the variables and methods of a class. No division can directly access the variables of another division. Subclasses have either to inherit or to replace a method group as a whole. In addition, Stata and Guttag use algebraic specification techniques and the notion of behavioral subtyping (Liskov and Wing, 1994) to specify precisely what a subclass is allowed to do when overriding an inherited method group.

It is worthwhile looking closely at Stata and Guttag's approach. They split state *and* behavior defined by a class into groups and require strict abstractional barriers between these groups. Note that this is different from Lamping's approach; Stata–Guttag method groups encapsulate part of the state, whereas Lamping allows any dependency of methods on state. Effectively, Stata–Guttag groups can be viewed as *separate classes*, with the exception of one detail: all part classes together introduce a single 'self.' (This strict compartmentalization, leading to the almost total separation of the groups within a class, had previously been rejected by Lamping in his proposal; Lamping, 1993, pp. 207–208.)

It is interesting to compare the Stata–Guttag approach with a hypothetical one that introduces just one group per class and uses object composition instead of class composition. (Object composition is covered in detail further below in section 7.7.) If all classes consist of just one Stata–Guttag group, then subclasses either can change nothing or have to replace everything. Obviously, this makes implementation inheritance a useless mechanism in the hypothetical approach. Instead of forming a subclass that replaces everything, one could create a new class that is merely a subtype of the same type as the old class. Figure 7.4 illustrates this: the diagram on the left shows class B inheriting from class A (and

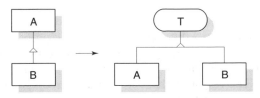

Figure 7.4   A fully overriding subclass versus a new class under a common supertype.

replacing everything). The diagram on the right shows independent classes A and B that simply implement the same type, that is the same interface. In other words, instead of introducing a class and opening it for implementation inheritance, a fully abstract class, that is a pure interface or type, is introduced. In this case, multiple classes can implement this interface. The result fully decouples implementation decisions but maintains polymorphism through the shared supertype.

To close the circle, consider what needs to be done to transform a Stata–Guttag class (one that contains multiple groups) into a set of classes that each contain a single group. Essentially, the lost 'self' needs to be compensated for. The common 'self' in a Stata–Guttag class allows methods in each of the groups of the class to invoke methods in each of the other groups of the class. The binding by a common 'self' allows such calls to refer to the most specific overriding version of a group, just as is true for any self-recursive invocation of methods of an object.

Conceptually, to transform a Stata–Guttag class into a set of single-group classes, each of the group classes receives an instance variable referring to instances of each of the other group classes. Figure 7.5 illustrates this transformation for a Stata–Guttag class with three groups.

Obviously, all essential properties of the transformed class have been preserved. 'Subclasses' can still be formed by replacing some of the single-group classes. Inter-group recursion within the original class is replaced by inter-object recursion. Clients now refer to instances of several classes, so the concept of object identity needs to be treated with care. By making any one of the part classes the *main part*, this problem can be overcome. The identity of the whole is then just the identity of the main part (part A in Figure 7.5).

As can be seen from the above transformation, classes in the Stata–Guttag approach are essentially reduced to providers of 'self.' Dropping classes (and therefore implementation inheritance) leads in the Stata–Guttag setting to compositions that are object based (instead of class based). There is no loss of functionality, although the increase in perceived complexity can be notable. The resulting object composition approach is more dynamic, as the part objects can be chosen at instantiation time rather than at class compilation time. Where meaningful, the object composition could even be changed during the composite lifetime.

The enclosing Stata–Guttag class has cost advantages. All part objects of such a class are instantiated simultaneously and can therefore be allocated contiguously.

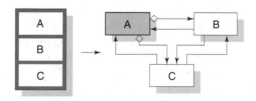

Figure 7.5 Transforming a Stata–Guttag class (with three groups) into three classes with one group each.

With all offsets between part objects statically known, there is no need to maintain references between part objects. Object composition is more dynamic and makes such optimizations far more difficult to implement.

Another disadvantage of object composition seems to be the quadratic number of references required between part objects. However, this is easily solved. Without significant loss in performance, it suffices to have all part objects refer to an arbitrarily chosen main part (as above for identification purposes). The main part maintains references to all other part objects. The resulting number of inter-part references is linear, and inter-part access cost merely increases from a single to a double indirection.

To summarize the above, closer analysis of the Stata–Guttag proposal leads to a surprising insight. Attempts at tight semantic control over classes and implementation inheritance naturally lead to a model that is much closer to object composition than to traditional class composition, that is implementation inheritance. This first glimpse at object composition should suffice at this point. A detailed coverage of object composition techniques follows below in section 7.7.

7.6.4 **Reuse contracts**

Stata and Guttag's work advocates a fairly restrictive use of implementation inheritance, much along the lines of object composition. However, there is room for less restrictive forms of implementation inheritance. For this to be manageable, a much better understanding of the coupling between classes and subclasses is required. In particular, a better understanding of base class evolution and its consequences for subclasses is required.

In 1996, Patrick Steyaert, Carine Lucas, Kim Mens, and Theo D'Hondt returned to the idea of statically verifiable annotations of the specialization interface (Steyaert *et al.*, 1996). They named the annotated interface a *reuse contract* with the intention that classes are reusable assets. Reuse contracts then determine how reuse happens. As with all contracts, reuse contracts bind at least two parties: classes and their subclasses. They coarsely specify structural aspects of a base class, so that subclasses can build on this specification. The aim is to gain a better understanding of the effects of what Steyaert *et al.* called *parent class exchange*, another name for the fragile base class problem.

Although following in the tradition of Lamping's (and Hauck's) work, reuse contracts are quite different. A reuse contract specifies only the *transitive hull* of the part of a call structure in a class that subclasses may rely upon. In other words, self-recursive calls, used in an implementation of a class, do not necessarily form part of the contract between that class and its subclasses. A reuse contract also mentions only those methods that should be relied upon by subclasses. In contrast, Lamping (and Hauck) specified the total call structure observable by clients regardless of whether or not clients are allowed to rely on that call structure. Below is the reuse contract of class Text.

```
reuse contract Text {
  abstract
    posToXCoord
    posToYCoord
    posFromCoord
  concrete
    caretPos
    setCaret
    max
    length
    read
    write  { caretPos, setCaret }
    delete  { caretPos, setCaret }
    type  { write, caretPos, setCaret }
    rubout  { delete, caretPos, setCaret }
}
```

Class Text does not define any methods that should be hidden from subclasses. Thus, none of Text's methods have been omitted. The listed dependencies are only among methods – Lamping's or Stata and Guttag's state representations or state partitions are not mentioned at all. Except for the concept of dropping information that ought to be irrelevant to subclass implementers, a reuse contract is just a specialization interface specification with less information.

The real innovation of the reuse contract approach is a set of modification operators. Using a sequence of applications of these operators, a contract can be modified to take a different shape. Changes described by such operator applications can explain the differences between base classes (base class evolution) as well as the differences between a subclass and its base class. The six operators introduced by Steyaert *et al.* are:

- *concretization* (inverse *abstraction*)
  replace abstract methods by concrete methods (replace concrete methods by abstract methods);
- *extension* (inverse *cancellation*)
  add new methods that depend on new or existing methods (remove methods without leaving methods that would depend on the removed methods);
- *refinement* (inverse *coarsening*)
  override methods, introducing new dependencies to possibly new methods (removing dependencies from methods, possibly removing methods that now are no longer being depended on).

Steyaert *et al.* then argue that, by recording the sequence of operations applied when constructing a subclass and when constructing a new base class, the compatibility of an existing subclass with the new base class can be checked. As reuse contracts and associated operators say nothing about semantics (and do not even

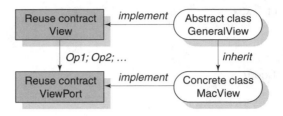

Figure 7.6 Co-evolution of reuse contracts and implementing classes.

refer to actual typing of methods), this check can only be conservative. However, they claim that it does eliminate a large number of errors that typically occur in practice.

Figure 7.6, which is adapted from Steyaert *et al.* (1996), shows how a class and its subclass both implement a reuse contract, and how these two reuse contracts are themselves related. In the figure, the sequence 'Op1; Op2; ...' refers to the sequence of operations applied to the base class's reuse contract to construct the subclass's reuse contract.

Figure 7.7, again based on Steyaert *et al.* (1996), shows how the reuse contracts of a class, its replacement, and one of its subclasses – before and after the replacement – are coupled by contract operators. In the figure, the labels Ops(derive) and Ops(exchange) refer to the sequences of operator applications that derive the subclass and the exchange base class respectively.

Steyaert *et al.* explain in detail what changes to a base contract would interfere with what derivations of subclasses. They claim that, where such interferences do not occur, a subclass will remain operational after the analyzed base class exchange. As the entire reuse contract approach is based merely on the transitive closure of relevant self-recursion, such a claim is not perfect. A subclass may depend on the ordering of calls – as demonstrated in the SimpleText class (p. 106). Such a dependency can be broken by a base class exchange without being noticed by reuse contracts.

Reuse contracts represent an interesting trade-off. On the one hand are the conditions that can be formally expressed and statically checked (for example by a compiler). On the other are the conditions sufficient to capture formally the

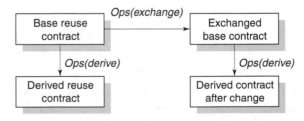

Figure 7.7 Exchange of a base contract.

behavior of a class. However, in the general case, these cannot be statically verified by a compiler.

7.7 From class to object composition

A prime motivation for implementation inheritance is the potential for flexible code reuse. In particular, it is usually emphasized that, in an inheritance-based scheme, evolutionary improvement of parent classes automatically improves subclasses. It is definitely true that the modification of parent classes leads to an automatic modification of subclasses. It is a different matter whether this leads to an improvement of the subclasses. The implicit web of self-recursive re-entrant invocations is difficult to control and could well stand in the way of evolution.

Object composition is a much simpler form of composition than implementation inheritance. However, object composition shares several of the often quoted advantages of implementation inheritance. What exactly is object composition? The idea is very simple and very much in the style of objects. Whenever an object does not have the means to perform some task locally, it can send messages to other objects, asking for support. If the helping object is considered a part of the helped object, this is called object composition. An object is a part of another one if references to it do not leave that other object. The part object is usually called an *inner object* because it can be seen as residing inside its owning object, the *outer object*.

Sending a message on from one object to another object is called *forwarding*. Note that, in the literature, the term *delegation* is also used in this context. However, technically, delegation has a different meaning, as will be explained further below. The combination of object composition and forwarding comes fairly close to what is achieved by implementation inheritance. However, it does not get so close that it also has the disadvantages of implementation inheritance.

An outer object does not reimplement the functionality of the inner object when it forwards messages. Hence, it *reuses* the implementation of the inner object. If the implementation of the inner object is changed, then this change will 'spread' to the outer object. The difference between object composition with forwarding and implementation inheritance is subtle. This difference is called 'implicit self-recursion' or 'possession of a common self.' If an object is an instance of a class, then it has exactly one identity, its 'self,' even if its class inherits from many other classes. However, if an outer object uses composition and forwarding, it does not share identity with its inner objects. There is no common 'self' to a composition of objects.

The difference does not show until a self-recursive invocation is studied. In the case of implementation inheritance, control in a self-recursive invocation always returns to the last overriding version of any method. That is, control can return from any of the involved superclasses back to any of the involved subclasses. Method invocation can cause up-calls in the subclass hierarchy. (In most diagrams, subclasses are drawn below their superclasses – up-calls in such a diagram point downwards. This convention unfortunately clashes with that of drawing layered architectures, where base layers are drawn below 'higher' layers. The latter convention lead to the name 'up-call' – see p. 48.) This is different in the case of forwarding. Once control has been passed from an outer to an inner object, self-invocations stay with the inner object. The outer object cannot possibly interfere with the flow of control inside the inner object.

To see why the lack of a common 'self' is a severe if subtle difference, consider the previous example of classes Text and SimpleText (p. 106). A naive attempt to implement the functionality of SimpleText by composing a text object with a simpleText object using forwarding would fail. The *implicit* self-recursive return of control from Text to SimpleText that is possible with inheritance does not occur under a forwarding regime. Hence, the subtle coupling between classes Text and SimpleText, as illustrated in Figures 7.2 and 7.3, cannot be reproduced using object composition and message forwarding alone. Figure 7.8 repeats a simplified version of the inheritance message chart of Figure 7.2 on its left. On its right, Figure 7.8 shows the forwarding message chart that would result from a simpleText object forwarding to an unmodified text object. (Note that class Text has abstract methods; assume that the text object is an instance of a subclass of Text that provides an arbitrary implementation for these methods.) Note that the chart on the right represents a malfunctioning simpleText object: its hideCaret and showCaret methods are not invoked. A working version based on object composition is introduced further below.

Obviously, the inner object (text) can be designed with interference of an outer object (simpleText) in mind. For example, the outer object's reference can be added to some of the operations as an additional parameter. For Figure 7.8, such a parameter on method write would solve the problem. Alternatively, the outer object

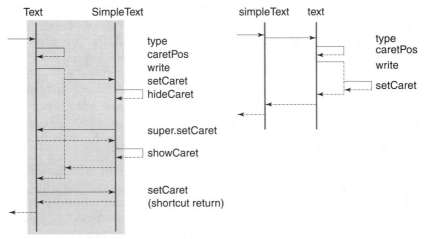

Figure 7.8   Comparing the control flow under inheritance (left) and forwarding (right) regimes.

could be registered with the inner object. Regardless of how it is achieved, the point is that recursion across multiple objects needs to be *designed* in, whereas in the case of implementation inheritance it can be *patched* in. This is sometimes called *planned* versus *unplanned reuse*. One could also say that it is about expected versus forced use. A more constructive view follows in the next section.

As a strong advantage, object composition is also naturally dynamic. An inner object can be picked at the time of creation of an outer object. In some cases, the inner object can even be replaced while the outer object continues to function. This sort of dynamics can be added to inheritance models as well, although this is not normally done. For example, Objective-C (NeXT, no date) allows specification of the superclass 'object' at object creation time. The object model of Newi (new world infrastructure; see Chapters 13 and 18) is another example following a similar approach.

7.8 Forwarding versus delegation (or making object composition as problematic as implementation inheritance)

Objects composed using object references and forwarding of messages lack the notion of an implicit common 'self.' As explained in the previous section, if such a common identity is required, it has to be designed in. This has far-reaching consequences. If an object was not designed for composition under a common identity, it cannot be used in such a context. An object may not have the mechanisms built in that are required to resend messages to an outer object. If so, it cannot be used as an inner or part object without affecting the common 'self.'

As argued above, the lack of an *implicit* common 'self' is a major strength of object composition based on forwarding. In contexts in which all part objects are under the control of a single organization or team, the requirement to make a common 'self' explicit everywhere may be considered overkill. After all, implementation inheritance works well for moderate numbers of classes, all of which are under local control and thus are whiteboxes. However, object composition has a second advantage over inheritance: it supports *dynamic* and *late* composition. Implementation inheritance can be augmented to approach the same degree of flexibility. Some examples of dynamic inheritance were briefly covered in the previous section. Making the 'inheritance link' dynamic blurs the distinction between class and object composition and eliminates the implementation advantages of (static) class composition. Languages that take this path include Objective-C (Pinson and Wiener, 1991) with its dynamic superclasses and Modula-3 (Nelson, 1991) with an option to bind methods at object creation time.

There is another way to close the gap between forwarding-based object composition and implementation inheritance-based class composition. Instead of making inheritance more dynamic, forwarding could be strengthened. The resulting approach to message passing is called *delegation*. To repeat: in much of the popular literature, the line between forwarding and delegation is not clearly drawn.

The difference is of such a fundamental nature that the price for this imprecision is a resulting lack of understanding.

The concept of message passing by delegation is relatively simple. Each message-send is classified either as a regular send (forwarding) or a self-recursive one (delegation). Whenever a message is delegated (instead of forwarded), the identity of the first delegator in the current message sequence is remembered. Any subsequently delegated message is dispatched back to the original delegator. Figures 7.9 and 7.10 illustrate the difference between forwarding and delegation. The two objects involved, niceText and text, are expected to share a common part of their interface. In terms of object composition, niceText is the outer object and text is the inner object. The idea is that niceText has a 'nicer' way to display marks, such as the caret. Messages from text to this shared interface are, under the delegation regime, rerouted to niceText. In the case of forwarding, this does not happen. For delegation to work, the delegator must share the delegate's delegation interface, much as a subclass shares the specialization interface of its superclass.

Delegation requires one further concept. Besides being able to send to the current 'self,' a method implementation should be able to call the base method in the object down the delegation chain. This is much like a 'super call' in class-based schemes. For example, niceText gets control when text delegates SetCaret. However, niceText does not fully implement the caret state and wants to invoke also the SetCaret code of text. This is not a normal forwarding send, as the current 'self' needs to be retained. It is also not a delegating send, as that would lead to an infinite regress (niceText is the current 'self;' under delegation it would just reinvoke its own SetCaret).

The mechanism that performs the equivalent of a 'super call' for objects is called *message resending*. As can be seen in Figure 7.10, niceText uses a resend to invoke text's SetCaret from within its own SetCaret. It is immediately obvious from the figures that the complexity of message sequences explodes when moving from forwarding to delegation. The interaction diagram looks similar to that in an implementation inheritance relation. As far as recursion structures are concerned, implementation inheritance and delegation are indeed equivalent (Stein, 1987).

Obviously, in the example shown in Figure 7.9, niceText will not function properly when using forwarding. By forwarding the InsertChar message to text, niceText

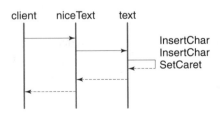

Figure 7.9 Forwarding.

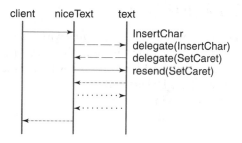

Figure 7.10   Delegation of messages InsertChar and SetCaret.

loses control until this call returns. However, text reacts to InsertChar by calling SetCaret to update the caret position – something that niceText really needs to know to update its caret display. If forwarding is the only option and text had not been designed with recursion through outer objects in mind, the programmer of niceText would have to resort to workarounds. For example, niceText could check on returning calls to text whether the state that it depends on has changed.

7.9   A brief review of delegation and inheritance

Delegation is a powerful programming tool. The point made so far has been that delegation introduces the same 'evils' as implementation inheritance. However, just as implementation inheritance is certainly an established and useful tool within components, so delegation could be put to use within similarly controlled units of encapsulation. The dynamics of a system based on object composition and delegation so gained is often cited as a prime advantage. It allows for direct manipulation systems that aim to make construction of software artifacts 'tangible' (for example Smith and Ungar, 1995). In such systems, objects are directly combined to form larger solutions, instead of separating compile time and runtime (classes and objects).

Languages that are based purely on objects, object composition, and delegation are usually called *prototype based languages*, as the role of classes is taken by objects that are cloned and then modified. The original proposal to investigate such languages goes back to an article by Henry Liebermann (Liebermann, 1986). The first concrete language proposal soon followed, introducing the language Self (Ungar and Smith, 1987). Since then, interest in delegation-based languages has increased, but none of these approaches has yet made it into mainstream commercially supported languages. This could change if the two approaches of inheritance and delegation are no longer seen as mutually exclusive philosophies. Recent work has focused on smoother transitions from delegation-based prototyping to inheritance-based production code (Dutoit *et al.*, 1996). In addition, it has been noted that the design spectrum between delegation and inheritance is more diverse than was previously thought (Malenfant, 1995).

To quote Gamma *et al.* (1995, p. 21):

> 'Delegation has a disadvantage that it shares with other techniques that make software more flexible through object composition: Dynamic, highly parametrized software is harder to understand than more static software. [...] Delegation is a good design choice only when it simplifies more than it complicates. [...] Delegation works best when it is used in highly stylized ways – that is, in standard patterns.'

A recent focus of research has been the disciplined use of delegation (for example Bardou and Dony, 1996). As delegation can be used to form a common 'self' across webs of objects, one could term such webs themselves as objects of a higher order. Such 'objects' are often called *split* or *fragmented* objects. In other words, instead of weaving arbitrary and overlapping domains of 'self' across webs of objects, a disciplined approach aims at structure and hierarchy. In a sense, delegation-based technology is lagging behind inheritance-based technology when it comes to aspects of discipline and modularity (for example Ungar, 1995). Inheritance-based approaches lag behind in the area of system dynamics and late composition. (This is considered further in Chapter 25.)

CHAPTER EIGHT

Aspects of scale and granularity

Partitioning a design into components is a subtle process that has a large impact on the success of the resulting components. Obviously, it is the exception that all components in the partitioning are designed from scratch. Fresh construction is usually acceptable only in the absence of usable components. Construction of a generalized component is only reasonable if it is expected that the component will find further applications. In the case of a mature component market, most necessary components can be acquired rather than constructed. The process of partitioning is then driven by two considerations: the requirements and the catalog of available components.

Nevertheless, as pointed out several times before, there are substantial benefits to introducing a component approach even in cases where component markets or even in-house component reuse are not yet foreseeable. Component-based architectures are inherently modular and as such have significant software engineering advantages. In particular, good modular architectures make dependencies explicit and help to reduce and control these dependencies. Also, good modular architectures are naturally layered, leading to a natural distribution of responsibilities. Once modularity has been established, it is easier to migrate part of a system to components by adopting relevant component interface standards. It is also possible that an outcome of the modularization effort is proposals for new component interface standards.

Where component frameworks or even entire component system designs can be adopted, the granularity of components in a system is predetermined. Today, this is the exception rather than the rule, and modularization is often the first step that needs to be taken. The important question of proper granularity then needs to be addressed.

The best size of a component depends on many different aspects. A system can readily be partitioned into units of varying size and coherence. Traditional units are procedural libraries, classes, and modules. The rules governing the partitioning vary from case to case. In particular, it is important to understand the implications of the granularity of a particular partitioning. This chapter covers a number of aspects of granularity and discusses the principal related concerns for an architect of a component-based system. It is argued that almost all relevant aspects

123

governing granularity demand fairly coarse-grained partitionings. Individual procedures or classes are thus frequently ruled out as components.

8.1 Units of abstraction

Abstraction is perhaps the most powerful tool available to a software engineer. Abstraction aims at reducing detail, making the thing that has been subjected to abstraction simpler to handle.

- With abstraction, less becomes possible in theory, but more becomes possible in practice.

The main benefit of an abstraction is the design expertise embodied in it, ready for reuse. Traditional abstraction aims at capturing functionality, resources, or state spaces. Objects are examples of abstractions that combine functionality and state. Abstractions usually build on lower-level abstractions, leading to a layered hierarchical design.

However, from a software architect's point of view, the hardest design problem is how abstractions such as objects should interact. To keep complexity under control, it is desirable to isolate objects as much as possible. However, if complex interactions can be handled by a library, the complexity for the library's clients may be reduced considerably. Thus, a focus of more recent efforts is to study object interactions in their own right.

Indeed, interaction patterns themselves can become the focus of abstraction. Examples in this category are 'active' libraries (those using callbacks) and frameworks (Chapter 9). Frameworks are libraries that define part of the interaction between certain objects. There is a deep conflict between the tight coupling required for effective interaction and the weak coupling required for strong and independent object abstractions. This conflict is addressed by frameworks: objects within a framework are coupled much more tightly than are objects across different frameworks.

A framework may completely hide its implementation, and only provide an abstract interface. Such a so-called blackbox framework (Johnson, 1994) acts as a unit of abstraction. Its classes are rarely meaningful if considered individually. Thus, the entire blackbox framework may form a component, where the classes that constitute it cannot. Of course, for a framework to serve as a useful component, it needs to be a possible unit of deployment. Such a *framework component* thus needs to come with useful defaults. As such a framework component can be specialized by plugging in components, it is also a *component framework*. Most conventional frameworks are not separately deployable and require specialization using class inheritance; instead of being components, they simply serve as prefactored implementation fragments to be completed by a programmer before deployment.

Nested frameworks constitute another challenge to component formation. Can an inner framework be a component in its own right? Obviously, the answer depends on the abstraction of the outer framework. If the outer framework can do without the inner, then there is no cyclic dependency. Without a cyclic dependency, both the inner and the outer framework can be components themselves, with the inner component listing the outer one as a prerequisite for it to function.

8.2   Units of accounting

In large systems, as are typical for enterprise solutions, the actual cost incurred by individual parts of a system and their use may need to be monitored. It thus becomes important to partition a system into units of accounting. If the chosen granularity is too fine, the accounting overhead becomes significant. If the granularity is too coarse, accounting is not precise enough to trace costs back to their exact causes.

As components are the units of deployment, it makes sense also to make them the units of accounting. In this way it becomes possible to link costs and benefits to acquired components and their vendors.

8.3   Units of analysis

Any system of at least medium size needs to be hierarchically partitioned into smaller units, and the coupling between those units should be as weak as possible. Only a good partitioning allows reliably to construct (synthesize) or to understand (analyze) a complex system. Examples where analysis of system parts is required are: verification according to a specification, testing, type checking, version control, re-engineering, and so on. Analysis is really the converse of synthesis. In fact, all phases of a software life cycle ask for one sort of analysis or the other.

The coupling between units determines the extent to which any form of analysis of one unit needs to take properties of other units into account. In an unstructured system in which all units are tightly entangled with all other units, separate analysis of units is hopeless and a global analysis must be undertaken.

Partitioning a system into bounded units of analysis is necessary in practice when a system becomes too large for a global analysis to be feasible. Even more important, partitioning into bounded units of analysis is necessary in principle, when a system is meant to be independently extensible. As components in such systems are added by the client on demand, there is no meaningful systems integration phase that the software engineer can rely on. Global analysis therefore cannot take place before it is too late (see Chapter 6).

Some forms of global analysis are unavoidable. A typical example is the final version check when integrating a component on demand. However, those 'last-minute' checks should only flag problems that are meaningful to the user, such as the correctable problem of a version mismatch.

It is advisable to aim for the smallest units of analysis possible. In some cases, such as local type checking, individual classes or even individual methods can form the units of analysis. Quite often, the units need to be larger and encompass interacting groups of objects bound by a certain contract. It can be useful to form strong static hierarchical boundaries, such as erected by modules or whole subsystems. However, the unit of analysis can never be bigger than the unit of deployment; thus *a component is the largest possible unit of (complete) analysis*.

8.4   Units of compilation

Compilation is a quite fundamental aspect, and many gradual variations between full interpretation, mixed compilation and interpretation (Gough *et al.*, 1992), just-in-time compilation, and fully static compilation are possible. As compilation involves checking and can thus be used to establish safety properties and the like, it is worthwhile considering the possible choices of units of compilation.

Incremental compilation can speed up the edit–compile–link–run cycle considerably. Increments can be applications, modules, classes, or statements. In a component software world, complete applications no longer exist, and thus the application as a unit of compilation is not relevant to this discussion.

Units of compilation relate to the units of analysis discussed above. The extent of the compiler's involvement is limited to confrontation of a trade-off when dealing with compilation units of finer granularity, such as classes. In particular, tight interaction with auxiliary constructs that are located outside the class but within a 'natural' module enclosing the class may require combined analysis. This can be simplified when compiling at the level of modules. For even larger units, compilation speed becomes an issue. Given a fast compiler (for example Wirth and Gutknecht, 1992), both modules and classes appear as reasonable units of compilation. Translating individual statements is only practical in interpreted languages.

To enable more global optimizations, compilation units should be as large as practically feasible. Components are the upper limit; modules may be a better compromise than classes. However, this performance argument becomes weaker when it is considered that just-in-time compilation or compilation on the fly (Franz, 1994) allows for cross-component optimization even *after* deployment.

8.5   Units of delivery

This section refers to units of delivery when it comes to the distribution of goods in a marketing sense. Today, applications, and sometimes components, are the typical units of delivery. Individual objects (or, better, classes) are rarely worth the administrative effort and cost of delivery. Surprisingly, the need to provide catalog entries, to market and maintain components, and to have clear and established interface contracts in place adds significant cost to something inherently as cheap to replicate as a software component. At the other extreme, it also costs to bundle just 'everything.' Such 'fatware' leads at least to tremendous training costs.

Individual classes are also rarely sufficiently self-contained to allow for separate deployment. In a system in which classes are the only structuring facility, it becomes very difficult to extract and package a suitable subset of classes, to ship them as a component. In practice, it becomes almost impossible to extract meaningful collections of classes from an unstructured collection that consists of thousands of classes. What is needed is a static higher order structuring facility, such as a module construct (Wirth, 1982; Szyperski, 1992a; Cardelli, 1997). Even modules may prove insufficient, and constructs such as systems (Cardelli, 1989), libraries (Apple, 1992), or subsystems may have to be introduced for more complex components.

8.6 Units of dispute

If a system composed of several components fails, component vendors tend to blame each other for the problem. To minimize this undesirable effect, it is vital that errors remain contained in individual components. This means that they should be clearly attributable to their particular component, and they should not endanger the system as a whole ('bug containment'). The most severe non-local errors are violations of memory integrity, that is dangling pointers and memory leaks.

In technical terms, safety means that invariants can be guaranteed. For a detailed discussion, see section 6.8. Information hiding on the level of objects (classes) allows invariants to be guaranteed over the hidden instance variables. For example, whenever the width of a rectangle is changed, the method that changes the width can also update an instance variable that contains the rectangle's area. In this way, the invariant 'area equals width times height' can be maintained. Safety can be increased if more global invariants (Holland, 1992) can be specified and enforced by a closed unit, that is if static information-hiding barriers can be erected. This is possible if information hiding is done at the level of modules or entire components, rather than at the level of individual objects or classes.

Languages either prevent errors or allow the component that caused the error that occurred to be pinpointed exactly. In a system composed of independently developed components, this helps clients to find out which vendor's software has failed. If a component's identity (boundary) could not be clearly determined, it would become very difficult or even impossible to determine which vendor was the culprit. An interesting problem is the propagation of exceptions across component boundaries. Normally, components should handle exceptions themselves, as no other component can be expected to have the inside knowledge to do so. However, some exceptions cannot be handled locally and need to be propagated. If the propagated exception had been declared as part of the contract, then calling components are expected to handle such exceptions in an orderly manner (or propagate them properly). Otherwise, the *calling* component failed. Exceptions that are propagated across components but not stated in the contract represent a failure of the *propagating* component.

8.7 | Units of extension

A component may not provide completely new functionality, but instead extend existing functionality or implement existing interfaces. Typically, several objects must be extended simultaneously. The coupling between the objects forming an extension is tighter than between extending and extended components. After all, under the paradigm of independent extensibility (Chapter 6), it is desirable to allow for the coexistence of several extensions of the same base.

For example, the file abstraction of an object-oriented operating system may define separate abstractions for files and for file access paths. A concrete implementation of the *file* abstraction would contain hidden information about the disk sectors occupied by the file. An implementation of the *access path* abstraction would contain the current position and hidden information, such as the disk sector of the current position. To implement these objects in an efficient and safe manner, it is necessary that the implementation of the access path object has direct access to the implementation of the file object. However, access to either implementation from outside the component must be prevented.

The lack of an access control scope that can enclose several objects is a fundamental weakness of most object-oriented programming languages. Notable exceptions are modular languages such as Modula-3 (Nelson, 1991), Oberon, Java, and Component Pascal. The designers of C++ acknowledge the problem by allowing private parts of a class to be selectively exposed to certain explicitly named 'friends' (Ellis and Stroustrup, 1994). Although perfectly general, this approach is entirely unstructured. The *namespace* construct that has been added to C++ merely provides units of name space management – it does not provide any access control. Java's packages are also interesting in that they are *open:* merely by declaring package membership of a new compilation unit, that unit gains full access to all package private and protected features of classes in that package. Java does not support *closed* packages, that is modules.

A unit of analysis must not be broken up into several units of extension. Otherwise, an extension could be integrated into a target system with incomplete context, in other words with a different context from that at the time of analysis. For example, a particular object may be less general than its interface seems to indicate because its implementation 'conspires' with another object's implementation that was part of the same unit of analysis. Analysis showed that these two objects, if used together, would have the required properties. However, if the object was deployed individually and some entirely different implementation would serve for the second object, then the former object is likely to fail. Hence, it would not be wise to sell this object as an individual product.

8.8 | Units of fault containment

Distributed systems must take into account classes of faults that are not under the control of any particular software component. For example, machines can fail and networks can have temporary or permanent communication failures. In such a situation, it is not a matter of isolating the 'guilty' component – such as discussed in section 8.6.

Instead, the question is how a system architecture can provide for subsystems that can contain certain classes of faults and thus shield the rest of the system. A fault-containing subsystem must itself be fault tolerant, that is it must tolerate and effectively mask the faults that it is meant to contain. The two ways to mask faults are physical or temporal redundancy. With physical redundancy, the critical parts of a fault-containing subsystem are replicated and the subsystem uses a highly reliable voting mechanism to present majority results to clients of the subsystem, that is the rest of the system. The use of redundant network resources allows recovery from faults using forward error correction techniques. With temporal redundancy, the subsystem has sufficient time to roll back to a check point and restart. Transaction monitors are a good example in this category.

Units of fault containment are very important on the level of overall system architecture. As indicated above, such units are usually of coarse granularity as they require explicit resourcing decisions and policies.

8.9 Units of instantiation

The standard unit of instantiation is an object. Larger or smaller units of instantiation would be conceivable with some object definitions. However, the one presented in this book leaves no choice; being a unit of instantiation is one of the defining characteristics of objects.

A component may package multiple classes (and required resources). It is not a useful unit of instantiation, as the contained classes need to be instantiated individually and independently. Forcing a component to contain exactly one class is not useful.

8.10 Units of loading

Once a component has been installed, it may be loaded on demand. In a networked environment, the component might not even be locally installed. Instead, the component is fetched from a remote site when needed (Arnold and Gosling, 1996). However it is done, a dynamic linking facility (DLLs) must be available. As classes in a component typically interact closely, loading one class would immediately cause the loading of the other classes. It is usually more efficient to load the whole component as a unit.

When loading a new component into an already running system, the version of the new component must be checked first. Loading must be prevented if the new component uses other components that are not available in this environment or which are of an incompatible version. Incompatibility due to version mismatches is the syntactic fragile base class problem. In essence, the problem is to 'avoid breaking clients that do not depend on details that have changed in a service's release or its interface' (see section 7.4.1). For maximum compatibility, version checking should occur per class or interface or even per method, rather than per component (Crelier, 1994).

Delaying version checking from load time to runtime, as done in Java, is problematic. Incompatibilities will then be detected only at unexpected moments midway through execution. This is too late to provide generic handling, as the executing code may have already committed changes. Hence, Java programmers would have to catch the version mismatch exception wherever a method invocation crosses load units. In Java, that would be on every call to a method of a public class, except for the one public class that can be local to a load unit.

When objects of different origins are loaded, name collisions may occur. There must be a mechanism to prevent such collisions. The safest way is to define a hierarchical naming scheme, where the top-level names are registered with a global naming authority. This is the case with Java or the BlackBox Component Framework (Oberon microsystems, 1997b) (an earlier version was known as Oberon/F; Oberon microsystems, 1994). An account of the Java-related issues has recently been published (Jordan and Van de Vanter, 1997).

Microsoft's COM is interesting in that it uses 128-bit numbers, so-called globally unique identifiers (GUIDs), to prevent name collisions. The scheme has been borrowed from the Open Software Foundation's distributed computing environment (OSF DCE), where such numbers are called universally unique (UUIDs). GUIDs are constructed out of the creating machine's network ID, the time of creation, and some other almost random sources. The algorithm makes it extremely unlikely that two GUIDs that have been generated independently will ever be the same.

The loading of new objects must not invalidate other already loaded objects merely by the fact of loading. This rules out the use of languages whose type systems require global analysis for type checking, for example as in original Eiffel (Meyer, 1990; Szyperski, 1996). [For Eiffel, a correction has recently been proposed (Meyer, 1996).] Languages that explicitly expect dynamic loading are sometimes called dynamic languages (Apple, 1992).

8.11   Units of locality

This section covers aspects of distributed computing. To avoid confusion with units of delivery, the term *unit of distribution* has been avoided. Microsoft coined the term *remoting* for distribution in this sense.

Component integration standards such as CORBA, DSOM, DCOM, and Java RMI provide facilities to access objects on a remote machine. In the resulting systems, locality to minimize communication cost is traded against distribution to maximize resource utilization. Modern distributed systems are arranged in a hierarchy of networks: from system-area networks connecting processors within cabinets, local-area networks (LANs), and various possible intermediate networks (wide-area networks), right to the Internet.

The communication cost increases with the network level used. Cross-process method invocations are significantly slower than in-process calls. Cross-machine calls across a LAN are even slower, and so on. Improving technology can be expected to deliver sustained bandwidth even over long distances. However, the high communication latency and therefore long observed round-trip delays over long distances will not change significantly. In other words, respecting locality preferences becomes increasingly important when moving up the network hierarchy.

Respecting locality essentially means keeping tightly coupled objects close together. Objects supported by the same component are likely to be coupled more strongly than objects in different components. It is therefore normally a useful strategy not to split up components across processes or machines.

A related aspect is the dynamic granularity of requests to a service. If a typical client needs to invoke many operations of a service to complete a single logical operation as seen by the client, then it is expensive to split client and service across machine boundaries. Hence, it is useful to design interfaces of units of locality, that is interfaces meant to serve cross-machine requests, in a way that minimizes the number of individual requests. For distributed computing, this is an important design rule. For example, attributes of objects can be grouped to be retrieved together rather than by calling a sequence of accessor methods, and operations can be offered in 'vector form' to perform the same operation on an array of arguments (Eichner *et al.*, 1997).

8.12   Units of maintenance

Software products are rarely perfect upon release. Usually it is necessary to distribute updates which correct errors, which are more efficient, or which add new features. If an update changes the inner workings of the component, depending client components may break, because they relied on a particular behavior of the classes from which they inherited. This is the semantic fragile base class problem: 'changing the inner workings of a provider, without violating the explicit contract, may still break clients' (section 7.4.2).

8.13   Units of system management

Certain parts of a system may require explicit management that goes beyond maintenance, as discussed above. To manage a system, it is useful to partition it into units of management, each of which can be individually monitored for availability, load, and so on.

Units of management can be individual components, but this solution may turn out to be too fine-grained to allow for efficient management of a large system. More likely, units of management will be subsystems located on server machines.

CHAPTER NINE

Patterns, frameworks, architectures

The discussions in the previous chapters should have helped to make one point clear: programming with objects and components is complex. Also, some of the ramifications in the case of large and complex systems are not yet fully mastered or even understood. A common reply to this generic concern is: 'So what? It works!' – but does it? The surprising answer is: yes, object-oriented programming does get you quite far. In view of the major problems covered in the previous chapters, how can this be explained?

The simple answer is: software engineers follow guidelines and good examples of working designs and architectures that help to make successful decisions. Instead of being based on a sufficiently strong theory and 'calculating' software designs, software engineers rather combine a little theory with a lot of experience. Reuse of architectural and design experience is probably the single most valuable strategy in the basket of reuse ideas. Also, it is not necessarily the hallmark of an immature engineering discipline to build firmly on examples and experience. All engineering disciplines are the same there: the creation of *products* that need to satisfy technical and non-technical criteria, including in-time production and marketing, *cannot* be based solely on theoretical 'calculation.' An educated mix is essential. Reuse of proven designs is the way in which *society* learns.

For a discipline to form a solid foundation grounded in experience, effective mechanisms need to be in place to communicate working examples. Software engineering spans a wide spectrum from the extremely small – one bit is about as small as anything can get – to the very large. Design reuse addresses an equally wide spectrum.

The architecture of component-based systems is significantly more demanding than that of traditional monolithic integrated solutions. In the context of component software, full comprehension of established design reuse techniques is most important.

This chapter briefly reviews the established approaches that help to reuse design on those levels that are relevant to component software. In particular, traditional design 'in-the-small' addressing individual algorithms or data structures is not covered. Full utilization of all presented design reuse methods assumes an established component-based *culture*. Initially, this is not the case, and the chapter therefore concludes by reviewing the issues of interoperability, legacy integration, and systems re-engineering.

9.1 Forms of design-level reuse

Reusing proven designs is essential, but there is no single reuse approach that covers all levels of granularity that software engineers have to face. Experience of how best to program 'in-the-small' needs to be conveyed very differently from that on how to best program 'in-the-large.' There is a huge difference between the problem of sorting a list of values and that of building complex interacting systems.

Design reuse can be understood as the attempt to *share* certain aspects of an approach across various projects. The following list names some of the established reuse techniques and for which sharing level they are best suited.

- sharing consistency: programming and scripting languages
- sharing concrete solution fragments: libraries
- sharing contracts: interfaces
- sharing interaction architectures: patterns
- sharing subsystem architectures: frameworks
- sharing overall structure: system architectures

Each of these techniques will be covered briefly in the following sections.

9.1.1 Sharing consistency: programming languages

One of the oldest forms of reusing proven methods is their casting into programming or scripting languages. A programming language can make some things easy, others difficult, and yet others impossible. By doing so, the language encodes a dogma of how things should be done. Over time, the language dogma combines with a culture of proven ways of doing things using the language: it becomes the *lingo* of a field.

For example, if a language makes it difficult or cumbersome to implement dynamic hash tables or associative arrays, then the language designer is effectively saying: these should not be implemented anyway. Although this may sound a little harsh, this is the message that a programmer will get. Naturally, such 'language dictate' can be largely eliminated by constructing languages in which 'everything goes.' Most successful languages are somewhere in the middle, striving for a balance between enforcement of 'good things' and flexibility to allow for the unforeseen. As projects grow in size and complexity, architecture gains importance. There is growing acceptance of the benefits of stringent languages, exemplified by the popular transition from C++ to Java.

A programming language cannot enforce good design, but it can exclude things that are likely to cause trouble. Thus, a programming language establishes consistency rails that protect programming efforts from certain classes of mistakes. It is known that a language, or better its implementation, the compiler, cannot statically verify a non-trivial program against its specification. Thus, enforcing correctness is out of the question. However, languages and their implementations can enforce static safety properties. The primary abstractional, structural, and compositional means of modern programming languages are:

- static type systems, including higher order mechanisms such as parametric polymorphism or bounded polymorphism
- functions, higher order functions, and functional composition
- closures or blocks
- lazy evaluation
- procedural abstractions
- exceptions and exception handling
- classes and implementation inheritance (subclassing)
- dynamic type systems and inclusion polymorphism (subtyping)
- support of an open object space (requires automatic memory management)
- late binding and type-driven dispatch
- support for concurrency and synchronization
- module and package systems.

Hybrid object-oriented languages are the most successful in contemporary component-oriented programming. Therefore, the following sections will concentrate on the programming models of such languages. Nevertheless, it is worthwhile noting that other language models, in particular the functional one, are promising. By the very nature of component-oriented programming, such alternative programming models could well start to blossom within components.

9.1.2 Sharing concrete solution fragments: libraries

Early programming languages attempted to provide all functions that should ever be used in multiple programs. An explosion of built-in functions was the result. For example, Pascal still had I/O concepts in the language (Wirth, 1971) while C no longer did (Kernighan and Ritchie, 1978). Since then, there has been a clear tendency to take specific functionality out of languages, in favor of abstractional and structural features. It was the birth of modular languages and their most prominent exemplar: Modula-2 (Wirth, 1982).

The central idea behind enhancing the sharing of proven solutions or, better, fragments thereof, is modular libraries or toolboxes. Such libraries can grow over time, without any need to change the language. For a coverage of the essence of traditional libraries, see Chapter 5.

Libraries are naturally layered on top of each other. Some modular languages, such as Component Pascal, even enforce layering by excluding circular dependencies between modules. Layers are of foremost importance to system architectures and are covered in more detail in section 9.1.6.

9.1.3 Sharing individual contracts: interfaces

Once providers of a service and clients of that service come separately into existence and are combined freely, the binding contract between providers and clients gains self-standing importance (see Chapter 5). Attaching contracts, formal and informal ones, to a named interface leaves implementers of providers and clients with verification obligations. Where a contract has been carefully crafted, providers and clients from fully independent sources will be able to interact properly.

Interfaces and their associated contracts are logically the smallest contractual unit in a system. The individual operations of an interface do not have meaning of their own. (If they do, the interface is probably poorly designed.) The operations bundled into an interface together form a minimal basis for interaction between providers and clients. As such, an interface and its contracts say nothing about the larger organizational structures – the architecture – of a system.

9.1.4 Sharing individual interaction architectures: patterns

An attempt to collect and catalog systematically the smallest recurring architectures in object-oriented software systems recently led to the cataloging of design patterns (Gamma, 1992; Gamma *et al.*, 1995). Gamma *et al.* (1995) define a pattern with the following four elements:

(1) a pattern name
(2) the problem that the pattern solves
    (a) includes conditions that must be met for the pattern to be applicable
(3) the solution to the problem brought by the pattern
    (a) elements involved, their roles, responsibilities, relationships, and collaborations
    (b) not a particular concrete design or implementation
(4) the consequences (results and trade-off) of applying the pattern
    (a) time and space trade-off
    (b) language and implementation issues
    (c) effects on flexibility, extensibility, portability.

In their catalog Gamma *et al.* identified 23 design patterns. Many more have since been identified and documented in an annual series of Pattern Languages of Programs (PLoP) conferences. The best are published in a book series (Coplien and Schmidt, 1995; Vlissides *et al.*, 1996). An example of a pattern already covered in the catalog by Gamma *et al.* that is particularly close to many examples in this book is the Observer pattern. It defines a one-to-many dependency between objects: when the one object changes, all its dependents are notified to perform updates as required. Using the notation of Gamma *et al.*, Figure 9.1 shows the class diagram of the Observer pattern. The attached 'notes' sketch implementations where this helps understanding the pattern. Otherwise, the notation is close to the OMT notation (Rumbaugh *et al.*, 1991).

The idea is that, once the problem has been isolated, a proper pattern can be chosen. The pattern then needs to be adapted to the specific circumstances. For example, an observable subject may need to be observed by *n* observers which are themselves unknown to the subject. The Observer pattern is chosen, but the pattern's Update method may need an additional argument to inform observers of what it is that has changed. A pattern catalog should contain a discussion of the common variations on a patterns theme, as demonstrated by Gamma *et al.*

Design patterns are microarchitectures. They describe the abstract interaction between objects collaborating to solve a particular problem. They are quite different from frameworks (described in the next section). Gamma *et al.* list the following differences between patterns and frameworks (Gamma *et al.*, 1995, p. 28):

- ■ 'Design patterns are more abstract and less specialized than frameworks. Frameworks are partial implementations of subsystems, while patterns have no immediate implementation at all; only examples of patterns can be found in implementations.'
- ■ 'Design patterns are smaller architectural elements than frameworks. Indeed, some patterns live on the granularity of individual methods – examples are the Template Method and the Factory Method patterns; most frameworks utilize several patterns.'

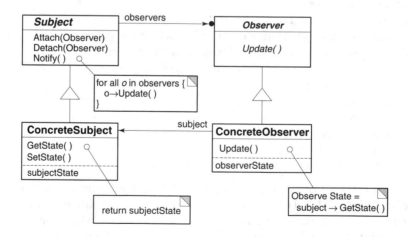

Figure 9.1 Observer pattern.

9.1.5 Sharing architectures: frameworks

Originally, frameworks were studied in the context of Smalltalk (Deutsch, 1989). Recently, frameworks gained much attention as a general approach in object-oriented programming (Gamma *et al.*, 1995; Lewis, 1995). A framework is a set of cooperating classes, some of which may be abstract, that make up a reusable design for a specific class of software. Although frameworks are not necessarily domain specific, they are usually concept specific. For example, a framework for OpenDoc parts does not say much about the specific functions of parts, but embodies the concepts that make a piece of software an OpenDoc part. (In a sense, OpenDoc was simultaneously too far ahead of its time in terms of technology and too late in terms of market penetration – it had to be abandoned by Apple in early 1997. OpenDoc has, however, been adopted as a standard by the OMG, and its full source code has been released into the public domain by IBM.)

Frameworks keep a number of their classes open for implementation inheritance, that is formation of subclasses. Some of these classes may be abstract, requiring implementation inheritance for the framework to work at all. Frameworks often provide default implementations to reduce the burden on lightweight usages of the framework. Instead of defining everything, a client merely needs to augment or replace those defaults that do not fit.

Traditional frameworks fully concentrate on classes and inheritance. However, there is no reason why a framework could not emphasize object composition instead. As implementation inheritance, even in the presence of reuse contracts (p. 114), tends to require knowledge of the superclass's implementations, it is often called *whitebox* reuse. Object composition, on the other hand, if based on forwarding rather than delegation, merely relies on the interfaces of the involved objects. It is therefore often called *blackbox* reuse. Frameworks are accordingly classified into whitebox and blackbox frameworks. Arbitrary 'shades of gray' can be formed by partially opening a blackbox framework for whitebox reuse.

An important role of a framework is its regulation of the interactions that the parts of the framework can engage in. By freezing certain design decisions in the framework, critical interoperation aspects can be fixed. A framework can thus significantly speed the creation of specific solutions out of the semifinished design provided by the framework.

Most frameworks apply multiple patterns in their design. For example, the most famous framework of all, the Smalltalk model view controller (MVC) framework (Krasner and Ope, 1988), can be dissected into three principal pattern applications (Observer, Composite, and Strategy). In addition, there are also some others of lesser importance to the MVC framework (for example Factory Method and Decorator) (Gamma *et al.*, 1995).

The MVC framework is a classic because it defines a number of *roles*, each of which is immediately intuitive. Models *represent* information, views *present* information, and controllers *interpret* user manipulation. In most cases, the same information can be presented in many different ways. For example, a text model can be presented in outline form or in page preview form. Less obviously, it can also be presented as a statistical summary showing the word count, a Flesch Reading Ease score, and other measures. Similarly, a vector of numbers can be presented as a table, a bar or pie chart, or again as a statistical summary. Orthogonal to the presentation style, presentations can also be different in their aspect by using scrolling, panning, or zooming. These are just a few examples, of course. The point is that *many* views can be attached to a single model. Controllers mediate between a model–view pair and manipulative actions taken by a user. Controllers are usually attached one-to-one to views. Figure 9.2 shows the resulting class diagram.

The small number of classes (Model, View, Controller) in Figure 9.2 may suggest that MVC could be seen as a pattern rather than as a framework. However, the figure is intentionally simplified. The apparently simple relation between model and view alone is covered by a pattern of its own: the Observer pattern (p. 136). The relation between view and controller is also non-trivial. A controller has to interact tightly with the way in which the view presents data. Thus, a controller directly depends on a specific view. The controller augments the functionality of the view by adding a strategy of how to interpret user events and map them to view operations. The corresponding pattern is called Strategy by Gamma *et al.* (1995). Note that the controller and view pair-wise refer to the same model – this is not easily shown in a class diagram. (This redundancy could be avoided by requiring the controller to acquire the model indirectly from the view.)

Figure 9.2 displays further relationships. First, it shows how user-triggered events reach a controller and how view presentations reach the display. What is more important, it also shows that arbitrary, other 'client' classes can directly operate on model, view, and controller. Remembering these 'other' players is important in the context of a framework, whereas it is of less importance in the context of patterns.

A framework integrates and concretizes a number of patterns to the degree required to ensure proper interleaving and interaction of the various patterns' participants. Indeed, a framework can be explained in terms of the patterns it uses (Johnson, 1992). A framework thus adds a higher level of architecture but also the infrastructure that integrates the lower-level abstractions, often usefully described using patterns. The degree of *enforcement* of integration rules depends on the framework technology used. If the framework is a set of Smalltalk classes,

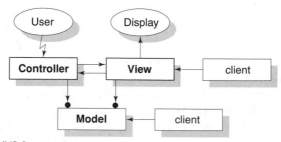

Figure 9.2 The MVC framework.

there is no strict enforcement that a programmer could not breach. If the framework is encapsulated into 'sealed' modules or packages whose implementations are inaccessible, enforcement can be quite strict.

Framework design can be bottom up and pattern driven (for example Schmid, 1995), or it can be top down and target driven. The bottom-up design works well where a framework domain is already well understood, for example after some initial evolutionary cycles. Starting from proven patterns and working one's way up has the advantage of avoiding idiosyncratic solutions in the small, problematic solutions that should be replaced by application of an established pattern. As with all bottom-up design work, there is a danger of constructing 'shopping centers' of fragmentary solutions, without a sharp focus. [The term 'shopping list' approach goes back to Meyer (1988), who advocated it as a good strategy for class design. This strategy does not work well in practice – anything beyond trivial ADTs does not have a 'complete' set of operations.]

Top-down design of a framework is preferable where a framework domain has not yet been sufficiently explored but where the target domain to be served by the framework is well understood. A framework domain is the set of rules and roles and their semantic models codified in a framework itself. A target domain is the set of interactions and entities found in a concrete outcome of a domain analysis effort. It is important to keep the two separated. Framework domains are technical and in a sense 'introverted,' whereas target domains are application oriented or 'extroverted.' A single framework is meant to address multiple concrete targets – otherwise the attempt to form a generalized architecture has failed.

An example will make this clearer. Assume that the ideas of the MVC separation were not yet known, but that there was a firm understanding of what it means to edit interactively some visualized data in a window system. In this case, an entire family of target domains are understood, corresponding to the various kinds of documents to be edited. Also, the domains' entities are known: specific documents, windows, and users. Finding a family of closely related target domains is a good indication that a framework should be considered. Under the assumption that no such framework already exists, the question is: how can the target domain entities and their interactions be distilled to form the framework domain? In the example, how can the abstractions and mutual interactions of models, views, and controllers(!) be found?

There is no simple answer. Concrete designs and implementations for specific targets can be found using one of the several object-oriented analysis and design techniques. However, substantial design and domain experience is required to determine what a good framework would be. Making the framework too rigid may unnecessarily rule out relevant targets. Making it too flexible will lead to inefficiency, undue complexity, and probably both. It is helpful for a first sketch to pick a small number of concrete targets and work on appropriate designs and implementations without aiming for a framework. Resting on this target domain expertise, a framework design can be attempted. Quite a number of iterations should be expected before a framework design settles and becomes stable.

9.1.6 Sharing overall structure: system architectures

A few basic principles can be learned from successful software architectures of the past:

- layering, strict and non-strict
- hierarchies or heterarchies.

The idea of a strictly layered approach to software architecture is old. One of the first clear presentations of the idea, in the context of an operating system's architecture, was Dijkstra's article on the THE operating system (Dijkstra, 1968). (THE stands for the Dutch acronym of Technological University, Eindhoven, Dijkstra's affiliation at the time.) The benefits of layered architectures in terms of development effort and cost have been empirically verified (Zweben *et al.*, 1995). Shaw and Garlan (1996) recently published an introduction to some of the issues of software architecture. For a bibliography see their architecture Web site (http://www.sei.cmu.edu/technology/architecture/).

In a *strictly layered* system, the implementation of one layer can only be based on the operations made available by the layer immediately below. Figure 9.3 shows two popular ways to depict layered architectures.

The 'onion model' emphasizes the encapsulating property of strict layers but introduces a bias toward the expected relative size of the layers. There is no strict technical need for lower layers to be 'smaller' than higher ones.

Strict layering introduces a very powerful property to a system's architecture. A layered system can be understood incrementally, layer by layer, whether bottom up or top down. This is possible because each layer can be fully understood by understanding its implementation, relative to the interfaces it uses from the layer immediately below, and the interfaces it offers to the layer immediately above.

Strict layering has several downsides however. It hinders extensibility and it can introduce unacceptable performance penalties. Extensibility is threatened because a new higher-level component can only build on what is provided by the next lower layer. Although some layer further below, ultimately the hardware, may well support the new extension, the next lower layer may not. The percolation of requests through a deep hierarchy of layers can lead to performance problems. The extensibility issue can be addressed by allowing extensions on every

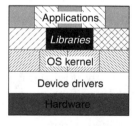
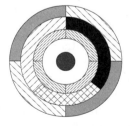

Figure 9.3 Strictly layered architectures and the strict 'onion model.'

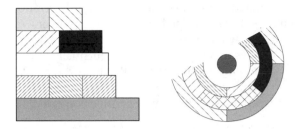

Figure 9.4 Extensible strict layering.

level of the architecture. Where operations can be bundled and bulk requests can be issued, performance problems in a layered system can normally be resolved. If operations cannot be batched, and resulting latencies introduced by the layering cannot be tolerated, the number of layers has to be reduced.

Figure 9.4 shows typical depictions of extensible layered architectures. In principle, the idea is that every extension should still reside on a single layer. Hence, if an extension on one layer needs to access services of a layer below the next lower layer, then intermediate extensions need to be devised. In practice, this principle is often breached. For example, instead of extending the *clib* (C library) layer, many Unix applications directly access the kernel where required.

The practice of accessing not only the next lower layer but any of the lower layers leads to *non-strict layering*. Figure 9.5 shows non-strict layering as it is often depicted. Non-strict layering can solve extensibility and performance problems by eliminating intermediate layers where useful. However, it destroys the main property of strict layering: that a layer creates an abstraction that is affected solely by the implementations forming that layer. In a non-strict layering, there is no obvious way to 'slice' a component that extends down to lower layers to gather all implementations belonging to a given layer.

Obviously, a non-strict layering is harder to visualize – there can be conflicts that make a complete diagram of the shape used in Figure 9.5 impossible. Is this relevant? Architecture is very much about striving for balances between understandability, functionality, and economy so it does matter if an architecture gets too complex to draw a simple overview diagram.

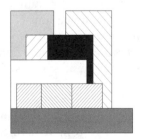

Figure 9.5 Non-strict layering.

It has been advocated before that each level of a description should involve three to seven entities. The reasoning behind this range is sometimes based on the human perceptive system and its natural ability to comprehend aggregates of up to around seven entities *at once* rather than sequentially and incrementally. An early proponent of this philosophy was Leo Brodie (Brodie, 1984). Many similar statements can be found in the literature on architecture or in discussions about architecture. For example, Kent Beck wrote (Anderson *et al.*, 1993, p. 358):

> 'The first test I apply [in my consulting practice] is whether staff can explain the system to me in 3–5 objects. If they can't, there is no explicit architecture. More often than not these projects are in trouble.'

It may seem strange to base architectural decisions on such vague criteria of human perceptibility. All other aspects, such as functionality and cost-effectiveness, certainly ask for due attention as well. However, they all fade to gray when the perceived complexity of an architecture prevents understandability and thus prevents effective teaching, maintenance, and evolution.

9.1.7 Systems of subsystems – framework hierarchies

To what extent do patterns and frameworks address architectural concerns? Patterns are microarchitectures; frameworks are subsystem architectures. Most larger, fully functional systems will introduce multiple frameworks. However, interaction across frameworks is a difficult problem that needs to be addressed on a yet higher architectural level. If formation of good frameworks is difficult, then conception of good system architectures is truly hard.

There is a compelling reason not to stop at the architectural level of frameworks but to move on to entire systems. Independently designed frameworks are very difficult to combine as they each aim to take control (see next section). By the very nature of frameworks, they aim at the regulation and possibly enforcement of part interaction. Unless there is a clear higher-level view of where, when, and how parts of frameworks overlap or interact, there is no handle for the framework architect to ensure proper inter-framework cooperation.

Systems are usually modeled as a *hierarchical* composition of subsystems. It should thus be possible to *lift* the concept of frameworks to higher levels. Traditional class frameworks are partial combinations of classes – partial because they need to be completed when instantiating a framework. A logical extension of this approach leads to *subsystem frameworks*. Subsystem frameworks prestructure larger systems by partially combining the key subsystems. Just as class frameworks use abstract classes for combination of sets of concrete classes, subsystem frameworks could use abstract subsystems.

The above vision of hierarchies of frameworks sounds straightforward. Experience however teaches that moving from structures with a fixed number of abstractional levels on to general hierarchical structures can introduce substantial complication. For example, Chapter 21 contains an example of lifting the 'flat' MVC framework to a hierarchical MVC framework. The result is *not* a framework hierarchy but a single framework covering a hierarchical structure. Nevertheless, the complexities introduced compared with plain MVC are truly substantial.

Another complexity of framework hierarchies needs to be faced. All previous attempts that aimed at merely replicating proven abstractional tools from a lower level to higher levels failed. For example, a class is not a procedural closure, a module or package is not a class, and a subsystem is not a module. In all these cases the lower-level abstraction is not perfectly suited to capture the higher-level needs. There are two reasons, and both can be understood as an 'impedance mismatch.' First, a lower-level abstraction is naturally closer to concrete detail, such as the execution order or the data representation. Retaining the lower-level's degree of detail overburdens a higher-level abstraction. Second, a higher-level abstraction introduces new organizational roles, for example to increase the degrees of independence and autonomy of responsible producers. Ignoring the new organizational roles leads to a complete failure of the introduced abstraction.

The discipline area is still too young to venture a general attempt at framework hierarchies. The next step has to be a close study of *second-order frameworks*, frameworks of subsystems that each by themselves can be structured and understood using traditional (first-order) frameworks. Attempts in this direction are component frameworks (see Chapter 21 for a detailed discussion.)

To conclude, system architecture is a means to capture an overall generic approach that makes it more likely that concrete systems following the architecture will be understandable, maintainable, evolvable, and economic. It is this integrating principle, covering technology *and* market, that links software architecture to its great role model and justifies its name.

9.2 Interoperability, legacies and re-engineering

Existing solutions to problems are the cornerstone of working organizations. Such solutions naturally age and eventually become a 'legacy' from earlier software engineering eras. Abrupt abandoning of legacy solutions and their instant replacement by something 'new and better' is not normally an option. Instead, solutions must be sought that enable smooth transitions and gradual replacement (for example Brodie and Stonebreaker, 1995).

A cardinal problem in many cases is the absence of a clear overall architecture of the legacy system, combined with refined architectures on lower levels of abstraction. Not surprisingly, some sort of architecture is usually present at the time a new system is first conceived. Naturally, this initial architecture proves inadequate as the system evolves, but instead of carefully evolving the architecture as well, it is often left behind. As the system evolves independently of a maintained architecture, it 'deteriorates' over time. Migration to new technologies then becomes a problem of *re-engineering,* and often even of *reverse engineering*, without guiding high-level documents. Then, legacy becomes a major burden.

To prevent deterioration of architecture, systems need to be *refactored* periodically. A clear benefit of component-based architectures is their support of localized refactoring. Refactoring within a component is easiest, but a hierarchical overall architecture also enables selective refactoring of subsystems. Refactoring has increasingly widespread effects as it is taken further up the hierarchy of an overall architecture. It is thus useful to design a hierarchical architecture from the beginning with refactoring in mind. In particular, coupling needs to decrease quickly when moving to higher levels of the hierarchy.

A separate but related aspect is *interoperability* across time and space. Interoperability across time is often called backward and forward compatibility. The issue is: how can two software systems, separated either by evolution over time or by independent development over space, cooperate? On a semantic level, this requires shared definitions. On an infrastructural level, it requires shared 'wiring.' It is the latter aspect that is often referred to as interoperability (Valdès, 1994).

Introduction of new technologies without the simultaneous introduction of adequate architectural approaches addressing all relevant levels can have disastrous effects. In the wake of early adoptions of object-oriented technology, architecture in-the-large has often been neglected. Objects were happily created and wired, all across a system. Layers were not introduced or not respected. Lines between a base and its extensions were not drawn or breached. The result is that object-oriented legacy is already a problem – after only a few years of adoption by the industry (for example Casais *et al.*, 1996). For example, the European Commission under the Esprit program is currently providing funding for a major project on evolution and re-engineering of 'object-oriented legacy systems' (FAMOOS Consortium, 1996).

With the arguments presented in Chapter 7 in mind, it is not surprising that a lack of overall architecture in object-oriented systems is much *worse* than in traditional procedural systems. This is increasingly understood today and often leads to a shattering of initial 'OO illusions.' While it is a difficult task to move software to other procedural libraries, it is a truly formidable task to attempt migration to a different class framework. Very few traditional class frameworks have been designed to be interoperable with other frameworks. Implementations that specialize a certain class framework are intimately coupled to their framework. Independent evolution of the framework is already a problem (see, for example, discussion of the fragile base class problem in Chapter 7). Exchange of the framework for another is almost impossible.

Interoperability on a global scale, as pushed by the Internet and its Worldwide Web, introduces a new dimension. Architecture on the top level now has to be global itself. It has to span borders, organizations, customers, and vendors alike. There is room for multiple architectures – not everything needs to integrate with everything else on the highest semantic level. For example, OMG's object management architecture (OMA) is one such ambitious attempt to standardize parts of a global architecture (Chapter 13).

CHAPTER TEN

Programming: shades of gray

It is sometimes thought that component software ends programming for most, leaving it to those specialists who create new components. The majority is expected merely to compose components; a task that is often called component assembly. If this was true, if programming was limited to the inside of a component, then this chapter and most of this book would be off-target.

What is programming? Programming a system is the activity of adding or changing functionality by combining or recombining existing or newly devised abstract entities according to a (programming) model. Programming can happen on all levels of a system. Programmable gate arrays lower the limits down to almost the gate level. Is there an upper limit? It is sometimes claimed that, from certain abstractional levels upwards, programming changes into *scripting*. Others claim that programming can be replaced by visual construction techniques. Such claims are not immediately helpful; their banishing of programming to the lower levels does no justice to this general concept.

In this chapter the various forms of programming, as they are propagated today, are put into perspective and related to the theme of component software and software architecture.

10.1 Different programming methods for different programmers

It is helpful to differentiate between programming tasks of varying complexity and audiences that are expected to perform these tasks. Here is a list of some exemplary activities that are not normally identified with programming, but which nevertheless are closely related:

- requirements engineering
- visual application building and component assembly
- scripting.

In all cases, the key is to consider the corresponding programming model. For requirements engineering, the programming model introduces entities of the application domain and ways to express relations and transitions over time. Executable requirement specifications are indeed preferable, especially in cases where ill-captured requirements can pose major safety threats (Leveson, 1995). The key difference to programming in the narrower sense is the total irrelevance of performance or resource consumption of the executable specification. Execution is merely used as a tool for validation.

Visual application building rests on a programming model of plug-and-play of prefabricated components. The number of components that are combined is usually quite small and the mutual dependencies between these components take simple standard forms. Thus, visual builders are an option. Programming on this level concentrates mostly on functionality. Performance and resource consumption are expected to be dominated by the components used, rather than by their particular 'wiring.'

Scripting is quite similar to application building. Approaches based on scripting admit that the actual 'wiring' may need more than just 'connections.' Scripting allows programs to be attached to connections – either at the source end (events) or at the target end (hooks). Unlike mainstream component programming, scripts usually do not introduce new components but simply 'wire' existing ones. Scripts can be seen as introducing behavior but no new state. Scripting is thus similar to traditional procedural or functional programming, and most scripting languages are indeed quite procedural in nature. Performance and resource consumption are expected to be dominated by the components used rather than the scripts. The actual script execution engines therefore usually deliver mediocre to poor performance.

Scripts themselves are sometimes grouped into new abstract units, so-called *script components* (Nierstrasz *et al.*, 1992). This terminology hints at the possibility of scripting scripts and ultimately at the fact that scripting *is* programming. 'Script component' is not quite the right term, however. Script package or script module would be more appropriate terms, but would still ignore the fact that a script itself does not introduce new (persistent) state. Of course, there is nothing to stop a 'scripting' language from introducing persistent state – it then simply turns into a normal programming language.

Following the above arguments, it is mainly the different programming models and the programming goals that make the difference. Scripting aims at late and high-level 'gluing.' Another dimension can be explored when considering graphical instead of textual programming, whether or not for scripting purposes. Graphical or visual programming is programming, and will remain programming, even if animation, virtual reality, and other media are used. This is so because the intellectual skills required are essentially the same. However, the audiences addressed by these different approaches to programming are likely to be quite different.

There is a proverb that holds that a picture says more than a thousand words. Kristen Nygaard countered that the opposite is also true: a word says more than a thousand pictures (Nygaards' dinner speech '25 years Simula,' ECOOP92,

Utrecht, The Netherlands). The point is that a true abstraction is necessarily represented symbolically, whereas a concrete real-world object may be represented (photo)graphically *or* by using its name. The photo may say much more than the name, but no picture can capture the full depth of the meaning of a symbol. Using icons instead of words merely adds new 'words' to the language; icons and words are both symbols rather than direct presentations of the 'real thing.'

Symbols are not only appropriate but inevitable when referring to abstraction: an abstraction is not a 'real thing.' The introduction of symbolic reference and abstraction is certainly among the foremost achievements of civilization. Without it, thinking remains at the level of the individual and concrete. Neither the future nor the past can be referred to; strategy, planning, generalization, and reflection remain out of reach. Crippling general programming by insisting on total 'concreteness' and 'tangibility' of everything is a mistake. In other words, graphical or visual programming cannot be about removing symbolism or eliminating metaphors used to visualize the abstract. Graphical notations, such as class diagrams, can indeed be entirely symbolic and unconcrete.

Graphical or visual programming can be the preferred method when the number of entities involved in any one 'view' is relatively small. Such forms of programming can also be appropriate where the relations and interactions between these entities are mostly regular. The human perceptive system can most efficiently spot minor irregularities in large and mostly regular structures. It can also evaluate 'at once' all relations between a small number of entities. Another possibility is the visual presentation of a large number of attributes using carefully selected visual properties (dimensions), including color, texture, spatial distribution, and temporal patterns such as flashing. Where such conditions are met, a graphical presentation can excel. In all other cases, more abstract methods, tabular, formula based, or textual, are more appropriate. In particular, these more abstract methods are more space economic, easier to change, and tend to be more precise as to what is actually specified and what not. Finally, graphical notations do not lend themselves to formal reasoning. To counter a common counterexample: in electrical engineering, graphical circuit schemata are used less and less frequently and usually only on the level of high-level diagrams or individual patterns. The wiring of more complex circuitry is expressed and verified using special formal languages.

10.2 Programming to a system

The proper abstractions to support programming obviously depend on the *programming model*. Traditional programming models are primarily based on the composition of library-provided procedural abstractions and a model of strict and immediate evaluation. In such a context, the programming style is caller driven. Interfaces list call points: procedures, also called entry points. This does not change when moving from procedures to objects. As long as objects remain passive, computation remains caller driven and interfaces list call points ('methods'). The model stays the same, even when considering higher-order programming, where procedure or object references are passed around, stored, and applied without static reference to the actual procedure or object.

The programming model changes when primarily looking at *connections* between objects rather than callers. A connection is really just a binding between a caller and a callee. However, connections are symmetric whereas traditional procedure invocation models are asymmetrically caller controlled. Caller and callee are just the two ends of a connection. Neither of them is in charge of the actual binding. Interfaces in such a setting need to describe both call and calling points. A terminology introduced by Microsoft for its Connectable Objects approach is to speak of incoming and outgoing interfaces. Incoming interfaces are the traditional ones, listing call points. Outgoing interfaces declare what operations a component could invoke if it was properly connected. In other models, such outgoing interfaces are called *raisable events* or just events.

10.3   Connection-oriented programming

Components may need to call other components to perform. This corresponds to normal programming in which abstractions depend on other abstractions. It is also said that normal programmed calls correspond to a *pull model* of programming. The information is 'pulled' in as needed. However, it may also be necessary for a component to be called by another component whenever that other component encounters a particular event. For example, in the observer pattern (Chapter 9) the observed object notifies its observers whenever its state has changed. However, it is not the observed object but the notified observers that depend on the notification. This is an important point. Notification or event propagation work in the reverse direction of traditional programming models: they implement a *push model*. Information is 'pushed' out as it arises, rather than being pulled by a procedure call or method invocation.

In a traditional pull model, the caller knows what service to call. This can be generalized by introducing increasing degrees of late binding or indirections. With such indirections in place, it makes sense to say that caller and callee are 'connected' by establishing the binding. In a push model, indirections are normally unavoidable: in most cases, the pushing source cannot statically know the interested sinks. On an implementation level, indirections in push and pull models are handled in the same way. In procedural settings, procedure variables are used. In object-oriented settings, references to objects of base types can be used as a method invocation always introduces one level of indirection.

By replacing statically chained call dependencies by indirections that can be configured at runtime, *connection-oriented programming* is introduced. Increasingly, the connection mechanisms are factored out as separate services. Examples are event or message services. It is even possible, although restrictive, to build communication middleware entirely on the concept of messages and message distribution. This is called *message-oriented middleware* (MOM). However, in object-oriented middleware, such as DCOM or CORBA, event and message services are of equal importance.

Connection-oriented programming is important when 'wiring' prefabricated components or objects provided by such components. This is one occasion when an analogy with integrated circuits (ICs) helps. ICs have various pins, some of which carry input and others of which carry output signals. The technical documentation of an IC clearly and equally specifies the role of input *and* output signals. In traditional software systems there has been a bias toward 'input signals.' Connection-oriented programming requires symmetry of 'connectors' for input and output. The corresponding interfaces are called *incoming* and *outgoing* interfaces. An incoming interface corresponds to traditional procedural or method interfaces. The analogy with IC signals is that calls come in on incoming interfaces, whereas calls go out on outgoing interfaces.

It is important to understand that the distinction between incoming and outgoing interfaces is about the direction of calls as seen by a component, not the flow of information. In particular, the parameters of a traditional incoming interface operation can, of course, be used to return values. It is thus easy to confuse return parameters with outgoing interfaces. The point is whether a call 'through' that interface originates within or outside the component. Being incoming or outgoing is thus *not* a property of an interface in isolation. Every interface defines a clear call direction from interface client (caller) to interface provider (callee). Interfaces are incoming or outgoing with respect to a given component. Declaring outgoing interfaces of a component corresponds to declaring the events or messages that this component could emit.

The traditional model is asymmetric. Although the callee does not know anything about the callers, a caller has to hold explicitly a reference or a static link to the callee. Interfaces on which a component depends are simply imported. Explicit parametrization using procedure references (callbacks) or object references are the only way to 'connect' a caller dynamically to a callee. The idea of outgoing interfaces or event models is to normalize this approach and to allow external tools to connect objects with a given outgoing interface to objects supporting a matching incoming interface. In a type-safe setting, connections can only be made if the incoming interface is the same as or a subtype of the outgoing interface (see Chapter 6).

Figure 10.1 illustrates the connection of two objects by symbolically 'wiring' outgoing to incoming interfaces using the COM notation (Chapter 14). Component object C1 has outgoing interfaces B and V and incoming interfaces A and U. Component object C2 has outgoing interfaces A and Y and incoming interfaces B and X. Connections have been established between the A and B interfaces of the two components.

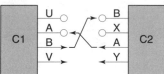

Figure 10.1 Connections, outgoing, and incoming interfaces.

Note that connections *per se* are independent of concepts of import, export, or layering. For example, a component framework may provide a common layer that defines various interfaces. A component for this framework imports the common layer and declares which of these interfaces it uses in incoming, outgoing, or both roles. It is then possible that several mutually independent components provide objects that, based on the common interface definitions, can be connected in a type-safe manner. These connections then exist *horizontally* within the layer of the components, or logically in a higher layer that establishes the connections. Such a separate connection layer or the connected objects themselves may need to provide *persistence* of connections. This is important when the connected objects themselves are persistent and the connections are supposed to persist as well.

10.4 | Connection-oriented programming: advanced concepts

Once connections are emphasized as entities of their own, other connecting networks come to mind. For example, a single caller could be connected to a set of callees to create *multicast* connections. Intermediate abstractions, sometimes called *channels* or *groups*, can also be introduced, so that callers (sources) communicate through an additional indirection with a set of callees (sinks). Multiple callers can then use the same group. Callees can be added to or removed from such a group without contacting every caller that is currently using the group.

Figure 10.2 shows how C1's outgoing B interface can be connected to two incoming B interfaces. Technically, this requires a single call, here issued by C1, to be mapped to multiple calls, here to C2 and C3. Note that the connection of multiple outgoing interfaces to a single incoming interface is also possible and even quite common. This is nothing new; even the simplest procedural abstractions allow the same procedure to be called from many different call sites.

Figure 10.3 shows how an event channel or group can be used to decouple the connections callers-to-group and group-to-callees. Note that the group itself is represented by another component object, G. There is nothing special about groups or channels, except that they 'promise,' as part of their interface contracts, to relay incoming calls to outgoing interfaces. Obviously, this can be extended to provide other useful services. For example, a channel may filter calls, count calls, delay

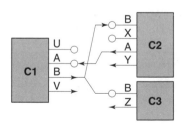

Figure 10.2 Multiple connections.

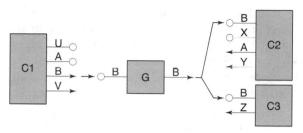

Figure 10.3 Separating the message target group from the message sources and sinks or, in message terms, separating the event channel from the event sources and sinks.

calls, log calls, or record calls for later replay. It is easy to see that such abstract calling fabrics are very useful and that their existence makes the connection model truly powerful.

Interesting questions arise when the issue is the construction of *generic* group or channel services. If a group supports a specific set of interfaces, such as interface B in Figure 10.3, then the group's implementation is straightforward. It simply passes on all incoming calls to the incoming interfaces of all callees registered with the group. It is not productive to construct simple multicasting services repeatedly for all sorts of interfaces. Even if the construction is performed automatically by a tool, it leads to a large number of logically identical objects to which callers and callees have to be connected.

To program generic group or channel services, calls of operations with arbitrary signatures need to be dealt with generically. A paradigm that fits well is that of *typed message passing*. If calls always go through the same procedures or methods when being relayed between components, but carry different messages, then the construction of generic group or channel services is easy. In the presence of runtime type information, functionality such as message type-dependent filtering is also straightforward to realize. Typed messages are often called *event objects*.

The following sample code illustrates this concept of message passing. The notation used is Component Pascal (Appendix A).

```
DEFINITION MessageGroups;
   TYPE
      Sink(A) = POINTER TO ABSTRACT RECORD
         (s: Sink(A)) Receive (VAR message: A), NEW, ABSTRACT
      END;
      Group(A) = POINTER TO ABSTRACT RECORD
         (g: Group(A)) Register (s: Sink(A)), NEW, ABSTRACT;
         (g: Group(A)) Unregister (s: Sink(A)), NEW, ABSTRACT;
         (g: Group(A)) Send (VAR message: A), NEW, ABSTRACT
      END;
END MessageGroups.
```

Component Pascal requires explicit naming and typing of the receiver object, called 'this' or 'self' in other languages. The receiver is specified in the form of an additional parameter list with exactly one parameter, placed *before* the operation's name. Methods have *attributes*. Attribute NEW marks a method as new, that is not overriding a base type method. (Note that a record declared with no base type has base type ANYREC.) Attribute ABSTRACT works as expected and marks the method as abstract.

Parametrization of types to express parametric polymorphism is a proposed language extension (Roe and Szyperski, 1997) and is currently under consideration for Component Pascal. In module Messages this is used to ensure that a group accepts only matching messages and sinks. Parametrization is achieved by naming any number of type parameters that can only be replaced by record types. In any specific context, all occurrences of a type parameter are guaranteed to refer to a type of identical bound. (The proposed parametric polymorphism is statically checked, does not conflict with separate compilation, has no runtime overhead, and does not lead to any object code duplication.)

In this example, the types of groups and sinks are parametrized to show that these types could be used in conjunction with an arbitrary message base type. For example, a sink that only accepts messages of type MyMessage would be declared as:

```
TYPE
   MyMessage = RECORD ... END;
   MySink = RECORD (MessageGroups.Sink(MyMessage)) ... END;
```

With a slight modification, a similar declaration can be used to declare that sinks can accept messages of type MyMessage or any of its subtypes:

```
TYPE
   MyMessage = EXTENSIBLE RECORD ... END;
```

The attribute EXTENSIBLE indicates that, although MyMessage is a concrete record type, it is still open for extension, that is not a final type. (Concrete types in Component Pascal are final by default.)

Below is the implementation of a module that offers a group implementation that broadcasts calls.

```
MODULE Broadcast;
   IMPORT Sets, MessageGroups;
   TYPE
      BCaster(A) = POINTER TO RECORD(MessageGroups.Group(A))
         sinks: Sets.Set(MessageGroups.Sink(A))
      END;
```

```
PROCEDURE<A> SendOne (s: MessageGroups.Sink(A); VAR message: A);
(* aux for Send *)
BEGIN s.Send(message)
END SendOne;

PROCEDURE<A> (g: BCaster(A)) Register (s: MessageGroups.Sink(A));
BEGIN g.sinks.Include(s)
END Register;

PROCEDURE<A> (g: BCaster(A)) Unregister (s: MessageGroups.Sink(A));
BEGIN g.sinks.Exclude(s)
END Unregister;

PROCEDURE<A> (g: BCaster(A)) Send (VAR message: A);
BEGIN Sets.Do(g.sinks, SendOne, m)
END Send;

PROCEDURE<A> New* (): MessageGroups.Group(A);   (* simple factory *)
    VAR bc: BCaster(A);
BEGIN
    NEW(bc); bc.sinks := Sets.New();
    RETURN bc
END New;
END Broadcast.
```

Note that in Component Pascal an identifier that is followed by an asterisk is exported from its defining module and thus visible in importing modules. In the example above, procedure Broadcast.New is thus exported from module Broadcast. The group implementation in module Broadcast rests on a simple generic implementation of sets. The type parametrization of procedures (and methods) uses angular brackets rather than parentheses to indicate an important difference. Procedures are never explicitly parametrized; instead, at every call site, the proper type arguments are inferred from the arguments passed to the procedure.

The definition of the Sets module, as used in this example, is shown below.

```
DEFINITION Sets;
    TYPE
        Set(A) = POINTER TO LIMITED RECORD
            (s: Set(A)) Include (elem: POINTER TO A);
            (s: Set(A)) Exclude (elem: POINTER TO A);
            (s: Set(A)) Contains (elem: POINTER TO A): BOOLEAN;
            (s: Set(A)) Size (): INTEGER
        END;
        Op(A,B) = PROCEDURE (elem: POINTER TO A; VAR arg: B);
    PROCEDURE<A> New (): Set(A);
    PROCEDURE<A,B> Do (s: Set(A); op: Op(A,B); VAR arg: B);
    (* other definitions deleted *)
END Sets.
```

In Component Pascal, the record attribute LIMITED prevents extension of the attributed record and restricts instantiation of such records to the defining module. In the example, only module Sets can allocate a new Set object. The broadcaster's method Send uses the procedure Sets.Do to call the auxiliary procedure SendOne once for each element of the set. Note that Sets.Do takes an arbitrary argument that it passes on to the operation it applies. Unlike Java, Component Pascal can express 'unboxed' constructed types. The generic argument can be allocated in the caller's stack frame; there is thus no need for heap allocation and subsequent garbage collection.

Below is a simple test module that uses the above message group abstraction and broadcasting service.

```
MODULE TestClient;
  IMPORT Strings, Out, MessageGroups, Broadcast;
  TYPE
    Message = RECORD
      famousWords: Strings.String
    END;
    Sink = POINTER TO RECORD (MessageGroups.Sink(Message))
      name: Strings.String
    END;
  VAR
    sink1, sink2, sink3: Sink;
    group: MessageGroups.Group(Message);
    hello: Message;
  PROCEDURE (s: Sink) Receive (IN m: Message);
  BEGIN
    Out.String("sink " + s.name + " received message: " +
            m.famousWords); Out.Ln
  END Receive;

  PROCEDURE NewSink (IN name: ARRAY OF CHAR): Sink;
    VAR s: Sink;
  BEGIN
    NEW(s); s.name := Strings.NewFrom(name); RETURN s
  END NewSink;
BEGIN
  Out.String("start of test"); Out.Ln;
  sink1 := NewSink("ONE");
  sink2 := NewSink("TWO");
  sink3 := NewSink("THREE");
  group := Broadcast.New();
  group.Register(sink1);   (* dynamic connect of sink1 to group *)
  group.Register(sink2);   (* dynamic connect of sink2 to group *)
  group.Register(sink3);   (* dynamic connect of sink3 to group *)
```

```
hello.famousWords := Strings.NewFrom("Hello World!");
group.Send(hello);   (* static connection here: source sends to group *)
Out.String("end of test"); Out.Ln
END TestClient.
```

The two remaining modules used by TestClient are Strings and Out. The relevant parts of their respective definitions are listed below.

```
DEFINITION Strings;
   TYPE String = POINTER TO ARRAY OF CHAR;
   PROCEDURE NewFrom (s: ARRAY OF CHAR): String;
   (* other definitions deleted *)
END Strings.

DEFINITION Out;
   PROCEDURE String (s: ARRAY OF CHAR);
   PROCEDURE Ln;
   (* other definitions deleted *)
END Out.
```

Executing TestClient will create three sample sinks, a broadcast group and a sample message. The three sinks are registered with the group. The message is then broadcast to all three sinks. Once TestClient terminates, the resulting output text will show the following five lines:

```
start of test
sink ONE received message: Hello World!
sink TWO received message: Hello World!
sink THREE received message: Hello World!
end of test
```

10.5 Events and messages

As can be seen from the above example, all that is required is to declare message objects and pass them around. With slight variations, this is the model of events in JavaBeans (Chapter 15), the CORBA Event Service (Chapter 13), or of COM's connection points and the Microsoft messaging service (Chapter 14). In the Component Pascal example above, a caller (a source) has to go through two steps:

(1) Create a message object and initialize its fields.
(2) Send the message object to the sinks.

Step 2 in CORBA is always through a channel abstraction defined by the Event Service. In JavaBeans or COM, such an indirection must be explicitly 'wired' in. Otherwise, JavaBeans and COM events travel directly from source to sink, with no system-imposed indirection. COM uses separate *sink* objects per connection to the same receiving COM object, whereas JavaBeans uses a complex *demultiplexing adapter* approach to separate calls from different sources.

The two-step approach of event signaling has three potential disadvantages:

(1) Making event objects first-class (heap allocated) can be expensive.
(2) Event objects of the wrong type could be passed.
(3) Event objects could be passed that have not been properly initialized.

All of these problems can be solved by proper programming language support. The first problem disappears where a language supports 'unboxed' object types – and Java is among the few languages that do not. Then, event objects can be allocated on the call stack, as any other argument passed to a called procedure or method.

In typed languages, for normal procedure or method invocations, the argument list is statically checked by the compiler. It is not possible to pass wrong numbers or ill-typed arguments. The second problem arises because of the desire to make event channels or groups generic. JavaBeans, for example, recommends the use of specific event object types in event-handling methods. The same is possible with the CORBA Event Service. In Java, it is not possible to construct generic channels or groups that are statically type safe. If the message's type, or at least a sufficiently narrow common base type, is known to the sources and sinks, then parametric polymorphism solves the second problem. The above experimental version of Component Pascal supports parametric polymorphism; the MessageGroups and Broadcast examples above are parametrized with the message type and will handle only this message type or a subtype thereof.

It may be necessary to send a wide variety of messages through the same channel. The type parameter in such a case is necessarily imprecise – it could be as imprecise as the base type of all messages. If such an imprecise type bound is required, the second problem naturally remains: a sink has to expect messages that it cannot handle – and therefore should ignore. If such a message is sent erroneously instead of one that the sink would understand, then hard-to-track errors occur. Unfortunately, a sink cannot simply raise an exception when it receives a message that it does not understand. Under the broadcasting discipline, some other sink addressed by the same message may well understand it.

The third problem, the use of only partially initialized event objects, is caused by code explicitly filling in fields of a new event object. It can be solved by using message or event constructors. In Java, this is achieved by making the fields of an event object non-public, providing accessor methods, and using a constructor to initialize the event object. This is workable but expensive. The solution in Component Pascal would be to export message or event fields in a *read-only* mode. Initialization also happens in a constructor procedure, but access is as efficient as with public fields.

Unless raisable events or outgoing interfaces form part of the definition of a component, it is not clear what events a particular object may raise. The solution is to make such information part of a component's definition. JavaBeans proposes an interesting way for doing so. Instead of introducing a notion of separate 'outgoing interfaces,' JavaBeans relies on the Java core reflection mechanism. Reflection is used to extract dynamically those methods from a Java interface that follow certain naming and signature conventions (Chapter 15).

For example, to allow the connection of callees (called *listeners* in JavaBeans), a bean's interface must contain a method for each event type that it is capable of 'listening' to. These methods must not have a return value and take only one parameter of a type that is a subtype of *java.util.EventObject*. Event-handling methods that follow this 'design pattern' can be singled out automatically by using the reflection facilities to traverse all methods of an interface and inspecting the methods' signatures and return types.

A similar 'design pattern' is used to find methods that support addition and removal of listener registrations. Such methods must not return anything, have a method name that starts with 'add' or 'remove' followed by the name of the listener type, and take a single parameter of this listener type. JavaBeans also defines a mechanism for a bean to override the automatic inference of event sources and handlers (Chapter 15).

10.6 Events versus calls

Firing an event is similar to calling a procedure or a method. However, the target of the event is totally unknown to the source of the event and there can be multiple targets for a single event fired. Event firing is not normally expected to return any results. Firing events is done as a service to other objects, not to fulfill local needs. Event models can be seen as a generalization of notification mechanisms, such as the one introduced in the Observer design pattern (p. 136).

At times, however, it is useful for an event mechanism to be able to return a result. For example, an event can be fired to check whether any of the unknown listeners satisfies a certain criterion. Pure event services, such as the CORBA Event Service or JavaBeans, do not allow for the return of values. The motivation is simple; as events may be sent to multiple listeners, it is not clear what to do if multiple listeners want to return a result. There is an obvious solution however. An event object can carry a reference to a collector object, which is often identical with the object that fired the event. Event sinks can then send results back to the collector object.

Other mechanisms, such as COM's Connectable Objects, directly support the returning of results in the event object. With interposed channels or other intermediate objects, special care is required. A typical approach is to set a flag in the event object, indicating that a result is returned. If the flag was set on arrival of an event, an event handler can no longer return a result. In this way, the first event handler with a result can report it. Other strategies that resolve conflicts among multiple replies are also possible, such as returning the largest or smallest value.

10.7 | Ordering of events – causality, races, and glitches

Event-based communication is asynchronous. The relative order in which events arrive at their sinks is not well defined in most cases. Consider the scenario in Figure 10.4. Source A fires event e1 while sinks B and C are listening. Sink B receives event e1 and immediately fires event e2, for which C and D are listening.

The ordering of events, as observed by C, is not defined. For example, in a single-threaded system it is likely that e2 arrives at C before e1. The event passing is handled by an invocation on B that, before it returns, causes an invocation on C to deliver e2. It is common that an event service specifies the relative event ordering only weakly. It is usually guaranteed that a sink receives events from the *same* source in the order in which they were sent. Figure 10.5 illustrates two possible arrival orders, of the events e1 and e2, at sink C.

The top ordering in Figure 10.5 is the *natural order* (breadth first), that is the order that is closest to the intuition behind event distribution. The bottom ordering is the *recursive call order* (depth first), that is the natural ordering in systems that do not use intermediate buffers and separate threads to distribute events.

There is one substantial difference between these two orderings. The natural order preserves *causality*, whereas the recursive call order does not. The firing of event e2 by B is *caused* by C's receipt of e1. In a causality-based logic, the receipt of e1 *happened before* the sending of e2. C should therefore first receive e1 and then e2. Preserving causality in group communication mechanisms has been studied thoroughly in the context of distributed systems (for example Birman, 1985), and yet it is not normally considered a feature in event services. The natural emergence of the recursive call order makes it much cheaper to implement than any other ordering.

Consider the following example. A model notifies its two views. As a result of the notification, the first view fires an event that, among other targets, reaches the second view. If the second view receives this event before it received the original model notification, it may not be in a consistent state and ready to handle the event. The situation becomes very severe in systems that support recursive embedding of document parts. For a particular solution provided by the BlackBox component framework see Chapter 21.

The asynchronous nature of event models can be compared with the asynchronous propagation of signals in electronic circuits. It can happen that an event reaches its target 'just before' the target moves to a consistent state. After receiving the event, the target may make this inconsistency observable to other objects

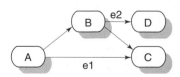

Figure 10.4   Event propagation.

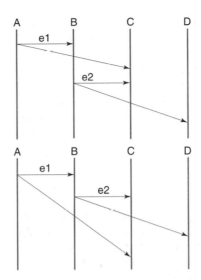

Figure 10.5   Event ordering: natural order (top) versus recursive call order (bottom).

for a short time, before reaching a consistent state again. In an electronic system, this transitory condition is referred to as a *glitch*, and resulting errors can be difficult to track down. As with electronic systems, introduction of a delay mechanism can solve the problem. In a software system, such a delay is caused by buffering the event and propagating it only after processing whatever is required to bring the event target up to date.

Another effect with an analogy in electronic systems is a *race condition*. If the relative ordering of event arrivals depends on dynamic conditions, then the events may arrive in the right order in some cases and in a wrong order in others. In a sense, the events compete in a 'race' to reach their targets first. In electronic systems, race conditions are affected by the inherent non-determinism of the *exact* timing of signals. This is not an issue in software systems. The analogy holds nevertheless: non-determinism in time is replaced by the very large number of possible state sequences in a complex component software system.

Preserving sufficiently strong order – such as causal order – and avoiding glitches and races is a tricky but important aspect of a component system's architecture. In some cases, component frameworks can be used to enforce well-formed interactions that avoid these problems (Chapter 21). In other cases, special programming methodologies can be used to avoid such problems from the outset (Chapter 22).

10.8   Very late binding: dispatch interfaces and metaprogramming

Connection-orientation, notifications, and events are all cases of late binding. The binding between caller and callee is not established before runtime, although the type of interface is known at compile time. Occasionally, it may even be necessary to find out at runtime the *types* of interfaces that a connected object supports. It may therefore even be necessary to delay type checking until runtime.

A typical example is a system in which a top-level interpreter can dynamically invoke precompiled operations. If these precompiled components are acquired dynamically, then runtime exploration of their interfaces may be necessary. A good example is a Web browser that supports scripting of documents that contain arbitrary controls or applets. The script author and the control 'know' what is involved, but the intermediate Web browser, serving as a container for the embedded controls, does not.

Provided that a component comes with enough information to be *self-describing*, the interfaces supported by the component can be dynamically explored. The means to do so differ from approach to approach, but the fundamental problem is always the same: preserve information available at compile time for inspection at runtime. Making such information about a system available within that system is called *reification*. A system that uses this information about itself in its normal course of execution is said to be *reflective*. Programming a system to not only use reified information but also to manipulate this information is called *meta-programming*. (For a good treatment of the issues involved see the literature on meta-programming, for example Kiczales *et al.*, 1991.)

Very few mainstream services support full meta-programming. One of the few examples is IBM's system object model (SOM), which fully supports meta-programming. For example, a program based on SOM can define new interfaces, synthesize matching new classes at runtime, and then create instances of the new classes. SOM goes as far as allowing for the interception of the actual execution model. This is used by distributed SOM (DSOM), which is really just a library sitting on top of SOM and using SOM's meta-services to intercept operations and transparently support distribution.

Flavors of meta-programming are to a lesser degree supported by all approaches. Java 1.1 introduced the *Java Core Reflection Service*. The name has been well chosen: the service does not allow interception or manipulation at the meta-level. However, it extends the rudimentary runtime type information available in the Java language (instanceof operator, p. 225). The Java language facilities merely allow an object to be probed for implementation of statically known interfaces. The reflection services allow enumeration and inspection of all facets of an object, a class, or an interface. For example, it is possible to write code which, for a particular method, inspects the signature, assembles the required parameters, and invokes the method. Obviously, this takes the compiler's type checking out of the loop and the reflection service has to perform checks at runtime.

The approach taken for COM is quite similar. A COM component can be equipped with a *type library*. The COM library supports dynamic inspection of all interfaces revealed in type libraries. Interfaces of a certain canonical form, called dispatch interfaces, can be invoked dynamically. This is more restrictive than the Java approach, which allows for dynamic invocation of any method in any interface or class. A dispatch interface essentially has just one interesting operation: Invoke. Operation Invoke takes an operation selector, called 'dispatch ID,' and a generic variant structure with the selected operation's arguments. However, this variant restricts the types of possible arguments to dispatch operations.

Using dispatch interfaces is substantially more expensive than calling operations directly. Component providers are thus encouraged to make dispatch interface operations also available in standard method form. An interface that offers both forms is called a *dual interface* (p. 210). Dual interfaces can be synthesized automatically, given a normal interface that respects the restrictions on signatures imposed by dispatching. This takes a substantial burden and source of error off the programmer. Dispatch interfaces are synthesized by Microsoft's J++ Java compiler. The current COM standard does not support full meta-programming – however the recently proposed COM+ does.

Finally, in CORBA, interface repositories serve these purposes. The interface repository reifies all OMG IDL information. This information can be used to check whether a certain object implements a specific interface. Dynamic invocation interfaces and dynamic stub interfaces allow calls to be dynamically dispatched either on the client's or at the object server's end. The current CORBA standard does not support full meta-programming. A request for proposals for a meta-object facility is in progress. The SOM services are a strong contender.

Dispatch interfaces make it easy to construct generic relay or adapter services, as discussed in the section on message groups above, without the need to synthesize special proxies or other non-generic code. All dispatch interfaces use the same single binary calling convention. Invocations can therefore be stored, forwarded, logged, filtered, or duplicated at will and generically for *all possible* dispatch interfaces. Similar generic implementations based on reflection services are possible but far less efficient. A dispatch interface thus sits in the middle between regular interfaces and fully dynamic reflection-based operation.

Some vendors of high-level components have taken the strategic decision to support only dispatch interfaces. Considering automatic generation of dispatch interfaces from given regular interfaces, this decision does not seem wise. It amounts to always using reflection services in Java, even when the interface is statically known. For operations that individually are quite expensive, this can be justified and is the justification for inefficient scripting engines. Otherwise, it simply cripples efficient direct programmability of components and should be avoided. Dual interfaces, where possible, are the best compromise – and are recommended for COM.

Besides being less efficient, reflection-based approaches and dispatch interfaces share another disadvantage over regular interfaces. Both are also statically less type safe than regular interfaces. Runtime type safety can be and still is enforced, but at the cost of additional runtime overheads and the possibility of exceptions. This cost is unavoidable for truly dynamic situations requiring very late binding. However, reflection and dispatch interfaces should be avoided where regular interfaces would do.

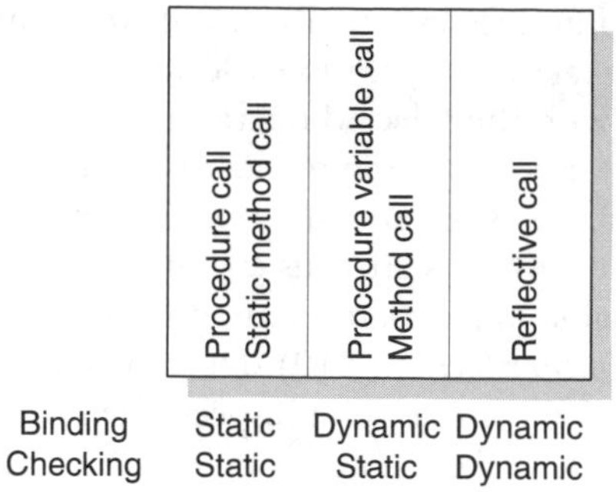

Figure 10.6   Spectrum of checking and binding times.

It is useful to view the different calling and binding styles as a spectrum. The calls on one end of the spectrum are bound and checked statically at compile time: procedure calls and static method calls. The calls at the other end of the spectrum are bound and checked dynamically at runtime: reflective calls. In between these two extremes lies the important case where checking is done statically but binding is dynamic: procedure variables and method dispatch. The spectrum is illustrated in Figure 10.6.

10.9   Degrees of freedom: sandboxing versus static safety

The importance of safety in a software component world has been stated repeatedly already. The issue is of such vital importance that the selection of programming languages that guarantee safety does play a key role in component-oriented programming. Safety guaranteed by a language does not necessarily interfere with efficiency. Effects on efficiency are negligible or even positive when a combination of compile-time and load-time checks is used to establish safety in a largely static way. This is the strategy taken by Java or Component Pascal. Provided that the language implementation can be trusted, the final component can execute efficient compiled native in-process code.

If the implementation language does not provide strong guarantees *or* its implementation cannot be trusted, lower-level runtime protection is required. Traditionally, operating systems achieved this objective by means of *process isolation*. By using hardware protection facilities to separate processes fully, mutual interference, even in the case of erroneous or malicious processes, can be controlled. For component software such strict isolation is often too expensive. Components need to interact frequently and efficiently.

An approach pioneered by Wahbe (1992) is called *software fault isolation* or *sandboxing*. The idea is to augment component code at load time to prevent it from accessing addresses for which it has no authorization. The overheads incurred are much lower than for hardware protection schemes and support protection at a much finer level of granularity.

10.10 Recording versus scripting

Event models and dispatch interfaces support the logging of activities. Replay while all involved objects are still 'alive' is also straightforward, although the replayed sequence may not make sense, depending on the state of the objects involved. A useful application of operation recording and replay is user-controlled multilevel undo and redo of commands. Other examples are systems that use checkpointing and replay to provide fault tolerance.

Unfortunately, recording of events is not enough in the case of automatic creation of scripts. Many scriptable systems provide utilities that record user activities and turn them into scripts for later replay. The key difference from the low-level recording discussed so far is that a recorded script should be applicable in *similar* rather than identical situations. It is thus too precise to record the object identities of objects involved in the recorded command. Instead, it is essential to use a symbolic object reference that is understood in the object's context. On replay, a script is then interpreted within the current context and symbolic references are resolved within this context.

One of the few fully generic scripting architectures that supports this level of genericity is the open scripting architecture (OSA) that forms part of OpenDoc and therefore the OMG's object management architecture (OMA). To a lesser degree of generality, COM also supports a scripting service, ActiveX Scripting, that solely relies on COM dispatch interfaces. (See Part Three for more information on these approaches.)

CHAPTER ELEVEN

What others say

The literature offers a number of definitions of what software components are or should be. Definitions range from the term component to the semantics of components and component systems. Most of these definitions are close to the ones used in this book, but not all are, and the various differences are certainly worth a closer look. For comparison, the definition from Chapter 4 is repeated here:

> 'A software component is a unit of composition with contractually specified interfaces and explicit context dependencies only. A software component can be deployed independently and is subject to composition by third parties.'

Note that a corollary of this definition, as explained in Chapter 4, is that software components are 'binary' units that are composed without modification.

11.1 Grady Booch (1987)

In his book *Software Components with Ada: Structures, Tools, and Subsystems*, Booch (1987) states:

> 'A reusable software component is a logically cohesive, loosely coupled module that denotes a single abstraction.'

This definition fully ignores environmental dependencies, except for stating that there should be few ('loosely coupled'). Independent deployability is not required. Also, Booch concentrates on source-level components.

11.2 Oscar Nierstrasz and Dennis Tsichritzis (1992 and 1995)

In their 1992 *Communications of the ACM* article, Nierstrasz *et al*. discussed component software in a form already quite close to the viewpoint taken in this book. They discussed the issues of component composition and scripting. They introduced the notion of script components that allows scripts to be encapsulated.

The book *Object-Oriented Software Composition* (Nierstrasz and Tsichritzis, 1995) contains an article by Nierstrasz and Dami with the following compact definition:

'A software component is a static abstraction with plugs.'

'Plugs' refers to the in and outgoing interfaces. The static aspect is according to the definition in this book; it allows components to be stored in repositories. Independent deployability is not covered. However, as composition and composability are central to their discussion, third-party composition is among the requirements.

The emphasis is on composition at system build-time. This leaves aside issues of late composition at runtime. Market issues are not touched upon.

11.3   Gio Wiederhold, Peter Wegner, and Stefano Ceri (1992)

In their important 1992 article 'Megaprogramming,' Wiederhold *et al.* state:

'Megaprogramming is a technology for programming with large modules called megamodules that capture the functionality of services provided by large organizations like banks, airline reservation systems, and city transportation systems.'

Megamodules correspond to subsystems, that is 'large' components. They further state:

'Megamodules are internally homogeneous, independently maintained software systems [...] Each megamodule describes its externally accessible data structures and operations and has an internally consistent behavior.'

They indirectly capture the contractual nature of such 'megamodule' interfaces by emphasizing:

'Megamodules are [...] managed by a community with its own terminology, goals, knowledge, and programming traditions. [...] The concepts, terminology, and interpretation paradigm of a megamodule is called its ontology.'

They then discuss aspects of megamodule composition, megaprogramming system architecture, and even megaprogramming languages and compilation. Despite their unusual terminology, at least in the context of this book, they described a large number of important issues of component software and component-oriented programming. Given the underdeveloped state of middleware in 1992, this article showed quite some foresight.

11.4   Ivar Jacobson (1993)

In his book *Object-Oriented Software Engineering*, Jacobson (1993) states:

> 'By components we mean already implemented units that we use to enhance the programming language constructs. These are used during programming and correspond to the components in the building industry.'

Jacobson's definition deviates from the one in this book. His component concept is wider and includes 'components' such as macros or templates. This makes sense if components are seen as only appearing during 'programming,' whereas the software components as understood in this book retain their isolatable character at product deployment time.

11.5   Meta Group (1994)

In a 1994 white paper, the Meta Group states (in the context of OpenDoc):

> 'Software components are defined as prefabricated, pretested, self-contained, reusable software modules – bundles of data and procedures – that perform specific functions.'

The basic notion is in line with this book, but the refinement 'bundles of data and procedures' is not. Simple procedural modules are possible components, but a component can encompass more powerful abstractions than just 'data and procedures.' In particular, a component can provide object-oriented abstractions and can be backed by its own set of resources.

11.6   Jed Harris (1995)

In their book on distributed objects, Orfali *et al*. cite Jed Harris, then the president of the Component Integration Labs. The CI Labs primarily looked after OpenDoc and maintained registries for extension types and semantic event types. Jed Harris is quoted as defining a component as follows:

> 'A component is a piece of software small enough to create and maintain, big enough to deploy and support, and with standard interfaces for interoperability.'

11.7   Ovum Report on Distributed Objects (1995)

In its 1995 report, Ovum defines componentware as:

> 'Software designed to enable application elements to work together that were constructed independently by different developers using different languages, tools and computing environments.'

Individual components are viewed as:

'Small blocks of code that can collaborate at runtime.'

Furthermore, it emphasizes the importance of object-oriented middleware, such as CORBA ORBs or Microsoft's DCOM:

'It is only with the availability of ORBs that componentware becomes technically feasible. This is because ORBs provide a way of bridging some of the differences inherent in assembling applications from components written in different languages on and for different operating systems.'

11.8   Robert Orfali, Dan Harkey, and Jeri Edwards (1995, 1996)

In a February 1995 *Datamation* article, Orfali and Harkey state:

'A component is a factory debugged software subsystem.'

In their book *The Essential Distributed Objects Survival Guide*, Orfali *et al.* (1996) broaden the definition of components by listing a number of minimal requirements (pp. 34–35). They also present a number of desirable requirements (pp. 36–37). The following is a brief summary of their minimal and desirable requirements. Note the lack of separation between objects and classes and thus the positioning of components as 'better' objects.

'A "minimalist component:"

- is a marketable entity: self-contained, shrink-wrapped, binary.

- is not a complete application.

- is usable in unpredicted combinations: 'plug-and-play' within 'suites of components.'

- has a well-specified interface: can be implemented using objects, procedural code, or by encapsulating existing code.

- is an interoperable object: can be invoked across processes, machines, networks, languages, operating systems, and tools.

- is an extended object: supports encapsulation, inheritance, and polymorphism.'

They move on to define:

'A "supercomponent" adds support for: security, licensing, versioning, life-cycle management, support for visual assembly, event notification, configuration and property management, scripting, metadata and introspection, transaction control and locking, persistence, relationships, ease of use, self-testing, semantic messaging, and self-installation.'

11.9   Johannes Sametinger (1997)

In his book *Software Engineering with Reusable Components*, Sametinger (1997) has a surprising definition of component, one that is somewhat at odds with this book:

> 'Reusable software components are self-contained, clearly identifiable pieces that describe and/or perform specific functions, have clear interfaces, appropriate documentation, and a defined reuse status.'

This is followed by a statement:

> 'We clearly take the (conservative) approach of defining existing abstractions as components.'

Code fragments, such as individual functions or macros, are explicitly included as candidates for components. Also included are pieces that merely 'describe' rather than 'perform' (implement) functionality. Sametinger explains:

> 'We use the term piece in our definition to indicate that components can have a variety of different forms, for example source code, documentation, executable code.'

His notion of software components is thus a vast superset of the one considered in this book. He claims that his superset conforms with the definitions given in the Nato standard for the development of reusable software components (Brown, 1994).

The essential aspect of independent deployability is indirectly covered by the requirement for self-containedness and identifiability. Clear provided interfaces are mentioned. Required interfaces are handled implicitly as a part of self-containedness. In particular, Sametinger distinguishes between execution and composition platforms. An *execution platform* is the environment required for a component to execute – obviously not an issue for documentation components. A *composition platform* is the environment within which a component can interoperate with other components. For example, the Java VM is an execution platform, whereas a specific framework is a composition platform.

PART THREE

State
of the art

This part presents a survey and analysis of the current best practice of component technology. Three main approaches (CORBA, COM, Java) are looked at in some detail and set into technical and strategic perspective. The technically detailed presentations help to form a solid understanding of each of the approaches – as is required for any useful comparison and evaluation.

CHAPTER TWELVE

Object and component 'wiring' standards

Wiring is the fabric that connects electrical components. Plumbing is essentially the same whether for gas, water, or sewerage systems. Standards on this level are important for components to be connectable at all. However, care must be taken not to overestimate the value of wiring standards. It would, for example, be easy to have identical plumbing standards for oxygen and flammable gases. There is a very good reason for making these two standards totally incompatible. Sometimes, compatibility would obviously be useful but has never been achieved: the enormous worldwide spectrum of phone jacks is an example.

This chapter reviews the features of software component wiring. The following chapters then go into the details of the more prominent wiring standardization attempts.

12.1 Where it all came from

Until recently, interoperability of software was limited to binary calling conventions at the procedural level. Every operating system defines calling conventions, and all language implementations respect the calling conventions of their platforms. Surprisingly, however, none of the traditional operating systems supported procedural calls across process boundaries. Even system calls to an operating system's inner services frequently follow non-standard calling conventions. To grant regular language implementations access to such services, standard libraries that shield system calls are usually provided by OS vendors.

As procedural interactions were confined to process boundaries, operating systems support a wide variety of mechanisms for inter-process communication (IPC). Typical examples are files, pipes, sockets, semaphores, and shared memory. Apart from Unix sockets, by now a quasi-standard supported on most platforms, none of these mechanisms is portable across platforms.

An advantage of all IPC mechanisms – with the exception of shared memory, which has scaling problems – is that they can easily be extended to work across networks right up to the Internet. This is a direct consequence of the traditional process model, in which each process creates the illusion of a separate virtual machine on a physical host.

All these IPC mechanisms operate on the level of bits and bytes – quite far from the well-ordered world of procedures with typed parameters. Implementing complex interactions on top of such mechanisms is painful and error prone. This was soon recognized, and *remote procedure calls* were proposed as early as 1984 (Birrel and Nelson, 1984).

The idea is to replace the local callee's end and the remote caller's end by *stubs*. The caller uses strictly local calling conventions and seems to call a local callee. In reality, it calls a local stub that *marshals (linearizes)* the parameters and sends them to the remote end. At that end, another stub receives the parameters, *unmarshals (delinearizes)* them, and calls the true callee. The callee procedure itself, just as the caller, follows local calling conventions and is unaware of being called remotely. The marshaling and unmarshaling are responsible for converting data values from their local representation to a network format and on to the remote representation. In this way, format differences, such as byte ordering of number representations, are bridged.

The *distributed computing environment* (DCE), a standard of the Open Software Foundation (part of the Open Group), is the most prominent service implementing remote procedure calls (RPCs) across heterogeneous platforms. At the other extreme, lightweight RPC variations can be used for inter-process communication on a single machine. Windows NT, for example, supports lightweight RPCs across processes and, with DCOM, full RPCs between machines. DCE also supports version control by attaching major version numbers to every service. Clients can specify what version of a service they expect.

A simultaneous advantage and burden of RPCs is the potential for transparency. Where the RPC 'glue' is automatically generated, neither clients nor providers need to be aware of non-local calling. This is an advantage as it simplifies the programming model by mapping all levels of communication (in-process, inter-process, and inter-machine) onto a single abstraction – that of a procedure call. It is also a burden, as it hides the significant cost difference between a local, an inter-process, and an inter-machine call. On most current architectures, inter-process calls are ten to a thousand times slower than local calls. Inter-machine calls are again ten to ten thousand times slower than inter-process calls.

To automate the creation of stubs, DCE introduced an interface definition language (IDL). For each remotely callable procedure, IDL specifies the number, passing modes, and types of parameters, as well as the types of possible return values. To ensure that communication across machine boundaries works, any IDL has to fix the ranges of basic types, for example specify that integers are 32-bit 2th complement values. DCE also introduced the concept of universally unique identifiers (UUIDs): names synthesized using an algorithm that for all practical purposes guarantees uniqueness (until year 3500: Rogerson, 1997). UUIDs are unreadable and meaningless for humans. They are much like social security numbers or license plate numbers.

Procedure calls, with their binary calling conventions, provide a well-proven 'wiring' standard. However, they do not directly support remote method invocations as required by objects. If combined with dynamic link libraries (DLLs), remote procedure calls get close to forming a useful basis for component wiring. Services can be located by name (the name of the DLL), are bound dynamically rather than at compile time, and can be remote. Why did procedural libraries not take off as major software component forms? In fact, they did. Libraries are still by far the most successful form of software components. Libraries can be and are sold in binary form. The question should rather be: what are the limitations of this approach?

12.2   From procedures to objects

Object invocations differ from procedural invocations primarily in their very late, data-driven selection of code to call. A method call, unless optimized, inspects the class of the receiving object and picks the method implementation provided by that class. Also, a method always provides, as another parameter, a reference to the object to which the message was sent. Most advantages of object-oriented programming result from these two properties of method calls.

It is interesting to see that current object invocations do *not* follow standard calling conventions. The reason is simple: as contemporary operating systems and their libraries have procedural interfaces, there never was a need for OS vendors to define method calling conventions. As a result, code compiled using different compilers does not interoperate, even if implemented in the same language. To be generally useful, an object-oriented library must thus be distributed in source form. This is a simple reason why binary class libraries are far less popular than procedural ones.

It is possible to implement method calls on top of the machinery that implements procedure calls. For example, IBM's System Object Model does just that (Chapter 13). In SOM, all language bindings simply call SOM library procedures and the SOM runtime then dynamically selects the methods to be called. Microsoft's COM is also quite close to just using procedural calling conventions, although it does rely on tables of procedure variables, also called dispatch tables, containing function pointers. This is not a problem as procedure variables have been part of calling conventions for a long time. For example, some DLL loaders rely on procedure variables to perform dynamic linking.

12.3   The fine print

If, on the binary level, procedural calling conventions almost suffice, why have so many different and competing proposals? There are other important aspects that need to be considered and standardized to achieve interoperability. Questions to be answered include: How are interfaces specified? How are object references handled as they leave their local process? How are services located? How is component evolution handled?

12.3.1 Specification of interfaces and object references

What exactly is an interface? All current approaches uniformly define an interface as a collection of named operations, each with a defined signature and possibly a return type. The signature of an operation defines the number, types, and passing modes of parameters.

What does an interface connect to? Here, the approaches differ. Those based on traditional object models define a one-to-one relation between interfaces and objects (CORBA, SOM). An object provides the state and implementation behind one interface. Other approaches associate many interfaces with a single object (Java) or many interfaces with many objects in a component object (COM). Obviously, as soon as there can be multiple objects behind an interface, the question of identity arises and needs to be addressed; COM provides a special interface for this purpose.

How are interfaces specified? All approaches follow the DCE lead and use an IDL. Unfortunately not *the* IDL, as there are several competing proposals. In particular, OMG IDL and COM IDL are the two strongest competitors. The so-called Java IDL is simply a mapping for Java to the OMG IDL and thus not an IDL in the true sense.

What are object references? How are they handled when passed as an argument in a remote method invocation? Again, the approaches differ, but all have mechanisms to map locally meaningful references to references that retain meaning across machine and network boundaries.

12.3.2 Interface relations and polymorphism

All approaches provide for polymorphism. In all cases, an entity with a known interface can be one of many different possible implementations. Also, in all cases an implementation can provide more than is specified by the interface.

When it comes to details, the approaches all differ. CORBA follows a traditional object model. An object has a single interface, although this interface may be composed of other interfaces using multiple interface inheritance. The actual interface provided may be a subtype of the interface expected. The additional capabilities can be explored dynamically. COM has immutable interfaces that, once published, cannot be extended or modified. However, a COM object can have multiple interfaces. The set of provided interfaces can vary and can be explored dynamically. A Java object can also implement multiple interfaces, although this is closer to multiple interface inheritance than to COM's totally separate interfaces.

12.3.3 Naming and locating of services

How are interfaces named? How are they related to each other? No two approaches agree. COM draws on DCE's UUIDs but uses a modified form, called globally unique identifiers (GUIDs). GUIDs are used to name uniquely a variety of entities, including interfaces (IIDs), groups of interfaces called categories (CATIDs), and classes (CLSIDs). OMG CORBA originally left unique naming to individual implementations, relying on language bindings to maintain program portability. In CORBA 2.0, globally unique Repository IDs have been introduced. These can either be DCE UUIDs or strings similar to the familiar universal resource locators (URLs) used in the Worldwide Web.

Given a name, all services provide some sort of registry or repository to help locate the corresponding service. On top of this directory-like function, all approaches offer some degree of *meta-information* on the available services. The minimum that is supported by all is the runtime test of the types of the offered interfaces, the runtime reflection of interfaces, and the dynamic creation of new instances.

12.3.4 Compound documents

Among the first practical approaches to software components were compound document models. Compound documents are a model in which components and composition are intuitively meaningful to those composing: the users. The Xerox Star system was first, based on research results of the Xerox Palo Alto Research Center (PARC), but failed to capture significant market and mind share. A first breakthrough was Apple's Hypercard, with its simple and intuitive composition and usage model, but creating new components was a pain. Microsoft's Visual Basic followed, with a reasonable programming model for Visual Basic controls (VBXs). General documents followed, with Microsoft's OLE 2 (now just OLE) and Apple's (later CI Labs) OpenDoc. Recently, Web pages with embedded objects, such as applets, added a new dimension. Apple's CyberDog integrates the Web and documents, as does Microsoft's latest Internet Explorer.

The concept is simple. Instead of confronting users with many different applications, each with their own 'self-centered' idea of what a document is, users deal only with documents. If parts of a document need the support of different 'applications,' then it is the system's problem to find and start these where needed. For this document-centric paradigm to be intuitive, it is necessary that embedded document parts can be manipulated in-place, even if they are supported each by a different 'application.' Figure 12.1 shows a compound document: a form embedded in a text. In the form, there is another text, some controls, and a clock. The inner text has focus and is ready for in-place editing.

In Visual Basic, all documents are forms. However, a form can contain controls and the list of possible controls is open. Users become component assemblers, simply by placing controls in forms and adding some Basic scripts to connect controls. The resulting flexibility and productivity created one of the first software component markets. What was called control, with simple things as selection boxes and entry fields in mind, turned out to be a powerful concept. The market quickly offered entire spreadsheets and process automation tools as Visual Basic 'controls.'

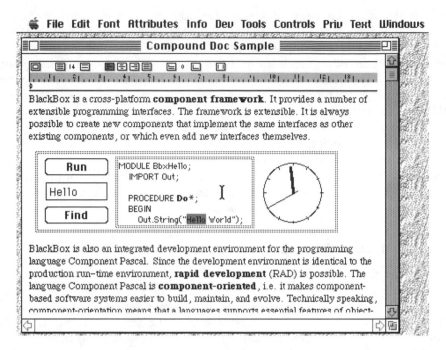

Figure 12.1 Compound document (this example was created using the OpenDoc-like look-and-feel of BlackBox for the Mac OS).

In OLE, the concept was taken a step further. First, arbitrary containers were allowed. Besides the Visual Basic forms, Word texts, Excel spreadsheets, PowerPoint slides, and so on, all became OLE containers. Also, the concept of 'control' was generalized to arbitrary document servers. However, the biggest change was that components could be document containers and servers at the same time. As a result, a Word text can be used to annotate an Excel spreadsheet, which again might be embedded in another Word text.

OpenDoc is the result of an effort to engineer a compound document framework from scratch. As a result, OpenDoc has several advantages over OLE, but until today it had only a very small customer base. One of the few 'killer' applications built on top of OpenDoc is Apple's CyberDog, a revolutionary integrated browser for the Web.

The final compound document example is the Web with objects embedded in HTML pages. Browsers present a uniform document model for all Web pages. The embedded objects, such as Java applets, can then add specifics as needed. Although a recent development, Web pages can be seen as a step back from OLE or OpenDoc to Visual Basic. Web containers are as static as Visual Basic forms. The embedded objects cannot themselves be containers and therefore are rather like Visual Basic controls. (The latest version of Visual Basic promises full support of ActiveX objects, which can be containers.)

12.4 | Which way?

Based on the above developments and ideas, a number of approaches are trying to capture their share of the emerging component markets. The next three chapters (Chapters 13 to 15) present a detailed technical account of the three major approaches followed today: the CORBA-centered standards, which emerged mainly from the world of enterprise computing; the COM-centered standards, which evolved out of Microsoft's dominance of the desktop area; and, finally, Sun's Java-centered standards, which developed around the Internet, and the Web in particular. Chapter 16 briefly covers a few further approaches and Chapter 17 presents a strategic comparison of the main approaches. Chapters 18 and 19 conclude with hints at ongoing efforts on domain-specific standards and at a number of open problems.

CHAPTER THIRTEEN

The OMG way: CORBA and OMA

The Object Management Group (OMG), founded in 1989, is by far the largest consortium in the computing industry. OMG operates as a non-profit organization aiming at the standardization of 'whatever it takes' to achieve interoperability on all levels of an open market for 'objects.' At the time of writing, more than 700 member companies had joined OMG.

13.1 At the heart: the object request broker

Originally, OMG efforts concentrated on solving one fundamental problem: how can distributed object-oriented systems implemented in different languages and running on different platforms interact? Far from the problems of distributed computing, such simple phenomena as total incommunicado between code generated by two C++ compilers on the *same* platform stopped integration efforts right at the start. Differing object models from language to language made this worse. Differences between platforms coupled by low-level socket communication or, in better cases, by remote procedure call (RPC) packages completed the picture of deep gaps everywhere. The first years of OMG went into tackling these basic 'wiring' problems. The outcome was the *Common Object Request Broker Architecture* (CORBA) in its initial version, 1.1, released in 1991, followed by minor improvements in version 1.2. Today's highly successful standard is CORBA 2.0, released in July 1995 and updated in July 1996 (OMG, 1997a).

From the beginning, the goal behind CORBA was to enable open interconnection of a wide variety of languages, implementations, and platforms. Thus, OMG never settled on binary standards: everything is carefully standardized to allow for many different implementations and to allow individual vendors of CORBA-compliant products to add value. The downside of this very open approach is that individual CORBA-compliant products cannot interoperate on an efficient binary level, but must engage in costly high-level protocols. The most prominent, although only moderately efficient, interoperability protocol is OMG's Internet inter-ORB protocol (IIOP), standardized with CORBA 2.0 in July 1995. Any ORB claiming interoperability compliance has to support IIOP. A promi-

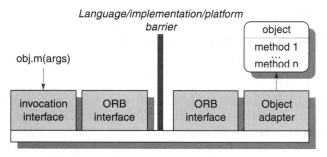

Figure 13.1 Simplified structure of an ORB-based system.

nent example is the Visigenic ORB 'Visibroker', which is part of Netscape Communicator browsers. In the July 1996 update of the CORBA 2.0 standard, an *interworking standard* was added, which specifies the interworking of CORBA-based systems with systems based on Microsoft's COM (Chapter 14).

CORBA essentially has three parts: a set of invocation interfaces, the object request broker (ORB), and a set of object adapters. Invocations of object-oriented operations, also called method invocations, require late binding of the implementation. The method implementing the invoked operation is selected based on the object implementation to which the receiving object's reference refers. Invocation interfaces enable various degrees of late binding. They also marshal an invocation's arguments such that the ORB core can locate the receiver object and the invoked method and transport the arguments. At the receiving end, an object adapter unmarshals the arguments and invokes the requested method on the receiver object. Figure 13.1 illustrates the basic CORBA structure in simplified form.

For invocation interfaces and object adapters to work, two essential requirements need to be met. First, all object interfaces need to be described in a common language. Secondly, all languages used must have *bindings* to the common language. The first condition enables construction of generic marshaling and unmarshaling mechanisms. The second allows calls from or to a particular language to be related to the common language. This common language formed an essential part of CORBA from the beginning and is called OMG interface definition language (OMG IDL). Here is an example of an OMG IDL specification:

```
module Example {
  struct Date {
    unsigned short Day;
    unsigned short Month;
    unsigned short Year;
  }
  interface Ufo {
    readonly attribute unsigned long ID;
    readonly attribute string Name;
```

```
    readonly attribute Date FirstContact;
    unsigned long Contacts ();
    void RegisterContact (Date dateOfContact);
  }
}
```

Bindings to OMG IDL are available for several languages, including C, C++, Smalltalk, and Java. Once interfaces are expressed in OMG IDL, they can be compiled using an OMG IDL compiler and deposited in an *interface repository*, which every ORB must have. Through the ORB interface, compiled interfaces can be retrieved from the interface repository. Also, when compiling program fragments that can provide implementations of such interfaces, these program fragments, called object servers, can be registered with the ORB's *implementation repository*. An ORB is capable of loading and starting an object server when receiving invocation requests for an object of that server. An object adapter is responsible for telling an ORB which new object is served by which server.

To enable efficient marshaling and unmarshaling of arguments, an ORB-specific OMG IDL compiler must be used to generate *stubs* and *skeletons*. A stub can be instantiated and then looks like a local object, but forwards all invocations through the ORB to the real target object. In other approaches, stubs are called (client-side) proxy objects. A skeleton receives invocations, unmarshals arguments, and directly invokes the target method. Although not mentioned so far, a skeleton also accepts return values, marshals these, and sends them back to the stub for unmarshaling and final returning. In other approaches, skeletons are called (server-side) stubs.

Stubs and skeletons are good solutions when dealing with regular method invocations. However, sometimes this binding is too static and the operation to be invoked needs to be selected at runtime. CORBA provides a dynamic invocation interface (DII) for this purpose; CORBA 2.0 added a dynamic skeleton interface (DSI). These interfaces allow for the dynamic selection of methods either at the client's end (DII) or at the server's end (DSI). Both interfaces use a universal data structure for arguments to cater with methods of arbitrary signature. IONA's Orbix, for example, generates stubs that translate static invocations to non-local objects into sequences of DII calls. The Orbix ORB itself handles only the universal dynamic invocation structures. Figure 13.2 gives a more detailed view of CORBA and its interaction with the OMG IDL.

It is important to understand that the separation into calling client and called object does not impose an asymmetric architecture, such as client–server computing. The same process can be both issuing and receiving calls. Distribution of functionality to machines is left to the system's architect using CORBA. The only asymmetry is introduced by the object adapter. Programs that need to function as object servers need to register with the ORB via the object adapter. In theory, there can be different object adapters for the same ORB, but so far OMG has standardized only one: the basic object adapter (BOA).

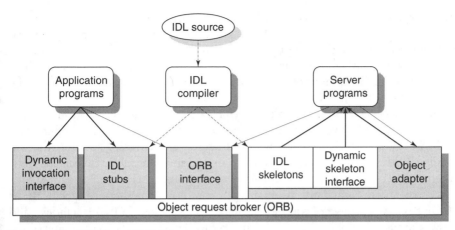

Figure 13.2 CORBA and OMG IDL.

Once an object server is registered with an ORB, the ORB 'knows' how to activate that server when needed. To determine on which machine to activate the server, each registered object has a home machine that is used to start the server on. Pure application programs that only call objects, but do not export any of their own, do not register with an ORB and therefore cannot be started by an ORB.

The OMG IDL distinguishes between basic and constructed data types and CORBA object references. Data types include integers, floats, characters, strings, structures, sequences, and multidimensional fixed-size arrays. All data types are passed by value; CORBA objects themselves cannot be passed. CORBA object references are opaque types and different from the references used within a bound language and cost more than the native references.

The ORB interface provides operations to turn a native reference into a CORBA reference and back. It also provides operations to turn a CORBA reference into a unique but proprietary ORB-specific string and back. Such strings can be used to store CORBA references – and are typically used within IIOP exchanges. A CORBA reference is defined to have indefinite lifetime – that is it will never be reused. The attempt to retrieve the associated object may of course fail if that object has been deleted in the meantime.

13.2   From CORBA to OMA

CORBA 2.0-compliant ORB implementations are now available from several vendors on many platforms. The above discussion should have made clear that an ORB is essentially a remote method invocation service. As such, ORBs promise a much cleaner model to program distributed systems than services based on remote procedure calls or even lower-level abstractions. Indeed, the most common use of ORBs in industry is to replace sockets and remote procedure calls in applications spanning several server machines. The pure 'wiring' standard established with CORBA is thus successful. However, above this basic 'wiring,' programmers were still left alone. Although the communicating ends may be on different machines and may be implemented in different languages, they need to share many conventions to interoperate. As a result, the ends are still most likely to be developed by the same team.

Being aware of this shortcoming, OMG started to broaden its focus long ago. Today, the OMG's overall effort is called the object management architecture (OMA) (OMG, 1997b). It revolves around the CORBA 2.0 specification, including OMG IDL, language bindings, invocation interfaces, object adapters, interface and implementation repositories, and object servers. The OMA adds three new areas of standardization: a set of common object service specifications (CORBAservices), a set of common facility specifications (CORBAfacilities), and a set of application object specifications. Figure 13.3 presents an overview of the OMA.

Object services support all CORBA-based programs in a way that is independent of specific domains or application models. Object services concentrate on the fundamental building blocks of any distributed solution, such as event propagation, transactions, or licensing. Common facilities are either horizontal or vertical component frameworks. Horizontal facilities are still domain independent, but focus on specific application models. The most prominent, and most complex, standardized horizontal facility is that for compound documents. Finally, application objects add domain-specific entities that could be plugged into component frameworks. The most prominent class of application objects are business objects: objects that directly represent abstractions used in specific businesses.

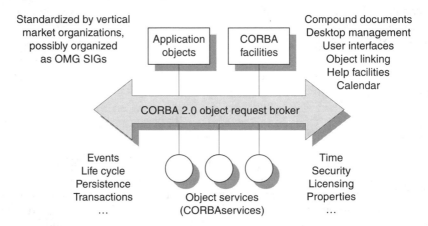

Figure 13.3 The OMG's object management architecture (OMA).

13.3 Common object service specifications (CORBAservices)

CORBAservices currently specifies 16 object services, one of which (change management) is still in the standardization mill. The following sections present brief summaries of the 16 services, in two categories, each in alphabetical order. The first category covers the services relevant for today's enterprise computing applications using CORBA. These applications typically use CORBA objects as modules and CORBA as a convenient communications middleware. The relevant services are those that support large-scale operations. The second category covers the services aiming at finer-grained use of objects. Although certainly of value and potential, these latter services are today of lesser practical importance.

13.3.1 Services supporting enterprise distributed computing

Naming service

Objects always have a unique ID used internally. This service also allows arbitrary names to be associated with an object. Names are unique within a naming context and naming contexts form a hierarchy. The resulting naming tree is quite similar to directory structures in file systems.

Object security service

A robust security service is clearly of paramount importance for distributed systems spanning more than a single trusted organizational domain. The security service needs to be pervasive. All interoperating ORBs, and other interworking systems, need to collaborate, and a security policy needs to be established for all involved organizational units.

Today's ORBs do not yet support the security service. A common approach is therefore to rely on platform-specific security services offered by various operating systems and secure network transports, such as Netscape's secure sockets layer (SSL).

An important access point to the security service is already built into the basic object adapter. For each incoming request, the adapter can provide the object server with the name of the *principal* that issued the request. (A principal is the human user in whose name the request was issued.)

Object trader service

This service allows providers to announce their services by registering *offers*. Clients can use a trader to locate services by description. A trader organizes services into trading contexts. Clients can search for services, based on parts of descriptions and keywords, within selected contexts. The trader returns a list of offers that match the query. Whereas the naming service can be compared to White Pages, this service can be compared to Yellow Pages.

Object transaction service

The object transaction service (OTS) is one of the most important services to build distributed applications. The OTS was standardized by OMG in December 1994, but even in early 1997 first compliant implementations were available only in beta release form. An OTS implementation must support flat, and optionally can support nested, transactions. It is possible to integrate non-CORBA transactions that comply with the X/Open distributed transaction processing standard. Integration with transactions spanning multiple and heterogeneous ORBs is also possible.

In the context of component-based systems, nested transactions seem unavoidable. It should be possible for a component implementation to create a transactional closure for a sequence of operations without having to declare this in the component interfaces. The principle of independent extensibility then requires support of nested transactions. Flat transactions, the only ones guaranteed to be supported in a compliant OTS implementation, are of limited value in a component system.

The OTS automatically maintains a current transaction context that is propagated along with all ORB-mediated requests and passed on to non-ORB transactional activities. For CORBA objects, the context is passed to any object that implements interface TransactionalObject. The current context can be requested from the ORB and thus is always available. The transaction operations *begin*, *commit*, and *rollback* are defined on the current context.

All objects that are modified under a transaction and require transactional control register with the OTS coordinator object. The relevant coordinator can be retrieved from the current context. A resource can indicate that it understands nested transactions. Resources have to implement interface Resource, which is used by the coordinator to run a *two-phase commit protocol*. (It is known that two-phase commit may deadlock in a fully distributed implementation. Three-phase commit protocols are known to avoid this problem, but at a higher cost per transaction. The OTS approach requires the coordinator to be logically centralized.)

Once robust OTS implementations become available, ORBs can grow from 'better sockets' to 'better transaction-processing (TP) monitors.' This may well open a substantial market for ORBs, although essentially replacing the existing one for TP monitors. For example, BEA Systems' Tuxedo is expected to be available in an OTS-compliant version during 1997.

13.3.2 Services supporting architectures using fine-grained objects

Change management service

This service is not yet standardized. The idea is to support version tracking and manage compatibility in an evolving system. Versioning affects many areas of the OMA. A persistent object may require support by an outdated server version. An implementation may support some, but not all, back-versions. After being published using OMG IDL, an interface may need to be developed further. A new version of the interface is then published. Hence, the compatibility of clients and providers built using different interface versions needs to be addressed.

Concurrency service

This service supports acquisition and release of locks on resources. Locks can be acquired either within a transactional context (see object transaction service below) or within a non-transactional context. Locks acquired on behalf of a transaction will be released as part of a transaction's rollback.

Locks can be acquired in one of several lock modes, such as read, write, and upgrade. A read lock allows for multiple readers whereas a write lock ensures single writers. An upgrade lock is a read lock that can be upgraded to a write lock because it guarantees mutually exclusive read access.

Locks are acquired out of locksets. Each protected resource holds a lockset that determines what kind of locks and how many of them are available. A lockset factory interface supports creation of new locksets. Locksets are either transactional or non-transactional and can be related to other locksets. A lock coordinator object can be used to release all locks held in related locksets.

Event notification service

This service allows event objects that can be sent from event suppliers to event consumers to be defined. Event objects are immutable: information flows strictly in one direction, from supplier to consumer. Events travel through event channels that decouple supplier from consumer. Events can be typed (described using OMG IDL) and channels can be used to filter events according to their type.

The event channel supports both the 'push' and the 'pull' model of event notification. In the 'push' model, the event supplier calls a push method on the event channel, which reacts by calling the push method of all registered consumers. In the 'pull' model, the consumer calls the pull method of the event channel, effectively polling the channel for events. The channel then calls a pull method on the registered suppliers and returns an event object if it finds a supplier that returns an event object.

Externalization service

This service supports mapping of an object web to a stream and back. The process of first externalizing the objects and then internalizing them again creates a copy of the corresponding object web. The externalization service does not maintain referential integrity. It merely preserves the references between objects externalized together. Externalization can thus be used to copy object webs by value. References to other objects can be maintained explicitly by using ORB provided string identifiers for these references.

To become externalizable, an object needs to implement the Streamable interface. Externalization of an object is requested by invoking an externalize method on an object implementing the Stream interface. This stream object invokes the externalize_to_stream method of the streamable object and passes an object implementing the StreamIO interface. The streamable object can then use this streamIO object to write any of the OMG IDL defined data types or to write embedded objects. The streamable object can also externalize an entire graph of objects defined using the relationship service.

Licensing service

As soon as components are used to assemble solutions, there needs to be a way to obtain licenses for all but freeware components. The licensing service supports a variety of different licensing models. The service defines just two interfaces (abstractions): license service manager and producer-specific license service. If an object is bound by a license agreement it can itself use the license service manager to find out whether its use is legitimate.

A licensed object contacts the license service manager and obtains a reference to a producer-specific license service object. All further activities are with this specific object. The licensed object informs the specific service object that its use has started and passes information such as the component name and version, the object reference, and a user context. The specific service object checks whether for this user context a valid license exists and advises the licensed object about actions to be taken. For example, the licensed object may switch to demo mode or offer a grace period if no valid license exists or if the license has expired. The actual licensing policy is thus fully encapsulated by the licensed object and the producer-specific license service object.

Once operating, the producer-specific license service object periodically sends event notifications to the licensed object, which replies by reporting usage statistics. Alternatively, the licensed object could actively report at regular intervals. The reports can be used to maintain a usage profile or to implement license expiration policies. Finally, if the user stops using the licensed object, it informs the specific service object, which then stops sending events.

Lifecycle service

This service supports creation, copying, moving, and deletion of objects and related groups of objects. Containment and reference relations used to handle groups of objects are described using the relationships service described below. Where containment relations are used, copies are deep – all contained objects are also copied. To support object creation, the lifecycle service supports registry and retrieval of factory objects. Once the needed factory object has been retrieved, it can be used to create new objects.

Surprisingly, the lifecycle service offers a destroy operation to get rid of objects or groups of objects but does not help to determine *when* to destroy objects. This is a significant shortcoming of CORBA: subtle distributed memory management issues are simply left for higher levels to solve. By comparison, DCOM supports distributed reference counting and Java even supports distributed garbage collection.

In current enterprise applications built using CORBA, this is not normally an issue: the 'objects' used are usually of unbounded lifetime, and each represents a traditional server program. In such a setting, CORBA is used as a communication middleware for modules distributed across a networked environment. Also, to be fair, distributed reference counting or garbage collection work well as long as there are no network or machine failures. To solve the distributed memory management problem in the presence of such failures requires embedding in a transaction context. Long-lived transactions are necessary to manage properly the lifetime of longer-lived objects.

Object collections service

The collection service was standardized in October 1996. The idea is to provide collections of various abstract topologies, such as bags, sets, queues, lists, or trees. The role model is the Smalltalk collection classes library (Goldberg and Robson, 1983, 1989). It is debatable whether the CORBA collection service, based on the relatively heavyweight model of CORBA objects, will ever be competitive with native object collection libraries. At the same time, object databases may be better suited to transfer 'collections' of various shapes and with various properties across ORBs. Only time will tell.

Object query service

This service helps to locate objects by attributes. It is similar to the object trader service, but instead of locating servers it locates object instances. Queries are based on the attributes that objects make public or accessible through operations. Two query languages are supported: the Object Database Management Group's ODMG-93 object query language (OQL) and SQL with object extensions. A single common query language is under development.

The query service defines its own simple collection service – a subset of the general collection service. Collections are used while processing queries to form result sets and are then returned to the querying client. These simple collections provide ordered set semantics, including operations to add and remove elements or sets of elements. The service also provides an Iterator interface to support enumeration of the elements of a collection.

The query service defines four query-related entities, each with its OMG IDL-defined interface: query objects, query evaluators, query managers, and queryable collections. A query object encapsulates the query itself and operates in two stages: first, the query is prepared and then the query is executed. A query evaluator can take a query and operate over a queryable collection to process the query and return a result: again a collection. A query manager creates query objects and delegates queries to the relevant query evaluators. The querying client finally uses an iterator to work through the collection of returned results.

Persistent object service

Object persistence is the property of an object to survive the termination of the program that created it. The persistent object service (POS) is the service that supports persistence of CORBA objects. Clearly, POS is a key service and was standardized by OMG in early 1994. Nevertheless, it took implementations until mid-1996 to appear in the first beta releases. Some reports on implementation attempts even pointed out severe technical problems with the specification and its expected interoperation with other object services, in particular with the object relationships service (Kleindienst *et al.*, 1996). In addition, it emerged that the POS did not solve the 'right' problems. In particular, it is still left to application code to request object storage. The POS specification is currently under revision by OMG.

The fundamental idea behind POS is to provide an abstraction layer that shields persistent objects from the persistence mechanism. For example, objects can be stored in files, in relational or object databases, or in structured storage as used by compound document architectures. There are only two basic operations: storing an object and retrieving an object. However, three properties of objects make these operations a non-trivial undertaking.

First, objects have an observable identity, that is they are *not* referentially transparent. A persistence service must thus ensure that object integrity is preserved. If an object that has been stored before is stored, then the original copy is updated and a reference to that is stored. Likewise, if an object that has been retrieved before is retrieved, and is still reachable, then a reference to the previously retrieved object is returned.

Secondly, objects refer to each other and thus form an object web. These references need to be maintained across persistent storage of objects in a web. It must be possible to distinguish between essential and transitory object references; otherwise a large number of temporary objects would be dragged into the persistent store. Also, if multiple persistent stores are used, relations must be kept across such stores. In addition to programming language level references, a POS must also support relations introduced using the object relationships service.

Thirdly, objects are units of encapsulation. Despite their storage in persistent stores, an object's contents should be protected against direct manipulation, bypassing the object's encapsulation barrier. Of course, this level of protection is only feasible with certain persistent stores.

POS works by defining four entities: *persistent objects* (POs), *persistent object managers* (POMs), *persistent data services* (PDSs), and *datastores*. Persistent objects have a *persistent identifier* (PID), a string that identifies the location of the object within a datastore. PIDs are created using a PID factory. POs are created using a PO factory. Datastores hold the persistent objects in an address space-independent way. Persistent data services perform the actual transport of objects to and from datastores.

A persistent object manager is used to shield POs from specific persistent data services. The information in a PID is used to locate and relay calls to the relevant PDS. A PDS provides an interface to a particular datastore. All PDSs implement the OMG IDL-specified PDS interface. In addition, they may implement one or more further *protocols* that allow POs that also implement such a protocol to support the mapping of a PO to a particular datastore. The simplest protocol is that used by the separate externalization service to map objects to streams and back. Other protocols allow for random access to objects in a persistent store. As these protocols require the cooperation of the involved objects with the persistence service, they are sometimes called *conspiracies* (Orfali *et al.*, 1996).

Properties service

This service allows arbitrary *properties* to be associated with objects which implement at least interface PropertySet. Properties can be added, retrieved, and deleted individually or in groups. If an object also implements interface PropertySetDef, properties can be further controlled to be of one of four *property modes*. Properties can thus be normal (can be modified or deleted), read-only (can be deleted but not modified), fixed-normal (can be modified but not deleted), or fixed-read-only.

The property service does not interpret any of the properties associated with an object. Properties are useful for programs that need generically to attach information to arbitrary objects. An important example is system administration tools that attach 'stickers' in order to track objects efficiently.

Relationship service

The relationship service allows general relations between objects to be specified and maintained. Rather than resorting to language-level pointers or references, this service introduces an associative model that allows relations over objects to be created without changing the involved objects at all.

The relationship service introduces a large number of abstractions, each with its own OMG IDL-defined interface. Fundamental are the notions of *identifiable objects, nodes, roles*, and *relationships*. An object needs to implement only the interface IdentifiableObject to participate in relationship webs. This interface introduces only one method used to query whether two objects are to be considered identical. Objects participate in relationships indirectly: an object can have many roles, and in each role it can participate in many relationships. Predefined relationships cover *reference* and *containment*. For this purpose, the predefined roles *contains, containedIn, references*, and *referenced* are used.

Nodes are used to associate an object with its relationships. Traversal of a relationship web is supported by *traversal objects*, which start at a specified node and use a *traversal-criteria object* to restrict the traversal to certain roles or relationships. A callback model is used to enable processing as the traversal proceeds. Factories are used to create new nodes, roles, relationships, or traversal objects.

Time service

This service deals with the inaccuracies inherent in a distributed system with multiple asynchronous clocks. In many applications, realtime information is used to correlate internal events, such as creation of files, with universal time. A time service has to ensure that such correlation is possible within reasonable error margins and that non-causal correlation is avoided. As an example, consider the creation of a new object as a reaction to another object firing an event. Non-causal time-based information would result when assigning a 'date of birth' time stamp to a new object that predates the first object – a typical result of a non-causal time service.

13.4 CORBA 2.0- and CORBAservices-compliant implementations

By mid-1997, no implementations existed for many of the services. In addition, few ORBs were already fully CORBA 2.0 compliant. Further, in the case of some object service specifications, it became clear that the service as standardized was not quite as useful as intended. For example, the persistent object service was selected for respecification in 1997.

The following three families of ORB implementations are exemplary for a large number of implementations currently available.

13.4.1 Orbix

IONA's Orbix is an ORB that is available for a particularly large number of platforms. It supports C++ and Smalltalk bindings; Java is likely to follow soon. Orbix is implemented as a pair of dynamic link libraries, one for the client and one for the server interface. In addition, a demon process is used to handle activation on demand for incoming requests.

Orbix/Desktop for Windows is an Orbix implementation that runs under Windows and implements a local COM interface supporting COM dual interfaces (Chapter 13).

Orbix/Web is a version of Orbix implemented in Java and solely communicating via IIOP. Orbix/Web simply travels with applets and other Java objects to the client machine. Even with Visigenic's Visibroker ORB built into Netscape Communicator, Orbix/Web remains useful as most Web browsers currently do not have a built-in ORB.

13.4.2 Visibroker

Visigenic attracted some attention when Netscape announced that it would use Visigenic's Visibroker for Java as the in-built ORB in its Communicator product.

Like Orbix/Web, Visibroker for Java is a CORBA 2.0-compliant ORB implementation written entirely in Java. Visibroker uses IIOP for all requests, in other words also for those between two Visibroker ORBs.

An interesting feature of Visibroker is its support for multiple object replicas. Client requests are forwarded to one of the replicas to balance load and to survive server crashes.

13.4.3 System object model (SOM)

IBM's System Object Model was originally developed independently from CORBA as part of the OS/2 workplace shell. Later, it was made first CORBA 1.2 and then CORBA 2.0 compliant. In fact, distributed computing is supported by the distributed SOM libraries, which build on SOM. In this section, DSOM is considered to be an integral part of SOM. SOM implements a superset of the CORBA standard and supports services that are only now under consideration for the CORBAfacilities set. In addition, SOM defines a binary standard.

Two features of SOM stand out: support for meta-programming and support or binary compatibility across binary releases. The SOM meta-programming model largely follows the Smalltalk example (Goldberg and Robson, 1983): every class is itself an object and as such an instance of a metaclass. All metaclasses are instances of a single class, Metaclass, which is its own metaclass. SOM goes beyond the reflective capabilities of CORBA: SOM allows classes to be constructed or modified dynamically. For example, it is possible to add a new method to an existing class without disturbing any of the existing instances of that class. A comparable meta-programming facility is under consideration for the CORBAfacilities set.

Versioning and binary compatibility are supported by the notion of a *release order* (Forman *et al.*, 1995). For example, adding new methods to a later release does not alter the dispatch indices used by code compiled against an older release. SOM comes with precise rules as to which changes in a release maintain, and which other changes break, binary compatibility with previous releases. Binary compatibility is a very important issue in a component world. It is unthinkable to ask all vendors of dependent components – and the vendors of components dependent on these components, and so on – to recompile and redistribute within any reasonable time. This is the syntactic fragile base class (FBC) problem (section 7.4.1).

SOM guarantees binary compatibility across a large number of base class changes, including refactoring of class hierarchies, as long as the required methods remain available and of compatible signature. As a special case, SOM guarantees that, if no interface changes took place, then building the next release of a component is guaranteed to preserve binary compatibility with clients compiled against the previous release. This effectively solves the syntactic FBC problem, but obviously cannot address the semantic FBC problem.

13.5   CORBAfacilities

CORBAfacilities can be split into facilities for horizontal (general) and for vertical (domain-specific) support. In both cases, a facility defines a specific component framework that can be used to integrate components. Vertical facilities have not yet been standardized, but work is in progress for areas as diverse as image processing and computer-integrated manufacturing. CORBAfacilities, when they reached critical mass, will raise the level of the 'wiring' standards. Everyone has to follow suit eventually if the current envelope is pushed further out. Overall productivity may improve, but, to achieve a sustainable competitive edge, proprietary specialized components that plug into some of these component frameworks are required.

The horizontal facility areas established so far address four important issues, but most of these standards have yet to be finalized and implemented. The first area is *user interfaces*: printing, email, compound documents, automation and scripting, and object linking are covered. The second area, *information management*, covers structured storage, universal data transfer, and meta-data. The third area is *system management* and covers a wide variety of needs, such as instrumentation, monitoring, or logging. Finally, the fourth area is *task management*, including the concepts of workflow, rules, and agents.

The areas are not entirely orthogonal. Indeed, in 1996, the OMG adopted a modified version of Apple's OpenDoc as the standard distributed document component facility, supporting compound documents, object linking, automation, scripting, and structured storage. Thus, OpenDoc covers aspects from at least two common facility areas. The original OpenDoc required IBM's SOM to operate – and this is the version that was commercially supported. However, the CORBA OpenDoc standard merely assumes CORBA 2.0 and CORBAservices and as such has not yet been implemented. OpenDoc is one of the few component frameworks available today and is described in some detail in Chapter 21.

Individual component instances embedded as *parts* into OpenDoc documents are called Live Objects. Like ActiveX objects (Chapter 14), Live Objects can be both containers and embedded parts: a container part can itself embed other parts. As such, Live Objects are far superior to simpler visual components, such as OLE controls (but not ActiveX controls) or JavaBeans (as specified today). Also, OpenDoc is one of the few component frameworks for this market. Neither ActiveX nor JavaBeans currently provides anything similar. An integration of JavaBeans into OpenDoc was attempted in 1996 by IBM (project 'Arabica'). Early in 1997, IBM released all OpenDoc source code to the public. [The future direction is to expand JavaBeans to a full document model (project 'Blue JavaBeans'.) A JavaBeans bridge to ActiveX is available from JavaSoft.]

Further CORBAfacilities standards that are currently being addressed by the OMG Domain Technology Committee include the business object facility, the electronic payments facility, and the medical facilities dubbed CORBAmed.

13.6 Application objects

This is the top-most category in the OMA. Application objects serve a specific application domain. The standardization process is thus farmed out from OMG to more specialized organizations, which then report to OMG, proposing a standard. Some of these specialized organizations are formed as special interest groups (SIGs) of the OMG itself. The most prominent example is the Business Object Management SIG (BOMSIG), although it has not yet produced significant standard proposals.

Business objects are application objects that directly make sense to people in a specific business domain. Common examples are customer or stock objects. More interesting examples are truly domain specific: for example, an object might represent a chemical reactor, a portfolio, or a car in a company's fleet. The OMG Business Object Domain Task Force is currently requesting proposals for a common business object standard as well as a business object facility.

Application and business objects are obviously the most long-term aspect of the OMA. They cannot be fully specified before the underlying infrastructure, with all necessary services and facilities, is in place. Several evolutionary cycles for each application object standard are realistically required to get it roughly 'right.' Evolution needs to be based on use experience. Evolution cannot take place before robust and practical implementations of services and facilities are available and deployed.

Non-CORBA business objects have already begun to surface. One such example is the New World Infrastructure approach (Newi) by Integrated Objects (Sims, 1994). A Newi object is almost fully self-contained. It may inherit from other Newi objects, but this relation is established dynamically (dynamic inheritance or delegation). A Newi object assumes very little about its environment and is thus easily transported into different contexts, provided the Newi runtime is available. Newi objects need to evolve to benefit from technologies such as JavaBeans or ActiveX – both are described in the following chapters. Otherwise, Newi will be overtaken by the evolution of these more tightly integrated objects.

A radically different example is the component-oriented realtime operating system Portos and its development environment Denia, developed by Oberon microsystems (1997). Portos supports application objects for industrial control systems. It uses an unconventional programming model that makes the individual components and the interaction of their instances natural and intuitive for process engineers (often trained electrical or mechanical engineers rather than software engineers). See Chapter 21 for more information on Portos.

To summarize, despite several successful examples of application object models, the time is probably not yet right for general standards. GTE's Michael Brodie recently conceded that 'distributed object computing' in general still requires highly trained staff to deliver at all, and that costs are currently likely to exceed benefits (Brodie, 1996).

CHAPTER FOURTEEN

The Microsoft way:
DCOM, OLE, and ActiveX

In a sense, Microsoft is taking the easiest route. Instead of proposing a global standard and hoping to port its own systems to it, it re-engineered its existing application base. Component technology was introduced gradually, gaining leverage from the twofold success of Visual Basic controls (non-object-oriented components!) and object linking and embedding (OLE).

Microsoft is not trying to converge its approaches on OMG standards. However, Java is taken seriously insofar as Java complements Microsoft's offerings. In many ways, Java is a better choice than C++ when implementing component object model (COM) components. Once robust implementations and strong native compilers are widely available, Java will be a serious contender for Microsoft platform programming. However, more recent Java efforts have encroached on COM and OLE territory, threatening competition instead of offering complementary functions. Not surprisingly, Microsoft is hesitant to follow these younger Java efforts.

14.1 The fundamental wiring model: COM

COM is Microsoft's foundation on which all component software on its platforms is based. In addition, COM is made available on the Macintosh by Microsoft and on many other platforms by third parties, such as Software AG, DEC, and Hewlett-Packard. This section provides a detailed and technical account of the inner working of COM. Although COM is simple, it is also different from standard object models, and a detailed understanding helps to compare COM with other approaches.

COM is a *binary standard*: it specifies nothing about how particular programming languages may be bound to it. COM does not even specify what a component or an object is. It neither requires nor prevents the use of objects to implement components. The one fundamental entity that COM does define is an *interface*. On the binary level, an interface is represented as a pointer to an interface node. The only specified part of an interface node is another pointer held in the first field of the interface node. This second pointer is defined to point to a table of procedure variables (function pointers). As these tables are derived from the tables used to implement virtual functions (methods) in languages such as C++, they are also called *vtables*. Figure 14.1 shows a COM interface on the 'binary' level.

The double indirection – clients see a pointer to a pointer to the vtable – seems odd. Indeed, very few descriptions of COM in the literature that are not of the most technical nature explain what this extra indirection is for. To understand this point, it is necessary to elaborate on another detail of the COM calling conventions: the specification of what exactly is *passed* when calling an operation from an interface.

Methods of an object have one additional parameter: the object they belong to. This parameter is sometimes called *self* or *this*. Its declaration is hidden in most object-oriented languages, but a few, including Component Pascal, make it explicit. The point is that the interface pointer is passed as a self parameter to any of the interface's operations. This allows operations in a COM interface to exhibit true object characteristics. In particular, the interface node can be used to refer internally to instance variables. It is even possible to attach instance variables directly to the interface node, but this is not normally done. It is, however, quite common to store pointers that simplify the look-up of instance variables and the location of other interfaces.

A COM component is free to contain implementations for any number of interfaces. The entire implementation can be a single class, but it does not have to be. A component can just as well contain many classes that are used to instantiate objects of just as many different kinds. These objects then collectively provide the implementation of the interfaces provided by the component. Figure 14.2 shows a component that provides three different interfaces and uses two different objects to implement these.

In Figure 14.2, object 1 implements interfaces A and B, whereas object 2 implements interface C. The gray pointers between the interface nodes are used internally: it must be possible to get from each node to each other node. The unusual layout of objects and vtables is just what COM prescribes if such an n-to-m relation between objects and interfaces is desired. However, without proper language support, it is not likely that many components will take such a complex shape. What is important, though, is that there is no single object identity that

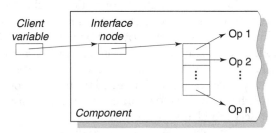

Figure 14.1 Binary representation of a COM interface.

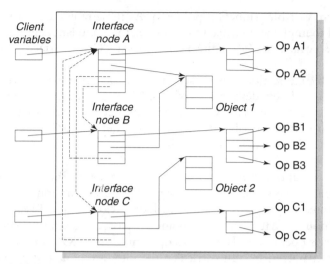

Figure 14.2   A COM object with multiple interfaces.

ever leaves the component and represents the entire COM object. A COM component is not necessarily a traditional class and a COM object is not necessarily a traditional single-bodied object. However, a COM object can be such a traditional object and all of its interfaces can be implemented using a single class using multiple inheritance (Rogerson, 1997).

There are two important questions to be answered at this point. How does a client learn about other interfaces and how does a client compare the identity of COM objects? Surprisingly, these two questions are closely related. Every COM interface has a common first method named QueryInterface. Thus, the first slot of the function table of any COM interface points to a QueryInterface operation. There are two further methods shared by all interfaces. These are explained below.

QueryInterface takes the name of an interface, checks whether the current COM object supports the named interface, and, if so, returns the corresponding interface reference. An error indication is returned if the interface queried for is not supported. On the level of QueryInterface, interfaces are named using *interface identifiers* (IIDs). An IID is a GUID (Chapter 12): a 128-bit number guaranteed to be globally unique. COM uses GUIDs for other purposes also.

As every interface has a QueryInterface operation, a client can get from any provided interface to any other. Once a client has a reference to at least one interface, it can obtain access to all others provided by the same COM object. Recall that interface nodes are separate and therefore cannot serve to identify a COM object uniquely. However, COM requires that a given COM object returns the same interface node pointer each time it is asked for the IUnknown interface. As all COM objects must have an IUnknown interface, the identity of the IUnknown interface node can serve to identify the entire COM object.

A common way to depict a COM object is to draw it as boxes with plugs. As every COM object has an IUnknown interface, which also identifies the COM

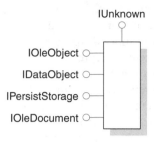

Figure 14.3 Depiction of a COM object.

object, it is common to show the IUnknown interface on top of a COM object's diagram. Figure 14.3 shows an example of a COM object diagram – in this case, an ActiveX document object.

Back to the IUnknown interface. Of course, its 'real' name is its IID '00000000-0000-0000-C000-000000000046,' but for the sake of convenience all interfaces also have a readable name. By convention, such readable interface names start with I. Unlike IIDs, there is no guarantee that readable names are unique. Thus, all programmed references to interfaces use IIDs.

The primary use of IUnknown is to identify a COM object in the most abstract, that is without requiring any specific functionality. A reference to an IUnknown interface can thus be compared to a reference of type ANY or Object in object-oriented languages. In a sense, IUnknown is a misnomer. It is not an unknown interface; rather it is the only interface guaranteed always to be present. However, a reference to an IUnknown interface is a reference to a potentially otherwise totally unknown COM object, one with no known interfaces.

The IUnknown interface supports just the three mandatory methods of any COM interface. The first mandatory method is QueryInterface, as described above. The other two mandatory methods of any COM interface are called AddRef and Release. Together with some rules about when to call them, they serve to control an object's lifetime, as explained further below. Using a simplified COM IDL-like notation, IUnknown is defined as:

```
[ uuid(00000000-0000-0000-C000-000000000046) ]
interface IUnknown {
    HRESULT QueryInterface
        ([in] const IID iid, [out, iid_is(iid)] IUnknown iid);
    unsigned long AddRef ();
    unsigned long Release ();
}
```

The type HRESULT is used by most COM interface methods to indicate success or failure of a call. QueryInterface uses it to indicate whether the requested interface is supported. If an interface belongs to a remote object, then HRESULT may also indicate network failures.

Every COM object performs *reference counting* either for the object in its entirety or separately for each of its interface nodes. Where a COM object uses a single shared reference count, it cannot deallocate an interface node, although this particular node may have no remaining references. This is normally acceptable, and sharing of a single reference count is the usual approach. In some cases, interface nodes may be resource intensive, for example because they maintain a large cache structure. A separate reference count for such an interface node can then be used to release that node as early as possible.

Upon creation of an object or node, the reference count is initialized to 1 before handing out a first reference. Each time a copy of a reference is created, the count must be incremented (AddRef). Each time a reference is given up, the count must be decremented (Release). As soon as a reference count reaches zero, the COM object has become unreachable and should therefore self-destruct. As part of its destruction it has to release all references to other objects that it might still hold, calling their Release methods. This leads to a recursive destruction of all objects exclusively held by the object under destruction. Finally, the destructed object returns the memory space it occupied.

Reference counting is a form of cooperative garbage collection. As long as all involved components play by the rules and cooperate, memory will be safely deallocated. At least, objects will never be deallocated while references still exist. Reference counting has the well-known problem that it cannot deal with cyclic references. Consider the two objects in Figure 14.4.

The two objects are, as a whole, unreachable: no other object still has a reference to any of the two. However, the mutual reference keeps both objects' reference counts above zero and thus prevents deallocation. Obviously, this is only a special case. The general case is a cycle of references through an arbitrary number of objects, all of which keep each other mutually 'alive.' As cyclic structures are very common, COM defines a set of rules that govern the use of AddRef and Release in the presence of cycles. These rules are complex and prone to error. In addition, they differ from situation to situation. The idea, however, is always the same: at least one of the objects in a cycle has another method that breaks the cycle, making the objects in the cycle collectible. The difficulty lies in specifying exactly when this extra method is to be called.

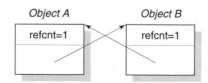

Figure 14.4   Cyclic references between objects.

<table>
<tr><td>**14.2**</td><td>## COM object reuse</td></tr>
</table>

COM does not support any form of implementation inheritance (although COM+ does). As explained in Chapter 7, this can be seen as a feature rather than a weakness. (Note that COM does not define or 'care about' how an individual component is internally realized. A component may well consist of classes that, within the component, use implementation inheritance.) In any case, lack of implementation inheritance does not mean lack of support for reuse. COM supports two forms of object composition to enable object reuse (Chapter 7). The two forms are called *containment* and *aggregation*.

Containment is just the simple object composition technique already explained in Chapter 7: one object holds an exclusive reference to another. The former, also called the outer object, thus conceptually contains the latter, the inner object. If requests to the outer object need to be handled by the inner object, the outer object simply forwards the request to the inner object. Forwarding is nothing but calling a method of the inner object to implement a call to a method of the outer object.

For example, Figure 14.5 shows how an outer object's IStream interface is implemented by forwarding calls to methods Read and Write to an inner object.

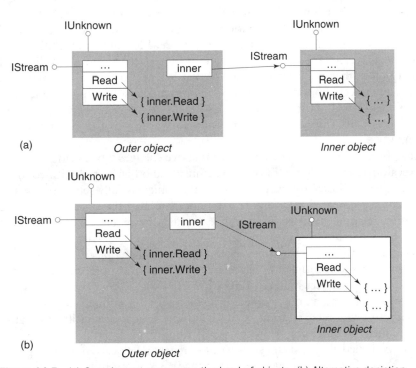

Figure 14.5 (a) Containment as seen on the level of objects. (b) Alternative depiction emphasizing the containment property.

Figure 14.5a shows that containment is really no more than normal object use. Figure 14.5b uses a different depiction of the *same* situation, this time illustrating the containment relation.

Containment suffices to reuse implementations contained in other components. In particular, containment is completely transparent to clients of an outer object. A client calling an interface function cannot tell whether the call is handled by the object providing the interface or whether it is forwarded and handled by another object.

If deep containment hierarchies occur, or if the forwarded methods themselves are relatively cheap operations, then containment can become a performance problem. For this reason, COM defines its second reuse form: aggregation. The basic idea of aggregation is simple. Instead of forwarding requests, an inner object's interface reference could be handed out directly to an outer object's client. Calls on this interface would then go directly to the inner object, saving the cost of forwarding. Of course, aggregation is only useful where the outer object does not wish to intercept calls, for example to perform some filtering or additional processing. Also, it is important to retain transparency: a client of the outer object should have no way of telling that a particular interface has been aggregated from an inner object.

Although with containment the inner object is unaware of being contained, aggregation needs the inner object to collaborate. A COM object has the choice of whether or not to support aggregation. If it does, it can become an aggregated inner object. Why is this collaborative effort required? Recall that all COM interfaces support QueryInterface. If an inner object's interface is exposed to clients of the outer object, then the QueryInterface of that inner object's interface must still cover the interfaces supported by the outer object. The solution is simple. The inner object learns about the outer object's IUnknown interface when it is aggregated. Calls to its QueryInterface are then forwarded to the outer object's QueryInterface.

Figure 14.6 shows how the scenario from above changes when using aggregation. Recall that the depiction of one object inside another, just as with containment, has merely illustrative purposes. The inner object is fully self-standing and most likely implemented by a different component than the outer object. The aggregation relation manifests itself in the mutual object references established between the inner and the outer object.

Aggregation can go any number of levels deep. Inner objects, on whatever level, always refer to the IUnknown interface of the outermost object. For internal purposes, an outer object retains a direct reference to an inner object's original IUnknown. In this way, an outer object can still query for an inner object's interfaces, without being referred to its own IUnknown. As is clearly visible in Figure 14.6, the inner and outer objects in an aggregation setting maintain mutual references. As explained above, such cycles would prevent deallocation of aggregates. Thus, COM has special, and again error-prone, rules about how to manipulate the reference counts involved in order for the scheme to work.

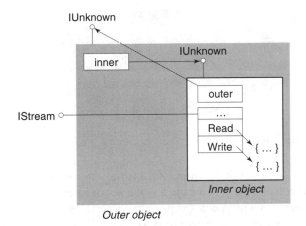

Figure 14.6 Aggregation.

Aggregation, as a pure performance tool, if compared to containment, is probably meaningful only for deeply nested constructions. This is one of the reasons why aggregation in COM practice is less important than containment. Another reason is the increase in complexity. Nevertheless, aggregation can be put to work where efficient reuse of component functionality is needed. The resulting performance is as good as that of a directly implemented interface as aggregated interfaces shortcircuit all aggregation levels.

Aggregation can be used to construct efficient generic wrappers ('blind aggregation' of arbitrary interfaces). For example, this is used by the Microsoft transaction server to attach new interfaces to otherwise unmodified COM objects (section 14.12.1).

14.3 Interfaces and polymorphism

COM interfaces can be derived from other COM interfaces using (single) interface inheritance. In fact, all COM interfaces directly or indirectly inherit from IUnknown, the common base type of the interface hierarchy. Besides IUnknown, there are only two other important base interfaces that are commonly inherited from: IDispatch and IPersist. Otherwise, interface inheritance in COM is rarely used. Why is this?

Surprisingly, interface inheritance in COM has *nothing* to do with the polymorphism COM supports. For example, assume that a client holds a reference to an interface, say IDispatch. In reality, the interface that the client refers to can be of any subtype of IDispatch. In other words, the function table may contain additional methods over and above those required by IDispatch. However, and this point is important, there is no way for the client to find out! If the client wants a more specific interface, it has to use QueryInterface. It is of no relevance to the client whether the returned interface node is actually the one QueryInterface was issued on, but this time guaranteeing the extra methods.

Figure 14.7 COM types are sets of interface IDs; subtypes are supersets.

The true nature of polymorphism in COM is the support of *sets of interfaces* by COM objects. The type of a COM object is the set of interface identifiers of the interfaces it supports. A subtype is a superset of interfaces. For example, assume that a client requires an object to support the following set of interfaces: {IOleDocumentView, IOleInPlaceActiveObject, IOleInPlaceObject}. An object that supports the set of interfaces {IOleDocumentView, IOleInPlaceActiveObject, IOleInPlaceObject, IOleCommandTarget, IPrint} obviously satisfies the client's requirements and could thus, from a subtyping point of view, be used. Figure 14.7 illustrates this.

One way to test whether a COM object satisfies all requirements is to call QueryInterface once for each required interface. For example, an ActiveX document container may need to check that an object offered for insertion into one of its documents satisfies the minimal requirements for an ActiveX container control.

14.3.1 Categories

Instantiating a COM object and issuing a large number of QueryInterface requests, just to verify that all the requested interfaces are indeed implemented, is too inefficient. To support efficient handling of sets of interfaces, COM defines *categories*. A category has its own identifier (CATID), again a globally unique identifier. Categories are roughly defined as sets of interface identifiers. A COM object can be a member of any number of categories, and categories among themselves are totally unrelated. Figure 14.8 illustrates the situation using set diagrams.

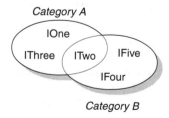

Figure 14.8   COM categories.

The two categories A and B both require three interfaces. They overlap in that both require ITwo.

Categories have to serve a second purpose, one that is a little irritating. COM allows a component to return an 'E_NOTIMPL' error code for any of the methods of an interface. This is quite catastrophic and subverts the idea of COM interfaces as contracts to some extent. A client still has to be prepared for a provider, despite its announced support of an interface, to choose not to implement one or the other method. The resulting coding style is ugly to say the least. Categories help to clean up this situation. A category specifies not only which interfaces must at least be supported, but also which methods in these interfaces must at least be implemented.

Finally, categories also have a contractual nature. For example, a category can specify not only that an object provides the universal data transfer interfaces, but also that it knows about specific data formats or media.

Categories also pose a problem: who maintains the list of categories? If categories are produced in large numbers, they become useless. Categories only make sense if a provider and a client agree in advance. Currently, the definition of categories is largely left to Microsoft. However, a strong vendor of, say, some innovative new container could cause a new category to become widely accepted. As CATIDs are GUIDs, the doors are open wide.

14.3.2 Interfaces and versioning

Once published, a COM interface and its specification must not be changed in any way. This addresses both the syntactic and the semantic fragile base class problem (Chapter 7) by avoidance. In other words, an IID in COM serves also to identify the version of an interface. As interfaces are always requested by IID, all participants in a system agree on the version of an interface. The problem of transitive version clashes mentioned in the CORBA discussion (Chapter 13) does not occur with COM.

A component may choose to implement several versions of an interface – but these are handled like any other set of different interfaces. Using this strategy, a COM-based system can concurrently support the old and the new while allowing for a gradual migration. A similar strategy would be hard or at least unnatural to implement in systems in which the multiple interfaces implemented by a single object are merged into the namespace of a single class. This is a problem with approaches to binary compatibility that are based on conventional object models, such as Java or CORBA.

14.4 COM object creation and the COM library

So far, the described COM mechanisms are self-sufficient. As long as COM components follow the rules, no further runtime support is needed. What is left unexplained, however, is how COM objects come to life. The question is: what information does some executing code have that could allow it to request a new COM object?

IIDs are obviously not enough. By the very definition of interfaces, there can be any number of different kinds of providers that support a specific interface. Asking for a service by asking for an interface is like asking for something with wheels, without specifying whether this should be a bike, a car, a train, or something else. Instead of asking for a service by interface, the service should be retrieved by *class*.

To identify classes of COM objects, COM defines *class identifiers* (CLSIDs). A CLSID is also a globally unique identifier (GUID). COM defines a procedural library interface to request new object instances based on their CLSID. As this interface is static and procedural, a bootstrapping problem is avoided. Programs can ask for objects without first having to know about an object that knows how to create objects.

The simplest way to create a new COM object is to call CoCreateInstance. (All COM library procedure names start with Co for COM. This can be confusing, as the prefix 'co' usually suggests some sort of concurrency.) This function takes a CLSID and an IID. It then creates a new instance of the specified class (CLSID) and returns an interface of the requested type (IID). An error indication is returned if COM failed to locate or start a server implementing the requested CLSID, or if the specified class does not support the requested interface.

When creating a COM object that is instantiating a COM class, COM needs to map the given CLSID to an actual component that contains the requested class. COM supports a *system registry* for this purpose, which is similar to the CORBA implementation repository. The registry specifies which servers are available and which classes they support. Servers can be of one of three different kinds. *In-process servers* support objects that live in the client's process. *Local servers* support objects on the same machine, but in a separate process. *Remote servers* support objects on a different machine. CoCreateInstance accepts an additional parameter that can be used to specify what kinds of servers would be acceptable.

CoCreateInstance consults the registry (through its local service control manager, SCM) to locate the server and, unless already active, loads and starts it. For an in-process server, this involves loading and linking a dynamic link library (DLL). For a local server, a separate executable (EXE) is loaded. Finally, for a remote machine, the service control manager on the remote machine is contacted to load and start the required server on that machine.

A COM server has a defined structure. It contains one or more classes that it implements. For each class, it also implements a *factory object*. (In COM, factory objects are called class factories. This name can be misleading, as not classes but instances of classes are created by a factory.) A factory is an object that supports interface IClassFactory – or IClassFactory2, where licensing is required. COM needs to use factories because COM objects need not be of simple single-object nature and their creation therefore needs to be specified by their component rather than a system-provided service. Figure 14.9 shows a COM server that supports two COM classes (coclasses), each with its factory.

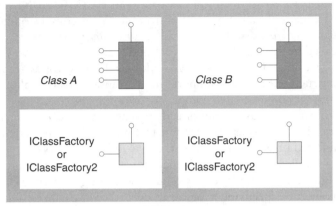

COM server

Figure 14.9 COM server with two coclasses, each with a factory.

Upon start-up, a *self-registering server* creates a factory object for each of its classes and registers it with COM. CoCreateInstance uses the factory objects to create instances. For improved performance, a client can also ask for direct access to the factory, using CoGetClassObject. This is useful in cases where many new objects are required.

Often, clients ask not for a specific class, but for something more generic. For example, instead of using the CLSID for 'Microsoft Word,' a client may use the CLSID for 'rich text.' To support such generic CLSIDs and enable configuration, COM allows one class to *emulate* another. Emulation configurations are kept in the system registry. For example, an emulation entry may specify that the emulation for class 'rich text' is done by class 'Microsoft Word.'

14.5   Initializing objects, persistence, structured storage, monikers

COM uses a two-phase approach to object initialization. After creating a COM object using CoCreateInstance or a factory object, the object still needs to be initialized. This is like creating a new object in C++ or Java with a constructor that takes no arguments: required storage is allocated, but no useful data is loaded into the new object. Once created, an object must be initialized. There are many ways to do this and the client has control over which method to use. This two-phase approach is more flexible than the use of constructors.

The most direct way to initialize an object is to ask it to load its data from a file, a stream, or some other data store. COM defines a family of interfaces for this purpose that are all derived from IPersist and named IPersistFile, IPersistStream, and so on. This direct approach is useful where a client wants to take control over the source of data to be used for initialization.

A standard place to store an object's data is in a COM *structured storage*. A structured storage is like a file system within a file. A structured storage simply is a tree structure. The root of the tree is called a *root storage*, the tree's other inner nodes are called *storages*, and the tree's leaf nodes are called *streams*. Streams are the 'files' in a structured storage; storage nodes are the 'directories.' From NT 5.0 on, COM's structured storages support simple transactions that allow an entire structured storage to be updated completely or not at all.

COM also defines a way to refer directly to a persistent object 'by name.' Such references can be used to ask the system to find and load the required server, create the referred object, and initialize the new object from its source. Such object names are called *monikers*, that is nicknames. Monikers are really objects in their own right. Rather than referring to an object using a unique ID, a moniker refers to an object by specifying a logical access path. For example, a moniker can refer to the spreadsheet object named '1997 Revenue,' embedded in the document 'The previous millennium,' and stored at a certain place specified by a URL. Quite often, monikers refer to objects stored within a structured storage.

To summarize, COM does not directly support persistent objects. Instead, classes and data are kept separate and object identity is not preserved across externalization–internalization cycles. In other words, when attempting to load the 'same' object twice, two objects with different identities are created. Likewise, asking a moniker twice for an object yields two different objects, although probably of identical class and with identical initial state. Therefore, where preservation of inter-object relations is required, this needs to be handled explicitly. Consider the example illustrated in Figure 14.10, in which two objects (A and B) share a third (C). In this example, when loading the objects from a persistent store, C must be loaded only once and a reference to C must then be passed to A and B.

In the presence of shared references across component boundaries, the task of preserving sharing becomes involved. Without a general persistence service, COM offers just a building block: monikers. Monikers are explained in section 14.9. Recently, for COM+, refined support for object persistence has been added.

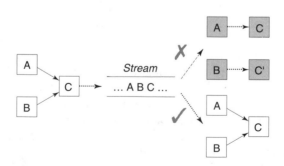

Figure 14.10   Preservation of sharing.

14.6 From COM to distributed COM (DCOM)

Distributed COM transparently expands the concepts and services of COM. DCOM builds on the client-side proxy objects and the server-side stub objects already present in COM, where they are used only to support inter-process communication. DCOM services were already hinted at when mentioning remote servers above.

To support transparent communication across process boundaries or across machine boundaries, COM creates proxy objects on the client's end and stub objects on the server's end. For the communication between processes within a single machine, proxies and stubs merely need to map all simple data types to and from streams of bytes. As the sending and receiving processes execute on the same machine, there is no need to worry about how data types are represented. Things are slightly more complex when an interface reference is passed – still between processes on the same machine.

An interface reference sent across process boundaries needs to be mapped to an *object reference* that retains meaning across process boundaries. When receiving such an object reference, COM needs to make sure that a corresponding proxy object exists on the receiving end. COM then selects the corresponding interface of that proxy and passes this reference instead of the original one, which would refer to an interface in the 'wrong' process. Figure 14.11 illustrates this approach.

Figure 14.11 shows a client issuing a call on object A. The called method takes a single parameter, referring to an interface of object B. As object A is in another process, the call is mediated by a local proxy object. The proxy determines an object identifier (OID) for object B and an interface pointer identifier (IPID) for the particular interface being passed. The OID and the IPID are sent together with the client process's ID to a stub in the server process. The stub uses the OID to locate the local proxy for object B and the IPID to locate the particular inter-

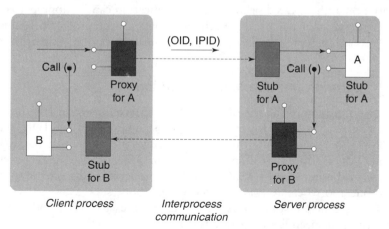

Client process   Interprocess   Server process
                   communication

Figure 14.11 Marshaling and unmarshaling of interface references across processes on a single machine. (Simplified: in COM proxies and stubs are *per interface*.)

face. The stub then issues the original call, on behalf of the client. It passes the interface reference of the local B proxy to object A, the receiver of the call.

The machinery used by DCOM is quite similar. There are two differences: representations of data types can differ across machines and object references need to contain more information than provided by just OIDs and IPIDs. To deal with differences in data representations, DCOM marshals data into a representation called network data representation (NDR), a platform-independent format. To form machine-independent object references, DCOM combines the OID and IPID with information that suffices to locate an *object exporter*. An object exporter is an object provided by DCOM that knows how to bind the objects exported by a server. Each object exporter has a unique ID (OXID), and this OXID is included in an object reference.

If the object exporter has been contacted recently, the OXID is known locally, together with contact information of the remote machine. This caching mechanism speeds up the resolution of object references, even in the presence of large numbers of objects. However, if the object exporter referred to in an object reference is seen the first time, a final field of the object reference is consulted. This field contains the symbolic information (a URL-like string binding) needed to contact the *OXID resolver object* on the remote machine. The remote OXID resolver is contacted and the contact information for the remote object exporter with the given OXID is retrieved.

In addition to this low-level machinery to connect COM objects across machine boundaries, DCOM also provides higher-level mechanisms to speed up remote operations, to provide security, and to detect remote machine failures (using 'ping' messages). The security mechanism is quite involved and supports various levels of security at various levels of granularity. There can be default security settings for machines, individual COM servers on machines, and individual COM interfaces in servers. All accesses can be protected by access control lists (ACLs) and based on authenticated principles. Authentication can be done per connection, per message, or per packet. Exchanged data can be protected against unwanted access (encrypted) or just protected against tampering (fingerprinted).

14.7   Meta-information and automation

COM does not require the use of a specific interface definition language, as it really is a binary standard. However, to use the standard Microsoft IDL compiler (MIDL) it is necessary to use the COM IDL. Despite the similar name, COM IDL and OMG IDL are two different languages. Once interfaces and classes have been described using COM IDL, the MIDL compiler is used to create stubs and proxies, but also to create *type libraries*. Other tools, such as Visual J++ and Visual C++, generate stubs, proxies, and type libraries directly and thus completely bypass the need for a separate IDL.

A type library is used by COM to provide runtime type information for all interfaces and classes described in a type library. Using the CLSID of a class, clients can query the COM registry for type information on that class. If a corresponding type library exists, the registry returns an ITypeLib interface that can be used to browse the type library. For each interface or class, an ITypeInfo interface can be retrieved and used to obtain type information on that specific object. Available information includes the number and type of parameters of a method. Also included are the categories to which a class belongs. For each interface, attributes are available to indicate dispinterfaces (dispatch interfaces, see section 14.8.2), dual interfaces, outgoing interfaces, and more.

In the context of COM, 'automation support' means programmability. Essentially, everything that provides COM interfaces, regular, dispatch, dual, or outgoing, is programmable in the sense of COM. Together with type libraries, services such as scripting systems can be built. COM automation fully relies on COM interfaces and type library information. There is no concept of semantic messages, as defined in OpenDoc's open scripting architecture (p. 283).

14.8 Other COM services

In addition to the forementioned wiring and structured storage services, COM also provides several other general services. There is a trend for services originally introduced for OLE or some other higher-level technologies to move down into the COM domain to form a wide basis for other technologies. Important COM services include uniform data transfer, dispatch interfaces, and outgoing interfaces (connectable objects). These services are introduced briefly in the remainder of this section.

14.8.1 Uniform data transfer

Uniform data transfer allows for the unified implementation of all sorts of data transfer mechanisms. Examples are clipboards, drag and drop facilities, files, streams, and so on. All that is required of a COM object to participate in such a data transfer is to implement interface IDataObject. Objects doing so are called *data objects* and function as both universal data sources and targets.

Obviously, source and target need to agree on a number of things for such a transfer to work and make sense. This agreement is based on a mutually understood data format and a mutually agreed transfer medium. Both can be specified using parameters to the methods of IDataObject.

Some additional interfaces support drag and drop-like mechanisms and object linking, where a transfer target needs to be notified of future data source changes. As drag and drop has wider applicability than just compound documents, this machinery is now considered to be part of COM rather than OLE. Uniform data transfer also supports 'lazy evaluation' of transferred data: large items can be kept at their source until they are truly needed. Finally, uniform data transfer defines a number of standard data formats.

14.8.2 Dispatch interfaces (dispinterfaces) and dual interfaces

Dispatch interfaces (dispinterfaces) have a fixed number of methods defined in interface IDispatch. A dispinterface combines all methods of a regular interface into a single method: Invoke. Method Invoke uses a variant record type to combine all possible parameters into one. This record is self-describing to the extent that each field is a pair of type and value. The actual method to call is specified by a dispatch ID (DISPID), which is simply the number of the method. DISPIDs are unique only within one dispinterface. IDispatch adds only four methods to those defined in IUnknown. The arguments are stylized in the following summary and will vary depending on the language binding used.

```
interface IDispatch : IUnknown {
    HRESULT GetTypeInfoCount ([out] bool available);
    HRESULT GetTypeInfo (unsigned int itinfo, [out] ITypeInfo typeinfo);
    HRESULT GetIDsOfNames ([in] names[], [out] DISPID dispid[]);
    HRESULT Invoke ([in] DISPID dispID, [in] DISPPARAMS dispParams,
        [out] VARIANT result, [out] EXCEPINFO einfo, [out] int argErr);
}
```

Dispinterfaces have one principal advantage: they always look the same. It is therefore easy to implement services that generically forward or broadcast dispinterface calls. Very prominent examples of such generic forwarding mechanisms are found in interpreters such as Visual Basic. Using dispinterfaces, an interpreter can call arbitrary operations without requiring that the interpreter itself is compiled against all these interfaces.

Dispinterfaces have several disadvantages. Obvious is the performance penalty. Furthermore, dispinterfaces restrict dispatch operations to parameters of a limited set of types (those covered by the VARIANT type), and to at most one return value. Finally, dispinterfaces introduce considerable complexity per interface implementation, instead of providing an adequate service.

The performance disadvantage can be compensated by so-called *dual interfaces*. A dual interface is both a dispinterface and a regular interface. It starts off with the IDispatch methods, including Invoke, and concludes by also providing all dispatched methods directly. With a dual interface, clients compiled against the interface can call methods directly, whereas other clients can use the more dynamic but less efficient dispatch mechanism.

Dispinterfaces could be avoided: modern meta-programming support would allow the same for arbitrary methods in arbitrary interfaces. By comparison, the CORBA dynamic invocation and dynamic stub interfaces support a much cleaner model for dynamic invocations at client or server end, without any of the dispinterface restrictions. Generic broadcasting and forwarding in CORBA can be achieved by using both the dynamic invocation and the dynamic stub interface. As a result, the ORB transfers the abstract parameter list and other invocation information without performing a final dispatch to the target method. By using a static invocation via IDL-generated stubs and a dynamic skeleton inter-face at the server's end, the ORB can be used to translate a static invocation into a dynamic one that can then be used to forward or broadcast the request.

14.8.3 Outgoing interfaces and connectable objects

An outgoing interface is an interface that a COM object would use (rather than provide) *if* it is 'connected' to an object that provides this interface. The intention is that, by specifying an outgoing interface, a COM object can announce that it could proactively provide useful information to any object that provided that in-terface. In essence, outgoing interfaces support the registration of other objects that wish to 'listen' for notifications.

To become a full *connectable object*, a COM object has to declare outgoing interfaces. It also has to implement interface IConnectionPointContainer. Finally, for each outgoing interface, it has to provide one connection point object which, in addition to calling the outgoing interface, also implements interface IConnectionPoint.

Using IConnectionPointContainer, the various connection point objects of a connectable object can be found and enumerated. For each connection point, IConnectionPoint can be used to establish, enumerate, and tear down connec-tions. A connection is established by passing an interface reference of another object to the connection point. When it wants to call a method of an outgoing interface, a connectable object iterates over all presently registered connections. For each registered connection, that is for each registered interface reference, the required method is invoked.

Connectable objects provide a uniform way to implement change propaga-tion. As outgoing and incoming interfaces are matched, the propagation can take the form of regular method invocations instead of requiring the creation of event objects. Connections are thus efficient.

14.9   Compound documents and OLE

Object linking and embedding (OLE) is Microsoft's compound document stand-ard. OLE was created to blend legacy applications, with their own application-centric view of the world, into a single document-centric paradigm. It is also possible to create objects that only exist within an OLE setting; ActiveX objects are the best example. However, OLE continues to support also stand-alone appli-cations with varying degrees of OLE integration. This pragmatic aspect makes many OLE technologies suboptimal or unnecessarily complex when compared with a design such as OpenDoc. However, it also allows for a smooth transition path, protecting investments into developments and user training, and therefore preserving the client base.

As with every technology on top of COM, OLE can be summarized as a (large) collection of predefined COM interfaces. Several of the key technologies required by OLE are delivered by COM services. This includes structured storage, monikers, uniform data transfer including drag and drop, connectable objects, and automation support (Chappel, 1996).

The OLE compound document's approach distinguishes between document containers and document servers. A document server provides some content model and the capabilities to display and manipulate that content. A document container has no native content, but can accept parts provided by arbitrary document servers. Many document containers are also document servers, that is they support foreign parts but also have their native content. Most of the popular 'heavyweights,' such as Microsoft's Office applications, Word, Excel, PowerPoint, and so on, are combined servers and containers. For example, Excel has a native content model of spreadsheet-arranged cells of data and formulae. Excel is also a container. As such, it can accept, say, insertion of a Word text object.

Fundamental to the user's illusion of working with a single document is the ability to edit everything where it is displayed. This is called in-place editing. In the example, Excel would allow Word to take over when the user wants to edit the embedded text object. In fact, Word opens a window for this purpose; the window is opened just over the place where Excel was displaying the text object. It is not apparent to the user that Word opened a window. The user sees only the text being activated after double clicking on it, ready for editing using the familiar Word tools.

In-place activation is a tricky business. The container has to hand off part of the container's screen estate to the server of an embedded part. Also, and more difficult, the container and server have to agree on how to handle other parts of the user interface. For example, menus and toolbars need to be changed as well. The OLE approach to in-place activation is generally to change all menus, toolbars, and other window adornments to those required by the activated server. For menus and toolbars, container and server can agree on a merger. For example, the File menu stays with the (outermost) container: filing operations normally operate on the entire document.

Besides embedding, OLE also supports linking of document parts. *Nomen est omen*. Linking rests on monikers: a container stores a moniker to the linked object. In addition, the linked object advises the container of changes. The technology to do so could be connectable objects, but for historical reasons a separate, less general, mechanism is used: sink advisory interfaces for data objects.

The OLE user interface guidelines do not allow in-place activation or editing of linked parts. Instead, a fully separate document window is opened to edit a linked part. This simplifies the user's view of things, as a linked part could be linked to multiple containers. Editing in a separate document window is also an option for embedded parts and is useful when embedded parts are too small for reasonable in-place editing.

14.10 OLE containers and servers

The interaction of containers and servers is complex by nature. A large number of details have to be addressed to enable the smooth cooperation required for a well-integrated document-centric 'look and feel.' In the case of OLE, things are further complicated by the support of stand-alone applications with OLE integration.

Recall that COM distinguishes in-process, local, and remote servers. OLE has to provide ways to enable document integration for configurations of all three server types. As windows can only be written to by their owning processes, things are complicated for all but in-process servers.

For local (out-of-process) servers, the situation is quite different. There needs to exist a 'representative' of the server object, executing in the container process. Such a representative is called an *in-process handler*. It implements functions that, among other things, draw to the container's window. A generic default in-process handler is part of the OLE infrastructure, but custom handlers can be used to fine-tune performance and functionality. Perhaps surprisingly, remote servers do not add a significant additional burden for the OLE programmer: DCOM hides the details and the local server technology carries over. This transparency can be deceptive however. Whereas a local server is unlikely to crash individually, a remote server may well become unreachable or fail. COM-based applications thus have to expect a potential error indication on each method invocation – to be prepared for interactions with a remote server.

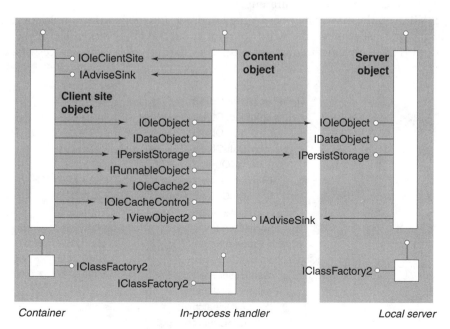

Figure 14.12 OLE document container and server interfaces.

The interaction between document containers and document servers is governed by two interfaces provided by a container's *client site object* and seven interfaces provided by a server's *content object*. That does not mean that servers are more difficult to implement than containers. In the end, containers have to call the operations of all the server interfaces. Indeed, it is generally more difficult to implement document containers. Figure 14.12 shows the split of interfaces across document container and server.

Figure 14.12 also shows the interaction between the in-process handler, implementing the content object seen by the container, and the local server, implementing the actual server object. As can be seen, the in-process handler is really supporting a separate class with its own factory. The factories could also use the simpler IClassFactory interface. As IClassFactory2 supports licensing, and licensing is most useful for controls, this is the choice shown in the figure.

14.11   Controls: from Visual Basic via OLE to ActiveX

Visual Basic controls (VBXs) were the first successful component technology released by Microsoft – first after their operating systems, of course. Visual Basic uses a simple and fixed model in which controls are embedded into forms. A form binds the embedded controls together and allows the attachment of scripts that enable the controls to interact. Entire applications can be assembled rather than programmed, simply by composing controls into forms, although the final scripting again is a form of programming.

VBXs on the market number by the hundreds and range from simple controls in the original sense of the word to 'mini applications.' For example, there are controls that implement entire spreadsheets, charting tools, word processors, or

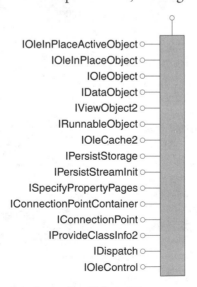

IOleInPlaceActiveObject
IOleInPlaceObject
IOleObject
IDataObject
IViewObject2
IRunnableObject
IOleCache2
IPersistStorage
IPersistStreamInit
ISpecifyPropertyPages
IConnectionPointContainer
IConnectionPoint
IProvideClassInfo2
IDispatch
IOleControl

Figure 14.13   Mandatory interfaces of an OLE control.

database connectivity tools. Despite this variety and the obvious potential, VBXs have some severe problems. The main disadvantages are the tight coupling of VBXs to Visual Basic, and Visual Basic's restrictive form model that a VBX cannot escape from. OLE controls (OCXs) were introduced to migrate the useful VBX concept to a more powerful platform, that of general OLE containers. OCXs are COM objects whereas VBXs are not.

To qualify as an OLE control, a COM object has to implement a large number of interfaces (Figure 14.13). Essentially, an OLE control implements all of an OLE document server's interfaces, plus a few more to emit events. The (good) idea was that a container could expect substantial functionality from a control. The unfortunate downside was that even the most minimal controls had to carry so much baggage that implementing OCXs was far less attractive than it was for VBXs. The extra baggage is particularly painful when considering competition with things as lightweight as Java applets. Downloading across the Internet makes lean components mandatory.

When OLE controls were finally renamed to *ActiveX controls*, the requirements were also revised. ActiveX control is therefore not just a new name for OLE control, but is also a new specification. An ActiveX control has to be implemented by a self-registering server. Self-registration allows a server, when started and asked to do so, to register its classes with the COM registry. This is useful where a server's code has just been downloaded, for example from the Internet. In addition, all that is required is the implementation of IUnknown.

ActiveX controls are really just COM objects supported by a special server. However, the ActiveX control specification is not empty. It does define a large number of features and interactions, but leaves *all* of them optional. A control supports only what is required for it to function. A full-blown control can even be a container itself, a so-called *container control*. Recent extensions of the control specifications, dubbed 'Controls 96,' allow controls to take arbitrary, non-rectangular shapes and to be 'Internet-aware,' that is they are able to handle slow links.

ActiveX controls have regular COM interfaces, but they also have outgoing interfaces (p. 211). These are very important, as controls are sources of *events* that are used by the control to signal changes. Recall that an outgoing interface is essentially an announcement of the availability of a notification mechanism. All interested objects register matching incoming interfaces with the object implementing the outgoing interface. Unfortunately, there is a dilemma in this case.

Of course, ActiveX controls can announce any number and kinds of outgoing interfaces. These may very well make sense to other controls or to script programmers, but not to the container. The container cannot possibly provide all interfaces that some control might want to be connected to. The solution to this problem is the use of outgoing dispinterfaces, which, as with all dispinterfaces, have a fixed static form: the one defined in IDispatch (p. 210). A container can dynamically construct such dispinterfaces as needed by reading the control's type library. The dispinterfaces then allow for dynamic handling and forwarding by a container. This mechanism is the reason that an ActiveX control that wishes to signal events has to come with a type library.

Another important aspect of almost all ActiveX controls is that they have *properties*. Containers can also have properties. Properties are settings that a user or application assembler can use to fine-tune looks and behavior. ActiveX defines a number of interfaces that can be used to handle properties. These interfaces are used by controls to examine the properties of its container. They are also used by the container to examine and modify the properties of embedded controls.

An ActiveX container is an OLE container with a few additional properties. Such a container cannot rely on anything when interacting with an embedded control. Therefore, it has to inspect what interface a control supports and react accordingly. Testing for a large number of interfaces can be expensive, and the category identifiers (CATIDs, p. 202) come in handy. Although it is now trivial to implement a new ActiveX control, it is also much more difficult to implement a useful container. However, because the number of containers is much smaller than the number of controls, this is the right trade-off. Unfortunately, many so-called ActiveX containers on the market today do not fully conform to the ActiveX specification and function only when embedded controls do implement the numerous OLE control interfaces.

14.12 Services

Like the various CORBAservices, Microsoft offers a number of key services that build on DCOM. A fundamental service in any distributed infrastructure is a directory service. The Windows Registry, a generalization of the system registry required by COM, serves this purpose. Security services are build into the DCOM extension of COM, as briefly outlined in section 14.6. A simple licensing service has been part of COM since the introduction of OCXs. Some important services have recently been announced or released, including a transaction server and a messaging server. Because of its several interesting features, the transaction server is discussed below.

14.12.1 Microsoft transaction server

The transaction server supports online transaction processing of COM-based applications. It maintains a pool of threads to control performance in the presence of large numbers of requests to large numbers of COM objects. Requests are queued until one of the pooled threads becomes available to handle it. The server also manages the mapping of components to server processes automatically. This can be used to group components according to security or fault isolation requirements. Like the thread pool, the server also maintains database connection pools, amortizing the cost of establishment and tear-down of connections over large numbers of requests. Finally, the server supports multiple resource managers, such as multiple databases.

The transaction server currently does not address fault tolerance issues beyond the properties of transactions. It also does not address load balancing across available machines. Currently, the server only supports Microsoft's SQL Server and databases with ODBC interfaces. Support for other protocols has been announced, including IBM's SNA LU6.2, transaction internet protocol (TIP), and XA.

An interesting feature of the transaction server is its transparent addition of transactional capabilities to existing COM components. By setting a property in the registry, a component can be marked transactional. At component object creation time, the transaction server then intercepts and adds transactional closures to the component's operations using COM containment. It uses COM aggregation to add transactional interfaces to objects as required. The server automatically detects references to other COM objects by a transactional component and extends transactional handling to these as well. Despite this automation, component developers need to be aware of transactions to keep exclusive locking of resources to a minimum. For components that need to be directly aware of transactions, a new library call – GetObjectContext – is provided to retrieve the current transactional context. Also, a new interface – IObjectContext – has been defined to access such a context.

14.12.2 COM+

In October 1997, Microsoft released COM+, an extension of COM. COM+ combines COM with lightweight object models such as that required by a Java virtual machine. COM+ is restricted to in-process objects; across processes or machines, COM (DCOM) is used. Because it defines more abstract memory (and disk) representations than COM, it is a more general architecture than the Java virtual machine, supporting a broad spectrum of programming languages and code file formats. Unlike COM, its runtime infrastructure can be systematically extended by third-party components such as debuggers or profilers. Within a process, the reference counting problems of COM are eliminated by providing true garbage collection. COM+ supports all types required to cover Java, including interfaces, classes, implementation inheritance, and field access. However, it is advisable to utilize only COM's strengths and avoid implementation inheritance (and the semantic fragile base class problem!) across different components.

Extensive use of meta-data makes COM+ well suited for Java, Component Pascal, Visual Basic, or scripting languages (compiled or interpreted) and obviates the need to implement dispinterfaces. Many standard services, including security and transactions, are scheduled for COM+. Although similar in scope to the CORBA object services, they are more focused and better integrated. The ability to mix COM and COM+ components should make transition smooth, virtually guaranteeing the success of this new standard. There are many technical advantages: COM+ is a standard object model which is as flexible as possible, but as concrete as necessary to allow for binary compatibility of shrink-wrapped components; it is a virtual machine architecture for dynamic languages such as Java, including scripting languages; provides a standardized infrastructure for third-party, low-level tool components; supports garbage collection, eliminating unsafe manual life-cycle management of objects; and supports safe and efficient in-process cooperation between components.

CHAPTER FIFTEEN

The Sun way: Java and JavaBeans

Java is a true phenomenon in the industry. Java is one of the very few success stories of the 1990s: a new programming language, which, together with its own view of the world, really made an impact. Sun released Java in alpha form in early 1995 and, although it was hardly known and very little used before early 1996, it is now one of the most commonly used buzzwords. It seems that the time was ripe for the message that there is more to come in the way of programming languages than was at first commonly believed. However, it was not the language that attracted attention originally. Other, and perhaps better, languages had failed before. The real attractor was the concept of *applets*, mini applications that function within a Web page.

Java was designed to allow an applet to execute in the same process as a client's Web browser without posing an unacceptable security threat. For this purpose, Java the language was designed to allow a compiler to check an applet's code for safety. The idea is that an applet that passes the compiler's checks cannot be a security threat. As the compiled code can still be tampered with, it is again checked at load time. The verified applet is then known to be safe and can thus be subjected to strong security policies. None of this would be possible with most of the established programming languages, including C++ and Object Pascal. Security policies can, of course, be enforced for languages that are usually interpreted, such as Smalltalk or Visual Basic. Java, however, was designed to allow for the compilation to efficient executables at the target site. This is done by so-called *just-in-time (JIT) compilers*.

As an aside, it is possible to base security policies on trust in applet vendors. Authentication techniques can be used to make sure that a received applet has not been tampered with and indeed comes from the announced vendor. If that vendor is trusted, the applet can be loaded, even if it has come in binary form. This is largely the approach taken by Microsoft's ActiveX ('authenticode'). An obvious disadvantage is that no one will ever trust the large number of small developers providing the Web community with applets. Ruling out this source of applets would seriously cripple the usefulness of applets on the Web. A combination of the two approaches is best and is now also supported by Java: 'signed applets.' If a downloaded applet is signed and authenticated to come from a trusted source, it can be given more privileges than an applet that does not pass this test.

The second winning aspect of Java is the *Java virtual machine* (JVM). Java compilers normally compile Java into Java byte code, a format that is understood by the JVM. By implementing the JVM on all relevant platforms, Java packages compiled to byte code are platform independent. This is a major advantage when downloading applets from the Internet. The true advantage is not so much the JVM but the Java class file and JAR archive formats (see section 17.3).

None of the advantages of Java are technically new. Safe languages existed before, including efficiently compilable ones (Reiser and Wirth, 1992). Virtual machines with byte code instruction sets go back to the early times of the Pascal p-machine (Nori *et al.*, 1981) and the Smalltalk 80 virtual machine (Krasner, 1983). Even the concept of object integration into the Web had been demonstrated before. The principal achievement with Java was to pull it all together and release it in a very timely fashion.

This chapter presents a detailed account of the Java language, the Java component model JavaBeans, and a number of relevant Java services. In line with the arguments of component safety by construction, the safety features of Java and their interaction with the Java security mechanisms are explored in detail. The introduction to the Java language is important because much of JavaBeans directly builds on the properties of the language.

15.1 Java, the language

Java is an almost pure object-oriented language. It makes some admissions: not everything is an object. All Java code resides in methods of classes. All state resides in attributes of classes. All classes except Object inherit interface and implementation from exactly one other class. Non-object types are the primitive types (boolean, byte, short, int, long, float, double) and interface types. Objects are either instances of classes or arrays. Objects can be created but not explicitly deallocated; Java uses an automatic garbage collector for safety. A class can implement any number of interfaces and interfaces can be in a multiple interface inheritance relation.

All Java classes and interfaces belong to packages. (Since Java 1.1, a class can also be nested inside another class or even inside a method.) Packages introduce a level of encapsulation on top of that introduced by classes. The default mode for access protection allows arbitrary access across classes in the same package. Packages form a hierarchy, but only the package immediately enclosing a class or an interface affects encapsulation and protection. Outer packages merely serve to manage name spaces. All naming in Java is relative to the package name paths formed by appending the names of inner packages to those of outer packages. It is recommended that a globally unique name is used for a top-level package; a typical candidate is a registered Internet domain name.

A fully qualified name of a feature of a class takes the form *package.Type.feature*. Here, *package* is the path name of the package, *Type* is the name of the class or interface, and *feature* is the name of the method or attribute referred to. If Internet domain names are used, a package name can take a form such as com.sun.javasoft. To use another package, the using package can always use fully qualified names to refer to the other package. However, such names can become quite lengthy. By explicitly importing some or all the types of the other package, these types names become directly available in the importing package: *Type.feature* then suffices.

Figure 15.1 shows the graphical notation used here for Java packages, inter-faces, classes, attributes, and methods. The notation is similar to OMT class dia-grams. Note that Java also has *final* classes: classes that cannot be further ex-tended, that is that they cannot be inherited from. In addition, and not shown in the notational overview, Java methods can be *final* (not overridable) or *static* (class instead of instance methods). Interfaces *extend* any number of other interfaces. Classes extend exactly one other class – except for class java.lang.Object, which has no base class. Classes can also *implement* any number of interfaces.

Figure 15.2 uses the concrete example of the java.awt.image package and its relation to the java.lang package. Note that java.awt.image is a subpackage of java.awt. As stated before, there is no special relation between a package and a subpackage that goes beyond the structure added to the namespace. In particular, both java.awt and java.awt.image contain interfaces and classes.

The line between the Java languages and some of the fundamental class librar-ies is not easy to draw. In particular, there are three packages required by the Java *language* specification (Gosling *et al.*, 1996): java.lang, java.util, and java.io. The package java.lang is even deeply intertwined with the language specification it-

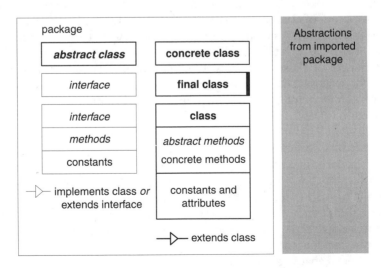

Figure 15.1   Java structuring constructs – abstract classes, abstract methods, and interfaces are set in italics.

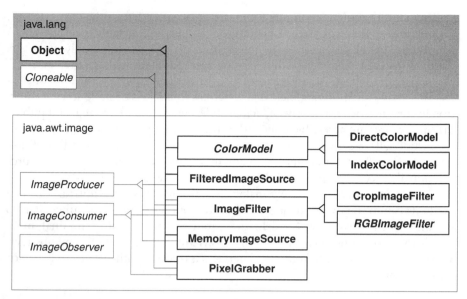

Figure 15.2 The java.awt.image package.

self. Many classes and interfaces in this package receive special treatment by the language rules. It would be fair to say that the otherwise modestly sized language Java really includes the definition of java.lang. Unfortunately, in JDK 1.0, java.lang alone defines 21 classes and two interfaces, all of which are available in any Java package automatically. This makes Java quite a large language. Just as an indication, these classes and interfaces together introduce 354 methods. Both numbers, the number of classes in java.lang and the number of methods in these classes, have been substantially increased in JDK 1.1.

The interweaving of language and standard package constructs is worse than it seems. Not only are all interfaces and classes of package java.lang automatically injected into any other package, but the language itself builds on some java.lang classes. In particular, these are the classes Object, String, and Throwable, which are entangled with the null reference, the array type constructors, the string literals, and the throw statement respectively. Under the transitive closure over the types used in the signatures of Object, String, and Throwable, the list expands to include classes Class, ClassLoader, and several subclasses of Throwable. (Because Java supports arbitrary and possibly circular dependencies across packages, one 'glitch' in java.lang, possibly an oversight, went by unnoticed. The class Throwable relies on type java.io.PrintStream – in a debugging method called printStackTrace. The language specification does not explain this method and it should probably be considered deleted. If not, it indirectly causes the classes PrintStream, FilteredOutputStream, and OutputStream from package java.io to be pulled into the language itself.)

The definition of access rights for entire packages is left to the environment. Java defines two access levels for interfaces and classes: default (package-wide) and public. In the former case the interface or class is accessible only within its defining package, not even within sub- or superpackages; in the latter case it is accessible everywhere. Access rights can be further controlled on the level of class features, that is methods and fields. Java defines four levels of static access protection for features of a class: private, default (package-wide), protected, and public. Private features are accessible only within their defining class. Default accessibility includes all classes within the same package. Protected features can in addition be accessed within their defining class and in its subclasses. Finally, public features are globally accessible, provided the containing package is.

Fields can be final, effectively making them constants once initialized. Final methods cannot be overridden. Static features belong to the class rather than to instances of the class. Interface fields are implicitly public, static, and final, making them global constants. Interface methods are implicitly public and abstract. With these restrictions enforced, Java interfaces introduce neither state nor behavior – they are pure types.

15.1.1 Interfaces versus classes

Probably the most innovative aspect of Java is its separation of interfaces and classes in a way that permits single implementation inheritance combined with multiple interface inheritance. This separation eliminates the diamond import problem (p. 99) while preserving the important possibility of a class to be compatible with multiple independent interfaces. The diamond import problem is eliminated because interfaces introduce neither state nor behavior. Thus, there can be no conflicts beyond name clashes in a class that implements multiple interfaces. Java offers no complete solution to the name conflict problem. If two interfaces introduce methods of the same name and signature but of different return type, then no class can simultaneously implement both interfaces.

Consider the following example involving both classes and interfaces. The standard package java.util defines the class Observable and the interface Observer, as shown below.

```
package java.util;
public class Observable extends Object {
    public void addObserver (Observer o);
    public void deleteObserver (Observer o);
    public void deleteObservers;
    public int countObservers ();
    public void notifyObservers ();
    public void notifyObservers (Object arg);
    protected void setChanged ();
    protected void clearChanged ();
```

```
  public boolean hasChanged ();
}
public interface Observer {
  void update (Observable o, Object arg);
}
```

The idea is that observable objects are instances of classes that extend (inherit from) Observable. Class Observable maintains a list of observers and a flag indicating whether the observable object has changed. Observers have to implement interface Observer. All registered observers will be called when the observable object calls notifyObservers. Figure 15.3 shows a simple class diagram using Observable and Observer to implement a simple model view scheme. (The dot at the tip of the arrowheaded line, from Observable to Observer, is the OMT notation showing that one Observable instance can refer to many observers.)

Observable and Observer aim to support the observer design pattern (Gamma *et al.*, 1995). This patterns is most prominently used in conjunction with model view separations in user interfaces (Chapter 9). The Observer interface certainly demonstrates a good use of interfaces in Java. However, the Observable class has a design flaw. (Observer and Observable are not used in any of the standard Java packages and were superseded in the JavaBeans standard; JavaSoft, 1996.)

The problem is that Observable is a class and not an interface. This forces restructuring of a class hierarchy in cases where a class already depends on a superclass different from Object and where instances of this class now should become observable. Why was this done? Observable as it stands does too much. It contains a concrete implementation of the list of observers and the notification broadcast. It also implements an occasional 'object has changed' flag. (If anything, it would seem that Observable should provide a counter for outstanding changes to account for nested calls to setChanged and clearChanged/notifyObservers.)

A simple solution is not to use the Observer/Observable approach. However, to study some further aspects of Java, assume that the interface Observable should be used, but that the observable object already extends some other class. Class Observable cannot therefore be used directly. The astute reader will notice that, again, the situation can be saved by using object composition. To do so, a trivial subclass of Observable needs to be implemented:

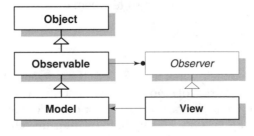

Figure 15.3 Model view construction using Observable and Observer.

```
package fix.it;
public class ObserverRegistry extends java.util.Observable {
  private Object owner;   // reference to the observable object
  public ObserverRegistry (Object trueObservable) {   // constructor
    owner = trueObservable;
  }
  public Object getTrueObservable () {
    return owner;
  }
  public void setChanged() {
    super.setChanged()
  }
  public void clearChanged() {
    super.setChanged()
  }
}
```

This trivial subclass removes the protected access mode from methods setChanged and clearChanged. Instances of TrulyObservable can now be used as part objects of observable objects. Because observers get a reference to an Observable, ObserverRegistry provides a method, getTrueObservable, to get to the object that has actually changed. The registry's constructor sets this reference. For example:

```
package fixed.it;
import fix.it.*;
public class StringBufferModel extends StringBuffer {
  private ObserverRegistry obReg = new ObserverRegistry(this);
  public ObserverRegistry getObserverRegistry () {
    return obReg;
  }
  public void setLength (int newLength)
    throws IndexOutOfBoundsException
  {
    super.setLength(newLength);
    obReg.setChanged();
    obReg.notifyObservers();   // could tell them what has changed ...
  }
  // other StringBuffer methods
}
```

Class StringBufferModel extends the standard class java.lang.StringBuffer, a helper class to support composition of strings. As a string buffer is a mutable object, it is a good candidate for a model view scenario. For example, a text entry field could be implemented as a view onto a string buffer. Unfortunately, StringBufferModel cannot extend Observable directly, as it already extends StringBuffer. StringBuffer was not designed to serve as the superclass of something observable and so extends Object instead of Observable. StringBufferModel solves this by using an ObserverRegistry object instead. Below is the sketch of an observer object displaying a StringBufferModel object's contents.

```
package fixed.it;
import java.util.*;
public class StringBufferView implements Observer {
   private StringBufferModel buf;
   public StringBufferView (StringBufferModel b) {
      buf = b;
      b.getObserverRegistry().addObserver(this);
   }
   public void update (Observable o, Object arg) {
      ObserverRegistry reg = (ObserverRegistry)o;   // checked cast
      Object observable = reg.getTrueObservable();
      if (observable != buf) throw new IllegalArgumentException();
      // ... get changes from buf and update display
   }
}
```

This concludes the example on how to use interfaces and object composition in Java. The example showed only classes implementing a single interface, but the extension to multiple interfaces is straightforward. Where unresolvable naming conflicts occur, a Java compiler rejects a class trying to implement conflicting interfaces. In all other cases there is no interference whatsoever between multiple implemented interfaces. One question remains to be answered though. How can a client that has a reference of a certain interface or class type find out what other interfaces or classes the referenced object supports? The answer is twofold. Java provides a type-test operator, instanceof, that can be used to query at runtime. Java also has checked type casts that can be used to cast the reference to another class or interface. Here is an example:

```
interface Blue { ... }
interface Green { ... }
class FunThing implements Blue, Green { ... }
```

A client holding a Blue reference can test whether the object also supports a Green interface, although Blue and Green themselves are totally independent types:

```
Blue thing = new FunThing ();
Green part = null;
if (thing instanceof Green)   // type test
   part = (Green) thing;   // checked type cast, from Blue to Green
```

15.1.2 Exceptions and exception handling

The Observer/Observable example above introduced another feature of Java: exception handling. Exceptions and runtime errors are reflected in Java as exception or error objects. These are either explicitly thrown, for example the throw statement in StringBufferView, or thrown by the runtime system, for example on out-of-bounds indexing into an array. All exception and error objects are instances of classes that are derived from class Throwable. Such throwable objects can be caught by a catch branch of a try statement. For example, the notifyObservers method in class Observable could be protected against exceptions raised by notified observers:

```
public void notifyObservers () {
    for (Observer ob = first(), ob != null, ob = next()) {
        try {
            ob.update(this, null);   // observer may throw an exception
        }
        catch (Exception ex) {
            // ignore exception and continue with next observer
        }
    }
}
```

In the example, it is not apparent just by looking at the declaration of method update that it might throw an exception. Exception types for which this is legal are called *unchecked exceptions*. Java also has exception types that can only be thrown by a method's implementation, if the method declaration announced this possibility. Such declared exceptions are called *checked exceptions*. For example:

```
class AttemptFailed extends Exception { }
class Probe {
    public void goForIt (int x) throws AttemptFailed {
        if (x != 42) throw new AttemptFailed();
    }
}
class Agent {
    public void trustMe (Probe p) {
        p.goForIt(6 * 7);   // compile-time error!
    }
}
```

Class Agent cannot be compiled. Method trustMe neither declares that it may throw the user-defined exception AttemptFailed nor catches this exception should it be thrown. Note that this check based on static annotations adds a degree of robustness to software. In the example, Agent happens to 'know' what Probe needs to avoid failure. Hence, Probe will actually never throw an exception when called from within trustMe. However, a future version of Probe may do so. After all, this possibility has even been declared and is thus part of the contract between Probe and Agent.

15.1.3 Threads and synchronization

Java defines a model of concurrency and synchronization and is thus a concurrent object-oriented language. The unit of concurrency is a *thread*. Threads are orthogonal to objects, which are therefore passive. Threads can only communicate through side-effects or synchronization. A thread executes statements and moves from object to object as it executes method invocations. Threads can be dynamically created, pre-empted, suspended, resumed, and terminated. Each thread belongs to a thread group specified at thread creation time. Threads belonging to separate thread groups can be mutually protected against thread state modifications. Threads can be assigned one of ten priority levels and can be in either user or demon mode. A thread group may impose limits on the maximum priority of its threads. However, priorities are hints only and are not supported by current virtual machines. Thread termination is not automatically propagated to child threads. A Java application terminates when the last user thread has terminated, irrespective of the possible continuation of demon threads. Figure 15.4 shows the states in which a thread can exist and the possible state transitions. The states and transitions are explained below.

Javas threads are lightweight: on any given virtual machine, they all execute in the same address space. As threads may be pre-empted, this raises the question of

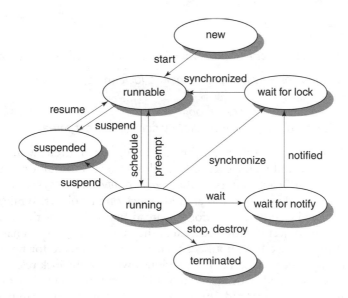

Figure 15.4   States and state transitions of Java threads.

how concurrent access is regulated. The language specification requires atomic and sequential ordering of access operations on values of primitive types and reference types. (As a concession to efficient implementation on contemporary 32-bit architectures, there are no such requirements for Java's 64-bit types *long* and *double*.) For consistent access to larger units, such as multiple fields of an object or multiple objects, explicit synchronization is required.

Java supports thread synchronization either on entrance to a *synchronized method* or on entrance to a *synchronized statement*. Synchronization forces a thread to acquire a lock on an object before proceeding. There is exactly one lock associated with each object. If the thread in question already holds a lock on that object, it can continue. (This is an important rule avoiding deadlocks in a common situation: a thread re-entering an object.) Synchronized methods use the lock of the object to which they belong. Below is an example of a wrapper for the unsynchronized stacks provided by the standard library class java.util.Stack:

```
class SynchStack {
    java.util.Stack stack = new java.util.Stack;
    public synchronized void push (Object item) {
        stack.push(item)
    }
    public synchronized Object pop () {
        return(stack.pop())
    }
    public synchronized boolean empty () {
        return(stack.empty())
    }
}
```

The synchronized statement takes the object to be locked as an argument:

```
...   // thread may or may not already hold a lock on obj
synchronized (obj) {
    ...   // thread now holds lock on obj
}    // lock released, unless it was already held by current thread
```

Without any further measures, a thread waiting for an event would have to poll variables. To avoid inefficiencies, Java allows threads to *wait* on any object. For this reason, class Object defines methods *wait*, *notify*, and *notifyAll*. These methods can only be called in a context that holds a lock on that object. While waiting, the lock is released. Upon notification, a thread first reacquires the lock before proceeding. If the object is currently locked, then the notified thread has to wait. If multiple threads have been notified, then they will compete for the lock and acquire it, in any order, as soon as the previous owner of the lock releases it.

A thread is associated with an owning object at thread creation time. It is through this object that a thread can be suspended, resumed, or terminated. The owning object can also be used to move a thread between user and demon status before the thread is first started. Objects that own a thread are instances (of a subclass) of class java.lang.Thread; below is an excerpt:

```
public class Thread implements Runnable {
    public Thread ();   // default constructor; use method run
    public Thread (Runnable runObject);   // use method run of runObject
    public void run ();
    public void start () throws IllegalThreadStateException;
    public void stop () throws SecurityException;
    public void suspend () throws SecurityException;
    public void resume () throws SecurityException;
    public void setPriority (int newPriority)
        throws SecurityException, IllegalArgumentException;
    public void setDaemon (boolean on)
        throws SecurityException, IllegalThreadStateException;
    public void destroy () throws SecurityException;
    // other methods deleted ...
}
```

A thread object can itself define the outermost method to be executed by the new thread: method run in class Thread. Alternatively, the thread object is constructed with a reference to an object that implements interface Runnable. In the latter case, thread execution starts by calling the run method of that other object. Either way, the thread terminates if the outermost method returns. A thread also terminates when its outermost method throws an exception or when its owning objects stop or destroy methods are called. (Method stop sends a ThreadDeath exception to the thread, whereas destroy terminates the thread immediately and with no clean-up. Objects locked by a destroyed thread remain locked. This is the last resort in case a thread catches ThreadDeath and thereby refuses to terminate.)

15.2 JavaBeans

Java versions before 1.1 mainly targeted two products: applets and applications. Neither qualify as components – an applet is really just a mini application launched by a browser or other environment. Although applets can be arranged to appear together on a Web page, there is nothing that allows these applets to interact. Any interaction has to be performed on the server end. An applet instance is thus well isolated from whatever executes in the same environment. An applet is also only a degenerate component because it cannot come with resources or even all classes that it needs to execute. Instead, resources and further class files need to be downloaded one by one from the applet's server.

JavaBeans, released in October 1996, aims to fill the gap and make a new kind of product possible: Java components, called 'beans' (JavaSoft, 1996). It is unfortunate that the clear distinction between class and object in Java is not carried through in JavaBeans. Although a bean really is a component (a set of classes and resources), its customized and connected instances are also called beans. This is confusing. In the following, *bean* refers to the component and *bean instance* to the component object. 'Bean object' would be too confusing, because a bean usually consists of many Java objects.

The current JavaBeans specification does not address issues of containers or other higher-level document-related functions. A bean is expected to support mainly small to medium-sized controls, similar to OLE controls or non-container ActiveX controls. JavaBeans has been designed to enable the integration of a bean into container environments defined outside Java. For example, there is an ActiveX bridge available from JavaSoft that allows a bean instance to function as a control in an ActiveX container. Similar bridges can be expected for OpenDoc or other document-centric environments.

Beans have been designed with a dual usage model in mind: bean instances are first assembled by an assembly tool such as an application builder, at 'design time,' and are then used at 'runtime.' A bean instance can customize appearance and functionality dynamically by checking whether it is design time or runtime. One of the ideas is that it should be possible to strip the design time code from a bean when shipping an assembled application. A bean instance can also inquire, at 'runtime,' whether it is used interactively, that is whether a graphical user inter-face is available. Thus, a bean instance can behave differently when being run on a server or as part of a batch job, rather than interactively.

The main aspects of the bean model are:

- *Events*. Beans can announce that their instances are potential sources or listeners of specific types of events. An assembly tool can then connect listeners to sources.
- *Properties*. Beans expose a set of instance properties through pairs of getter and setter methods. Properties can be used for customization or programmatically. Property changes can trigger events and properties can be constrained. A constrained property can only be changed if the change is not vetoed.
- *Introspection*. A bean can be inspected by an assembly tool to find out about the properties, events, and methods that a particular bean sup-ports.
- *Customization*. Using the assembly tool, a bean instance can be custom-ized by setting its properties.
- *Persistence*. Customized and connected bean instances need to be saved for reloading at the time of application use.

15.2.1 Events and connections

Events in the JDK 1.1 terminology – and as used in JavaBeans – are objects created by an *event source* and propagated to all currently registered *event listeners*. Thus, event-based communication generally has multicast semantics. However, it is possible to flag an event source as requiring unicast semantics: such a source accepts at most one listener at any one time. Event-based communication is similar to the COM Connectable Objects approach and also can be seen as a generalization of the Observer pattern (Chapter 9).

An event object should not have public fields and should usually be considered immutable. Mutation of event objects in the presence of multicast semantics is subtle. However, where mutation of an event object during propagation is required, these changes should be encapsulated by methods of the event object. The JavaBeans specification gives coordinate transformations as an example: a mouse-click event may need to be transformed to local coordinates to make sense to a listener.

Listeners need to implement an interface that extends the empty 'marker' interface java.beans.EventListener and that has a receiving method for each event the listener listens to. For example:

```
interface UserSleepsListener extends java.util.EventListener {
    void userSleeps (UserSleepsEvent e);
}
```

A listener can implement a given event listener interface only once. If it is registered with multiple event sources that all can fire the same event, the listener has to determine where an event came from before handling it. This can be simplified by interposing an *event adapter*. An event adapter implements a listener interface and holds references to listeners. Thus, an event adapter is both an event listener and an event source. A separate adapter can be registered with each of the event sources. Each adapter then calls a different method of the listener. Thus, event adapters can be used to *demultiplex* events. In principle, event adapters can perform arbitrary event-filtering functions. Note that in the absence of method types and method variables, event adapters lead either to an explosion of classes or to slow and unnatural generic solutions based on the reflection service. Such generic demultiplexing adapters are indeed proposed in the JavaBeans specification (JavaSoft, 1996, pp. 35–37). In Java 1.1, this problem has been reduced by supporting in-line construction of lightweight adapter classes: so-called anonymous inner classes, somewhat similar to Smalltalk blocks.

An event source needs to provide pairs of listener register and unregister methods:

```
public void addUserSleepsListener (UserSleepsListener l);
public void removeUserSleepsListener (UserSleepsListener l);
```

If a source requires unicast semantics, it can throw a TooManyListenersException:

```
public void addUserSleepsListener (UserSleepsListener l)
    throws java.util.TooManyListenersException;
```

Event propagation in a multicast environment introduces a number of subtle problems. The set of listeners can change while an event is propagated. JavaBeans does not specify how this is addressed, but a typical way is to copy the vector of registered listeners before starting a multicast. Also, exceptions may occur while the multicast is in progress; again, JavaBeans does not specify whether or not the multicast should still continue to address the remaining listeners. Finally, a listener may itself issue an event broadcast upon reception of an event. This raises the difficult problem of relative event ordering; JavaBeans does not specify any constraints on the ordering of event delivery (see section 10.7 for a detailed discussion of the ordering issues of event-based programming).

Event ordering issues are aggravated in multithreaded environments such as Java. For example, an event source may hold locks that are required by event listeners to process events. The result would be a deadlock. Indeed, the authors of the JavaBeans specification (JavaSoft, 1996, p. 31):

> 'strongly recommend that event sources should avoid holding their own internal locks when they call event listener methods.'

This is clearly subtle. It is not even clear whether this recipe can even be followed without breaking encapsulation. It may not be at all easy to determine whether and which locks the event source already holds. More precise advice continues:

> 'Specifically, [...] they should avoid using a synchronized method to fire an event and should instead merely use a synchronized block to locate the target listeners and then call the event listeners from unsynchronized code.'

Although this specific advice clearly needs to be followed, it is not sufficient to avoid subtle deadlocks that result from a combination of multithreading and event-based communication.

15.2.2 Properties

A bean can define a number of properties of arbitrary types. A property is a discrete named attribute that can affect a bean instance's appearance or behavior. Properties may be used by scripting environments, can be accessed programmatically by calling getter and setter methods, or can be accessed using property sheets at assembly time or runtime. Typical properties are persistent attributes of a bean instance. Property changes at assembly time are used to customize a bean instance. A property change at runtime may be part of the interaction with the user, another bean instance, or the environment.

Access to properties is through a pair of methods. For example, the setter and getter methods for a property 'background color' might take the following form:

```
public java.awt.Color getBackground ();
public void setBackground (java.awt.Color color);
```

To optimize the common case where an array of property values needs to be maintained, *indexed properties* are also supported. The corresponding setter and getter methods simply take an index or an entire array of values:

```
public java.awt.Color getSpectrum (int index);
public java.awt.Color[] getSpectrum ();
public void setSpectrum (int index, java.awt.Color color);
public void setSpectrum (java.awt.Color[] colors);
```

A property can be *bound*. Changes to a bound property trigger the firing of a property change event. Registered listeners will receive an event object of type java.beans.PropertyChangeEvent that encapsulates the locale-independent name of the property and its old and new value:

```
public class PropertyChangeEvent extends java.util.EventObject {
    public Object getNewValue ();
    public Object getOldValue ();
    public String getPropertyName ();
}
```

The methods required to register and unregister property change listeners are:

```
public void addPropertyChangeListener
            (PropertyChangeListener x);
public void removePropertyChangeListener
            (PropertyChangeListener x);
```

The interface java.beans.PropertyChangeListener introduces the method to be called on property changes:

```
void propertyChange (PropertyChangeEvent evt);
```

A property can also be *constrained*. For a constrained property, the property setter method is declared to throw PropertyVetoExceptions. Whenever a change of a constrained property is attempted, a VetoableChangeEvent is passed to all registered *vetoable-change* listeners. Each of these listeners may throw a java.beans.PropertyVetoException. If at least one does, the property change is vetoed and will not take place. If no veto exception is thrown, the property is changed in the usual way and a PropertyChangeEvent is passed to all change listeners.

The methods required to register and unregister vetoable property change listeners are:

```
public void addVetoableChangeListener
    (VetoableChangeListener x);
public void removeVetoableChangeListener
    (VetoableChangeListener x);
```

The interface java.beans.VetoableChangeListener introduces the method to be called on property changes:

```
public void vetoableChange (VetoableChangeEvent evt)
    throws PropertyVetoException;
```

Normally, properties are edited by property editors as determined by a java.beans.PropertyEditorManager object. This object maintains a registry to map between Java types and appropriate *property editor classes*. However, a bean can override this selection by specifying a property editor class to be used when editing a particular property of that bean. Furthermore, where customization of a bean is complex or involves many properties, a bean can also nominate a *customizer class* that implements a specific customization interface. A customizer will normally take a separate dialog window, whereas typical property editors are controls. Thus, property editors can be used in the dialog implemented by a customizer.

15.2.3 Introspection

Events and properties are supported by a combination of new standard interfaces and classes. Examples are EventListener, EventObject, EventSetDescriptor, and PropertyDescriptor; for more information on the property and event models, see the following sections. The use of interfaces such as EventListener allows an assembly tool using the reflection services (see below) to discover support of certain features by a given bean. In addition, JavaBeans introduces the new notion of method patterns. [In the JavaBeans specification, these are called 'design patterns' (JavaSoft, 1996). This is highly confusing. The term 'method pattern' used here is much closer to what is meant.] A method pattern is a combination of rules for the formation of a method's signature, its return type, and even its name. Method patterns allow for the lightweight classification of individual methods of an interface or a class. For example, here is the method pattern used to indicate a pair of getter and setter methods for a specific property:

```
public <PropertyType> get<PropertyName> ();
public void set<PropertyName> (<PropertyType> a);
```

For a property 'background' of type java.awt.Color, this pattern yields the following two methods:

```
public java.awt.Color getBackground ();
public void setBackground (java.awt.Color color);
```

The use of conventional names in method patterns can be avoided: a bean can implement interface java.beans.BeanInfo. If this interface is implemented, an assembly tool will use it to query a bean instance explicitly for the names of property getters, property setters, and event source registration methods. The signatures prescribed by the patterns still need to be followed of course; otherwise the assembly could not take place. The following excerpts from class BeanInfo and related classes (JavaBeans 1.00-A) hint at how BeanInfo information can be used to find out about the supported events, properties, and exposed methods:

```
package java.beans;
public interface BeanInfo {
```

```
    public abstract BeanInfo[] getAdditionalBeanInfo ();
      // current info takes precedence over additional bean info
    public abstract BeanDescriptor getBeanDescriptor ();
    public abstract EventSetDescriptor[] getEventSetDescriptors ();
    public abstract MethodDescriptor[] getMethodDescriptors ();
    public abstract PropertyDescriptor[] getPropertyDescriptors ();
  }
  public class FeatureDescriptor {
    public Enumeration attributeNames ();
    public Object getValue (String attributeName);
    public void setValue (String attributeName, Object value);
      // setValue and getValue allow to associate arbitrary named attributes
      // with a feature
    public boolean isExpert ();   // feature for expert users only
    public boolean isHidden ();   // feature for tool-use only
  }
  public class BeanDescriptor extends FeatureDescriptor {
    public Class getBeanClass ();   // the class representing the entire bean
    public Class getCustomizerClass ();   // null, if the bean has no customizer
  }
  public class EventSetDescriptor extends FeatureDescriptor {
    public java.lang.reflect.Method getAddListenerMethod ();
    public java.lang.reflect.Method getRemoveListenerMethod ();
    public java.lang.reflect.Method[] getListenerMethods ();
    public Class getListenerType();
    public boolean isUnicast ();   // this is a unicast event source:
                                   // at most one listener
  }
  public class MethodDescriptor extends FeatureDescriptor {
    public java.lang.reflect.Method getMethod ();
  }
  public class PropertyDescriptor extends FeatureDescriptor {
    public Class getPropertyEditorClass ();
    public Class getPropertyType ();
    public java.lang.reflect.Method getReadMethod ();
    public java.lang.reflect.Method getWriteMethod ();
    public boolean isBound ();   // change of bound property fires
                                 // PropertyChange event
    public boolean isConstrained ();   // attempted change may be vetoed
  }
```

Method patterns are an interesting deviation from the established Java design principles. Normally, a Java class that has a certain property, or implements a certain functionality, signals this by implementing a corresponding interface. Consider the following hypothetical substitution of the method pattern for property getters and setters. A standard empty interface Property is provided. For each property, a subinterface is defined. A bean class that has some of these properties then has to implement the corresponding property interfaces:

```
interface BackgroundProp extends Property {    // hypothetical!
    public Color getBackground ();
    public void setBackground (Color color);
}
```

The names of the set and get method should still contain the property name to avoid conflicts with set and get methods from other property interfaces. Java reflection could now be used directly to look for property interfaces in a class; the triggering key would be extension of interface Property rather than detection of methods of a certain pattern. It is not clear why this straightforward use of interfaces and reflection, instead of method patterns, was not used for the specification of JavaBeans. This is particularly surprising as a similar approach *is* used for event listener interfaces.

15.2.4 JAR files – packaging of beans

Java class files were the only pre-beans means of packaging Java components in pre-1.1 JDKs. All that a Java class file can contain is a single compiled class or interface. A class file also contains all meta-information about the compiled context. Resources cannot be included in a class file.

The limitations of class files were already revealed with Java applets: a browser had to contact the applet's server repeatedly to retrieve further class files and resource files needed by the applet. With more general software components (beans), the situation became unbearable. To ship a component, many separate files would need to be distributed.

The problem is solved by using Java Archive (JAR) files to package a JavaBean. Technically, a JAR file is a ZIP-format archive file that optionally includes a manifest file. Manifest files can be used to provide information on the contents of an archive file (see below). The archive includes entries for:

- a set of class files;
- a set of serialized objects that is often used for bean prototype instances;
- optional help files in HTML;
- optional localization information used by the bean to localize itself;
- optional icons held in *.icon* files in GIF format;
- other resource files needed by the bean.

The serialized prototype contained in the JAR file allows a bean to be shipped in an initialized default form. Serialization is performed using the object serialization service (section 15.3.2). New instances of such a bean are created by deserializing the prototype, effectively producing a copy.

There can be multiple beans in a single JAR file: potentially, each of the contained classes can be a bean and each of the serialized objects can be a bean instance. The manifest file in the JAR file can be used to name the beans in the JAR file.

15.2.5 Java AWT enhancements

The Java abstract windowing toolkit (AWT) is central to any Java development providing a graphical user interface. In recognition of the needs added by true components (beans) and of the problems introduced by some JDK 1.0 design decisions, the AWT in JDK 1.1 has been substantially improved. Further improvements, such as support for drag-and-drop gestures, have already been announced for post-1.1 releases. Here is a short summary of the most important additions and changes, as seen in the context of beans:

- *Delegation-based event model* – perhaps the most dramatic change in JDK 1.1. The previous event model was based on inheriting from component classes and overriding event handler methods. The subtle interaction of super-calls, open lists of possible events, and local handling decision procedures was found to be too complex and error-prone. The 1.1 model has been described above (section 15.2.1). 'Delegation-based' is a misnomer, following the unfortunate example of the use of the term delegation in COM. The 1.1 JDK really provides a *forwarding-based* event model. Object connection and composition are used in favor of implementation inheritance.
- *Data transfer and clipboard support* – like the COM universal data transfer service, the 1.1 AWT defines the notions of transferable data items. Internet MIME (multipurpose Internet mail extensions) types are used to interact with non-Java applications. Data transfer between Java applications can also directly use Java classes.
- *Lightweight user interface framework* – in JDK 1.0, most user interface components (buttons, list boxes, and so on) relied on native implementation in so-called 'peer classes.' This has the advantage that a Java application truly looks and feels like a native one. In JDK 1.1, so-called 'lightweight components' are available that implement look-and-feel in a way that is independent of native peers. Whatever look-and-feel is selected, it will be consistent across all platforms.
- *Printing* – printing was not really supported before JDK 1.1. The new printing model is straightforward. Graphical components that do not explicitly handle printing will be printed using their screen rendering methods. Thus, for simple components, printing is free. However, the printing model does not address the subtleties resulting from printing an

embedded contents that itself has to spread over multiple pages. (This is addressed, for example, by the ActiveX printing model, which allows embedded controls to print across several pages in cooperation with their container.)

15.3 Other Java services

There have been many recent additions to the services standardized for Java. Notable examples are the many new core interfaces added in version 1.1 of the Java Development Kit (JDK), including object serialization, remote method invocation (RMI), and reflection. A further enhancement is the specification of the Java native interface (JNI). Other services new to JDK 1.1, but not discussed here, include: the Java database connectivity (JDBC) SQL access interface to databases, support for internationalization and localization, the notion of signed applets (similar to signed ActiveX objects), and new math packages supporting arbitrary precision integers and decimals, for example to represent precisely and to manipulate large monetary values. A Java to OMG IDL binding is expected to be finalized before the end of 1997. Special packagings of Java have been announced to address the demands of various markets, for example Personal Java, Enterprise Java, Embedded Java, or Smartcard Java.

15.3.1 Reflection

The JDK 1.1 core reflection service significantly enhances the limited reflective capabilities of the 1.0 JDK. Reflection in 1.0 was limited to a few possibilities. One could get the class object for a given object or a class object by name – possibly causing the corresponding class to be loaded. A class object could be used to create new instances of that class provided the class has a default constructor, that is one that takes no arguments.

The Java reflection service, curbed by the active security policy, allows:

- inspection of classes and interfaces for their fields and methods;
- construction of new class instances and new arrays;
- access to and modification of fields of objects and classes;
- access to and modification of elements of arrays;
- invocation of methods on objects and classes.

The reflection service thus now covers all the Java language's features. The Java language-level access control mechanisms, such as privacy of a field, are enforced. (Unrestricted access can be useful to implement trusted low-level services, such as portable debuggers. A special interface for such unrestricted access has been announced but is not part of JDK 1.1.) To enable reflective operations, the reflection service introduces a package java.lang.reflect. (The default import of java.lang into all packages makes java.lang itself effectively inextensible; otherwise there would be a risk of name clashes with existing packages. The introduction of java.lang.reflect, instead of introducing the new classes into java.lang itself, avoids the conflict.)

- Classes Field, Method, and Constructor: these provide reflective information about the field, method, or constructor that they describe and allow for type-safe use of this field, method, or constructor. All three are final and without public constructors. All three implement interface Member, which makes it possible to find out how the member is called and to determine the member's modifiers and to which class or interface it belongs. Below are excerpts of some of these interfaces and classes:

```
public interface Member {
  public abstract Class getDeclaringClass ();
      public abstract String getName ();
      public abstract int getModifiers ();   // decode using class
                                             // Modifiers
  }
      public final class Field implements Member {
      public Class getType ();
      public Object get (Object obj)   // if static field, obj is ignored
        throws NullPointerException, IllegalArgumentException,
            IllegalAccessException;
      public boolean getBoolean (Object obj)
        throws NullPointerException, IllegalArgumentException,
            IllegalAccessException;
      // similar for all other primitive types; avoids wrapping in get
      public void set (Object obj, Object value)
        throws NullPointerException, IllegalArgumentException,
            IllegalAccessException;
      public void setBoolean (Object obj, Boolean z)
        throws NullPointerException, IllegalArgumentException,
            IllegalAccessException;
      // similar for all other primitive types; avoids wrapping in set
  }
      public final class Method implements Member {
      public Class getReturnType ();
      public Class[] getParameterTypes ();
      public Class[] getExceptionTypes ();
      public Object invoke (Object obj, Object[] args)   // returns null if
                                                         // return type void
        throws NullPointerException, IllegalArgumentException,
            IllegalAccessException, InvocationTargetException;
          // wrapper for exception thrown by invoked method
  }
```

■ Class Class (still in java.lang, not java.lang.reflect) has methods to return instances of these classes when querying for the features of a particular class. The important methods of class Class are:

```java
public final class Class {
    public static Class forName (String className) throws
            ClassNotFoundException;
    public Object newInstance () throws InstantiationException,
            IllegalAccessException;
    public boolean isInstance (Object obj);
    public boolean isInterface ();
    public boolean isArray ();
    public boolean isPrimitive ();
    public String getName ();
    public int getModifiers ();   // decode using class Modifiers
    public ClassLoader getClassLoader ();
    public Class getSuperclass ();   // null if primitive, interface,
                                     // or class Object
    public Class[] getInterfaces ();
    public Class getComponentType ();   // type of array components;
                                        // null if not array
    public Class getDeclaringClass ();   // declaring class of inner
                                         // class or interface
    public Class[] getClasses ();   // public inner classes or
                                    // interfaces, incl. inherited ones
    public Field[] getFields ();   // public accessible fields, incl.
                                   // inherited ones
    public Method[] getMethods ();   //public methods, incl.
                                     // inherited ones
    public Constructor[] getConstructors ();   // public constructors
    public Class[] getDeclaredClasses () throws SecurityException;
        // all inner classes or interfaces, excl. inherited ones
    public Field[] getDeclaredFields () throws SecurityException;
        // all fields, excl. inherited ones
    public Method[] getDeclaredMethods () throws
            SecurityException;
        // all methods, excl. inherited ones
    public Constructor[] getDeclaredConstructors () throws
            SecurityException;
    // all constructors
    // further methods to get (declared) field, method, constructor,
    // or class by name
}
```

- Constant objects (public static final) for the languages primitive types. For example, there is an object java.lang.Boolean.TYPE that is the Class object for primitive type boolean. Class Array supports dynamic construction and use of arrays. Class Modifier simplifies the inspection of modifier information on classes, fields, and methods.

```
public final class Modifier {
    public static boolean isPublic (int modifiers);
    // true if modifiers incl. public
    // similar for private, static, final, synchronized, volatile,
    // transient, native, interface, abstract – note that "interface"
    // is viewed as a class modifier!
}
```

15.3.2 Object serialization

Up to JDK 1.0.2, Java did not support serialization of objects into byte streams; only primitive types were supported. If an application wanted to write an entire web of objects to an output stream, it needed to traverse and serialize the objects itself, using some ad hoc encoding scheme. The Java object serialization service overcomes this by defining a standard serial encoding scheme and by providing the mechanisms to code and decode ('serialize' and 'deserialize') webs of objects.

To be serializable, an object has to implement either interface java.io.Serializable or interface java.io.Externalizable. In addition, all fields that should not be serialized need to be marked with the modifier *transient*. This is important, because fields may refer to huge computed structures, such as caches, or to values that are inherently bound to the current JVM incarnation, such as descriptors of open files. For objects implementing Serializable, sufficient information is written to a stream such that deserialization continues to work, even if different (but compatible) versions of classes are used. Methods readObject and writeObject can be implemented to control further what information is written or to append further information to the stream. If these methods are not implemented, all non-transient fields referring to serializable objects are automatically serialized. Shared references to objects are preserved.

To make serialization safe and configurable, methods readObject and writeObject are private! Therefore, there can be one such method per subclass level. Reflection is used to find these methods for each extension level. If these methods exist, they should call a method defaultReadObject (or defaultWriteObject) before handling additional private data. In any case, readObject and writeObject on a given class extension level handle only the fields introduced in this level, not those in subclasses or superclasses.

If interface Externalizable is used, none of the object's fields are automatically handled and it is up to the object to save and store its contents. Externalizable has methods writeExternal and readExternal for this purpose. These methods are public, and objects implementing Externalizable open themselves for access to their state that bypasses their regular public interface. This requires some care to avoid safety problems.

A simple versioning scheme is supported: a serializable class can claim to be a different version of a certain class by declaring a unique *serial version ID*. A serial version ID is a 64-bit hash code ('fingerprint') computed over the name of a class and all implemented interfaces' features of that class, including the features' types or signatures. It does not cover superclasses, because each extension level has its own serial version ID and is responsible for its own evolution. The serial version ID is computed automatically when an instance of a class is serialized and that class does not declare a serial version ID. However, if it does, then the class declares to be compatible with the class that originally had this ID. The readObject method can be used to read serialized state from other versions and thus preserve compatibility with serialized versions.

Object serialization creates a stream of bytes in a single-pass process, that is with no back-patching. Hence, while still serializing a web of objects, the part of the stream that has been produced already can be forwarded to filters or the destination. The stream is fully self-describing down to the level of Java primitive types: every value in the stream is preceded by a tag that describes the type of the following item. Compared with compact native formats, this can be quite costly. However, the added robustness of the serial format probably outweighs the higher cost.

A major drawback of the current serialization service is the missing support for graceful degradation in the case of missing or incompatible classes at the receiving end. For example, if the serialized object is a document, then it should be possible to deserialize and use that document even if some of its embedded objects cannot (currently) be supported on the receiving platform. The current service simply throws a ClassNotFound exception and does not offer means to resynchronize and continue deserialization. In the document example, it would also be desirable if an unsupported object could be kept in serialized form to include it when serializing the document again. This is also not supported by the current serialization service.

15.3.3 Java distributed object model

Distributed computing is mainly supported by the object serialization service (as described above) and the remote method invocation (RMI) service, both introduced with JDK 1.1. A distributed object is handled via references of interface type – it is not possible to refer to a remote object's class or any of its superclasses. Interfaces that can be accessed remotely have to be derived from java.rmi.Remote. A remote operation can always fail as a result of network or remote hardware problems. All methods of a remote interface are therefore required to declare the checked exception java.rmi.RemoteException. Parameter passing to remote operations is interesting. If an argument is of remote interface type, then the reference will be passed. In all other cases, passing is by value, that is the argument is serialized at the call site and deserialized before invoking the remote interface. Java objects are not necessarily serializable. An attempt to pass a non-serializable object by value raises a runtime exception. If Java RMI conventions were made parts of the language, then the compiler could statically enforce that only serializable objects are passed by value and that all methods declare RemoteException.

The Java distribution model extends garbage collection as well. Fully distributed garbage collection is supported, based on a careful book-keeping of which objects may have remote references to them. The collector is based on the work for Network Objects (Birrel, 1993). Distributed garbage collection is the most outstanding feature of Java RMI compared with any other approach in the mainstream today.

The Java distributed object model has a number of quirks however. First, Java RMI interferes with the notion of object identity in Java. Second, Java RMI interferes with the Java locking system's semantics, which normally prevents self-inflicted deadlocks. These two problems are explained below.

Object identity is affected by Java RMI as a result of its model of implementing remote references. If a remote interface reference is passed around, proxy objects are created on remote sites. A reference to a remote interface, once passed in a remote method invocation, is thus *not* a reference to the remote object but a reference to the local proxy of that object. Even if such a remote reference is sent back to the object's home server, it will still point to a proxy: a proxy in the same server that the object itself is residing in. It is thus not possible to send out a reference, get it back, and compare it against a local object to see whether the returned reference matches that of the local object.

Self-inflicted deadlocks are caused by locking systems that do not allow a thread to re-enter a locked area. In regular Java, threads can acquire locks any number of times without causing a deadlock. In Java RMI, the situation is different. The notion of a thread identity does not span multiple machines. If a remote invocation performs a nested remote invocation back to the original requester, then a *distributed deadlock* can occur. Such a deadlock is caused by the original requester holding locks that are also needed by the recursive callback.

The special handling of identities by Java RMI has further effects. Several methods defined in java.lang.Object had been introduced with the Java object identity model in mind. Under Java RMI, the Object method's equivalents, hashCode and toString, need to be implemented differently. Proper handling can be achieved by extending class java.rmi.RemoteObject when creating a class that implements remote interfaces. Obviously, this precludes extending some other class and it may therefore be necessary to override these three methods 'manually'.

The situation is slightly worse for the Object methods getClass, notify, notifyAll, and wait. These are declared final in java.lang.Object and cannot be adjusted by RemoteObject or another class. Although none of these methods malfunctions in the context of Java RMI, they all have potentially unexpected semantics. When operating on remote references, all these methods operate on the proxy object.

For getClass, this makes the synthesized proxy class visible, instead of returning the real class of the remote object. For the wait and notify operations, there is no synchronization between the local proxy and the remote object.

Today, the Java distributed object model lacks services. The only available service is a simple name server implemented in class java.rmi.Naming. (Naming is an interesting class: it is a final class with only static methods.) It merely supports binding, unbinding, and look-up of remote object references based on URLs. It is also possible to list all URL–reference pairs registered on a particular host and port.

15.3.4 Java native interface

The Java native interface (JNI) specifies, for each platform, the native calling conventions when interfacing to native code outside the Java virtual machine. JNI also specifies how such external code can access Java objects for which references were passed. This includes the possibility of invoking Java methods. JNI does not specify a binary object model for Java, that is it does not specify how fields are accessed or methods are invoked within a particular Java virtual machine. Interoperation between Java virtual machines on the same platform remains an unresolved issue, as does interfacing with services such as just-in-time compilers. JNI allows native methods to:

- create, inspect, and update Java objects;
- call Java methods;
- catch and throw exceptions;
- load classes and obtain class information;
- perform runtime type checking.

The actual layout of objects is not exposed to native code. Instead, all access is through so-called JNI *interface pointers* that use a runtime structure identical to that of COM (Figure 15.5).

Despite the superficial closeness to COM, JNI is different and not automatically compatible with COM. A JNI interface pointer is used only to refer to a thread-specific context and does *not* correspond to an individual Java object. The

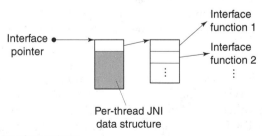

Figure 15.5   JNI interface pointer.

JNI interface does not include standard COM functions QueryInterface, AddRef, or Release. If these are added, the entire JVM could function as one COM component object. A native method is called with a JNI interface pointer as its first argument. Other arguments, including Java object references, are passed directly, but all access to Java objects is through functions provided by the JNI interface pointer.

For the Java garbage collector to work, the JVM keeps track of all references handed out to native methods. References are handed out as *local references,* and these are released by the JVM upon return of the native method. Native code can turn a local into a *global reference.* It is the responsibility of the native code to inform the JVM when a global reference is no longer needed.

All access to fields or invocation of methods of Java objects from native methods is performed using one of several accessor functions available through the JNI interface pointer. Below are two sample JNI functions that show how to invoke a Java object's method, using C++ notation:

```
JNIEnv *env;   // the JNI interface pointer
jmethodID mid =
    env->GetMethodID (classPtr, methodName, methodSignature);
// methodSignature is a string representing the mangled signature
jdouble result =
    env->CallDoubleMethod(obj, mid, args);
// factoring of GetMethodID useful to avoid repeated method lookup
```

JNI specifies how to 'mangle' signatures of methods. In the above example, this is used to resolve overloaded methods when performing a method look-up. As JNI does not reveal how a JVM implements objects or dispatches methods, access is relatively expensive.

15.4   Final notes – the case 'Java interfaces versus Java classes'

Java separates and supports classes and interfaces, where an interface is essentially a fully abstract class. As Java classes can be fully abstract, Java programmers have to choose whether to use an interface or an abstract class. It is interesting to observe the current trend away from the use of classes and toward the increasing use of interfaces. Since interfaces rule out implementation inheritance, this trend also favors object composition and message-forwarding techniques. A few examples of this ongoing trend are described below.

Whereas the non-distributed Java object model supports classes and interfaces, the distributed Java object model of JDK 1.1 restricts remote access to interfaces. In other words, where distribution is used or planned for, direct use of classes is not advisable and all access should be through interfaces.

JavaBeans still allows classes to surface on bean boundaries. Even implementation inheritance across bean boundaries is commonly used, although usually to inherit from base libraries, not from other beans. However, the JavaBeans specification (version 1.00-A) recommends not using the Java type test and guard operators (instanceof and checked narrowing cast). Instead, programmers should use the methods isInstanceOf and getInstanceOf in class java.beans.Beans. The intention is to provide a hook for post-1.00 beans that can be represented to the outside by more than one object, similar to the QueryInterface mechanism in COM.

Finally, the Java AWT event model has been changed from an inheritance-based solution in JDK 1.0 to a 'delegation-based' (really a forwarding-based) solution in JDK 1.1. In addition to the resulting advantages and increased flexibility, it was admitted that the 1.0 approach led to undue complexity and was a source of subtle errors.

The tension between interfaces and classes is clearly showing its first marks; the further development promises to be interesting. Indeed, JavaSoft recently started an effort, code named 'Glasgow,' to generalize JavaBeans. Besides drag and drop and other user-interface enhancements, this specification is supposed to support object composition based on containment and aggregation!

CHAPTER SIXTEEN

More customs than customers?

In addition to the approaches covered in some detail in the preceding chapters, there is at least one proprietary approach from each major company holding a stake in the computing game. Most have given in to some degree and promise compatibility with CORBA, COM, Java, or any combination thereof. However, the compatibility ends where the competitive edge of the company begins. This is only natural and part of the industry's normal evolution. In this chapter, some of these approaches are described, briefly and non-exhaustively.

16.1   Texas Instruments Composer

One of the longest established software vendors concentrating on enterprise applications in client–server environments is Texas Instruments. The TI Composer is a well-established approach to the component-based construction of such large applications. However, Composer largely rests on components specific to Composer and thus defines its own market. This is not surprising, as Composer has been around for a while. Interesting 'connectors' exist to interface Composer-built applications to other systems. For example, a connector is offered that connects Composer components to the SAP R/3 system.

The Composer notion of 'component' is relatively loose, ranging from whitebox procedural structures to application templates. Composition of components using Composer is carried out strictly at construction time. The approach relies heavily on source generation and adaptation. The deployed application is distributed across machines, but essentially is one application rather than a dynamic set of components. Connectors can be used to split such applications into separate systems, just as if these systems were constructed using non-Composer methods. Such systems would then correspond more closely to the notion of components as introduced in this book.

16.2 | Netscape ONE

Netscape's open network environment (ONE) is an amalgam of established technologies (Netscape, 1996). In particular, the central technologies that Netscape ONE rests on are:

- HTML, the Web's hypertext markup language, is seen as the universal description language for portable 'desktops,' or *webtops*. The vision is that all applications will eventually execute within an HTML-described outer shell.

- Java and JavaScript. JavaScript has been developed by Netscape and was originally called LiveScript. As a language, it is only superficially related to Java. The main integrating aspect is that JavaScript code can call applet methods. The reverse does not hold, although LiveConnect (see below) can be used to interconnect objects. In general, quite a 'zoo' of languages and approaches is used to target Web clients and servers, including JavaScript, Java, CGI scripting languages such as Perl, and so on.

- Netscape's Internet foundation classes (IFCs), Java classes for network-oriented programming, and a Java- and platform-independent object model, called LiveConnect. IFC and LiveConnect compete with many of the more recent developments introduced with Java 1.1. For example, LiveConnect defines a Java runtime interface (JRI) that partially collides with the new Java native interface (JNI) developed by Sun. Object persistence, localization, and controls are further areas of competition.

- The Internet inter-ORB protocol (IIOP) – a text-based protocol to support interoperation of ORBs that adhere to the OMG CORBA 2.0 standard. By making IIOP part of every Netscape browser or server, this part of the CORBA standard could quickly gain importance. LiveConnect uses IIOP to connect Netscape clients and browsers across intranets and the Internet, but it could also be used to connect to other CORBA ORBs.

- A number of transport and application-specific protocols, such as HTTP (hypertext transport protocol), NNTP (network news transport protocol), SMTP (simple mail transport protocol), or POP3 (post office protocol, version 3).

- A set of security services, including Netscape's own SSL 3.0 (secure sockets layer) protocol and X.509v3 certificates.

Some of these pieces are technically suboptimal and the overall integration requires some 'glue.' However, all the mentioned parts exist, and most are already proven in practice – IIOP is one of the exceptions. For example, whereas the CORBA security service has been standardized only recently and is still lacking commercial implementations, Netscape's secure session layer has been on the market for about two years.

Netscape keeps its clients (browsers) and servers open for extensions beyond those that fit its Java-based component architecture. For this purpose, *plug-in* modules can be installed and integrated into a client or server. Plug-ins are necessary to make platform-specific facilities available to regular components operating on top of Netscape ONE. The need for plug-ins reveals a weakness of Java: Java is not usable as a system programming language. The best that Java can offer are native interfaces; Java code can invoke lower-level code, but Java cannot be used to implement this lower-level code itself.

Obviously, plug-in installation requires a significantly larger degree of trust than execution of an unsigned Java applet. In principle, plug-ins should be 'signed' components, that is cryptographically protected against tampering and marked with a tamperproof sign of origin. They demand the same level of trust as regular applications do.

16.3   IBM Visual Age and ComponentBroker

IBM provides a number of development environments under the collective Visual Age banner, including support for Basic, COBOL, C++, RPG, Smalltalk, and Java. Initially, these environments shared little more than their name, but increasingly there is support for a common object model based on CORBA/IIOP. Already, there is a market for Visual Age-based components.

Announced in May 1997, IBM is now offering ComponentBroker, a new approach to packaging existing software into components and supporting simple set-up of connections between such components. In its announcement it states that an 'estimated 70 percent of all code written today consists of interfaces, protocols and other procedures to establish linkage among various systems.' ComponentBroker is based on OMG standards to enable connectivity based on standard interfaces. In addition, ComponentBroker provides a system-wide management facility to control aspects such as security, adequate resourcing to satisfy demands, and proximity of location to improve performance.

ComponentBroker consists of the CBToolkit and the CBConnector. The toolkit facilitates development of components whereas the connector enables connection and management of components. The ComponentBroker programming model is to separate business objects from client views. Business objects encapsulate functionality according to business functions. Client views are visual objects. Each business object can be presented by one or more client views to users.

The Object Builder, part of the CBToolkit, generates source code skeletons for business 'objects,' based on OMG IDL and further specifications, targeting Java, C++, Smalltalk, or Object Cobol. Client views can also be generated to use ActiveX interfaces and live within ActiveX containers. The CBConnector Managed Object Framework is provided so that new classes can inherit all standard management interfaces and functionality. Services covered via this framework are: life cycle, externalization, naming, security, event, persistence, concurrency, and transaction services. A CB-specific service, the identity service, allows objects to be uniquely identified based on references relative to managed CBConnector domains.

The CBConnector application adapter framework can be used to create components that wrap existing applications and make them available to ComponentBroker-based solutions. An integrated transaction monitor concentrates and dispatches high volumes of requests. Clients are dynamically associated with their applications, supporting distribution across resources, scalability, and high availability.

CHAPTER SEVENTEEN

Strategic comparison

Given the abundance of technical detail that characterizes each of the approaches discussed so far, what are the *significant* differences and what are the *essential* shared attributes? What are the *strategic* consequences?

17.1 Shared attributes

Obviously, the shared attributes of the approaches discussed cannot help to make decisions as to which approach to follow. However, the rich sharing of attributes swing the decision in favor of the use of component software technology at all, whatever the concrete approach is. Understanding the shared attributes also helps to prevent fruitless arguments for minor points that are simply misunderstood as major differences.

All approaches rely on late binding mechanisms, encapsulation, and dynamic polymorphism (also called inclusion polymorphism or subtyping). All approaches support interface inheritance, although in the case of COM this is almost irrelevant. (COM's source of polymorphism is the interface class separation and the support of multiple interfaces for each class.) In other words, all approaches rely on some sort of object model.

In addition, there has been strong cross-fertilization over time. All approaches now support:

- compound documents with active embedded objects;
- a component transfer format: Java JAR files, COM structured storage, OpenDoc Bento;
- uniform data transfers, including drag and drop;
- events and event connections or channels, single and multicasting;
- meta-information: introspection, reflection;
- some form of persistence, serialization or externalization.

An often overlooked development is that the non-COM approaches slowly converge to support also what COM always had: component objects that can present themselves to their clients through multiple distinct objects. Doing so opens up the possibilities of dynamic configuration. This has now been acknowledged. OpenDoc defines the concept of extensions – separate objects of registered types that are associated with an OpenDoc part (a Live Object). CORBA has nothing similar to offer, although an approach similar to that of OpenDoc could be introduced. JavaBeans introduces a library indirection, java.beans.Beans, to replace the Java language's type tests (instanceof) and guards (checked casts). By doing so, future beans could present themselves to clients as a set of Java objects, rather than just a single object.

17.2 Differences

Once the decision to utilize software components has been taken, the next step is to choose an approach. Alternatively, based on the wide spectrum of shared attributes of many approaches, it can be useful to follow a small number of different approaches simultaneously. Proponents and third parties are likely to provide bridging solutions between the major approaches in particular. There are a number of recent examples in this direction. IONA's Orbix/Desktop for Windows is a CORBA/COM integration tool (IONA, 1996). IONA's Orbix/Web is an ORB in Java that can be downloaded by a Java applet. Finally, JavaSoft's ActiveX bridge allows JavaBeans instances to be embedded into ActiveX containers. Says IONA's chief technology officer, Annrai O'Toole:

> 'Our motto is incompatibility is business – it's a huge opportunity for us.'

Here is a (non-exhaustive) list of significant differences between the approaches:

- *Binary interfacing standard per platform*. A binary standard for component interaction *is* the heart of COM. Java, with JDK 1.1, defines the Java native interface (JNI), the design of which is based on COM, but which is quite Java specific. In particular, it is designed to create room for modern garbage collectors. CORBA still does not define binary standards. Binary standards are required by *Direct-to-** compilers that map constructs of a specific language directly to binary interfaces.
- *Source-level standards for compatibility and portability*. CORBA is particularly strong in standardizing language bindings that ensure source code compatibility across ORB implementations. Its position is strengthened by the large number of standardized service interfaces. The current practice of accessing ORB-specific functions on the object server side reduces the portability of CORBA-based servers. For Java, the agreement on the Java language specification solves the problem as long as no other languages are used to target the Java platform. Standardization of language bindings then becomes an issue. The Java libraries are already facing fragmentation, with JavaSoft and Microsoft offering competing services. COM does not have any concept of source-level standards or

standard language bindings. The COM interface market is also not standardized beyond Microsoft's *de facto* standards.

▪ *Grown versus forged standards.* COM, CORBA, and Java standards (in that order) have had ever shorter periods of evolution before forging 'standards'. Both COM (with OLE 1) and CORBA (1.2) have already gone through substantial revisions – with no true backwards compatibility. COM/OLE/ActiveX has many redundant mechanisms, for example outgoing interfaces and connectable objects (but also change notification interfaces, also known as advice interfaces) and dispatch interfaces (but also verb interfaces and, new in ActiveX, command target interfaces). A consequence of the varying lifetimes of the approaches is the difference in product variety on the markets today: there are several thousand ActiveX objects on the market, but there were only a few dozen Live Objects before dissolution of CI Labs, and there are only a few dozen beans.

▪ *Memory management, life cycles, and garbage collection.* CORBA today does not offer a general solution to the global memory management problem in a distributed object system. COM and DCOM rely on reference counting from the ground up, and so do OpenDoc and Apple's version of SOM – this works if every component plays by the rules. Java relies totally on garbage collection, and with the introduction of the Java remote method invocation (RMI) service in JDK 1.1 Java now also defines a distributed object model and supports distributed garbage collection.

▪ *Concepts for evolution and versioning.* COM insists on freezing interfaces and their specifications once they have been published together with their interface ID. This solves both the version and the migration problem. CORBA does not directly address this issue, but supports the weak notion of major and minor version numbers – SOM mechanisms that enhance binary compatibility are under consideration. The CORBA solution has problems because it allows a reference to an object of some version to be passed on to another object that expects an object of a different version: version checking is performed only at initial object creation time. Java addresses versioning only on the level of binary compatibility, for which a painstaking list of rules is given. It would seem that some of these rules go too far. For example, changing a constant's value from one release to another has no effect on precompiled clients, which simply stick to the old value. Instead of declaring such a client as broken when interfacing to the new version, the old client remains usable, although it is likely to malfunction. Component Pascal implementations use a per-interface fingerprinting algorithm to maintain compatibility on a fine granularity (Crelier, 1994).

▪ *Concept of categories.* Categories in COM are often overlooked – they are new and seem harmless but in fact introduce the concept of contractual binding to specifications encompassing any number of interfaces. A component can belong to any number of categories and a framework or other component can use category membership as a high-level assertion; neither Java nor CORBA has anything like it.

■ *Availability of industrial-strength implementations and applications*. Here, all approaches have their home fields. COM is strongest on the traditional desktop and Java on general Web clients (ActiveX on Windows Web clients). CORBA and now DCOM dominate servers, but Java is catching up. CORBA is strongest for traditional enterprise computing.

■ *Development environments*. COM is supported by a wide range of strong development environments. Environments for Java are still maturing. Environments for CORBA are entirely underdeveloped.

■ *Services*. CORBA now has a full set of standardized services; however, most of these still lack commercial implementations. COM has recently been supplemented by a number of key services, including a transaction server. Java services have been promised but so far are neither standardized nor available.

17.3 Consequences for infrastructure vendors

One of the most fundamental differences among the three main approaches considered here (OMA, COM, Java) is the degree of freedom they leave to *implementers of the approach*. To understand what is possible, it is useful to look at what exactly is fixed by an approach.

All three approaches define an object model – and do so in different ways. OMG also defines language bindings, the OMG IDL, sets of standard interfaces in IDL, and interoperability protocols (IIOP in particular). COM defines binary calling conventions and binary interface definitions of a set of standard interfaces; the COM IDL is defined *de facto*, as explained below. Java defines standard interfaces specified in the Java language. Additionally, Java defines the load file format, including all available meta-information, in class files and, since 1.1, Java archive (JAR) files. Finally, Java defines the stream format of serialized objects, that is objects externalized automatically using a standard strategy.

What are the consequences of such subtle differences? They mainly govern the number of variants that need to be implemented to support the opened spectrum. The OMA does not define a binary standard. Hence, it is necessary for an ORB vendor to provide language binding tools for each supported language. For COM, language implementations, including COM bindings, can be provided by independent vendors, as COM defines a binary standard. COM still offers significant leeway for different COM implementations: COM library, type libraries, proxy and stub implementation and generation (including DCOM), and the implementation of standard services. Finally, Java merely requires one class file compiler per language targeting the Java class-file format, independent of platforms.

A simple analysis shows that the above decisions work best for Java, second best for COM, and worst for OMA. Assume that there are L languages and P platforms to be supported. Ideally, for each language and each platform it should be possible to have multiple vendors.

With Java, each language vendor merely implements mappings to class files. With an average of VL vendors per language, $L*VL$ language implementations are created. For each platform, the native Java services have to be provided, possibly including a just-in-time compiler. This leads to $P*VP$ implementations, where VP is the average number of Java implementation vendors for each platform. With JDK 1.1, the JNI has been standardized. It reduces the burden on platform-specific developments by defining a single standard binary interface for each platform. This interface allows a particular Java VM implementation to be connected with platform-specific 'native' libraries that are themselves JVM independent. Unfortunately, Microsoft supports an incompatible low-level interface called Java raw interface or JRI.

With COM, each language vendor implements native code generation. With VLP being the average number of language vendors for each language–platform combination, $L*P*VLP$ language implementations are created. For each platform, a COM implementation needs to be devised. With VP average vendors per platform, this leads to $P*VP$ implementations.

With CORBA, each language vendor implements native code generation. As with COM, this leads to $L*P*VLP$ language implementations. For each platform an implementation of ORB and CORBAservices is required. However, CORBA vendors also need to provide language bindings, and these can differ between language vendors, even for the same language. This leads to $L*P*VPL$ CORBA implementations that differ at least in their language bindings. Here, VPL is the average number of language binding plus ORB vendors per language–vendor–platform combination.

Note that language and CORBA vendors can be distinct and that language vendors are independent. However, CORBA vendors may need to provide different bindings for each language vendor, even for the same language, because there are no fixed calling conventions. In other words, if all CORBA vendors want to support all language vendors, $L*P*VLP*VP$ implementations result.

Note that this is only part of the CORBA spectrum. Most ORB vendors deliver object adapters that go well beyond the common standard basic object adapter (BOA). Object servers therefore depend on the object adapter on which they built. Switching from one ORB to another is thus an option only at the client end.

What is wrong with *potentially* large numbers of offerings, as predicted for CORBA? The market becomes fragmented and thus the spectrum of options actually available is likely to be small. For example, picking a language that is not supported on all ORBs on all platforms restricts the options that a project would otherwise have. To support a language universally in the CORBA case, $P*VP$ bindings are required. It is not likely that this investment will be made for a large number of languages. For example, there are several direct-to-SOM compilers on the market that bind directly to SOM, avoiding the indirection of the OMG IDL. The effort required for such a direct-to-ORB compiler is significant. It is likely that such support will not be available for most ORBs. At the other extreme, for the Java approach the support of additional languages is cheap. Only one implementation per language is required to guarantee universal availability of that language, provided that there is at least one Java implementation for each platform.

A possible argument against the above line of reasoning would be to claim that the mentioned VP will be small. Assume that there is only one service vendor per platform, that is VP=1. For COM, this is a likely scenario and leads to P service implementations; the number of language implementations is unaffected and remains L*P*VLP. For CORBA, even today, the number of competing ORB vendors is quite large on the more popular platforms. The assumption is therefore less realistic. Nevertheless, the assumption does not help. L*P*VPL service implementations are still required. However, VPL is now likely to become *larger* as the market share of the single CORBA vendor on a platform allows for the support of more languages and language vendors.

The above becomes more concrete by substituting realistic numbers. There are around 10 important platforms and around 10 important languages. The Java model today supports, besides Java and after just two years on the market, languages such as Ada 95 (Intermetrics, 1997) or REXX (IBM, 1997). This is in spite of the aim of the Java model to be a single-language approach. The Java model also already covers all major platforms. The COM model today supports all major languages, including Java, but also C++, Component Pascal, Object Pascal, Visual Basic, Object Cobol, ML, and so on. It also covers most major platforms (via recent DCOM ports).

CORBA implementations are available for almost all platforms. Also, for many platforms, there is a choice between several ORB vendors. However, there is a tendency to support only a small number of languages. Often, C++ is the only language supported. Smalltalk used to be second choice but is rapidly losing support. Java is one of the candidates to fill this gap, and a Java OMG IDL mapping is about to be finalized; however, few ORB vendors currently support Java bindings. (IONA's Orbix/Web is interesting in that it implements a minimal ORB in Java that travels with applets and uses IIOP to interact with other ORBs.) The number of languages available for a given ORB is usually small, despite the availability of OMG IDL mappings for several languages. Today there is only one language available on all ORBs across all platforms: C++. The above analysis makes this outcome plausible and, in hindsight, quite predictable.

In summary, if too many dimensions are coupled to support the widest variety of solutions, most solutions will be limited to a small niche market. This will result in pruning, and variety is first hurt where it is least welcome: in the spectrum of language–platform combinations supported *uniformly*. This can be summarized succinctly as:

■ Maximizing the number of *possible* combinatorial variations minimizes the number of *available* variations.

In other words, where too much is possible, islands of mutual competition and partial incompatibility result and *a component market becomes highly unlikely*.

Thus, CORBA fails to deliver on one of its major promises: support of a wide variety of *available* (not just possible) solutions. CORBA was meant to be platform, ORB vendor, and language independent. Hence, it does not define sufficiently strong low-level integration standards that allow for efficient language-independent service and service-independent language implementations. Java seems to be the clear and obvious winner. However, there is one drawback. The Java class file format is tightly coupled to the language Java. Translation of other languages is suboptimal (Ada 95, Component Pascal) or impossible (C++). (The Java position, although not that of the Java language, might improve further if Java class files and Java VM are carefully generalized, for example in ways that efficiently support concepts such as in-line allocated objects, reference parameters, and overflow checks.) COM sits in the comfortable middle. It can support a very wide variety of languages at close to optimal efficiency.

The breakthrough for CORBA is still possible, *if* a strong enough vendor fills the gap left by OMG and defines a *de facto* binary standard on all relevant platforms. One possible candidate at the time of writing is Netscape, which is planning to introduce Visigenic's Visibroker ORB into its Web server and Communicator browser products. However, supporting a variety of languages would still take time, especially as users of these languages have to retarget their applications first.

In the meantime, cross-language solutions can be built using the CORBA C binding and the fact that all reasonable language implementations today can call C functions. Using C as a lingua franca has substantial disadvantages however. As C does not have a notion of objects, it offers a very low-level bridge between a safe object-oriented language and the safe and object-oriented CORBA world. Note that C++ cannot be used as the lingua franca because platforms do not define C++ calling conventions and thus bindings to third languages rarely exist. Note also that the use of the CORBA C binding is hampered because a number of commercial ORBs, including Orbix, do not support the C binding.

The strongest point in favor for COM, besides the compromise described above, is its migration path for old application code. COM is simple enough to support effective wrapping of legacy code into COM components. For example, COM enabled the migration of the originally monolithic Microsoft Office applications to the still coarse-grained collection of components that they are today (in Office 97). Wrappers for CORBA are possible, but are more involved and are ORB specific in a subtle and complicated way (for example Wallace and Wallnau, 1996). Wrappers for Java are possible, although in some cases the JNI may prove to be in the way of efficient wrappers.

17.4   Consequences for component vendors

Another interesting difference is the degree of freedom left to an implementer of a component targeting one of the approaches. Designers have to face a very large

number of decisions. Reducing the degrees of freedom of possible designs is a
'good thing,' as long as it does not affect feasibility. To cite Orfali *et al.* (1996,
p.522):

> 'Only the consumer gets freedom of choice; designers need freedom
> from choice.'

This citation is taken from an argument on why the more restrictive constraints of
OpenDoc, as compared with OLE, speak in favor of CORBA and against COM.
It is ironic that their argument *does* speak for particular aspects of OpenDoc but
also speaks *against* the generality of CORBA.

Most current approaches largely follow what could be called the 'toolkit philosophy,' as compared with one that defines frameworks or even system architectures.
Despite their names, CORBA (common object request broker architecture) and
OMA (object management architecture) are *not* architectures from the component vendor's point of view. CORBA is an architecture from the ORB implementer's point of view. The OMA does not go beyond the granularity of objects.
It could be seen as a global architecture on the level of ants.

One of the few component frameworks is OpenDoc. It defines an architecture
from the component vendor's point of view. Another one is the BlackBox component framework; this was also, from the beginning, designed as a component framework and thus as an architecture for component vendors to target.

Some of the cornerstones of a component architecture include regulation of
the interaction with other components, definition of the roles of components,
and standardization of user interface aspects for assembly and use. Component
frameworks are a partial answer; OpenDoc and BlackBox are first examples in
this direction. Component frameworks are focused architectures whereas component system architectures consider interaction across frameworks. By analogy, consider the architecture of a single building compared with that of a master-planned
city. Today, no component system architecture in this sense exists. (For a detailed
discussion of component architectures and frameworks see Part Four.)

CHAPTER EIGHTEEN

Efforts on domain standards

The importance of domain-specific standards has been recognized and several efforts aim at such standards.

18.1 OMG Domain Technology Committee

This committee of the OMG organizes 'domain task forces' to oversee the standardization of domain specific interfaces. Currently, active task forces are focusing on:

- *business objects* – common business object, business object facility, CORBAtransport;
- *manufacturing* – high-level requirements, product data management enablers;
- *electronic commerce* – electronic payment facility, asset and content management, enabling technologies and services;
- *telecommunications* – control and management of audio/video streams, topology, notification, intelligent networking with CORBA;
- *financial* – currency, insurance;
- *medical* – patient identification services, healthcare lexicon service.

18.2 OMG BOMSIG

Probably the oldest group is OMG's Business Object Model Special Interest Group (BOMSIG). Business objects, as defined by BOMSIG, have the characteristic property of directly representing entities that as such make sense in a certain business process. Entities can be people, goods, concepts, places, organizations, and so on. A business object populates a conceptual level that directly matches that of people working in its target business domain. As units of manipulation, combination, and communication, they therefore individually make sense to involved staff.

Business objects are still largely on the drawing board. The few systems that truly aim at this level so far form relatively small islands. One such system, the New World Infrastructure (Newi) by Integrated Objects has been on the market since 1994. Newi objects directly aim to be business objects, but compatibility

259

between Newi objects depends on the availability of the Newi infrastructure. Interoperation with other infrastructures is an immediate concern. In a sense, Newi objects are not very different from ActiveX Controls, JavaBeans, OpenDoc Live Objects, or BlackBox Views. In all cases, the idea is that the object can be presented to the user directly. Presentation in the form of an icon is the minimum; custom user interaction is the goal.

In all these examples, objects surface and become tangible for regular users. Allowing users to manipulate directly and compose such objects certainly has great potential. However, there is good reason to remain suspicious. Where are the domain-specific aspects? There is indeed fairly little there. In all cases all that is provided is an infrastructure that *could* be used to support domain-specific tasks.

The point, however, is missed. For business objects to collaborate in a way that truly solves domain-specific problems, these objects not only need to be domain specific, but also need to follow domain-specific standards for interaction. Where these specifications are fully provided by an individual organization, the main gain is that of using a powerful infrastructure, rather than creating component markets.

Only where successful component-based solutions are opened, relevant specifications are published, and *de facto* standardization is aimed for, will specialized component vendors be able to benefit.

18.3   Java domain standard efforts

Application programmer interfaces (APIs) are under development to support 'pure' Java solutions in specific domains. A first example that reached the stage of alpha releases in mid-1997 was the Java electronic commerce framework (JEFC) (JavaSoft, 1997). JEFC addresses the issues of secure electronic commerce, including support for smartcard systems. The current alpha release (0.6) already consists of nine commerce-specific and two security-related packages; together they introduce roughly 100 classes and 50 interfaces.

Further domain-specific Java frameworks are under development as part of IBM's San Francisco project (http://www.ibm.com/Java/SanFrancisco). San Francisco aims at the creation of a large number of *common business objects* that can be shared across many domains. On top of the common business object layer sits a layer supporting *core business processes*. This layer is populated by application frameworks that are specific to certain types of applications, such as general ledger or warehouse management. The topmost layer finally contains the individual applications. It is interesting to note that, in the context of San Francisco, the concept of components is reduced to class reuse. Component frameworks, as opposed to application frameworks, are not considered.

18.4   OLE for process control

An interesting example of domain-specific aspects that is completely off the track of desktop solutions comes from industrial automation. An effort to create signaling standards for process control led to COM-based standards called OLE for process control (OPC). In essence, OPC defines COM interfaces for classes of device drivers.

One of the first products directly targeting such a market has recently been announced: the realtime operating system Portos by Oberon microsystems (1997a). Portos supports a programming model that is very different from that found in traditional operating system kernels. The model is specifically designed to grant industrial engineers with backgrounds in mechanical or electrical engineering (rather than programmers) intuitive access. Portos and its cross-platform development environment Denia are covered in more detail in Chapter 21.

18.5 Industry associations

According to an IDC white paper (Steel, 1996), two kinds of industry associations are forming to establish relevant component standards. The first are groupings of information technology industry. The second are trade associations. A third, not mentioned in the white paper, could be general user associations.

18.5.1 Information technology industry groupings

Groupings of IT vendors have a simple interest in establishing interoperability standards. The members of the group can then believably position their products as pieces of a larger plan. As long as group members claim their own ground, they can join forces against their common competition. Some groupings are so large that they merely serve to push the envelope – examples are the OMG or the Open Group. The more relevant examples in the category of vendor groupings are much smaller in terms of their membership, and indeed have the primary purpose of increased competitiveness.

An example in this latter category is the Open Applications Group (OAG), founded in early 1995 and today comprising 17 corporate and five associate members, including IBM Manufacturing Solutions, NEW, Oracle, SAP, Siemens Nixdorf, and Texas Instruments. The OAG coordinates the standardization of interfaces for commercial domains and aims at the integration of business objects. To this end, the OAG has created their business object document (BOD) architecture. The aim is to enable the bridging of a very broad range of 'wiring' standards, including CORBA and COM, but also older standards such as Edifact. Thus, the BOD defines requests and replies in terms of formatted documents. This approach is relatively heavyweight, but also fairly robust. To date, the OAG has approved 82 interfaces (APIs) in areas such as general ledger, accounts payable, accounts receivable, purchasing, sales order management, and plant data collection. The OAG Web site covers all OAG standards. An example of using BODs to post a journal in a general ledger context can be found at http://www.oag.org/specs/Pndx_b.htm.

18.5.2 Trade associations

Users of information technology in a certain industry sector may form trade associations pushing for vertical standards that broaden the market for high-quality offerings that suit their needs. Again, the motive is obvious: the members of the association collectively gain strength against their competition.

Trade associations may control the quality of components and validate their standard compliance. Component vendors gain a competitive advantage where a trade association gave its approval.

18.5.3 User associations

An association formed by component users can create a forum to exchange know-how and to have a collective voice that will be heard by component vendors. In contrast to trade associations, user associations aim for very large memberships: mostly individuals or small organizations. It is conceivable that associations such as the ACM or the IEEE Computer Society could form branches that would represent the interests of component users in particular domains.

CHAPTER NINETEEN

Open problems

As has to be expected with a technology as young as that of component software, there are still a number of open problems. In this chapter, some of the more pressing problems are briefly reviewed.

19.1 Domain standards

The need to create working and accepted domain-specific standards was emphasized in the last chapter. Plumbing and wiring are not enough, but forging domain standards is also not a good answer. The OMG 'fast-track' mechanism to approve domain standards promises a normal turnaround of just six months. OMG insists that such proposals rest on proven technology. However, in a field in which even the wiring infrastructure barely exists, how can anyone claim to have proven domain-specific technology? Proposals must necessarily be based on experience with other and older technology.

It is of vital importance not to rush into standards and risk credibility. There is a need for a time of fierce competition and evolution of approaches before any approach can qualify for standardization. Processes that encourage independent exploration of markets and domains but also encourage submission of proposals for standardization later would be ideal. However, this is far from being realistic. Why would an organization that 'got it right' and has established its market position want to release crucial information?

The idea is that pushing for domain standards based on established but proprietary technology promises to expand the target market. The reason is that more customers will be willing to build on standards than on proprietary solutions. The proponent of a new standard is in a strong position based on products that already comply with the proposed standard. The relative market volume of the proponent is thus expected to grow, assuming that the proponent can defend its leading edge.

Unfortunately, things are not that easy. Initial competition for the best approach – and thus the absence of a single standard – benefits quick product evolution. Where incompatible standardization proposals emerge, the threat of 'standards by compromise' follows. This entire phenomenon is only too well known in traditional industries that lived with standards for a long time. Such traditional industries converge on standards *slowly* and often in painful shake-out processes. There is no fast track to working standards!

19.2 Rethinking the foundations of software engineering

From a software engineering point of view, component technology presents a number of novel challenges that question the applicability of many proven approaches. The key problem is the notion of independent extensibility that is so characteristic of any component-based system (Szyperski, 1996; see also Chapter 6). Late integration of components from independent sources eliminates the confidence usually drawn from integration testing in a traditional software engineering model. Also, extensibility needs to be 'architected' and designed into a system and all its parts – or the resulting system will not be extensible: components will not be independently producible and deployable.

To summarize, all facets of software engineering and the entire underlying approach need to be rethought. Throwing in large numbers of different technologies, each with even larger numbers of alternative ways of tackling a problem, is not helpful. There is an urgent need to unify methodologies, guiding architectures, and working examples. All this will take time to mature; investment into component technology at this time still needs to be seen as strategic rather than tactical.

19.3 But is it object oriented?

Object orientation has been 'evangelized' to such a degree over the past decade that for some it has become a synonym for quality rather than being a means to an end. Object oriented usually means that everything is partitioned into objects, each of which encapsulates state and behavior. Objects are instances of classes, which themselves are related by (traditional) inheritance. Finally, objects can be used in polymorphic contexts (for example Wegner, 1987). Wars of bitter arguments are fought over these requirements. It is interesting to subject the main approaches in the component field to these criteria.

Before looking at the various approaches, it is important to recall that Java adds a language model to its object model. In contrast, COM and CORBA are both language neutral and thus simply cannot impose certain restrictions required to make something 'object oriented' in the genuine programming languages sense.

The Java approach is quite clearly object oriented – with the defensible exception of some basic types, everything is done with objects. Objects are instances of classes. Classes can inherit implementation and interfaces. Polymorphism is introduced by subtype compatibility of both subclasses and 'subinterfaces.' Classes (not objects) are the units of encapsulation, although packages add a second level. The distribution technology (remote method invocation) makes object location transparent and allows for the free passing of Java's object references across process and processor boundaries. Object references in Java are not of a persistent nature, but persistence could be supported by a service.

COM bases everything on component objects that are accessible through sets of interface references; object references do not exist. COM objects are instances of classes, but classes are in no inheritance relationship. COM interfaces can be in a single interface inheritance relation, but that is of little importance to COM. Polymorphism is introduced by allowing any number of classes to implement any set of interfaces. Encapsulation is addressed by limiting all interactions to object interfaces. Interface references can be transferred freely across process and processor boundaries. References are not of persistent nature and object identity across persistent forms is not a COM concept, but could be supported by a persistence service.

In CORBA, everything seems to be based on objects. Classes correspond to object implementations but are not related by inheritance. Interfaces are related by multiple interface inheritance. This is also the basis for polymorphism in CORBA. Encapsulation is addressed by limiting all interactions to object interfaces.

Basic types are not CORBA objects, but neither are many complex data types such as sequences and structures. All CORBA types, including object references, are collected into a generic type *any*. Fully excluded are 'small' objects, called *serverless* objects, for which the cost of the CORBA model could be prohibitive. CORBA does not make object location fully transparent as it distinguishes between local object references and CORBA object references. The latter are themselves not so small objects and can be converted into string form (and back). Object references and their 'stringified' forms are guaranteed to be of indefinite validity. CORBA object references are too expensive to replace all component-internal references.

To make an object a CORBA object, its class needs to inherit from interface CORBA and the object needs to be registered with the ORB, which returns a fresh object reference. CORBA objects are too expensive to make all objects used within a component CORBA objects. A hidden mechanism to mediate automatically between internal and CORBA references, as available in Java RMI or DCOM, does not exist. OMG IDL does not allow the use of normal object references in operation definitions – only OMG IDL basic types, constructed types, and CORBA object references are allowed. A particular language binding could automatically call ORB services to map an internal reference to a CORBA reference (and back). This is possible as long as the referred object is a CORBA object, that is, registered with the ORB. For SOM, special direct-to-SOM compilers are available that make most ORB interactions transparent to the programmer.

In summary, *none* of the discussed approaches is 'object oriented.' Java comes closest, but does not establish objects as the units of encapsulation. COM and CORBA units of encapsulation are, at best, individual object servers. Neither COM nor CORBA specifies at all how objects located in the same server can interact. CORBA separates internal references, such as those used by Java or C++, from external references: CORBA object references. The actual conversion to and from external references is optimized by some ORBs in the case of local invocations. However, the bipartite nature of the world of references and thus the world of objects cannot be hidden. Both Java and COM exhibit local references and use external references only 'under the hood' (in RMI or DCOM) when marshaling references for remote calls.

It should be noted that it is not very relevant that none of the approaches is 'object oriented.' The important question is: what can these approaches do and not do? All three approaches seem to be able to carry the weight of coarse-grained partitionings, in which individual objects exposed by the approach are relatively large. Both COM and Java can also handle smaller objects efficiently, although it is most likely that only Java programmers will do so. COM naturally asks for clustering of multiple and possibly many non-exposed objects into one COM object. References to the non-exposed objects are of no meaning outside that COM object.

Having multiple non-COM objects within a single COM object is not an efficiency requirement. Clearly, COM is efficient enough to make all objects COM objects. (A COM method invocation on an interface in the same process is as cheap as or slightly cheaper than a C++ method invocation.) Microsoft's J++ takes advantage of this and can make any Java object a COM object. J++ maps Java interfaces to COM interfaces and Java classes to COM classes. As COM does not directly expose classes, Java's implementation inheritance remains banned inside Java. J++ automatically implements QueryInterface and reference counting. Finally, J++ automatically synthesizes class factories and dispatch interfaces with all the argument checking required by COM.

The J++ automation of QueryInterface and reference counting was pioneered by Oberon microsystems' Direct-to-COM compiler (DTC) and their Safer OLE technology, both extensions to the BlackBox component builder. DTC does not impose some of the restrictions of J++, such as ignoring the case of method names. DTC also faithfully models the COM notion of in, out, and inout parameters that cannot be handled by Java.

19.4 Object mobility and mobile agents

An issue not directly addressed by any of these approaches is object mobility. All assume that an object resides in some object server and that all that is passed around are references to that object. For objects providing services, this is a useful assumption. If required, the entire object server can be migrated to another machine, for example, to rebalance load.

However, there is another role that objects can play. An object can simply encapsulate data through a normalizing access interface. Where small amounts of data need to be communicated, it is often preferable to send the object itself rather than a reference. CORBA forces the programmer to transfer such 'small' objects by stripping the object off the data and transferring the data without any encapsulation whatsoever. OMG IDL offers a host of traditional data type constructors for this purpose. COM and Java offer no direct support at all. The so-called uniform data transfer services offered by COM and CORBA are far too heavyweight for transfers of small amounts of data.

What would be needed is an indication that an object itself should be sent, instead of its reference. None of the approaches have direct facilities to do so. Object serialization, as offered by Java, comes close, but it still seems to be too expensive for the frequent exchange of 'small' but encapsulated data objects. A current OMG standardization effort aiming at object transfer by value addresses this concern.

A related issue is mobile 'agents.' In this case, the requirement is not the efficient and lightweight transfer of small objects but the transparent transfer of objects representing agents roaming across a network. Any fixed binding of objects to object servers needs to be avoided in this context unless, of course, the notion of object server is made so lightweight that an entire object server could become an 'agent.'

Java applets seem to be mobile objects. In reality, all that is mobile is the component implementing the applet. JavaBeans are moved around in JAR files. As long as a bean cannot modify the contents of the JAR file from which it was instantiated, the unit of mobility is still just a component, not an object. If a bean could modify the JAR file from which it was instantiated, it would jeopardize other beans instantiated from the same file. To make an applet or a bean a truly mobile object, new mechanisms are needed. Recent research in this direction at IBM Japan goes under the name of 'aglets' (Lange and Chang, 1996) and has been submitted to OMG as a proposed standard for a mobile agent facility.

Here, object serialization can offer an answer, if combined with proper infrastructure for orderly 'beaming' of mobile objects. An object needs to be taken out of its current environment, not just serialized, and implanted into a new environment, probably after security checks. Then it needs to be revived. Parts of the answers have been pioneered at Digital's System Research Center with its work on network objects for Modula-3 (Birrel *et al.*, 1994). At the same center, the approach has been taken further with the Obliq language and system. Obliq addresses critical-safety issues of mobile objects by imposing a *static* scoping rule across sites of activation (Cardelli, 1994).

19.5　Foundations: better contracts for better components

Component software and the widespread use of software components will dramatically increase the demands put on component developers. There are two reasons. First, the technology underlying component software is more complex than that underlying traditional software. Second, the use of third-party components encourages the 'outsourcing' of risk: customers will set much higher standards on bought components than on in-house developments. Some sceptics even predict that there will be no significant component markets before the year 2001 – because of the quality problems (Rösch, 1997).

As quality, and in particular security, are a major concern when using components on the Internet, neither Java nor ActiveX objects has been doing particularly well in today's Web. For example, a study in March 1997 showed that, out of 20 million Web pages, only 30 000 used Java and fewer than 1000 used ActiveX objects (Leach and Moeller, 1997).

However, components can only be of high quality – and customers can only insist on such quality – if the requirements are clearly specified. The specifications of the contracts that bind components thus need to be improved much further. The current best practice of listing interfaces with informal descriptions is by no means enough for a stable component world. Where components already function, this is largely because of a dominating vendor setting *de facto* benchmarks. For example, whatever the OLE specifications may say, an OLE component had better work with Word and Excel.

Experience with Java 1.0 and substantial incompatibilities between different JVMs, but even between different versions of the same JVM, led to a test suite of around 10 000 tests with the 1.1 release. (In the second half of 1996, John Gough and the author held a university course on Java. Students were asked to implement some simple applets, using a system of their choice. The applets handed in frequently worked only on one particular version of one particular Java implementation. Indeed, few 'platform-independent' components are so picky when it comes to platforms they run on.)

Particular points that should be addressed in improved contract specifications are:

- Specification of re-entrance conditions. Sequential and concurrent cases need to be covered differently.
- Specification of self-recursive patterns or, alternatively, abstaining from inheritance and implicit delegation across component boundaries. Of course, explicit re-entrance patterns remain.
- Specification of bounds on execution time and resource needs. Compositions break unexpectedly where parts have unspecified time or resource demands that can be satisfied for each part but not for the whole. The situation becomes very difficult where bounds of the whole are not additively related to bounds of parts.
- Specification of other non-functional properties, as indicated in section 5.2.2.

Current IDLs describe contracts at the 'plumbing' or 'wiring' level. All that is firmly captured is what is required to marshal data properly when communicating across process, processor, or machine architecture boundaries. This is, of course, essential to enable 'wiring' at all. Also, it should not be expected that significant parts of contracts will ever make it into the IDL parts processed by an IDL compiler. Contract specifications, formal or informal, will remain largely for the human programmer. Their precise specification, formal where reasonable, should nevertheless accompany the machine-level interfaces. An explicit and unambiguous link must exist between an interface and its contractual specification.

The COM requirement that a published interface has to remain immutable is grounded in the idea that an interface comes with a specification. Thus, the real requirement is that the specification must stay the same. A COM unique interface ID could thus be seen as linking a specification to an interface. The recent introduction of categories into COM goes one step further. A category identifier links a unique identifier to a specification spanning multiple interfaces of a component, conceptually promising its proper embedding into a larger pattern of interoperation, perhaps a component framework.

In a similar attempt, Java specifications rely more and more on the use of empty interfaces or classes, called *markers*. These are used to specify certain characteristics of a class derived from such a marker interface or class. For example, the interface java.lang.Clonable is empty. It should be 'implemented' by a Java class that supports cloning – but cloning itself is based on the clone method in class java.lang.Object. Another example is java.util.EventListener to mark all classes that 'listen' for events. Both COM's categories and Java's empty interfaces allow for runtime inquiries to check whether a certain component does or does not obey a certain contract.

CORBA finally defines *repository IDs* that associate a unique id with an OMG IDL-specified type. The interoperation standard uses these ids to match entries in interface repositories of independent ORBs. Although repository IDs are very similar to COM IIDs, they are not normally associated with interfaces at interface definition time. Although CORBA 2.0 introduced an IDL pragma to specify the repository ID of an interface, this is rarely used. Instead, repository IDs are usually automatically generated and assigned when registering an interface with an interface repository.

Obviously, this practice has to change for interoperation or interworking to work properly. A second transition is required in coding conventions – all code must refer to interfaces by repository IDs. Otherwise, version control is unsound (Chapter 12). Once these transitions are made, CORBA interfaces and COM interfaces will be much closer and the fundamental concept that meaning is attached to an interface by means of a unique identifier will have gained almost universal acceptance. Note that 'IDL-free' approaches to CORBA programming, such as direct generation of IDL from Java source or direct-to-SOM compilation, will have to follow suit. Unique identifiers will have to be associated with the source code. In the COM world, this is already common practice; examples are Oberon microsystems' Direct-to-COM compiler or Microsoft's J++.

PART FOUR

The next generation

This is the last technical part of this book. Combining the foundations laid in Part Two and the current approaches reviewed in Part Three, this part aims at opening perspectives for future technical development. The examples are naturally not taken from the future, but have been selected for their early adoption of one or another aspect expected to gain importance in the future. The chapters in this part are only weakly linked and can be read in any order. In particular, it is safe to skim over or skip any of the technical details.

Chapter 20 discusses the concept of component architectures. A set of technical definitions and a conceptual framework for component architectures is developed. Chapter 21 covers the important notion of component frameworks and presents three case studies of such frameworks, two targeting visual objects and one industrial automation. Chapter 22 covers a range of component development issues, including methodologies and aspects of programming languages. Chapter 23 briefly discusses the issues of component acquisition and distribution, the problem of finding components, and current attempts at solving this problem. Chapter 24 covers component assembly and Chapter 25 concludes with a discussion of some open problems.

CHAPTER TWENTY

Component architecture

As briefly outlined in Chapter 9, system architecture is the pivotal basis of any large-scale software technology and is of utmost importance for component-based systems. Only where an overall architecture is defined *and maintained* do evolution and maintenance of components and systems find the firm foundation they require. To name just a few of the cornerstones of a component architecture: interaction between components and their environment is regulated, the roles of components are defined, tool interfaces are standardized, and user interface aspects both for end users (where applicable) and for assemblers are regularized.

Where component vendors do not find a clearly established architecture, random architectures arise. For example, component vendors copy the sample implementations provided by infrastructure vendors or early adapters, without a precise understanding of what guided the various implementation decisions. The result is a quick blurring of even the crispest concepts; a component world emerges, full of redundancies, inconsistencies, and idiosyncrasies. Eventual collapse is preprogrammed.

It is not at all clear what a component architecture – better, a component system architecture – should look like. No current approach goes beyond individual component frameworks, as described in the next chapter. This chapter presents an attempt at conceptualizing the important area of component architecture. The driving point is to establish order within chaos. By carefully enabling independent extensibility in key areas of a system, degrees of freedom are introduced that remain for all time, that is for the lifetime of the architecture. Such degrees of freedom limit overall understanding *in principle*.

20.1 The roles of an architecture

People claim to be key or principal architects of one or the other software architecture, but it is usually unclear what that means. While software architecture is still maturing, much can be learnt from the role of architecture and architects in the 'real world.' In any system complex enough to ask for guiding rules for design and implementation, an architecture is needed. An architecture needs to create simultaneously the basis for independence *and* cooperation. Independence of system aspects is required to enable multiple sources of solution parts. Cooperation between these otherwise independent aspects is essential in any non-trivial architecture: the whole is more than the sum of its parts.

Architecture is about a holistic view of a system: often a system yet to be developed. More technically, an architecture defines overall invariants, that is properties that characterize any system built following this particular architecture. An architecture categorizes central resources to enable independence in the presence of competition for resources. Operating systems are a good example. An operating system partially defines the architecture for the overall system resting on it by defining how independent processes compete for resources.

An architecture prescribes proper frameworks for all involved mechanisms, limiting the degrees of freedom to curb variations and enable cooperation. An architecture includes all policy decisions required to enable interoperation across otherwise independent uses of the mechanisms. Policy decisions include the roles of components.

Architectures need to be based on the principal considerations of overall functionality, performance, reliability, and security. Detailed decisions can be left open, but guidance regarding expected levels of functionality and performance is required. For example, an architecture may exactly prescribe some details to ensure performance, reliability, or security. All too commonly aspects of performance, reliability, and security are ignored on architectural levels, emphasizing only functionality. The consequences can be literally fatal, depending on the deployment context. Thus, emphasis of these so-called non-functional aspects has a tradition in safety- or security-critical applications. To view all four aspects as prioritized facets of a whole in *any* software architecture remains an important goal.

20.2 Conceptualization – beyond objects?

At a conceptual level, it is obviously useful to introduce layers, to single out components, and to separate concerns. How much of this needs to 'survive' in a concrete realization of an architecture? More controversially, are granularities beyond objects really needed? Interestingly, it is sometimes claimed that a prime strength of objects is the isomorphism of objects and object relations as they show up in requirements, analysis, design, and implementation (for example Goldberg and Rubin, 1995). This is true either if nothing but objects count in all these phases or if everything that is more than one object can be isolated and represented by just one object. Doing so is largely the main thrust of 'pure' object-oriented approaches.

It is obviously not true that everything *is* just an object. However, it is true that anything that requires a group of objects to interact can be abstracted by designating a representative object that stands for the interacting group. In this context it becomes essential to distinguish between has-a (or contains-a) relations and uses-a relations. The representative object *has* a group of objects, whereas the objects in the group, possibly mediated by the representative, *use* each other. Relations between objects can be modeled as graphs, whereas objects are nodes and a relation introduces directed edges between such nodes. Distinguishing has-a from uses-a allows us to distinguish between inter-graph and intra-graph edges. Consider an externalization service that supports transfer of objects between contexts in time and space. Storing a compound document is an example. Intra-graph edges need to be followed in typical externalization activities. Inter-graph edges are not followed but abstractly maintained as 'links,' where links symbolically represent the target node of a directed edge. As a special case, links can also occur within a graph.

Unless particular care is taken, all objects are potentially in arbitrary uses-a or has-a relations. Arbitrary uses-a relations can introduce cyclic dependencies and threaten organizational structure. Arbitrary has-a relations can even be unsound: the has-a relation must be acyclic. Hierarchical design is the key to mastering complexity. Unless objects are conceptually allowed to contain other objects in their entirety, there is little hope of mastering complexity in a pure object-oriented approach. As soon as hierarchical designs are introduced, the question arises 'how could parts of such hierarchical designs be units of deployment?' It is therefore, and quite paradoxically, non-trivial to introduce the notion of components into object systems. The following section introduces definitions of structures at levels beyond objects (classes).

20.3 Definitions of key terms

The terms defined in this section help to construct an architectural terminology.

- A *component system architecture* consists of a set of platform decisions; a set of component frameworks; and an interoperation design for the component frameworks.

A *platform* is the substrate that allows for installation of components and component frameworks, such that these can be instantiated and activated. A platform can be *concrete* or *virtual*. Concrete platforms provide direct physical support, that is implement their services in hardware. Virtual platforms – also called platform abstractions or platform shields – emulate a platform on top of another, introducing a cost–flexibility trade-off. In practice, all platforms are virtual to some degree, and a sharp distinction is academic. The conceptual distance, or gap, between a virtual platform and its underlying platform generally has a tremendous impact on expected performance. Understanding this distance is thus very important.

- A *component framework* is a dedicated and focused architecture, usually around a few key mechanisms, and a fixed set of policies for mechanisms at the component level.

Component frameworks often implement protocols to connect participating components and enforce some of the policies set by the framework. The policies governing the use of the mechanisms that are used by the framework itself are not necessarily fixed. Instead, they can be left to higher-level architectures.

■ An *interoperation design* for component frameworks comprises the rules of interoperation among all the frameworks joined by the system architecture.

Such a design can be seen as a second-order component framework, with the (first-order) component frameworks as its plug-in (second-order) components. It is quite clearly established by now that this second level is required – a single-component framework for everything is illusory. It is less clear whether a third or even higher level will be needed, but the meta-architecture model hinted at here is scalable, allowing growth. (For a more detailed discussion, see section 20.4.)

■ A *component* is a set of normally simultaneously deployed atomic components.

This distinction between components and atomic components caters for the fact that most atomic components will never be deployed individually, although they could. Instead, most atomic components belong to a family of components and a typical deployment will cover the entire family.

■ An *atomic component* is a module and a set of resources.

Atomic components are the elementary units of deployment, versioning and replacement: although usually deployed in groups, individual deployment is possible. A module is thus an atomic component with no separate resources. (Java packages are *not* modules in this strict sense: the atomic units of deployment in Java are class files. A single package is compiled into many class files – one per public class.) The above technical definitions are in line with the broader definition of components in Chapter 4. In particular, there is room for other technical definitions that nevertheless respect the definition in Chapter 4.

■ A *module* is a set of classes and possibly non-object-oriented constructs, such as procedures or functions.

Obviously, a module may statically require the presence of other modules to function. Hence, a module can only be deployed if all modules that it depends on are also available. The dependency graph must be acyclic, or else a group of modules in a cyclic dependency relation would always require simultaneous deployment, violating the defining property of modules.

■ A *resource* is a 'frozen' collection of typed items.

The resource concept could include code resources to subsume modules; the point is that there are resources besides those generated by a compiler compiling a module or package. In a 'pure objects' approach, resources are externalized immutable objects: immutable because components have no persistent identity – duplicates cannot be distinguished. (Component instances have identity, of course.)

20.4 A tiered component architecture

A fundamental notion of traditional software architectures is that of layers (Chapter 9). Layers and hierarchical decomposition remain very useful in component systems. Each part of a component system, including the components themselves, can be layered; components may be located within particular layers of a larger architecture. To master the complexity of larger component systems, the architecture *itself* needs to be layered. It is important to distinguish clearly between the layers formed by an architecture and those formed by a meta-architecture. The layers formed by a meta-architecture are thus called *tiers*. Multitier client–server applications are an example of tiered architectures. However, the tiers proposed in the following differ from the tiers found in client–server architectures.

A component system architecture, as introduced above, arranges an open set of component frameworks. This is a *second-tier* architecture, in which each of the component frameworks introduces a *first-tier* architecture. It is important to notice the radical difference between tiers and traditional layers. Traditional layers, as seen from the bottom up, are of increasingly abstract and increasingly application-specific nature. In a well-balanced layered system, all layers have their performance and resource implications. In contrast, tiers are of decreasing performance and resource relevance but of increasing structural relevance. Different tiers focus on different degrees of integration, but all are of similar application relevance. Figure 20.1 illustrates the interplay of layers and tiers in a multilayer three-tier architecture. As depicted, higher tiers provide shared lower layers to accept lower tiers – tiers are depicted besides each other, whereas layers sit on top of each other.

Figure 20.2 shows how component instances communicate with each other either directly (for example using COM connectable objects, COM messaging service messages, CORBA events, or JavaBeans events) or indirectly through a component framework that mediates and regulates component interaction. The same choice reoccurs when component framework instances interact; the mediator in this case is a tier three instance. In Figure 20.2, CI stands for component

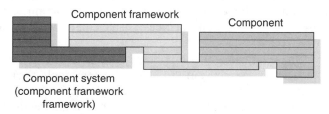

Component framework

Component

Component system
(component framework
framework)

Figure 20.1 A multilayer architecture with three tiers: components, component frameworks, and a component system.

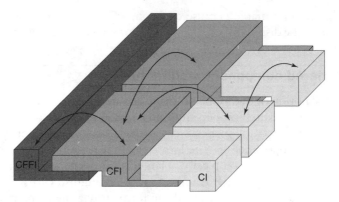

Figure 20.2 Free versus mediated interaction in a tiered architecture.

instance, CFI for component framework instance, and CFFI for component system (or component framework framework) instance.

In a world still largely dominated by monolithic software, not even first-tier architectures are commonplace. Note that objects and class frameworks do *not* form the lowest tier; the tier structure starts with deployable entities: components! Traditional class frameworks merely structure individual components, independent of the placement in a tiered architecture. Objects and class frameworks can be found *within* components; there, depending on the components' complexity, they can readily form their own layering and hierarchies, for example MFC in OLE or ODF in OpenDoc. However, all of a class framework's structure is flattened out when compiling a component. Unlike component frameworks, the line between a class framework and its instantiation is blurred, as the framework is immaterial at runtime, whereas the instances do not exist at compile time. This duality may explain the common confusion of the terms class and object.

As in the preceding section, it can be seen to be clearly established that a single first-tier architecture satisfying all demands of all components and all component applications will never emerge. Obviously, if it did, the tier model would be superfluous. What is more important, it is not even desirable to focus on a single unified first-tier architecture. Lightweight architectures that intentionally focus on one problem rather than trying to be everything for all enable the construction of lightweight components. Such components can be constructed with restrictive assumptions in mind. Lightweight components are most economical if their guiding architecture opens an important degree of extensibility while fixing other decisions.

The ability to have lightweight components is important; it creates richness in a market in which heavier weights can also blossom. For example, the many ActiveX 'heavyweights' become truly useful when combined with the many more lightweight objects, including controls in the original sense. Lightweight components can be made possible in two ways: by using multiple specialized component frameworks or by allowing components to leave unimplemented those features that they do not require. In the first case, the question of interoperation among component frameworks arises, and thus the concept of tiered architectures. In the second case, it becomes very difficult to compose components, as it is never clear which aspects are implemented. Indeed, most systems following the second approach simply do not even have a guiding first-tier architecture: there is no component framework at all.

CHAPTER TWENTY-ONE

Component frameworks

Component frameworks are the most important step to lift component software off the ground. Most current emphasis has been on the construction of individual components and on the basic 'wiring' support of components. It is thus highly unlikely that components developed independently under such conditions are able to cooperate usefully. The primary goal of component technology, independent deployment and assembly of components, is not achieved.

A component framework is a software entity that supports components conforming to certain standards and allows instances of these components to be 'plugged' into the component framework. The component framework establishes environmental conditions for the component instances and regulates the interaction between component instances. Component frameworks can come alone and create an island for certain components, or they can themselves cooperate with other components or component frameworks. It is thus natural to model component frameworks themselves as components. It is also straightforward to postulate higher-order component frameworks that regulate the interaction between component frameworks. For a general discussion, see the preceding chapter on component architecture.

Today, there are only few component frameworks on the market. Higher-order component frameworks seem necessary and unavoidable in the longer run, but certainly do not exist in the market today. This section therefore concentrates on first-order component frameworks, that is two-tier architectures. Two component frameworks for visual components are presented in some detail: OpenDoc and BlackBox. Finally, a non-visual component framework for hard realtime control applications is presented briefly.

21.1 Contributions of a component framework

What precisely is it that a component framework contributes to a system architecture? If its purpose is to collect 'useful' facilities, then it would be no more than a traditional 'toolbox'-style library. Since by construction, a component framework accepts dynamic insertion of component instances at runtime, it also has little in common with class frameworks. In fact, implementation inheritance is not normally used between a component framework and the components it supports.

The key contribution is partial enforcement of architectural principles. By forcing component instances to perform certain tasks through mechanisms under control of the component framework, the component framework can enforce policies. To use a concrete example, a component framework might enforce some ordering on event multicasts and thus exclude entire classes of subtle errors caused by glitches or races that could otherwise occur.

21.2   OpenDoc

21.2.1 Some initial remarks

The following remarks are closely tied to their time of writing (early 1997). However, the conclusions drawn are of more permanent value.

In early 1997, OpenDoc has been discontinued by Apple, and the supporting not-for-profit Component Integration Labs have been dissolved. The Live Objects certification and validation services have been terminated. For several important reasons, this brief discussion of OpenDoc has still been included in this book. First, OpenDoc is one of the few component frameworks (besides BlackBox, described in the next section) developed to product level. So far, neither JavaBeans nor OLE/ActiveX has anything similar to offer. Second, OpenDoc is an interesting design that serves well for a case study. Recently, IBM has frozen OpenDoc and released all source code to the public. Third, OpenDoc is an OMG standard CORBA facility and as such is still supported by a substantial industrial group, although only 'on paper.' The OMG standard and the available OpenDoc implementations differ substantially however. All existing OpenDoc implementations sit on top of IBM's SOM (Chapter 13), whereas the OMG OpenDoc version merely requires CORBA 2.0 and standard CORBA services.

In a sense, OpenDoc hit the market too early: at a time when the full potential of compound documents and visual components was still a well-kept 'secret.' Another unfortunate mistake was the positioning against OLE; whereas OpenDoc is a component framework, OLE merely defines a component environment. OpenDoc could have been (and still could be) a component framework for OLE and other component environments. Currently, every OLE container is its own component framework. The unifying rules are written down as part of the OLE and ActiveX specifications, but are not uniformly enforced. Many OLE and ActiveX developers feel that they are essentially programming extensions of the Microsoft Office applications or of Visual Basic. Nor is ActiveX a component framework or a set of component frameworks, although this is sometimes claimed. With the current development of the Internet Explorer (IE) into *the* generic ActiveX document shell, IE could become the *de facto* ActiveX component framework. Even the Office applications and Visual Basic would have to follow suit and conform to (and possibly use!) the IE component framework.

JavaBeans is currently a rather weak standard, focusing on the 'easy' part, that is on non-container components. This may well change over time, but some sort of reinvention of OpenDoc would then seem unavoidable.

21.2.2 Overview of OpenDoc

OpenDoc revolves around one fundamental concept: that of a *document part*. Every part belongs to a compound document and can itself be a container for other parts. Parts contain native data and, if they are containers, other parts. Every part has an associated *part editor*. Users can specify which part editors they prefer for which kinds of parts. By comparison, OLE does not support the simple configuration of editors for document parts. If an embedded part belongs to Word, it can be converted to another format. However, it is not possible to set a default, saying that this particular user wants all rich text parts to be handled by, say, Corel WordPerfect, as Word stores its parts not as rich text but as Word text. Hence, all text parts currently belonging to Word would first require conversion to rich text format. Then, a class emulation entry in the registry would be required to declare that all rich texts should be handled by WordPerfect.

OpenDoc defines structured files for compound documents, mechanisms for uniform data transfer, and a scripting architecture. All of these are similar in nature to the key technologies described in the chapter on OLE (Chapter 14). OpenDoc's uniform data transfer is quite similar to the services offered by COM uniform data transfer (p. 209). For packaging of parts, SOM is used in the available OpenDoc implementations. Part interfaces are distributed as compiled OMG IDL and accessed through SOM's interface repository. Part implementations are distributed as DLLs and accessed through SOM's implementation repository (or resources on the Mac). Parts always execute in the same process as their container: there is one process per compound document. Inter-process complexities and costs show in OpenDoc only when parts are linked or when parts themselves choose to communicate with other processes. Thus, if a single part is faulty, its entire enclosing document is at risk.

OpenDocs structured filing mechanism is called *Bento* (after Japanese compartmentalized food plates). Bento is generic and older than OpenDoc. In addition to OpenDoc, Bento is used in several other systems by several companies. Unlike COM structured storage, Bento has no concept of transactional modification. Bento does, however, naturally support the concept of document versioning: a Bento file can compactly store a tree of versions of a document. Instead of committing a change to the document, a new version with a delta can be stored. Bento provides a flexible model to store both streamed data and piece-list data. For example, it is possible to update lengthy data, such as a video clip, by updating affected pieces only, avoiding the costly copying of the entire item. Finally, Bento defines a rich architecture for generic annotations of a file's contents; these Bento *properties* can then be used to manipulate Bento files generically.

The support for multiple drafts of a single document has no current counterpart in OLE. It is, of course, possible to implement a container that does nothing but manage a series of drafts as embedded parts. The Office Binder mini-application can be used to do so manually. A drawback compared with Bento-based drafts is the redundant storage of unchanged parts from draft to draft.

The scripting architecture used with OpenDoc is the Open Scripting Architecture derived from Apple's AppleScript. Key concepts are scripting language independence, semantic events, and logical object specifiers. Object specifiers are similar to COM monikers (p. 205). Semantic events are events that have their semantics registered with a central authority and are therefore expected to be uniformly understood by all parts reacting to a particular semantic event. COM simply uses COM interfaces for the same purpose. Independence from a scripting language is achieved by compiling any script into sequences of abstract semantic event sends to targets defined using object specifiers.

With OpenDoc, three levels of scripting are distinguished: simple scripting, tinkering, and recording. Simple scripting drives parts from the outside. *Tinkering* refers to attaching scripts to semantic event handlers of parts. For this, parts have to be 'tinkerable,' that is they have to follow certain rules to allow for the attachment of scripts. If attached, a tinkering script can change the behavior of the tinkered part when receiving the corresponding semantic event. For *recordability*, a part has to funnel all internal events through its external tinkerable event handler. In this way, a generic service can be used to record event sequences and replay them later on the same or a similar part.

21.2.3 Programming a new OpenDoc part

New OpenDoc parts are realized by implementing new part editors that understand at least one, but possibly many, data formats. A part editor has to implement the approximately 60 methods of the ODPart interface – a fully abstract class. These methods support many different aspects of OpenDoc parts. The more important aspects are persistence, rendering and management of frames and facets, interaction with containing and contained parts, linking and event handling, and user interfacing. The user interfacing methods specifically support drag and drop, multilevel undo/redo, and part activation. Besides ODPart, OpenDoc defines almost 70 further classes, most of which are solely instantiated by OpenDoc. OpenDoc offers few concrete classes to subclass from – for most purposes, OpenDoc is a clean component framework.

An OpenDoc part essentially implements a single but large interface (ODPart). As this class has to cater for all possible OpenDoc parts, it introduces substantial mental overhead for the implementer of simple parts. To solve this problem, the OpenDoc development framework (ODF) has been developed. Unlike OpenDoc, the part framework is not a component but a traditional class framework. It defines a semifinished architecture sufficiently well for the majority of OpenDoc parts. Just by subclassing those classes of interest to the developer of a specific OpenDoc part, this framework promises to simplify greatly the task of implementing new OpenDoc parts. At the same time, it does not get in the way of the underlying OpenDoc component framework. For example, a programmer may still decide to implement the ODPart interface directly and ignore the part framework. Also, alternative part frameworks could be devised as needed. For example, IBM already provides a different OpenDoc framework.

21.2.4 The OpenDoc compound document model

On the outermost level, an OpenDoc document is supported by the OpenDoc document shell. This shell is the actual component framework. It enforces some of the principles of part interoperation and provides parts with their basic infrastructure. A document itself starts with a root part that is usually a container and contains a hierarchy of nested parts. Root parts take on some additional responsibility, such as mapping to sequences of pages when printing the document. Parts are embedded within other parts not directly but through an indirection: *frame* objects. A part uses a set of frames to manage the visual space it allocates to embedded parts. The size and shape of frames are negotiated between embedded part and container. When displaying part of a document in a window, or printing part of a document, OpenDoc creates *facet* objects. A facet maps a visible part of a frame to the used output device, which itself is abstracted by a canvas object. OpenDoc parts can have arbitrary shapes and so can ActiveX controls. JavaBeans still limits its visual objects to rectangular objects, although this is likely to change as well. Note that, in practice, rectangular visual objects cover almost all cases anyway.

An OpenDoc part can acquire various foci. For example, it can become the target of future keyboard input or it can own part of the menu bar. Ownership of a focus corresponds to exclusive access to a particular system resource. As OpenDoc defines many such foci, a deadlock could occur where multiple parts compete for multiple foci. To avoid this problem, OpenDoc uses a sophisticated two-phase locking protocol when parts try to acquire a set of foci.

Every OpenDoc part can be displayed either in a frame or as an icon. Thus, an OpenDoc document containing a set of icons 'looks and feels' like a file folder of typical graphical file managers. OpenDoc can indeed be used to unify fully compound documents and traditional graphical user interfaces, based on windows, icons, and drag and drop. An interesting early example is Apple's Cyberdog application, which uses OpenDoc to provide a graphical icon-based Web-browsing interface. Such a unification is called a *compound user interface*.

21.2.5 OpenDoc extensions

In essence, an OpenDoc part implements the single interface ODPart. This one interface may not suffice for some parts. To retain the properties of a component framework, OpenDoc does not rely on multiple inheritance to add further methods to a part's interface where needed. Instead, a part may implement any number of so-called OpenDoc *extensions*. Each extension defines a separate interface and extensions are implemented using separate objects that are returned by a part when asked whether it supports a particular extension.

To guarantee mutual understanding, extension interfaces are standardized and registered with a central authority. For comparison, COM solves the same problem in a similar way using its QueryInterface function. Instead of relying on a global registry, COM merely relies on globally unique IDs to separate independently developed interfaces and otherwise does not specify how independent vendors learn about useful common interfaces. The OpenDoc extension mechanism has an equally important role as QueryInterface in COM. It is supported by two methods, HasExtension and GetExtension, that are already defined in class ODObject, the root of the entire OpenDoc class hierarchy. In particular, ODPart is derived from ODObject – through two intermediate classes introducing reference counting and persistence.

21.2.6 Odd ends

OpenDoc had to fix what CORBA and even SOM left wide open: memory management. To do so, OpenDoc introduces reference counting, something that COM introduces right in the bottom layer. IBM's SOM itself has memory leaks, and Apple's version of SOM therefore also introduces reference counting. Where reference counting is uniformly used, as in COM or in OpenDoc, memory management problems can be solved. At the same time, reference counting fully relies on perfectly cooperating components; a misbehaved component can threaten the entire system's consistency. Automatic memory management as required by Java or Component Pascal, for example using garbage collection, is a much better solution.

Something that would explain the lack of success of OpenDoc is the platform dependence of OpenDoc part implementations. This is an odd point, as all OpenDoc interfaces are platform independent and OpenDoc does a reasonable job at shielding part implementers from platform-specific look and feel. For example, OpenDoc on OS/2 and OpenDoc on Mac OS look distinctively different and blend in well with the native look and feel of their host platforms.

So, what is it that makes parts inherently platform dependent – even the simplest ones? OpenDoc does not provide its own imaging model! Parts have to access the platform's imaging interfaces to render their contents. Total shielding of platform-specific issues is not necessarily desirable: it would lead to either a least common denominator syndrome or a massive duplication of efforts when porting OpenDoc itself. However, a minimal shield would go a long way to make at least simple parts source code compatible across OpenDoc platforms.

The BlackBox framework, discussed below, offers such a minimal shield – a shield that is sufficiently complete to implement portably the standard text and form containers. As a result, almost all BlackBox components are platform independent, without paying the price of total platform independence as advocated by Java. The Java AWT (abstract windowing toolkit) is a total shield and strictly limits what can be done, independent of the capabilities of the underlying platform.

21.3 | BlackBox component framework

The BlackBox component framework (formerly Oberon/F; Oberon microsystems, 1994) is part of the BlackBox component builder, a component-oriented rapid development tool and component-oriented programming environment by Oberon microsystems (1997b). The BlackBox component framework (BCF) is one of the few available component frameworks and, like OpenDoc, focuses on components for compound-document-based client applications with rich graphical user interfaces.

As the name suggests, BCF builds on the principles of blackboxes (abstraction) and reuse through object composition. Figure 21.1 presents an overview of the BlackBox architecture. The framework consists of a core set of layered modules and an open set of *subsystems*. Each subsystem is itself a set of layered modules. The component builder *is* the component framework extended by a development subsystem (providing compilation, debugging, browsing facilities, repository services, as well as documentation and source wizards).

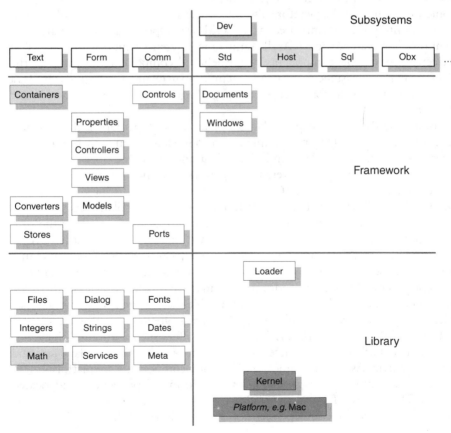

Figure 21.1   Architecture of the BlackBox component builder.

All parts of BlackBox, except for those shaded in Figure 21.1, are platform independent. The lightly shaded modules still have portable interfaces. Even the look and feel of the platform's native compound document architecture is abstracted from. Platform-specific features can be accessed, but components that refrain from doing so are themselves fully platform independent. The modules and subsystems on the left side of Figure 21.1 provide standard programming interfaces. Those on the right side are either optional (for example SQL or development subsystem), not normally imported by components (for example module Windows), or platform-specific (for example Host subsystem).

The BlackBox component framework focuses on visual components – a flexible concept, as proved by Visual Basic, OLE, and now ActiveX controls, JavaBeans, or Live Objects (OpenDoc parts). The cornerstone of visual components is their visual appearance and interaction with their containing and contained components. The central abstraction in BlackBox is thus a *view*. BlackBox views can be fully self-contained, that is have their embedded model and controller (editor). For more complex views, and container views in particular, a proper split into models, views, and controllers is used to enhance configurability and master complexity.

The BlackBox architecture is based on a number of novel patterns and approaches. Some of them are especially characteristic of BlackBox: the carrier–rider–mapper separation, the directory objects, the hierarchical model view separation, the container modes, and the cascaded message multicasting services. Each of these patterns and approaches is explained further in the following subsections.

21.3.1 Carrier–rider–mapper design pattern

This design pattern is ubiquitious in the BlackBox framework, and its uniform application greatly contributes to the understandability of the framework. The key idea is to separate data-carrying objects ('carriers'), access paths to data in these objects ('riders'), and data-formatting filters ('mappers').

A carrier maintains data that is logically accessible by position. The abstract carrier interface opens a dimension of extensibility: many concrete implementations can implement a given carrier interface. A rider encapsulates an access path to a carrier's data at a certain position. Riders are created by their carriers and usually have privileged access to the carrier's implementation. Therefore, a rider can efficiently maintain client-specific access state to a carrier. (The separation into carriers and riders is related to the iterator pattern; Gamma *et al.*, 1995.) Clients use the combination of a carrier's direct interface and provided rider interfaces to access a carrier.

Together, the carrier and rider interfaces form a 'bottleneck' interface that decouples clients from the potentially many carrier implementations. Mappers are used to provide interfaces that are more suitable for specific clients than the raw carrier and rider interfaces. Decoupled by the bottleneck interface, mappers form a dimension of extensibility that is orthogonal to that of carriers. Figure 21.2 illustrates the relations between clients, mappers, riders, and carriers.

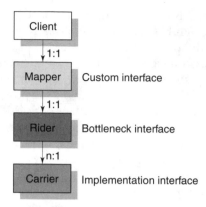

Figure 21.2 Carrier rider mapper separation.

The list below illustrates the rich use of this design pattern in the BlackBox framework:

File system abstraction layer

mapper	Stores.Reader, Stores.Writer	*internalize/externalize objects*
rider	Files.Rider	*random access byte read/write*
carrier	Files.File	*file abstraction (positional streams)*

Display system abstraction layer

mapper	Ports.Frame	*coordinate transformation*
rider	Ports.Rider	*clipping area*
carrier	Ports.Port	*pixelmap abstraction*

Text subsystem

mapper	TextMappers.Scanner, TextMappers.Formatter
rider	TextModels.Reader, TextModels.Writer
carrier	TextModels.Model

Form subsystem

mapper	*(no standard form mappers)*
rider	FormModels.Reader, FormModels.Writer
carrier	FormModels.Model

Using the file system abstraction as an example, the following Component Pascal fragment illustrates how a specific file object and a specific mapper are combined. The file object is implemented by some file system; the mapper used is the standard object writer controlling externalization:

```
VAR f: Files.File; w: Stores.Writer; pos: INTEGER;
...
f := ...;
w.ConnectTo(f); w.SetPos(pos)
```

The writer's ConnectTo method requests a new rider from the file and attaches it to the writer. In the example, this rider is then advanced to some position in the file. The writer is then able to handle requests to externalize objects by writing a linear sequence of bytes to the file.

21.3.2 Directory objects

Blackbox abstraction in BlackBox is taken to the extreme in that not even the names of implementations of abstract interfaces are made public. As a consequence, the use of language-level NEW statements (in Java, new functions) is ruled out as these would require the class name. Instead, new objects are created using factory objects or factory methods (Gamma *et al.*, 1995). Factory objects, which are called *directory objects* in BlackBox, are used where a new object is needed and no similar object is available. Such directory objects point to the currently selected default implementation in a certain context.

Each module introducing a new abstraction also provides a configurable directory object: the system-wide default for all cases for which no specific directory object is available. For example, consider the following excerpt of the file system abstraction:

```
DEFINITION Files;
   TYPE
      Locator = ...;
      Name = ...;
      File = ...;
      Directory = POINTER TO ABSTRACT RECORD
         (d: Directory) This (path: ARRAY OF CHAR): Locator, NEW, ABSTRACT;
         (d: Directory) New (loc: Locator): File, NEW, ABSTRACT;
         (d: Directory) Old (loc: Locator; name: Name): File, NEW, ABSTRACT;
         ...
      END;
   VAR dir-: Directory;   (* read-only variable *)
END Files.
```

Locators are abstract path names. A file directory object can be asked to open an existing 'old' file by name or to create a new one that initially has no name. (This application in the file system gave directory objects their name.) The standard file system is accessed through configuration variable Files.dir:

```
VAR f: Files.File;
...
f := Files.dir.Old( Files.dir.This("/dev"), "null" )
```

In many situations, an object of similar qualities to the one at hand is required. For example, when transforming an attributed data model, a buffer for temporary copies may be required. To avoid loss of specific attributions, the buffer and the data model should be instances of the same implementation. For such cases, BlackBox supports cloning of most objects, where a clone is an 'empty' copy of its original. Note that this is different from copying as the source object's specific state is dropped and a freshly initialized object is returned instead.

```
VAR t, t1: TextModels.Model;
...
t := ...;
t1 := TextModels.Clone(t);
t1.InsertCopy(t, 0, 42);   (* avoid loss of attributions *)
...   (* change t1—for example delete all lowercase characters *)
t.Replace(0, 42, t1, 0, t1.Length())   (* atomically replace with update *)
```

Consider a case where the implementation of text t adds new attributes to those defined in the standard text interface. For example, t1 might maintain an outline-level attribute. If t1 was created independently of t, support of this special attribute would not be guaranteed and the CopyStretchFrom operation would potentially have to drop this attribution. By using a clone, this loss is avoided as t and t1 are instances of the same text model implementation.

21.3.3 Hierarchical model view separation

The original model view controller (MVC) framework (Krasner and Pope, 1988) was flat and thus unable to support compound documents. BlackBox defines a compound document model that is easily mapped to standard platforms, such as OLE or OpenDoc. To the programmer, BlackBox presents a hierarchical version of the original MVC framework (HMVC).

The HMVC framework is designed to accommodate very lightweight visual components as well as fully fledged heavyweight container components. For example, a view that merely displays something need only implement a single method (Restore) and is immediately usable as a first-class citizen. This is in contrast to approaches that either only support simplistic non-container objects, such as today's JavaBeans, or complicate the implementation of even simple objects, such as OpenDoc or OLE/ActiveX.

Views in BlackBox provide visual presentation of data and can be context-sensitive, active, and interactive. A view is a rectangular display object, may be transparent, and can overlap other views. Views may be embedded recursively where some views also function as containers. A BlackBox compound document itself is an outer-level view. In addition to presenting visual information directly, a view can also function as an anchor for arbitrary objects 'under the hood.' For example, a view can be just an icon but refer to the results of a database search (Weck, 1996). Views are mapped by BlackBox to platform-specific abstractions, for example to both OLE containers and servers. The framework shields view programmers from platform-specific issues, including look and feel.

A view may have a separate model, enabling multiple views to display the same model in different ways or from different perspectives. Models represent and manage data presented by views. A view can also have a separate controller, enabling the configuration of a view with a controller of the user's choice. Controllers interact with users and interpret user input. The typical interaction of models, views, and controllers has already been explained and illustrated in Chapter 9 (p. 137).

Views and also, where present, models and controllers are all modelled as persistent objects in BlackBox. Their state is stored as part of the containing document. For models, persistence is an expected property. For views and controllers, an explanation is in order. First, the actual choices of view and controller implementations matter and should be preserved. For example, a model containing a table of numbers may be displayed graphically by one view and as a textual table by another. Likewise, one controller may support one style of editing such a view, whereas another controller may support a different style. Second, a view may be set to display a specific section of a model (for example scrolling) and may have various adjustable display properties (for example show or hide marks). These settings should also be preserved. Controllers may save the mode of a container view they belong to (see section 21.3.4).

In the HMVC approach, a model can contain nested views. This is important, as the choice of view settings of a nested view needs to be consistent across the possibly many views onto the outer model. Figure 21.3 shows a scenario in which a document is visible in two windows, one showing the document itself and the other showing separately an embedded view.

The document, as shown, consists of an outer text that contains several embedded game views (by coincidence, the game is also called BlackBox. It was invented by the English mathematician, Dr Eric W. Solomon, whose games are distinguished by being simple but very interesting). One of the embedded graphical game views is displayed a second time and this time enlarged in a separate window. Figure 21.4 shows how this scenario is supported by a hierarchy of an outer text view displaying a text model, which contains an embedded game view displaying a game model.

Documents in BlackBox are simply the root views of a model view hierarchy.

A root window uniquely displays a document, but an arbitrary number of child windows may display other sections of the same document or views embedded into that document. Child windows can be opened and closed freely – they represent no persistent state. Opening and closing root windows opens and closes documents. Closing a root window also closes all child windows onto the same document.

The root view of each window is a unique view to allow for separate scrolling, panning, and so on. The root view's models, and views embedded in this model, are shared with other windows displaying the same document. A view may be embedded in a model that is displayed by several views, possibly in several windows, and even on different display devices. Each individual visual appearance of

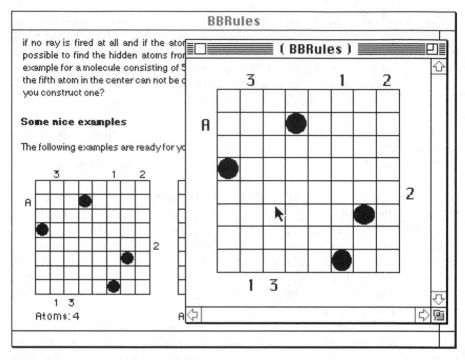

Figure 21.3   Scenario of a document displayed in two separate windows.

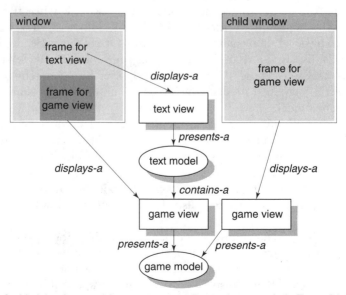

Figure 21.4   Models, views and frames corresponding to the scenario in Figure 21.3.

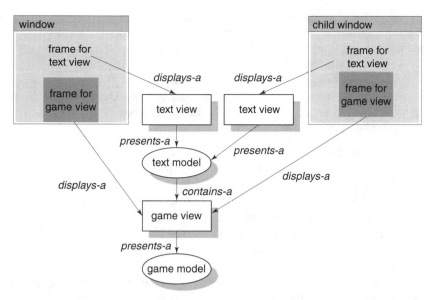

Figure 21.5 Models, views, and frames in the case of two windows onto the same document.

a view is represented by a *frame* object. Frames are mappers onto abstract display devices called *ports*. Whereas views in a document form a directed acyclic graph, frames form a tree for each window. Figure 21.5 shows how models, views, and frames are arranged when using a child window to display the original document rather than an embedded view.

21.3.4 Container modes

Traditional visual component systems distinguish the use of preassembled component instances from the assembly of component instances. An example of the former is filling in a predesigned form; an example of the latter is designing a new form. For example, a Visual Basic form either is under construction and its controls are inactive, or it is frozen and its controls are active. The same split is advocated for JavaBeans, where a bean is either in assembly or in use mode, differentiating between build and use time. For many applications, this split is justified: different people create and use forms.

However, compound document systems naturally unify construction and use of assemblies of visual component instances. For example, some outer levels of a compound document may be 'frozen,' that is turned into a fixed form, whereas at inner levels it is still possible to arrange new component instances. There is nothing wrong with filling component instances into the fields of a form if the form designer permitted this. A forms field could, besides text or numbers, easily accept pictures and other media encapsulated by instances of visual components.

Strictly separating build and use time is quite restrictive and rules out many advanced applications. At the same time, the strict separation also has its advantages: the user of a prefabricated form, for instance, cannot accidentally damage the form while trying to fill it in.

The BlackBox container framework has a unique concept to take advantage of the unification without losing control: *container modes*. Using a special editor, containers on any level of a document can be set into one of several modes. The four standard modes are listed below.

- *Edit mode*. The contents of the container can be selected, edited, and focused; this is the default used by a document editor where nested contents can be both edited and used, for example a text editor.
- *Layout mode*. The contents of the container can be selected and edited but not focused. This is the default used by a visual designer or component builder. Note that a BlackBox view can be *active* even if it is not focused – just like ActiveX and OpenDoc objects but not traditional OLE objects.
- *Browser mode*. The contents of the container can be selected and activated but not edited. This is similar to standard Web pages where HTML-defined text can be selected and embedded controls can be focused; a typical use is for online documentation and machine-generated reports.
- *Mask mode*. The contents of the container can be activated but neither selected nor edited; this is the default used by a predesigned form.

The other four combinations of selectable, editable, and focusable settings are also possible. For example, a container can be fully frozen by allowing none of these operations, or it can form a palette by permitting selections but neither editing nor focusing. (Permitting editing but not selecting seems less useful.)

- no edit, no select, no focus – *frozen*
- no edit, no select, focus – *mask*
- no edit, select, no focus – *palette*
- no edit, select, focus – *browser*
- edit, no select, no focus
- edit, no select, focus
- edit, select, no focus – *layout*
- edit, select, focus – *edit*.

The modes can be individually set for each container in a document, including the outermost one. Hence, a human designer or a programmed document generator can fully determine the degree of flexibility left to the 'user' of a document. Documents can thus range from fully static and immutable to freely editable templates. The mode-switching commands can be made unavailable to some users to prevent intentional misconduct.

21.3.5 **Cascaded message multicasting services**

BlackBox uses first-class *message objects* to decouple the sources of events from models, views, and display frames. Unlike ActiveX or JavaBeans, most BlackBox component instances do not need to be connected explicitly to cooperate – implicit connections are made and maintained by the framework. Essentially, change propagation is based on multicasts instead of registration of observers with observables. The result is a lightweight and intuitive programming model, but also a potential minefield for subtle errors. Message or event multicasting raises some important problems, as pointed out in section 10.7. In particular, the relative ordering of incoming messages needs to be looked at carefully.

For example, consider a model displayed by two views. A change to the model's contents causes a notification message to be multicast to all views displaying that model. If the first view decides, as a result of receiving the notification, to change the model's contents again, then a second notification message is multicast. As depicted in Figure 10.5 (p.159), there are two possibilities: the second view receives the two notifications either in the order sent or in the reverse order. In this example, a reverse order could be devastating, as the second view would receive incremental change notifications in non-causal order. If this view used these notifications to update its display incrementally, for example to avoid screen flicker, then an inconsistent display could result.

A general but very heavyweight solution to the ordering problem is to buffer all messages in queues and equip all recipients with their own threads. The messages are then delivered in causal order, where the separate threads allow for independent processing of messages. This approach is practicable in a truly distributed system with its physically separate processors. In a compound document setting, this approach would lead to a separate thread for every instance of every visual component used in any of the open documents. In addition, it would force all messages to be heap allocated.

The BlackBox component framework follows a different and more lightweight approach. Messages are normally allocated on the sender's stack frame and are delivered in natural recursive order (depth first), but the framework prohibits recursive sending of messages with overlapping semantics. When the first view in the above scenario tried to change the model's contents while a change notification was still in progress, the system would raise an exception. If the view still wanted to cause that change it would have to delay the change by registering a *deferred action* with the BlackBox framework. This action would be executed after the currently ongoing change notification terminated, causing nested change requests to be serialized.

If all BlackBox messages went through the same multicasting channel, the framework could not reasonably block nested message sends. To see why, consider the following typical message chain. The user pressed a key and, in reaction, the framework sent a message to the current focus view. The focus view delegated the message to its controller, which interpreted it and requested a change to the contents of its model. The model performed the change and sent a notification mes-

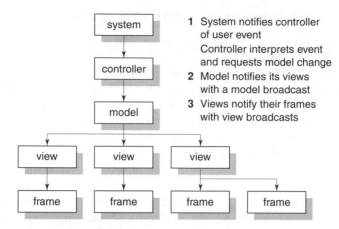

1 System notifies controller of user event

Controller interprets event and requests model change

2 Model notifies its views with a model broadcast

3 Views notify their frames with view broadcasts

Figure 21.6　Three-stage cascaded message propagation in BlackBox.

sage to its views. Each view computed the required changes to its displayed contents and sent a message to each of the frames displaying (part of) the view on one of the display devices. Figure 21.6 illustrates how BlackBox propagates messages in a three-stage cascade.

Obviously, it would be painful to force serialization of these logically non-interfering messages. To solve this problem, the BlackBox framework provides *cascaded message multicasting*. For each of the three messaging levels indicated above and numbered (1) to (3) in Figure 21.6, a separate multicasting mechanism with a separate recursion barrier is provided. First, a *controller message* is sent along the focus path – this is a forwarded singlecast, as any container on the way to the focused view can intercept and possibly modify the message. The view consuming this message, usually the focus view, can now request a model change. This change causes a *model message* to be multicast to all views displaying the model. Each of these views can then multicast a *view message* to all frames mapping the sending view onto one of the display devices.

The rules enforced by the framework are quite simple but catch most misbehaving components just as the error occurs rather than leaving behind visual 'trash' or even inconsistent document states. The first rule is that no model message can be sent by a model while another message being sent by the same model is still on its way. The second rule is that no view message can be sent by a view while another message sent by the same view is still on its way.

By using source-addressed messages, the system can limit distribution of messages to genuinely interested recipients *without* maintaining explicit dependency lists. In some exceptional cases, the source of a message needs to send a message to sinks that are not even aware of the source's identity; source addressing fails to handle such cases. Note that in such cases explicit dependency lists would not help either: the sink would not know with which source to register. For these occasions, BlackBox also supports *domaincasting* of model and view messages: such messages are sent to all views and frames, respectively, that belong to a given document. Finally, *omnicasting* of view messages can be used to broadcast to all currently open documents. The absence of a source address forces the framework to impose very strict recursion barriers on such messages. As a result, domaincasts can only be nested if addressing different documents, and omnicasts cannot be nested at all. In addition to these restrictions, omnicasts are also less efficient than domaincasts, which are less efficient than multicasts.

21.3.6 Advanced applications based on compound documents

The BlackBox compound document model is powerful and flexible enough to support radically different application models. In particular, the standard text containers provided allow for interesting user interface variations compared with the more traditional form containers. Essentially, interfaces based on text containers are more like Web pages than dialog boxes or forms, as known from Visual Basic style applications. However, both recursive container embedding and container modes allow for interfaces that go well beyond either Web-style interfaces or traditional forms. Also, as all BlackBox components have genuine programming interfaces, there is no need for separate automation or scripting interfaces. Using these programming interfaces, it is simple to synthesize on-the-fly user interfaces that exactly meet their requirements. This is similar to Web pages synthesized by CGI (common gateway interface) scripts, for example to report on the results of a search.

A first example of such novel interfaces is the BlackBox component builder's debugging support. For instance, it is possible to select a view in an open document and inspect its current state. The inspection command uses the BlackBox reflection mechanism to inspect the state of the selected view. It then generates a text displaying all fields of the view object together with the values that each field had at the time of inspection. The generated text contains controls (embedded views) to continue inspection. Link controls allow pointers (object references) to be chased and inspection of the objects to which they point. Folding controls allow expansion or collapse of parts of the inspected object to reveal or hide the state of subobjects. Figure 21.7 shows a typical screen, where a text view has been selected and state inspection requested. The user then asked for the state of the view's model. As all displayed information is just regular text, the displayed material can be dragged and dropped, for example to create an email message to a help desk, or to write a report.

A second example of the unusual interfaces that become possible when generating compound documents as user interfaces is the Debora discrete circuit simulator implemented using BlackBox (Heeb, 1993). Figure 21.8 shows a typical user interface, as synthesized by Debora. Again, the outer container is a text. This time, the actual simulation results are displayed by embedded trace views. A trace view is *text context aware*: if it finds that its container is a text, then it extracts the name of the signal that it should display from the surrounding text. In Figure 21.8, signal names are 'Clock,' 'Enable,' and so on. They correspond to names of signals in the simulated circuit – in this example, a cyclic 13-state counter.

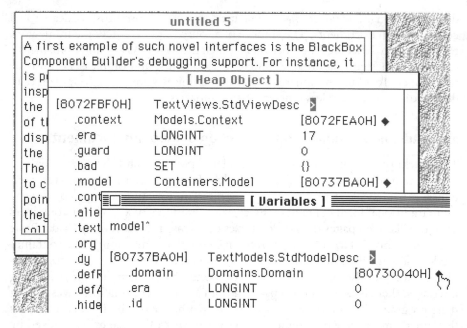

Figure 21.7 Interface generated by the BlackBox component builder's debugger.

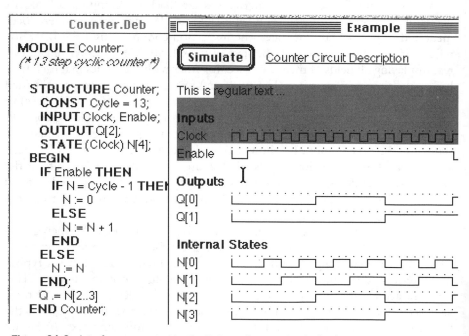

Figure 21.8 Interface generated by the Debora discrete circuit simulator.

21.4   **BlackBox versus OpenDoc**

In many ways, BlackBox is similar to OpenDoc. Both are component frameworks for mostly visual components. Both have the notions of general containers and recursive embedding. Both use compound documents for everything, including all of their user interface. This similarity is not surprising, as the BlackBox component framework is designed to allow for natural mapping to both OpenDoc and OLE.

Even on the level of compound document modeling, OpenDoc and BlackBox are at least superficially similar. Where OpenDoc uses parts, frames, facets, shapes, and canvases, BlackBox uses views, contexts, frames, port riders, and ports, respectively.

BlackBox is less complex – and thus less powerful – than OpenDoc in that it supports a more restrictive document model. For example, there is no generic support for document versioning. Also, BlackBox currently does not support general object linking, although it does support Web-like hyperlinking.

BlackBox goes beyond OpenDoc in that it also has a fully integrated development environment. Component Pascal is used as the one language for all purposes, from performance-critical low-level programming, to interfacing to external platform-specific dynamic link libraries, to implementation of new components, to scripting. This very broad use of a single language is unparalleled in the industry. Java, for example, is not advocated for scripting – JavaScript is used instead. Also, Java is not at all suitable for systems programming.

A proof of concept: all of BlackBox, including its garbage collector, compiler, top-level interpreter, reflection service, platform-specific interfacing, command and script packages, and all standard components are solely implemented in Component Pascal. This enormous bandwidth is possible because Component Pascal is a small, simple, efficient, and effective language that can be used in 'layers.' Script authors, for example, need not be aware of the majority of the language features. Implementors of simple components can still ignore substantial parts of the language. At the other extreme, no one but systems programmers need to be aware of the low-level features of the language. Language-established safety properties strictly hold for all but the low-level features – which can therefore be statically excluded at compile time, if desired.

However, BlackBox avoids the single language island syndrome by supporting the standard object model of the underlying platform, most prominently COM on Windows platforms. A Direct-to-COM binding of an extended Component Pascal compiler allows for native programming of COM components. Components programmed using any other language or environment can be used by BlackBox components – and vice versa. On COM platforms, BlackBox is fully OLE enabled; BlackBox is both an OLE server and an OLE container. OLE automation is fully available to the Component Pascal programmer or script author. Below is an example of a simple module that uses the Microsoft Excel spelling checker to check the spelling of the current focus text:

```
MODULE TestSpellcheck;
  IMPORT CtlExcel, TextControllers, TextMappers, TextViews;
  VAR app: CtlExcel.Application;
  PROCEDURE Next*;
    VAR c: TextControllers.Controller; s: TextMappers.Scanner;
      res, beg, pos: INTEGER; ch: CHAR;
  BEGIN
    c := TextControllers.Focus();
    IF c # NIL THEN   (* there is a focus controller and it is a text controller *)
      IF c.HasSelection() THEN
        c.GetSelection(beg, pos)   (* there is a selection; start checking
                                        at its end *)
      ELSIF c.HasCaret() THEN
        pos := c.CaretPos()   (* there is a caret; start checking at its
                                    position *)
      ELSE
        pos := 0   (* else start checking from the beginning of the text *)
      END;
      s.ConnectTo(c.text); s.SetPos(pos); s.Scan();
      WHILE ~s.rider.eot & ( (s.type # TextMappers.string)
      OR app.CheckSpelling(s.string, NIL, NIL) ) DO
        (* while there is more text and the current token either is not a
            word or is found in the dictionary, skip white space and scan
            in the next token *)
        s.Skip(ch); pos := s.Pos() - 1; s.Scan()
      END;
      IF ~s.rider.eot THEN
        (* found a word that is not in Excel's dictionary—select and show it *)
        TextViews.ShowRange(c.text, pos, s.Pos() - 1, TextViews.focusOnly);
        c.SetSelection(pos, s.Pos() - 1)
      ELSE
        c.SetCaret(c.text.Length()) (* checked entire text; remove selection *)
      END
    END
  END Next;
BEGIN
  app := CtlExcel.NewWorksheet().Application()
END TestSpellcheck.
```

This simple script module acquires a reference to an Excel application component object and stores it in a global variable. The result is efficient checking once Excel starts up. However, the Excel server is also locked in memory for the lifetime of module TestSpellcheck. A sophisticated implementation would release the Excel object, for example after the spelling checker had not been used for a while.

A fully functional education version of BlackBox for Windows (win32s) and Mac OS is available free of charge from Oberon microsystems' Web site (http://www.oberon.ch/).

21.5   Portos and Denia – a hard realtime component framework and its development environment

Examples of component software outside of graphical user interfaces and compound documents are still rare. To show that there is no technical reason for this, this section covers some technical detail of the Portos system.

Portos is a realtime operating system consisting of components (Figure 21.9), which are all implemented in Component Pascal. New components can be loaded at run-time if the system is connected to a server. Portos teams up with a rapid application development tool called Denia that is built on top of BlackBox. Integration of realtime process control components with workstation-located interactive components is possible, including full OLE integration on the workstation.

21.5.1 Structure of Portos

The Portos core is a small runtime environment for embedded or realtime systems. It incudes a heap manager and a proprietary garbage collector. The garbage collector runs in the background and is designed such that it never interferes with other tasks. In particular, it never disables interrupts, and thus does not impede fast and predictable realtime responses.

Figure 21.9 shows the overall structure of the Portos operating system. The rectangles represent individual Component Pascal modules. Rectangles with thick outlines are complete subsystems consisting of several modules (e.g. the Comm subsystem) or open collections of component implementations (e.g. device drivers implementing process peripherals).

The Comm subsystem is a component framework for reliable communication via serial byte streams. It supports extensibility in four independent dimensions: clients (e.g. the module loader), services (e.g. the debug server), channels (e.g. an Ethernet driver), and protocols (e.g. UDP/IP).

The process peripherals modules constitute a component framework for input/output of digital or analog data. It supports extensibility in three independent dimensions: applications (e.g. a process control program), device drivers (e.g. for a digital–analog converter), and scales (e.g. a linear transformation on the analog data read or written).

Various configurations of Portos are possible. At the least, the modules PortosKernel and PortosTasks are required. PortosKernel is a private module that contains some unsafe low-level facilities and the heap manager, including the asynchronous garbage collector. Module PortosTasks is the pivotal interface for developers of hard realtime applications. It is described in further detail below. These two modules are sufficient, provided that the application contains all necessary device drivers and is linked with them. A minimal Portos application that is

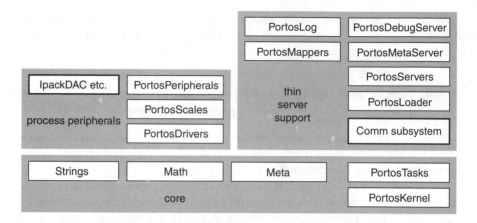

Figure 21.9   Modular structure of Portos.

linked together with the core fits into a 64-kB EPROM and 128 kB of RAM. A minimal Portos application that uses TCP/IP networking and supports downloading of new components over the network starts at about 128 kB of EPROM and 256 kB of RAM.

Optionally, module PortosThreads may be added. It implements a scheduler for prioritized threads, that is tasks which are not time critical. Their scheduler can be plugged into module PortosTasks. If desired, PortosThreads could be replaced by other threading mechanisms.

Several modules from the BlackBox component framework are available for Portos, in particular Meta (typesafe reflection facilities) and CommStreams (reliable serial communication). Several implementation modules are available for CommStreams, in particular for communication over V24 and over Ethernet via TCP/IP and UDP/IP. PPP, FTP, and other standard Internet services are provided as further options using this communication platform.

PortosLog is a simple console output service that uses the communication facilities to send output to a host computer running Denia (see next section) or a terminal program. Several optional modules implement server functionality that can be used during cross-development and for visualization purposes. In particular, a user can issue remote commands in Denia, which are executed on Portos. New modules can be installed on Portos in this way; debug output can be fetched; and controls (in the sense of ActiveX or BlackBox controls) can display and manipulate Portos state remotely.

PortosLoader is necessary to load new modules at runtime. In particular, new code files can be downloaded from the host using the communications facilities, and then loaded into memory.

Note that the code files contain native machine code, not intermediate byte code that would have to be interpreted. Module loading and unloading is fully dynamic, allowing for field upgrades of the software without downtime. The loader is an optional service that can be left out in closed embedded systems that have no communication facilities, and thus need to be fully linked.

21.5.2 **Realtime scheduler**

The central module of Portos is PortosTasks. It implements the following interface
(the version shown here is a slight simplification of the actual interface):

```
DEFINITION PortosTasks;
  TYPE
    (* monitor/signal synchronization primitive *)
    Synchronizer = POINTER TO EXTENSIBLE RECORD
      (s: Synchronizer) TryEnter (OUT done: BOOLEAN), NEW;(* non-blocking
                                                              enter *)
      (s: Synchronizer) Enter, NEW;   (* lock *)
      (s: Synchronizer) Exit, NEW;   (* unlock *)
      (s: Synchronizer) Notify, NEW;   (* wake up a waiting task *)
      (s: Synchronizer) NotifyAll, NEW;   (* wake up all waiting tasks *)
      (s: Synchronizer) Awaited (): BOOLEAN, NEW;   (* a task is waiting for
                                                        notification *)
      (s: Synchronizer) Wait (usec: INTEGER), NEW   (* await notify, with
                                                        timeout *)
    END;
    (* client process controlled by a task *)
    Handler = POINTER TO ABSTRACT RECORD
      (h: Handler) Run–, NEW, ABSTRACT;(* implements the task's behavior *)
      (h: Handler) HandleException–, NEW, EMPTY   (* optional exception
                                                      handler *)
    END;
    (* tasks control the concurrent execution of handlers *)
    Task = POINTER TO LIMITED RECORD
      (t: Task) Start, NEW;   (* make task ready for scheduling *)
      (t: Task) Stop, NEW;   (* make task inactive *)
      (t: Task) Suspend, NEW;   (* wait for resumption *)
      (t: Task) Resume, NEW   (* resume after suspension *)
    END;
  VAR current–: Task;   (* the currently executing task *)
  (* factory functions for normal, periodic, and sporadic (interrupt) tasks *)
  PROCEDURE NewTask (handler: Handler; duration, deadline: INTEGER):
              Task;
  PROCEDURE NewPeriodicTask (handler: Handler; duration, deadline:
              INTEGER; period: INTEGER): Task;
  PROCEDURE NewHarmonicTask (handler: Handler; duration, deadline:
              INTEGER; factor: INTEGER; periodicTask: Task): Task;
  PROCEDURE NewSporadicTask (handler: Handler; duration, deadline:
              INTEGER; minPeriod: INTEGER; eventType: INTEGER): Task;
  PROCEDURE Time (): INTEGER;
  PROCEDURE Sleep (usec: INTEGER);
END PortosTasks.
```

A combination of monitor and signal is used as a synchronization construct; its definition is compatible with the java.lang.Object class, in that it supports suitably defined Enter, Exit, Wait, Notify, and NotifyAll methods.

A task represents a concurrent process, which is implemented by a PortosTasks.Handler object. Handler objects contain an abstract method, Run, which implements the code of the process. An optional exception handler (as signified by EMPTY in the declaration) may be implemented. If it is left empty, the system's default exception handler is used, which writes symbolic debugging output to a host console if one is connected.

Tasks are inactive after they have been created with one of the NewTask factory functions. They can be started, stopped, suspended, resumed, and sent to sleep for some time. Unlike typical threads, a task may not run for an indefinite amount of time. Instead, a task (more precisely, its handler's Run method) must terminate before some deadline has passed or some amount of computation time has been consumed. If one of these constraints is violated, the handler's exception-handling method is called. This means that the hard realtime scheduler knows about time, and uses it for scheduling purposes ('Earliest Deadline First' scheduling). The interesting aspect here is that tasks can be safely composed, as long as there is sufficient computational power available. If the processor is saturated, the scheduler rejects new tasks ('admission testing'), rather than risking that some tasks may miss its deadline. This is an example of a component-oriented approach in the realtime domain, in stark contrast to the usual user-assigned priority schemes of many commercial realtime operating systems.

A Java version of Portos, called J*** CE, is largely identical to Portos, but provides Java interfaces to the kernel's services. Java objects are implemented using the Synchronizer type mentioned above. The scheduler, class loader, heap manager, and the realtime garbage collector for Componet Pascal and Java are identical. Timesharing tasks, which consume the computation time left by the hard realtime tasks, implement a prioritized scheduling mechanism as defined by Java. Thus they can be used as standard Java threads. J*** CE is fast because the kernel directly implements the runtime environment needed for Java; there are no inefficient translations or expensive kernel calls. The Portos/J*** CE core *is* the virtual machine, except that Java byte code is translated by a cross-compiler before downloading into the embedded system. This is important to obtain systems with minimal memory footprint, and with optimal and predictable speed.

21.5.3 Cross-development environment Denia

Denia is a cross-development environment for developing Portos applications. Denia is an extension of the BlackBox component builder described above. Denia adds functionality for the transfer of code files and data to and from an embedded system running Portos, a Component Pascal cross-compiler that produces 68k or PowerPC machine code, symbolic cross-debugging support, an interpreter for remote commands, and remote (visual) controls. Denia with BlackBox is available for Windows NT and Windows 95.

Basically, the developer opens one or several connections to an embedded processor running Portos. For simple systems, connections run over serial V24 lines. At the other extreme, several connections may be open simultaneously via TCP/IP, for example one connection to each of the processors of a multiprocessor system. Typically, such connections are made over a company's intranet, but it is also possible to log into a target on another continent via Internet; for example to perform remote diagnosis.

The cross-development tools such as the compiler and browser work in the same way as the regular local BlackBox tools. This means that the same development environment and programming language can be used to develop local visualization software, as well as the corresponding remote Portos application.

The BlackBox forms subsystem can be used to create dialog boxes as user interfaces to a remote Portos application. For this purpose, the complete set of BlackBox controls, such as command buttons, radio buttons, text entry fields, and so on, are available also as 'remote controls.' Using the standard BlackBox property inspector, remote controls can be linked to program variables of a Portos module.

CHAPTER TWENTY-TWO

Component development

Component-oriented programming is a young discipline, and much work remains to be done. This chapter briefly covers the aspects of programming methodology, environments, and languages. Methodologies are needed to allow for a cohesive approach to component system partitioning, component interaction, and component construction. Environments and languages can reflect and support chosen methodologies.

22.1 The methodology – component-oriented programming

Just as object-oriented programming (OOP) addresses the fundamental aspects of programming object-oriented solutions, component-oriented programming (COP) addresses the aspects of programming components. A definition of COP in the style of typical OOP definitions is (Szyperski, 1995):

> 'Component-oriented programming requires support of:
> – polymorphism (substitutability)
> – modular encapsulation (higher level information hiding)
> – late binding and loading (independent deployability)
> – safety (type and module safety).'

A proper methodology for component-oriented programming still needs to be found. Practically all existing methodologies work only *within* a component. The difficulties resulting from the complex interactions with other components are not adequately covered. The tiered architectural approach introduced in section 20.4 or other architectural approaches help to master complexity and guide system evolution. However, architecture alone does not suffice to guide the development of component frameworks and components. Many problems are still open. The following subsections should help to understand how extensive a 'complete' component development methodology would have to be. The subsections cover selected problems at different levels and hint at possible solutions.

22.1.1 **Problems of asynchrony**

All current component 'wiring' standards use one or other form of event propagation as one particularly flexible form of component instance assembly. The idea is simple: component instances that undergo a state change of expectedly wider interest post an event object. A separate event distribution mechanism accepts such event objects and delivers them to other component instances that have registered their interest. Component instances register their interest, because they may have to update their state to adjust to the changes indicated by the event object.

This seemingly simple mechanism introduces many subtle problems. Firstly, the 'natural' form of event distribution is multicasting, that is delivery of an event object to more than one recipient. While a multicast is in progress, the system is in an inconsistent state. This is observable by component instances, for example by using regular method invocations to query other component instances. Secondly, event object recipients are themselves free to post new events. All the problems associated with relative ordering of multicasts thus need to be considered. Thirdly, the set of recipients could change while a multicast is in progress. This requires particular attention to maintain well-defined semantics. Fourthly, some of the recipients might raise exceptions while handling received event objects and while the multicast is in progress. Again, careful definition of the system's behavior in such a case is required.

22.1.2 **Multithreading**

'Multithreading will rot your teeth.'

Swaine (1997, p. 93)

As Swaine explained in a subsequent publication, this and his other statements were intentionally provocative. He did not claim that they were wrong.

Multithreading is the concept of supporting multiple sequential activities concurrently over the same state space. The resulting increase in complexity over sequential programming is substantial. In particular, conflicts from concurrent writes (or reads and writes) to variables accessed by multiple threads need to be avoided. Synchronization of threads using some form of locking solves this problem but introduces a new one. Locking too conservatively or in the 'wrong' order can result in deadlocks.

The main focus of multithreading is the better distribution of performance as observed by clients issuing concurrent requests. However, note that *overall* performance is maximized by not using threads at all and by always serving the request with the shortest expected execution time first. Synchronization, even where deadlocks are avoided, can lead to substantial degradation of performance. Prolonged locking of frequently shared resources must be avoided. Also, propagation of exceptions across thread boundaries leads to the difficult problem of handling asynchronous exceptions. Finally, it is exceptionally difficult to debug code that uses multiple threads and complex interlocking patterns.

Obviously, none of these problems can be avoided where true concurrency needs to be dealt with. For example, if component instances execute on separate processors, then concurrent requests need to be handled. Complete locking of a component instance while one request is handled is possible, but may lead to deadlocks or poor response time.

A concept that would help to reduce complexity in many such cases is transactional programming. A transaction that fails to acquire all necessary locks would simply abort and could be retried later rather than deadlocking the system. However, few general-purpose programming methodologies support transactions and even fewer programming languages do.

22.1.3 Learning from circuit design

The problems of true concurrency, non-determinism, and synchronization are well known from other component technologies. Electronic circuit design, in particular, has a long tradition in addressing these issues. Although it is true that fully asynchronous circuits are often the best performers, they are also the most complex to design. Synchronous circuits synchronize all activities on component boundaries to *clock signals*. Design of component interaction can then be disentangled into *phases* – distinct clock cycles used to perform coordinated activities in a well-defined order.

A similar approach can be taken in software design. Instead of always directly driving computation as a result of invocation, invocations can be queued and processed in an order determined by system design rather than invocation occurrence. The resulting systems naturally use processes and asynchronous inter-process communication rather than threads with synchronous side-effects. An example of a synchronous approach from the domain of reactive hard realtime systems is Esterel (Berry and Gonthier, 1992).

Instead of using processes, more lightweight abstractions are also possible. For example, all computation can be split into *atomic actions* (Back and Kirki-Suonio, 1988). Actions are triggered by events queued by the system, but there is always at most one action executing within a single process. Availability of actions can be conditional. Ordering of activities is determined by a system scheduling policy based on the set of enabled (available) actions. Unlike processes, actions can easily communicate through side-effects on global state, as there is no true (observable) concurrency.

22.1.4 Living without implementation inheritance

The severe problems introduced by implementation inheritance across component boundaries is justification for advocating the use of simple object composition and message forwarding instead. However, a concern frequently raised when being faced with this alternative is the resulting clumsiness when *minor adaptations* of available implementations are needed. It is simple to subclass a class with dozens of methods and then override just a few of them. In contrast, it is tedious to create a new wrapper class that merely forwards all but a few method invocations. In addition to the implementation overhead, plain forwarding also introduces an avoidable runtime overhead, in both execution time and code space.

Where the methods of an object are grouped into interfaces, each with only a modest number of methods, COM-style aggregation helps to avoid the performance implications of forwarding. The implementation cost can also be hidden from the programmer by using various forms of automation.

One solution is to generate the code of a forwarder's class based on the interfaces of objects to forward to. The main disadvantage is that shared by all textual code generation approaches. As the generated code needs to be edited, changes to the target object interfaces require regeneration and re-editing, or manual adjustment of the generated code.

Another solution is to use a template mechanism, such as that of C++, to generate the required code at compile time. Rather than editing generated code, templates are parametrized. Final code is then generated by the compiler based on the template's instantiation arguments. This approach shares problems with all such 'glorified macro' techniques. First, the template itself cannot be type checked and the compiler may report confusing errors when processing template instantiations. Secondly, a template cannot be compiled separately, leading to code bloat and eliminating dynamic linking of template abstractions.

22.1.5 Nutshell classes

A third solution is to use implementation inheritance... What? Recall that there is nothing wrong with implementation inheritance from whitebox classes, that is classes that have been published in full source form and are guaranteed to be immutable. For component interfaces that are expected to be frequent targets for forwarding objects, a *nutshell class* that trivializes the programming of forwarders can be provided (Szyperski, 1992b). A nutshell class has the same interface as the object it is forwarding to, and all methods are implemented as plain forwards to the target object. Nutshell classes are themselves abstract, although all methods are implemented: it simply makes no sense to instantiate such a class. (It is interesting that some languages, including C++, have no way of expressing the fact that a class with no abstract methods is still abstract.) However, to create a useful forwarder that intercepts some of the method invocations, a nutshell class can be subclassed. The resulting overhead for the programmer is similar to that of plain implementation inheritance, except that forwarding instead of delegation semantics results.

22.1.6 Language support

A fourth, and probably preferred, solution would be language support. Where construction of a forwarder class is directly supported by the programming language, all disadvantages discussed so far can be avoided. The programming overhead is minimal and the runtime overhead in time and space has to be no different from that of implementation inheritance schemes. No mainstream language currently supports such a construct. For example, the C++ virtual base class mechanism does not allow for sharing of base class objects across separate objects. It also does not allow for dynamic change of base class objects, or for separate subclassing of a virtual base class. A language that does support dynamic inheritance from an object is Objective-C (NeXT; Pinson and Wiener, 1991).

22.1.7 Dynamic base objects with forwarding semantics

A hypothetical extension of Component Pascal would naturally introduce the required mechanism: where in standard Component Pascal the base type of a record is specified, a base pointer could be introduced instead. Consider the following example of a view interface:

```
TYPE
  View = POINTER TO ABSTRACT RECORD
    (v: View) Restore, NEW, ABSTRACT;
    (* many more methods *)
  END;
```

In Component Pascal, the type of text view objects that inherit interface and implementation from View would be:

```
TYPE
  TextView = POINTER TO RECORD (View)
    (v: TextView) Restore;
    (* implement other View methods *)
    (v: TextView) ThisText (): TextModel;
    (* other text view specific methods *)
  END;
```

The construction of TextView follows the traditional single implementation inheritance scheme. Using a slight modification of the base type notation, a forwarding mechanism could be introduced. For example, consider the type of objects that accept all View methods, but that intercept (at least) the Restore method. Expressed in the hypothetical extension of Component Pascal, this type is:

```
TYPE
  Decorator = POINTER TO ABSTRACT RECORD (v: View)
    (d: Decorator) Restore;
    (*other View method invocations are forwarded to base object v *)
```

```
  (d: Decorator) GetProperties ( ... ), NEW, ABSTRACT;
  (d: Decorator) SetProperties ( ... ), NEW, ABSTRACT
END;
PROCEDURE (d: Decorator) Restore;
BEGIN
  d.v.Restore;   (* forward to base object: restore it first *)
  ...  (* draw decoration *)
END Restore;
```

A Decorator object supposedly paints its base view plus some decoration, such as a border, based on editable properties. The details of the property mechanism are of no importance here. As Decorator objects use a dynamic reference to a View object, they can be added 'after the fact' to any existing view object, including ones that have already been 'decorated.' For example, Decorator could be used to decorate a TextView object, or to decorate any other instance of a subclass of View.

Note that, syntactically, the extension is limited to the introduction of a field name that optionally precedes the name of the base type. Semantically, if a method is left unimplemented in a wrapping object, requests are forwarded to the base object. The proposed semantics is forwarding, not delegation, to decouple the base object from the forwarder. This proposal is close to the one by Stroustrup (1987) for C++ but not adopted in the actual language (Stroustrup, 1994, section 12.7).

Note that Decorator still inherits from View and is a subtype of View. If View has fields or methods then these are inherited into Decorator. Also, if Decorator issues a supercall, rather than a base object forward, the called method belongs to the decorator object, not the view. This inclusion of a complete base type object in the wrapper *and* a reference to a forwardee compatible with the base type distinguishes this proposal from that of Stroustrup. In particular, this proposal allows a Decorator object to be passed into a context expecting a View object without bypassing the decorator. In Stroustrup's proposal, the view base object would be extracted from the decorator and passed into the View context. As a result, the decorator would be out of the loop and unable to perform its function.

A subtle point is the declaration of the base object using field syntax. In Component Pascal, the export status of record fields can be individually controlled to be module private (default), read-only exported, or fully exported. The same three export modes are possible for the base object field. If the field is not exported, then clients have no way of telling that this object uses a base object – all that is visible to module-external clients is that the type has a supertype. If the field is exported read-only, then the base object can be accessed but not replaced by module-external clients. This can be used to establish stable base objects that are set at creation time, but never again changed. Finally, if the field is fully exported, then any client can replace the base object. In the example, any client could take a decorator off its current view and wrap it around some new view.

The semantics of Decorator above can be explained using rewriting into stand-ard Component Pascal form.

```
TYPE
    DecoratorRewrite = POINTER TO ABSTRACT RECORD (View)
        v: View;
        (d: Decorator) Restore;
        (*other View method invocations are forwarded to base object v *)
        (d: Decorator) GetProperties ( ... ), NEW, ABSTRACT;
        (d: Decorator) SetProperties ( ... ), NEW, ABSTRACT
    END;
(* methods explicitly handled in Decorator are not changed: *)
PROCEDURE (d: DecoratorRewrite) Restore;
BEGIN
    d.v.Restore;   (* forward to base object: restore it first *)
    ...   (* draw decoration *)
END Restore;
(* rewrite all View methods that are not overridden in Decorator: *)
PROCEDURE (d: DecoratorRewrite) Method (...);
BEGIN
    d.v.Method(...) (* forward to base object *)
END Method;
```

Such a rewriting rule can be used to define the proposed forwarding mechanism.

22.1.8 Caller encapsulation

Another area that benefits from language support is that of interface definitions. When exposing an interface on a component boundary, two different intentions may be involved. On the one hand, component-external code may need to invoke operations of the exposed interface. On the other hand, component-internal code may need to invoke operations that implement the exposed interface. In COM terminology, this is the difference between incoming and outgoing interfaces. With the exception of Component Pascal, no languages properly support pure outgoing interfaces of components.

Consider the following example. The base class Object in Java defines a method finalize. This method is called by the runtime's garbage collector before deleting objects that became unreachable. The intention is that the object has a chance to release external resources that are out of reach of the garbage collector. For ex-ample, Java FileOutputStream objects implement the finalize method to release native file descriptors or similar resources that they may hold. Obviously, the finalize method is an 'outgoing' interface of the garbage collector – no other code should ever invoke it.

To express this constraint, Java uses *protected* methods – and Object.finalize is protected. A protected method can only be invoked by code in the introducing class, in one of its subclasses (some restrictions apply), or in the packages that contain the introducing class and the subclasses. In addition, a subclass can redeclare a protected method to be public and thus remove the protection for all direct or indirect instances of that subclass. Note that the Java package system is too weak to enforce protected-mode access fully. In the example of method finalize, the class Object is defined in package java.lang. Any new class file can claim to be part of the package java.lang and thus gain access to protected features of java.lang. Such a class can then freely call the finalize method of any object!

The properties of *protected* methods prevent most erroneous invocations of such methods. However, they are not strong enough to allow a base package to establish the strict invariant that no code outside this package may ever invoke such a method. The only way to achieve this in languages such as Java or C++ is to make the method *private*, which defeats the original purpose. To be a useful outgoing interface, it must be possible to implement such a method, but not to invoke it from outside a protected domain. (C++ has an odd construct: *private virtual* functions. These are methods that are not visible externally but can nevertheless be overridden by subclasses and, if so, made public by the subclass or be called from within such a subclass.)

The need to encapsulate the caller rather than the callee, as done by most traditional encapsulation constructs, should not be surprising, once the symmetry between incoming and outgoing interfaces is accepted. However, proper *caller encapsulation*, suitable for the construction of components, is missing in most languages. Languages in the Simula tradition, including Beta (Lehrmann Madsen *et al.*, 1993), support *inner* methods. On the level of classes, these come very close to caller encapsulation. No code outside the introducing base class can invoke the inner methods filled in by subclasses. Everyone can invoke the method itself, but execution of the base class code is guaranteed and can at least dynamically protect the base class against unwanted external callers.

A much simpler facility is available in Component Pascal. A method may be marked *implement only* and can then be overridden outside the defining module, just as a regularly exported method. However, no code outside the defining module can invoke such a method. As the mechanism, like all Component Pascal access protection, is on the level of modules (atomic components), calls can come from 'friend' classes or procedures in the same module. For example, the finalize method in Component Pascal is pervasively defined as:

```
TYPE
  ANYPTR = POINTER TO ANYREC;
  ANYREC = ABSTRACT RECORD
    (a: ANYPTR) FINALIZE–, NEW, EMPTY;
  END;
```

Type ANYREC is the implicit base type of all record types in Component Pascal, in much the same way as class Object is the implicit base class of all classes in Java. Component Pascal expresses access restrictions using *export marks* that follow newly

defined identifiers. There are only two kinds of export marks in the language: *
and –. An identifier marked * is exported, including its definition, from its defining module. A variable or field marked – is exported read-only, that is, it is write
protected outside its defining module. The * marks were introduced with Oberon
(Reiser and Wirth, 1992); the – marks followed in Oberon-2 (Mössenböck, 1993).

In Component Pascal, the – mark has been generalized: a method name marked
– exports the method override-only, that is, it is call protected outside its defining
module. (Overriding methods remain under the override-only protection.
Supercalls are legal within overriding code of call-protected methods.) The type
ANYREC is defined pervasively, that is, it is part of the language and defined outside any normal module. Thus, method FINALIZE can only be called by the runtime
system and the garbage collector in particular. Note that this is *not* a result of
including FINALIZE in the language rather than in a library. Any module can export override-only methods and thus statically guarantee that no other module
can contain a invocation of such a method.

Caller encapsulation is put to good use in several places in the BlackBox component framework. For example, key methods of views can be invoked only indirectly by the framework. If the framework has caught an exception on an earlier
invocation of the same method on the same view, it stops propagating these calls.
Faulty views thus degenerate without becoming fully useless or continuing to
disturb the system. BlackBox is one of the few systems in which a view embedded
into a compound document does not endanger the document as a whole. For
example, a view with a broken Restore method will be masked by the framework:
a gray raster overlays the view's display and no further calls to Restore will occur.
However, as the view's externalization may well function, the document can still
be saved – and reloaded with the view intact again, once its implementing component has been repaired.

Another example of caller encapsulation from the BlackBox framework is encapsulation of an object's Externalize and Internalize methods. The framework
can thus ensure that only newly allocated objects are asked to internalize themselves, protecting established objects from erroneous requests. The framework
also enforces the fact that the proper environment for externalization or internalization is established before these methods are called.

22.2   The environment – selecting target frameworks

A component object cannot function outside a defined environment. Component
frameworks define such environments. However, a component object can be designed to operate in multiple such environments simultaneously. Depending on
the component system architecture, frameworks are separated according to various roles. For example, each framework may take care of one particular mechanism that operates across components. In this case, a distribution framework may
be responsible for distribution of component instances across machines. A separate framework would be responsible for compound document integration. A

component may well need to interact with both frameworks to implement objects that can be distributed *and* that function within a compound document.

While the first component frameworks are just appearing on the market, proper integrating component system architectures are still missing. The dangers of investing heavily in solutions based on a single framework are well understood by now. Although application frameworks are very successful, it is also known that 'divorce' is almost impossible. It is already notoriously difficult to combine multiple traditional frameworks, as most of them have been designed in total isolation and insist on total control. However, it is even harder to migrate a solution from one framework to another one with similar functionality. This is commonly required as providers of frameworks go out of business, no longer support all the platforms required by an evolving solution, or 'better' frameworks become available. To address such problems, the first re-engineering projects for 'object-oriented legacy' are already attracting funding, for example in the European Union (FAMOOS Consortium, 1996).

22.3 | The tool – selecting the programming language

In principle, component programming could use almost any language – and almost any paradigm. Minimal requirements exist nevertheless. Component programming rests firmly on the polymorphic handling of other components. As interactions with other components need to be dynamic, late binding has to be supported. Safety-by-construction arguments additionally ask for support of encapsulation and safety – type *and* module safety (Chapter 6) – and thus for garbage collection in most cases. The object-oriented paradigm comes closest to expanding into the area of component-oriented programming, but other paradigms, such as the functional one, might also be suitable.

The number of programming languages that truly support component-oriented programming is still quite small. Many mainstream languages, such as COBOL, Object COBOL, FORTRAN, C, C++, Pascal, Object Pascal, Modula-2, Eiffel, or Smalltalk lack the support for encapsulation, polymorphism, type safety, module safety, or any combination of these. Probably the most prominent component-oriented language at this time is Java, although it has some defects when it comes to module safety (as explained below).

Other component-oriented languages are Modula-3, Oberon, Component Pascal, and Ada 95. None of these languages fully addresses the various language-level issues raised in the above section on component-oriented programming methodologies. Component Pascal probably comes closest, but there is still room for improvement. This should not be surprising, given the relative youth of component software technology. Most current language technology goes back to the late 1960s, including object-oriented polymorphism!

Both Java and Component Pascal support access protection on the level of packages or modules respectively. In this way, module safety can be established. Java has an open package system that is too weak in the area of module safety.

Even without replacing a single compiled and possibly signed file, packages can always be augmented with new classes – and these have full access to the mechanisms protected by that package! This loophole needs to be closed by additional extralingual means: packages need to be kept in protected directories of the file system or some other repository with access control.

In a context of dynamic acquisition of class files from remote servers, the situation is even more complex. Class files belonging to the same package would need to be authenticated to come from the same compiling source. To allow for more open settings, Java might benefit from a closed module construct, where each such module maps to exactly one compiled file for distribution.

CHAPTER TWENTY-THREE

Component distribution and acquisition

By definition, components are the units of deployment. The only reason for their existence is to allow integration of products from independent vendors to fulfill a shared purpose. Obviously, this requires a way of marketing components. The two technical sides of the problem are component distribution and component acquisition. Proper distribution and acquisition infrastructures are required, and these need to go far beyond pure connectivity, as provided by the Internet.

The Java applet role model is an example of a (so far) entirely chaotic approach. Distribution is not backed by marketing or serious cataloging efforts; acquisition is governed by browsing and random discovery. For a substantial and focused component market to develop, this needs to improve. As Java applets have been free until now, it is not surprising that neither distribution nor acquisition strategies have yet evolved.

The situation is different for the profit-bearing market of controls for Visual Basic or, now, ActiveX. There are thousands of controls on the market, and traditional distributors actively market these. Acquisition is backed by catalogs of available controls, but by and large still relies on trial-and-error matching.

Technically, what is required are precise specifications of what components do (and do not do) and what platform requirements they have. These specifications need to be organized into catalogs. Established component technologies in other engineering disciplines can lead the way. However, today it is not even clear how to specify a software component. Research has concentrated on how to catalog and retrieve components, but there are no methods that are proven and work with components of substantial complexity.

Microprocessors, for example, come with component specifications that effectively fill entire books. The same holds true for many other electronic, electrical, or mechanical components. Discovering components is only the main problem when focusing on components that are so lightweight and trivial that one has to expect 'millions' of offerings. However, it is not productive to assemble systems out of microscopic components. Component assortments that offer a hundred different implementations of stacks or queues are not what the component market is waiting for.

Component frameworks are the next problem. Components will only interact properly if installed together with the required frameworks. Thus, component frameworks become products in their own right. By necessity, there will be far fewer component frameworks than components, but a careful selection of frameworks is crucial to establish a successful component-based system. Component specifications thus need to list the frameworks that are either required or could optionally be also interfaced with. More specialized component frameworks could even become rather effective selection criteria when looking for components that need to support a chosen component framework.

The location of components and component vendors based on requirement profiles is also an open problem. How can component services be described to allow for efficient retrieval with high recall and high precision? An approach that shows some potential is based on ontological approaches. An ontology is a universe of discourse covering the knowledge about entities in that universe. A basis for such an approach is a standardized way to interchange knowledge. The ANSI X3T2 committee's working draft of the knowledge interchange format, developed at Stanford, proposes such a standard (http://logic.stanford.edu/kif/). Corinto, an Italy-based consortium founded in 1995 and jointly run by IBM, Apple, and Selfin, has a project called Reuse Center: an ontology-based repository for object-oriented software components (http://corinto.interbusiness.it/). A Stanford project specifically addresses knowledge-based CORBA component repositories (http://ksi.cpsc.ucalgary.ca/KAW/KAW96/gennari/).

A recent project at Stanford, the Computer Industry Project (SCIP), investigates the interaction of markets and technology that is so characteristic of components (http://www-gsb.stanford.edu/scip/sirp.html).

Another issue is the technical infrastructure required to establish electronic distribution channels. As components may have to be transferred as part of assemblies, there is a need to establish licensing schemes that distinguish several different forms of use. A component may be bought for purposes of unlimited use and royalty-free redistribution in assemblies. This is the common business model in today's controls market. Means that create a return proportional to the actual use of a component may be more satisfactory, both for component vendors and for vendors of products using assembled components. Pay-per-use schemes (Cox, 1990) would cater for this perfectly, but they rely on a refined and tamperproof infrastructure that can verify a component's licensing status and measure a component's use. The CORBA Licensing Service is an example; the COM Licensing Service comes close.

Pay-per-use raises further technical problems. The charges per use will in most cases be very low. Care needs to be taken to avoid charging-overheads higher than the actual charges. Also, service providers may want to charge their users a fixed subscription fee, but themselves pay the actual use charges to component providers. Viability of component markets could thus depend on either special hardware support in standard PCs, or on NCs (network computers), in which case use metering can be approximated by servers.

CHAPTER TWENTY-FOUR

Component assembly

Components are units of deployment, deployable by third parties, but are never deployed in isolation. Component instances interact with each other, usually mediated by one or more component frameworks. One obvious way of assembling systems out of components is by way of traditional programming. However, the reach and viability of components are much increased by enabling simpler forms of assembly to cover most common component applications – or to avoid separate assembly altogether.

24.1 Visual component assembly

Visual assembly of component instances is one way of simplifying the assembly process. JavaBeans components, for example, can distinguish between use and build time of their instances. A 'bean' can therefore exhibit special looks, for example building block icons; behavior, for example handles to connect instances to others; and guidance, for example dedicated online help to assist assembly personnel. During assembly, components are instantiated, and instances are connected using a uniform approach to connectable objects with outgoing and incoming interfaces. Both JavaBeans and COM support general connection paradigms for this purpose.

Where required, additional behavior is added using a scripting approach. A script is essentially a small program – usually a procedure – that intercepts an event on its path from source to sink and triggers special actions. The prototypical application builder supporting a dedicated scripting language is Visual Basic, although Apple's Hypercard was a precursor. (Hypercard failed to create a market for several reasons. It had a totally inadequate programming interface for new components. The set of standard properties that could be expected to be understood by all or most components was too small. Finally, the set of initial components was too small to show the full potential of the approach.) Following the assembly approach of Visual Basic, but underpinning it with a proper programming language and development environment, are Borland's Delphi and C++ Builder. In all these cases, there is a sharp distinction between building and using an application and thus a continued emphasis on the concept of applications.

24.2   Compound documents to supersede visual assembly

Where component instances are naturally visual (for example provide a visual user interface), dedicated builders or assembly environments can be unified with environments for regular use. With compound documents, integration of build and use environments is straightforward and natural: documents are applications and document editing is component (instance) assembly. In such a system, there need not be any gap between component assembly and component use. The transition can be smooth: using component assemblies, late assembly of further component instances, or programmed generation of further assemblies can all be combined to suit application needs. To be fully useful, the assembly mechanisms need to be available at use time, if so desired. The BlackBox component builder and framework follow this approach. There is no sharp distinction between component assembly and component use, although such a line can be drawn by not deploying required builder components.

Seamless integration of build and use environments, especially in the context of compound documents, forms the strongest and most productive case yet for rapid application development (RAD). Production quality components, prototype components, and throwaway use-once solutions can be freely combined. Requirements capturing and change request validation can be performed efficiently and effectively in this setting. Sufficiently trained end-users can continue to fine-tune their system – if that is organizationally desirable.

24.3   Components beyond graphical user interface environments

Most component software approaches proposed, and all that have gained a viable market share, have addressed client-side front-end or stand-alone interactive applications. The demanding nature of modern graphical user interfaces, combined with the relative regularity of user interfaces, makes reusable components particularly valuable assets. However, other areas of computing, and server-based solutions in particular, are also of rapidly increasing complexity. Nevertheless, development of component technology for servers and other non-interactive systems is lagging well behind that for interactive systems, and in particular that for compound document and Web-browsing systems.

For server-based components, the clear division between build and use time is more natural. Business objects, as proposed by Oliver Sims (Sims, 1994), were one of the first proposals for 'components everywhere.' With this idea in mind, the New World Infrastructure (Newi) system was created (Chapters 13 and 18). More recent examples are Java 'servlets': components that are designed to operate on a server but which can be assembled visually. While harmonizing well with many current models, including that favored by CORBA, assembly before use usually requires early decisions as to which component instances to place where in a distributed system. Recall that in most systems, including current CORBA implementations, there is little to no support for object migration that preserves existing object references, although migration facilities are discussed.

Another example of component standards not aiming for graphical user interface environments is OPC (OLE for process control), a set of interface standards for device drivers in the factory automation area (Chapter 18).

24.4 Managed and 'self-guided' component assembly

Component assembly is always about assembly of component *instances*. (Recall that a component instance, where the component has been implemented using object technology, is normally a web of objects.) Combining multiple *components* is, of course, also possible, but in fact closely resembles the traditional task of building higher-level libraries by using available lower-level ones. In other words, component (rather than component instance) assembly would merely be a new word for programming. Component instance assembly, however, is different. Rather than mixing the code and resources that implement components with the code that 'connects' instances, the two aspects are kept separate. Lightweight programming (scripting) can be used to connect instances, while programming new instantiable components is substantially more involved – and is better not done with scripting languages and interfaces.

There is a flip side to the above observations. As assembly focuses on instances, it can operate only on instances that can be predetermined at assembly time. This is negating one of the greatest potentials of software: the ability to create new instances at will and in any number. Where these new instances are always to be used in the same predefined configurations, deep copying of template assemblies (prototype assemblies) can be used. A common application for this can be found in compound document systems: form templates. A form template is a document that is copied each time that a fresh form, ready to be filled in, needs to be created.

If it is necessary to work with dynamic instances of components in unforeseeable configurations, the remaining possibilities are managed and self-guided assembly. Managed assembly rests on an automated assembly component that implements the policies that govern the dynamic assembly of instances. An example would be a system that used a rule base to synthesize forms according to the current situation. Self-guided assembly is similar, but uses rules that are carried by the component instances themselves. For example, a component instance could form a 'mobile agent,' an entity that migrates from server to server and which aggregates other component instances to assemble functionality based on the findings at the various servers. Obviously, this is a fairly far-fetched scenario. The point is that there is some potential beyond static assembly of component instances.

24.5 Component evolution

Component technology is late assembly. The potential of components increases with the further deferral of assembly (or binding). At the same time, the fragility of the overall system increases. Components will normally undergo regular product evolution. Installation of new versions will compete with running systems that expect older versions or even with existing instances of older versions of the same component. The later a component is retrieved from a repository and instantiated against already instantiated components, the greater the potential for version conflicts.

In distributed systems, it is not realistic to shut down all current instances of a component to install a new version. Binary interoperability across clients of different versions and instances of different versions needs to be planned in (Release-to-release binary compatibility). Actual upgrading of operational instances to newer versions is still an area of active research.

In realistic settings, it must be expected that various versions of the same component will have to coexist in a single system. Migration from one system generation to the next is the most important example. Besides coexistence of multiple versions, adaptation of incompatible or older software using wrapper components is required to address 'legacy migration' problems. (Without solving the legacy migration problem, component technology will not be able to play a major role in the foreseeable future.)

The most robust approach to supporting version coexistence and wrapper components is that of COM. As, once published, COM interfaces are by convention immutable, there is no versioning problem for individual interfaces. Instead, a component offering a new service version will have to use a new interface. The key advantage is that it is possible to support simultaneously the old interface with its old semantics and the new interface with the new semantics. Obviously, old interfaces can be retired once their support is withdrawn. The absence of such an old interface will lead to a well-defined error when coming across a client that still relies on this interface. (QueryInterface will return an indication that the interface is not supported.)

The versioning approach in CORBA is inferior in that it is still expected to merge all operations of all versions into a single interface. This does not support the notion of changing the semantics of an operation without also changing its name or signature. As a consequence, ever new operation names need to be introduced – and there is no simple means to retire old operations without threatening binary compatibility. Even SOM's release orders cannot resolve this problem.

Another problem with version management is transitivity. (This problem was brought to the attention of the author by Microsoft's Tony Williams.) If an object creates another object, CORBA-style versioning allows verification that the server supporting the new object is of a suitable version. However, once an object has been created, references to the object can be passed around without any further version checking. This is unsound because the component originally accepting the created version may have less strict requirements than the component receiving the object reference. In other words, it is not sufficient to check versions at object creation time only. In COM, this problem is solved by keeping interfaces of different versions completely separate; a reference to a component's interface has immutable semantics. A similar solution for CORBA would be possible on the basis of CORBA 2.0's Repository IDs, which also uniquely identify an interface and which are also expected to be changed when the interface semantics changes. However, the explicit use of Repository IDs in interface definitions and in client code is not yet established.

Java does not yet have a special version control mechanism. Versioning of interfaces is an essentially unsolved problem. In particular, Java does not address the problem of coexistence of clients and providers based on different versions of the same interface. A partial solution to the problem of compatibility of persistent objects across component versions is offered by the Java Object Serialization Service (p. 241).

However, Java does define elaborate rules on binary compatibility. Unfortunately, some of these rules are questionable. For example, many Java interfaces contain constants that are meant to be used as arguments to some of the interface's methods. When a Java client of such a class is compiled, these constants are hard coded into the generated class file and no version dependency is recorded. If the interface is then revised and constants are redefined or removed, previously compiled classes will continue to use the old constant values and pass them to methods of the new interface. This will not be discovered by the version check of the class loader and is considered a 'feature.' Merely recompiling such a client class then leads to potentially changed behavior. Since version tracking in Java is oblivious to such changes, hard to track problems can result.

CHAPTER TWENTY-FIVE

On the horizon

This chapter concludes the technical coverage of component software. The following sections introduce a number of emerging approaches, selected for their potential to set new directions. Some of the approaches are still in an academic stage, others are at the level of small market shares. This section may safely be skipped, but following it through broadens the perspective for possible future developments.

25.1 Advanced object composition

Recall the important properties of object composition in a component setting. Object composition is a useful technique across component boundaries. Class composition is too static for many component applications: the class to inherit from needs to be available at compile time. Object composition allows for the runtime extension of independently deployed components.

Object composition is usually based on message forwarding rather than on delegation. Unfortunately, forwarding-based object composition introduces conceptual complexity by eliminating the identity of the whole. In contrast, when composing classes, the resulting subclass generates whole objects with a single identity. However, when composing objects using message forwarding, a web of objects represents the whole. The part objects retain separate identities.

For the programmer, this loss of identity of the whole complicates the design process. Incoming messages have to be handled by the receiving part object in a way that does not threaten the consistency of the whole. To maintain consistency, one of the part objects must be designated the 'main' part. All other part objects have to be modeled as subordinates. The problem can be solved by using delegation-based object composition.

25.1.1 Delegation

Class composition based on implementation inheritance introduces subtle dependencies between base class and subclass. If used across components, these dependencies lead to the fragile base class problem. Object composition based on message forwarding does not suffer from this problem. However, if delegation is used, object composition is just as problematic as class composition.

Much research has been undertaken in recent years to develop a firm handle on the complex semantics of implementation inheritance. It is not yet clear whether this research effort will eventually succeed in producing a practicable method of harnessing implementation inheritance while preserving most of its flexibility. If such a method can be devised, then it will simultaneously solve the equivalent problem of delegation-based object composition. A restriction to selection of delegates at object creation time, with no dynamic changes allowed, may then become necessary to harness delegation.

Solving the problems of delegation across component boundaries is equivalent to solving the semantic fragile base class problem. Once solved, delegation-based object composition can be used to form composites at runtime that, as a whole, have a single identity. The language-level mechanisms have been around for a while (Ungar and Smith, 1987). Systems using delegation-based object composition with fine-grained objects initially performed poorly, but more recent work has demonstrated that good performance is achievable (Hölzle, 1995).

25.1.2 Split objects

A web of objects with a common identity established through delegation is sometimes called a *split object* (for example Astudillo, 1996; Bardou and Dony, 1996). The idea is to treat the split object as a whole and to maintain encapsulation for the whole. A fragment of a split object individually does not have object status as it shares its identity with all other fragments of the same split object. Delegation across split objects is excluded in this model, and delegation is thus disciplined to allow for system structure.

A possible direction for future research is *hierarchical split objects*. Each fragment of a split object could have private parts that internally are organized as split objects. This generalized model could form an interesting basis for recursive composition of objects out of fragments.

Another problem with split objects is *reorganization* (Astudillo, 1996). The fragments of a split object are exposed to clients to enable viewpoint-specific selection of features. Evolution of individual fragments is thus much easier than evolution of the fragmentation itself. Merging or splitting of fragments breaks existing clients.

25.1.3 Environmental acquisition

Closely related to delegation in split objects is the concept of objects that form parts of aggregates and acquire properties from their enclosing objects. Instead of forming a flat web of parts, as in the case of split objects, objects are embedded in a containment hierarchy. Delegation or forwarding of requests that cannot be handled by a part are sent up the containment hierarchy. The innermost enclosing container that can handle a request will do so.

Like split objects, environmental acquisition is a form of disciplined delegation.

25.1.4 Dynamic inheritance

Instead of strengthening the static properties of delegation, it is also possible to loosen those of implementation inheritance. The idea is to generalize the concept of a base class to that of a base object selected at object construction time. This is called *dynamic inheritance* or *configurable inheritance*. Stroustrup had proposed a scheme along these lines for C++ (Stroustrup, 1994, Section 12.7).

Usually, proposals for dynamic inheritance try to preserve the self-recursion semantics of inheritance and hence rely on delegation semantics between an object and its base object(s). An unusually lightweight proposal based on single inheritance and forwarding semantics can be found in Chapter 22.

25.2 | New forms of object and component abstraction

A fundamental property of objects is their uniform presentation of features irrespective of the actual client. Subtyping allows for objects that have more features than are statically known. However, for a traditional inheritance approach, all these features need to be grouped into classes, which then form a static inheritance graph. The number of different perspectives or viewpoints on an object is thus statically fixed.

Traditional inheritance only allows for the addition of subtypes. However, it may be necessary to present a viewpoint that is effectively a supertype of existing types. Most approaches would require refactoring of the class graph to introduce a new superclass. Few languages support the explicit *construction of supertypes*; Sather is one such language (Szyperski *et al.*, 1994; Omohundro and Stoutamire, 1996).

25.2.1 Subject-oriented programming

In 1993, Harrison and Ossher proposed the concept of *subject-oriented* programming. The idea is that a subject can associate state and behavior with an object identifier as required by that subject. Different subjects can then see the same 'object,' by referring to the same object identifier, as having different properties and behavior. Composition of subjects, that is composition of associations of state and behavior with object identifiers, has been studied more recently (Ossher *et al.*, 1995).

An approach similar to subject orientation, but much older, is the association of property lists with objects. Associated properties are only meaningful to those knowing certain property types, whereas objects abstractly maintain the union of associated properties. The concept of associated property lists goes back to early Lisp systems. However, object-oriented models do not normally support the generic association of properties with objects.

25.2.2 Aspect-oriented programming

Promoted by Kiczales (1994), aspect-oriented programming is about explicitly slicing programs according to the various aspects they address. By analogy, the engineering of a building is split into aspects of statics, safety, plumbing, electricity, ventilation, and so on. Instead of creating 'modules' for each section of the building that specify solutions to all these aspects, typical building plans are fully separated according to aspect. The binding concept are the physical coordinates of the building's shell.

Aspect-oriented programming aims to follow the lead of other engineering disciplines and support individual programming of separate aspects. Obviously, as in the building example, the various aspects are separate but not independent. Kiczales thus proposes a *weaver* tool that merges the aspect-oriented fragments into a whole. Weaving is a complex task as mutual dependencies among the fragments need to be respected.

25.3 Interesting combined approaches

Some recent products used surprising combinations of what were, until then, independent technologies to achieve significant symbioses. This section describes two examples of such products.

25.3.1 Webtops

IONA released its Orbix/Web in early 1997. Representing a lightweight IIOP-based ORB, Orbix/Web comes as a set of Java classes and travels together with applets to the browser. The applet can thus use ORB services and issue method invocations across IIOP. The approach of sending the entire ORB with the applet is radical but rather in the spirit of Java. The incorporation of Visigenic's ORB into Netscape Communicator will slow Orbix/Web, but it still has a market as not all browsers will have CORBA 2.0-compliant ORBs built in in the near future.

Once browsers enable access to corporate servers, they can be used as universal replacements for desktop metaphors. The browser becomes the 'desktop' or, rather, the Webtop.

25.3.2 Orbix on ISIS

Again using IONA's Orbix, another interesting product combines Orbix with ISIS, a commercial version of Birman's ISIS research system (Birman, 1985).

ISIS supports the concept of groups across a distributed system. Group membership and messaging are controlled to construct virtually synchronous semantics for the entire group. A typical application for ISIS is the fault-tolerance enhancement achieved by executing an application on multiple machines. ISIS then guarantees that the set of replicas will always be in a mutually consistent state.

By implementing an Orbix version on top of ISIS, the replication and fault-tolerant properties inherent to the underlying ISIS are retained and combined with the CORBA object communication model. An application of Orbix on ISIS, at the time of writing, was the Swiss Electronic Stock Exchange in Zurich.

PART FIVE

Markets and components

This part, which is of a non-technical nature, closes the circle and links up with Part One. The technical essence of Part Four is briefly rehashed where necessary to derive market- and profession-oriented consequences. Chapter 26 develops arguments for the markets that are likely to develop around component software in the future. Chapter 27 presents a similar analysis for some important new professions and their job profiles. Finally, Chapter 28 addresses the seemingly paradox situation that software component development obviously costs and therefore needs to be amortized – whereas people have the tendency not to pay for widely accessible information (and do not perceive software as 'hard' products).

CHAPTER TWENTY-SIX

Future markets

The Gartner Group report *Object Orientation for the Rest of Us* (March 1995), as cited in Orfali *et al*. (1996, p. 33), predicted that:

> 'Software components will foster emergence of three new markets: a component market, a component assembly tool market, and a market for custom applications developed using components.'

It is interesting that, out of the three markets mentioned, two are product markets and only one is a service market. Besides the one mentioned, a variety of further service markets will join in, and perhaps become even more important than the product markets. Whereas software component products on their own may be difficult to market, a combination with services strengthens the offering. The following brief discussion of markets thus distinguishes component, component tool, and component service markets. Development of custom applications is just one such service.

26.1 Components

The obvious market is the one for components targeting horizontal or vertical domains. To be more precise, each of these domains is likely to create its own market, as competition across domains is not likely to be strong.

Marketing components to recover the cost of their development (and make a profit) is a challenging problem of its own. Whereas the tools and services markets described in the following sections are fairly well understood, marketing of software components falls into unknown territory. There seems to be little that can be learned from traditional component markets in other engineering disciplines. Software components are too 'soft' to have direct analogies to warehouses and distributor chains. For a detailed discussion see Chapter 28.

26.2 Tools

Software component development and use are far more demanding on developers than traditional software development was. It can therefore be expected that component technology will raise the level of expectations on supporting tools. Most of the traditional tools of the software engineer will continue to be useful. In addition, a considerable number of new tools will be needed.

26.2.1 Component design and implementation tools

Component design rests on the environmental specifications – usually given by a component framework and an underlying component (or object) model. Ideally, component development should use rapid application development (RAD) methods to capture requirements quickly within a working component system. The same environment is used to prototype a component, within a characteristic environment, and to implement the component.

26.2.2 Component testing tools

Testing of components is possibly the single most demanding aspect of component technology. By definition, components can only be tested in a few, hopefully representative, configurations. Systematic approaches to testing of components are needed, and intense tool support for this purpose is likely to be required.

Faced with the extreme difficulties of component testing, two strategies seem advisable. The first strategy is to avoid errors statically wherever possible. For example, a safe and expressive language can allow a compiler or analyzing tool to catch substantial errors statically. Even better, a carefully crafted language can rule out entire classes of errors. Prominent examples are languages that have no explicit notion of memory deallocation: dangling references and memory leaks are simply eliminated. More subtle examples are language-enforced access modes and visibility rules eliminating programmed side effects that break encapsulation and thus invariants.

■ A rule of thumb is that most errors that can be caught using *automated* runtime debugging aids could be statically avoided, had a 'better' language been chosen for the implementation.

The second strategy is to make sure that components are deployed in such a way that faults leave logged traces. In this way, a failure in a production component system can at least be traced.

26.2.3 Component assembly tools

Components are assembled by instantiating and connecting component instances and by customizing component resources. While component instances at runtime may or may not correspond to visual entities, it is useful to assume that all component instances have a visual representation at assembly time. It is then possible to use powerful document-centric builder tools to assemble components, even if the runtime environment is a server or batch one. JavaBeans is a component standard that explicitly distinguishes between assembly time and runtime and that allows component instances to look and behave differently during assembly time and runtime.

An important aspect often overlooked by current 'builder tools' is that assembly itself needs to be automated. Software assembly is different from hardware assembly in that it is not necessary to assemble individual instances repeatedly – the entire assembled product can instead be cloned. However, a different aspect of assembly processes also still holds for software assembly. If future versions of components become available, then it is important that the assembly process can be repeated – only modified where necessary to live with or take advantage of the new component versions.

26.2.4 Component system diagnosis and maintenance

Related to component testing, it is important that an entire component system in the field can be diagnosed. Diagnosis is tricky, as the system is likely to consist of components from many different and independent vendors. Either a diagnosis tool has to concentrate selectively on the contributions made by those components from a selected set of vendors or, preferably, a diagnosis standard should be established and component vendors should provide diagnosis components that can be configured into the diagnosis tools.

Once diagnosis is possible, maintenance follows. It may be necessary to replace components and their instances and resources in a running system. To make diagnosis and maintenance at all feasible, a component system needs to be architected with these requirements in mind. The CORBA system management common facility is an example in this direction. Diagnosis and maintenance would normally be performed remotely. As these tasks require special clearances, overall security policies need to consider them.

26.3 Services

26.3.1 Component system and framework architects

As described in detail in the next chapter, the tasks of architecting component systems or component frameworks are extremely demanding. It is likely that most organizations will not develop the in-house expertise required to do so successfully. Independent architecture firms can concentrate the expertise and amortize it over projects for many customers.

Component system architects are likely to work with a few clients in a tight consultancy relation. Component framework architects, on the other hand, may well aim at open markets.

26.3.2 **Component assembly consultants**

Component assembly is supposedly simple enough to re-enable the use of customized software even by small organizations. Obviously, this is relative. The more demanding components are, the less obvious it is which ones to select from a large palette of possibilities. Consultants specializing in the mere assembly of components will find a broad market. Some may go further and offer custom production of the 'missing' components to create true custom solutions.

26.3.3 **Component configuration management**

With complex remote diagnosis and maintenance mechanisms in place, these tasks are a good opportunity for outsourcing. Part of a management contract could be the monitoring of component markets for the arrival of more suitable components. Other parts could be the development of gradual migration plans and the integration of new components into existing systems.

A particularly daunting task is the migration from monolithic solutions to component-based ones. Too many assumptions can pass undocumented in a monolithic solution. Reverse engineering can answer some of the questions. The parallel operation of the old and a proposed new system over an extended period is often the only way to convince everyone involved that the new system is capable of taking over. A practical example is the use of COM to support simultaneously system services from different generations.

For the parallel operation of systems from different generations and the extraction and analysis of observed differences, substantial expertise is required. It may even be necessary to emulate older hardware or software that itself is no longer available. The relevant detailed information could well be a critical trade secret. Likewise, the successful transition can be of vital importance for an entire business.

26.3.4 **Component warehouses, marketing, and consulting**

A traditional aspect of components is the necessary mediation between component providers and component users. Component warehouses, distributors, and marketing and consultancy firms all have their place. However, with software components all activities are likely to be fully electronic, for example via the Internet. It is not clear to what extent traditional component businesses find analogies in the software component markets.

Note that the Internet scenario assumes that the legal and practical protection offered by physical packaging becomes unnecessary. Today, software is cast on physical media, burdened with piles of printed material, and the resulting 'bricks' are shrink wrapped.

CHAPTER TWENTY-SEVEN

New professions

This chapter is speculative in nature. It is not intended to present polished job profiles. Instead, the goal is to point out the variety and complexity of the tasks involved and to suggest the creation of specialist areas. The following descriptions can be compared with traditional task descriptions, including those of system analysts and programmers. One of the most interesting phenomena that can be observed when performing such a comparison is the emphasis on independence in the component case.

Component technology does not make sense when it is addressed in a traditional top-down fashion. This needs to be reflected in the organizational structure. For example, while a component systems architect creates the foundations for a component framework architect to begin working, the two jobs are *not* in a traditional hierarchical order. It has to be expected that the two tasks are performed by independent organizations, mediated by market and standardization effects.

The independence of the various levels is emphasized further when realizing that a component can be made to function within multiple component frameworks. Likewise, a component framework can be made to function within multiple component systems. Component systems and component frameworks are likely candidates for (partial) standardization, whereas components are likely to remain 'free' and bound only by the standardized frameworks on which they depend.

Independence leads to independent evolution and necessarily to (technical) conflicts. There is no simple answer to this problem – weakly coordinated co-evolution in an industrial environment is probably the only way. However, an emphasis on architecture is crucial if independently developed interoperable components are to become reality.

27.1 Component system architect

The architecture of a component system is the single most important and at the same time by far the most demanding aspect. Components can only function when embedded in a component framework. A component system typically consists of many component frameworks. Each framework needs to obtain enough resources and control to enable and, where possible, to enforce a smooth interoperation of the components it integrates. Component frameworks are therefore at a much greater risk of mutual exclusion than are individual components. Correct interoperation of the component frameworks in a system is a prime objective of a component system architecture. A possible but not yet fully understood approach is to create system frameworks that integrate all component frameworks in a system.

The role of a component system architect would be to analyze system requirements, both of the existing systems and of systems planned for introduction. A main goal is to devise a system partitioning into component frameworks that combines interoperability of the frameworks with sufficient room for independent operation and evolution of the frameworks. For each of the component frameworks, the basis needs to be created for largely independent detailed work of a component framework architect.

A component system architect provides architecture for the architects: the architects of component frameworks. It is what city master-planning is to the architects of individual buildings.

27.2 Component framework architect

A component framework accepts the plug-in of components. It facilitates the interoperation of these components and partially enforces their organized interaction. The rules by which components have to 'play' to be acceptable for the framework need to be precise enough to allow largely independent creation and evolution of components.

A component framework architect needs to understand fully the horizontal or vertical domain that the framework in question should address. Both creation of new frameworks and evolution of established ones are required. Framework evolution has to respect two issues: preservation of compatibility with (most) existing components and preservation of interoperability rules established by (most) component systems using the framework.

A component framework is not just a design – it may itself contain substantial implementation parts. The framework implementation is the basis for the interoperation with other frameworks, for the rule of component interaction, and for the provision of component default behavior where applicable. Depending on the project size, separate programmers may be required to take the framework design and implement it.

For the component programmer, a component framework architect has to specify very precisely what the framework expects from and provides to a component. In the absence or impracticability of fully formal specifications of all aspects, it is particularly important to provide documents that help a component programmer form the right intuition about the concepts of the framework.

Component frameworks are complex and difficult to get 'right.' Iterative design of a component framework is unavoidable. It is likely that a framework design stabilizes only after the framework has been used by different people in multiple projects. It is difficult but crucial that the experience condensed in a successful framework design is properly documented.

27.3 Component programmer

Components are the 'leaves' of a component system. As such, they are the parts of greatest replaceability and cross-organizational exchange. Components do not have a bounded size. However, given that they form the units of configuration and assembly, it makes sense to concentrate on components with well-defined and bounded functionality.

A component programmer takes component framework specifications and specific component requirements and takes these through analysis and design to implementation of components. Traditional factoring into teams may be required for very large components. However, normally individual components remain in the bounds of what a single person can manage. (Back-up strategies may still ask for teams.)

27.4 Component assembler

Component systems with their frameworks and components do not perform any useful function unless customized to do so. The concept of traditional applications disappears with many component systems, for example to be replaced by document-centric computing. Nevertheless, the majority of users will continue to look for 'applications': solutions to concrete problems in their routine. Obviously, where a good solution can be found by a layperson's component assembly, this will be done. Highly specialized niches will find workable solutions where current technology has fallen short of offering the required flexibility per dollar ratio.

As 'end-users' become component assemblers, the state-of-the-art rises. Ad hoc crafted solutions are acceptable where they solve a problem and where the problem and its solution do *not* form part of the core business of the organization. To maintain a competitive edge, a business needs to do *better* in its core areas. Professional experienced component assembly staff fill this gap.

A component assembler (or composer) takes application requirements, selects appropriate components – and perhaps component frameworks – and assembles these. Component assembly may be largely automated by an available builder tool, or it may require substantial programming (or scripting) to provide the 'glue.' Which end of the scale a particular assembly task will end up at depends on the inherent complexity of the application domain and the number of sufficiently similar demands on the market. If, despite substantial complexity, the market is large enough, it is likely that components and builder tools that reduce the burden on the component assembler will be found.

The more individual the task, the more creativity and programming effort are required of the component assembler to create solutions based on components – and perhaps component frameworks – on the market. Free selection of component frameworks is not normally possible however. Higher-level organizational requirements often prescribe the use of a specific component framework. This may be done to optimize interoperability, to minimize training costs, or to reduce overall project cost.

An important role of a component assembler is to provide feedback on the feasibility and practicability of currently used frameworks and components. Unless already discovered during analysis, it is to be expected that the component assembler makes the final decision as to whether a solution can be based on available components. If not, a new component would need to be programmed. The decision as to whether to pursue such individual component development efforts or to loosen the requirements can have dramatic effects on the viability of the project and is thus left to management.

CHAPTER TWENTY-EIGHT

A component marketing paradox

Software, as its name suggests, is not a tangible product. In the literal sense, as the opposite of hardware, there is nothing physical or unique about a particular *copy* of a software artifact. Two copies of the same software artifact are indistinguishable.

When software is sold in bulky shrink-wrapped boxes that contain thousands of pages of printed documentation and enormous piles of software on media, customers seem to get something for their money. If the same functionality and documentation are made accessible through electronic distribution channels, the true 'softness' of the traded goods becomes obvious. Are people willing to pay for bits as they come in over the network link?

A significant trend over the past two years has been the total collapse of access charges to the Internet. Essentially, the Internet is now increasingly available at low and flat access rates, independent of the actual access pattern. This has a dramatic consequence: the Internet becomes so cheap that it will grow faster than ever before. The Internet already threatens other carriers. Telephony and fax, video conferencing, distributed groupware – everything will find its place on the Internet to make it the one and only total communication interconnect.

Software distribution is bound to move from stores to virtual stores. The appeal of printed and neatly bound documentation will for some time continue to create a 'physical' market. However, as devices get smaller, display technology improves, and browsing metaphors leave 'thumbing of pages' behind, this may also change. (With the introduction of CDs many believed in the continuing appeal of traditional LPs. With the exception of a small collectors' market, LPs have almost vanished since then.)

What would be the good of almost free Internet access if the *contents* provided were expensive? Alternative vendors will always try to steal the show of established content providers, by making the same functionality available for less. If a component is useful to many or all, then its availability merely raises the state-of-the-art. Everyone willing to remain competitive will have to get this component eventually. Early adopters may still be willing to pay and perhaps pay well. As the mainstream catches on, the market volume explodes, but the willingness to pay *anything* diminishes.

People have a tendency *not to pay* for information of common value. They are willing to pay for services where the services are obviously tailored to their needs. An attempt to charge for services, or soft products, that are mass marketed will fail in the absence of monopolies or cartels. The Internet creates a worldwide market, bridging all nations and local markets. Its physical infrastructure is increasingly distributed and redundant. For horizontal markets, upholding of monopolies or cartels in this environment is difficult if not impossible.

If customers do not want to pay for software components they download from the Internet, how should the investment into producing the components be amortized? This is the central component marketing paradox and its resolution is at the heart of success or failure of the software component approach. It is not likely that people will ever be willing to pay significant amounts for electronically acquired 'generalware' – components of widespread usefulness. Other profit-generating models have thus to be evaluated by developers and distributors of such generally useful components. The diversity and usefulness of the entire component 'market' are at stake.

28.1 Branding

The problem of a need to control quality and prices has been known for some time in most established commodity markets. How can vendors of bananas distinguish themselves from others? Are all bananas not equal? The answer is *branding*. Using focused marketing, a brand is carefully associated with hallmarks of quality, performance, affordability, and so on.

Establishing powerful brands will become important for software components as well. In a world in which access to many components will have to be inexpensive, it can become prohibitive to market individual components. Instead, users are encouraged to browse the catalogs carrying the 'right' brand. Such brands may well be established by wholesalers, brokers, or other intermediate agents rather than component manufacturers.

An interesting effect of branding is the possible creation of *de facto* monopolies. Although it is difficult to imagine actual monopolies in international component markets, it is readily conceivable that brands lead to extremely strong vendors or vending chains.

28.2 Pay-per-use

Brad Cox proposed models of pay-per-use (Cox, 1990, 1996). The infrastructure should guarantee that every use of a component is tracked and billed. This is an obvious model, and support in the form of licensing services has been built into both COM and CORBA. Java so far lacks a licensing service.

On second thoughts, the pay-per-use approach is flawed however. Software components are not necessarily at a level of granularity that makes any sense to end users. If a bill lists zillions of uses of ridiculous numbers of components, then customers will (rightfully) object and the service will collapse. *Transparency of cost* is essential. For example, just by browsing through Web pages, a user may receive and temporarily use an enormous number of applets (or ActiveX objects or...). Billing per use would be unacceptable unless the user is made aware of the cost *before* using an object. Normally, that would require prompting *before* entering a Web page. This model works as long as it is used sparingly and only for services that are of obvious and immediate value to the customer. It can be expected that users will simply ignore services that announce billing – and they will rightly refuse to pay unannounced bills.

A property of component software that makes pay-per-use particularly inadequate is the concept of late composition. Anyone and even automated services can combine components to form a new whole. Sub-billing of the part components involved is out of the question as that would not be transparent. Licensing of subcomponents by the assembling organization will work only where the composition (assembly) is not delayed until the last moment. However, it is just this possibility of delaying assembly until a concrete request comes in that makes software components particularly flexible. A solution would be a billing hierarchy. As a result, the end-user is billed only for the top-level components used directly, but the price will vary potentially from use to use as the subcomponent prices change. It is not clear whether customers would generally accept such a bazaar like situation.

Pay-per-use has an advantage however. If combined with a billing hierarchy to maintain billing transparency, income can be fairly distributed to all involved component vendors. Small component shops can exist even without massive marketing efforts. To some extent, this would be a developer's paradise. Although the above arguments make pay-per-use a not so obvious winner in the current component marketing strategy 'wars,' it should be noted that the required billing technology is at least almost ready.

Smart-card systems can be used conveniently to authenticate the principal: the real user willing to pay. The same cards can also hold the electronic cash for direct debit, or the credit information for later collective billing. The problems of local tampering with end points (PCs) largely disappear with the introduction of pure network computing. A network computer (NC) does not function autonomously and all customization is reduced to 'user profiles' kept in the network. On NCs, accounting and billing can be performed by the network in a highly reliable way.

Finally, service providers addressing end users may decide to accept flat fee subscriptions and deal with pay-per-use issues in internal agreements with component vendors. This model is particularly attractive where end users merely use NCs that cannot locally retain copies of components.

An interesting downside of pay-per-use has been proposed in an IDC white paper (Steel, 1996): currently dominating suppliers may have no interest in pay-per-use systems revealing the actual use profiles of the software they sell. The report claims that most companies currently have no clue how the software they have acquired is actually used – if at all. Pay-per-use systems offer an unparalleled degree of scrutiny: components that are not used will not be requested and will not be paid for. The percentage of mostly unused components in a best-selling mainstream application will become obvious.

28.3 Co-placement of advertisements

Instead of centering in on pay-per-use, it is instructive to compare the cost recovery methods used by other 'soft' media. Print media reached the point a long time ago, when the price tag at the local kiosk was lower than the actual production cost. 'Free to the air' television networks are even more extreme – as their name suggests, their services are free. In both cases, cost is recovered through advertising. Advertising is already becoming a major source of income on the Web.

Advertising ruins the quality of television offerings, but does so to a much lesser degree for print media. The reason is simple. Print media do not force the consumer into a sequential consumption mode. Content and advertisements compete for the reader's attention. Reading is a selective process. The same is true on the Web – advertisements there are better compared to those in print media than to the irritating interceptions on free television. Furthermore, advertising on the Web can be 'subject oriented.' Unlike print media, Web servers can attempt to build user profiles and make advertisements available in a more selective fashion. For example, the home page of an organization might display specific technical advertisements only to those users that in their (provided or generated) profiles indicate interest in technical matters. For this to be workable, the Web needs to be further developed, but technically this approach would clearly be possible.

There is a second-order component-marketing paradox when relying on returns through advertisements. Such advertisements obviously cannot advertise software components, as their vendors would not normally be willing or able to pay for advertisements – after all, they rely on advertisements to generate income. Hence, to break a seemingly vicious circle, advertisements for 'hard' products and individualized services are required. (As long as people are willing to pay high prices for carbonated, sugared, and colored water, or even just water, a steady income stream from advertisements can be guaranteed.) An interesting example is of a service industry, based on a freeware product, developed around the Linux operating system. Consultants charge for installing and maintaining Linux systems, although Linux itself and all its documentation is available free of charge.

28.4 Leveraging on newly created markets

Creators and providers of a domain-specific component system architecture or component framework can create new markets *if* the initially available infrastructure and functionality has critical mass. The latter is required for initial sufficiently broad user acceptance.

The first company to introduce a component approach to a domain traditionally dominated by monolithic solutions will initially be able to capture a large fraction of the new but still small market. During market formation, clients will be willing to pay for the new infrastructure and the first components – the approach offers a competitive edge. As further vendors enter the new market, the situation gradually changes to the one of established component markets as described above.

Companies with highly specialized domain expertise are required to break the initial ice. However, the market start-up effect that does allow for initial and substantial charges makes the effort worthwhile (Szyperski, 1997). Substantial initial capital is required to accumulate the critical mass before the new market can take off. The critical mass required is simple to estimate. The first successful component infrastructure must already come with sufficient quality components to provide an edge for early adopters.

The case must be convincing: an early adopter is likely to be willing to invest in the development of a few highly specialized components, but the bulk must already be there. As the new component approach has to compete with established monolithic software in the target market, the flexibility of component approaches needs to be fully leveraged. A good starting point is to analyze where current clients of the monolithic solutions compromise their internal business processes to live with the inflexible solutions. Only where such compromises can be expressed as costs that could be saved or productivity losses that could be removed will a more flexible approach based on component technology be competitive. Two important advantages of component technology that contribute to such savings are the reduction in time to market and the more flexible response to rapidly changing business conditions. Generally speaking, it is more important to adapt quickly than to reduce costs.

28.5 Leverage of integrative forces

Even where direct competitiveness of a component approach over established monolithic approaches is hard to establish, introduction of component technology can be worthwhile. The benefits are the software engineering advantages of component technology. Solutions that are well modularized into components are easier to maintain, evolve, and refactor. Careful selection of component frameworks and component system architectures allows for the integration of previously separate business processes. With components from independent vendors, integration is an implicit outcome of the underlying approach. With monolithic solutions from independent vendors, integration is difficult to achieve unless an industry leader sets standards that at least serve as a lowest common denominator. This is not likely when attempting to integrate across different domains.

Thus, where the target market covers sufficiently large organizations with investments in several domains, a joint effort to introduce component technology-based integration across some of these domains could pay off. Initial investments are even larger than in the case of creating a component market for an individual domain. Formation of common interest groups is likely to be required. The market start-up effect can again be expected to produce initial direct returns before a transition to an established market occurs.

A final note: in some cases, a component market will remain small and therefore never reach the 'established market' effects. Then the group of vendors and clients of components remains small; business remains a matter of mutual agreements rather than open markets. This is where small vendors are likely to blossom.

Epilogue

'Is this the end?'

The Doors

Unlike technologies, markets do have a tendency to function even when left unattended. Market forces do not automatically thrive on technical excellence. However, in a situation in which everything else is equal, technology can be the deciding competitive edge. Technological superiority of an approach needs to be established on a broad basis. It is difficult to evaluate all trade-offs, before a technology is put to use.

Software component technology, like all component technologies, can exist only in the combined 'force fields' of technology and markets. Understanding the technical factors, but also what is 'good enough' to hit the markets, is important. Time to market is crucial – the quality of an approach cannot be measured on the basis of technical merit alone.

This book has presented an attempt at a unique merger of technology and market aspects driving component software. In an area evolving as quickly and dramatically as this, much had to be left unsaid. Where approaches come and go, fundamental problems and principles stay. Fundamental aspects are therefore at the heart of this book. To make such aspects accessible and meaningful, strong links to current approaches are also drawn. It is the tension between what could be done and what can be done that leads to deeper insight – a tension that in the area of component software is not likely to be resolved soon.

Component Pascal versus Java

Despite the declared independence of components from programming languages (Component Liberation Act, 1997), components still need to be constructed somehow. Component construction itself can be performed using almost arbitrary programming languages, as long as the language and its implementation support the particular component standard's interface conventions. These conventions usually include notions of object or interface references. However, as argued in Chapters 5–7, there are obligations left with the component implementer that may ask for proper language support. Issues of primary concern are performance, component safety, and component framework safety.

This appendix compares two of today's few component-oriented programming languages. One, Java, is very well known; the other, Component Pascal, less so. The two languages evolved independently and have their roots in the two major language strands found today: C and Pascal respectively. (One might argue that Java really is rather more in line with the Pascal language family, inheriting many of its strengths from Oberon or Modula-3. The 'C touch' of Java can indeed be seen as a clever camouflage.) The following is a compact rehash of material discussed in more detail throughout this book.

The Component Pascal language report and further documents can be found on the Web (http://www.oberon.ch/).

Component Pascal and its more academic root, Oberon, rest on ten years of experience – 30 years since the introduction of Pascal. The language has been used for an extremely wide spectrum of tasks:

- low-level systems programming – device drivers, embedded systems, realtime programming, garbage collectors, operating system kernels, interrupt handlers;
- complex graphical user interfaces, compound document systems (OLE *and* OpenDoc), the BlackBox component framework;
- high-level scripting.

Component Pascal can be implemented efficiently. For example, the entire BlackBox component developer, including the garbage collector, is implemented in Component Pascal. At the same time, Component Pascal is a safe language. A simple proof of concept: Component Pascal can be compiled to Java byte code (however, some improvements to the Java virtual machine would enable more efficient mappings). There are few languages that are sufficiently safe to enable compilation to Java byte code. Another example is Ada 95, and the first 'Ada 95 applets' appeared in early 1997. A compilation to Java byte code is *not* possible for languages in the C family, including C itself, C++, and Objective C. It is also impossible for most languages in the Pascal family, including Pascal itself, Object Pascal, and Modula-2.

Why is this seemingly arbitrary observation relevant? Because the Java virtual machine performs safety checks as part of the loading process that establish minimal safety properties of a loaded class. These checks redundantly recheck what is already checked by the Java compiler, but safeguard against byte code sequences that have been tampered with. The above languages are all ruled out, because they cannot be mapped into the safe world of the Java virtual machine. Of course, crippled subsets of these languages could, but it is fair to say that such subsets really represent different languages. (Recall that Java is sometimes sold as a safe subset of C++.)

Statically established and, at load time, enforced safety properties allow a component infrastructure to execute multiple components efficiently within the same protection domain (Chapter 6).

Here are the areas where Component Pascal (CP) and Java use essentially identical approaches:

- Smallest unit of deployment (smallest component): CP, compiled module; Java, compilation unit (part of a package)/class file.
- Support for object-oriented programming: CP and Java, yes.
- Support for type-safe separate compilation: CP and Java, yes.
- Implementation inheritance: CP and Java, single.
- Open packages: CP, open packages, called subsystems, supported by environment rather than language; Java, open package system in language.
- Cross-class protection (replacement for 'friend' mechanisms *à la* C++): CP, module; Java, package.
- Runtime type system: CP, type test and type guard; Java, instanceof test and checked type cast.
- Meta-programming: CP and Java, reflection library.
- Basic types: CP and Java, platform independent, fixed ranges, Unicode; pointers, references: CP and Java, no C pointers, safe references only (called pointers in CP).
- Memory management: CP and Java, no explicit destruction, fully garbage collected.
- I/O: CP and Java, libraries, no language-level features.
- Interfacing with native platform: CP, yes, can directly interface with native APIs and DLLs; Java, yes, but needs wrapper classes.

■ Platform-independent 'executables': CP, encoded parse tree + native compiler on first load; Java, byte code + interpreter, optional native just-in-time compiler.

Here are areas where Component Pascal and Java differ:

■ Closed modules: CP, closed modules in language; Java, no closed modules (outer classes could almost serve as closed modules in Java 1.1, but the definition of 'protected' still grants package rather than module-level access to protected features, and subclasses can change attribution from protected to public access).

■ Expressiveness of protection system ('module safety'): CP, field access protection (no access, read-only, read/write), instantiation protection (not exported, abstract, module limited, public), caller encapsulation (not exported, override only, override or call, call), extension protection (not exported, not extensible, extensible); Java, field access protection (no access, read/write), instantiation protection (abstract, private, or public), caller encapsulation (private or public), extension protection (private, final, extensible).

■ Runtime checks on integer arithmetic: CP, full overflow checking; Java, division by zero check only, otherwise modulo semantics of overflowing computations (C heritage).

■ Exception handling: CP, left to libraries; Java, language level but also has unchecked exceptions against which only catch-all handlers offer protection, much the same as CP's library-based exception handling.

■ Multithreading and synchronization: CP, left to libraries; Java, language level plus libraries.

■ Interface inheritance: CP, not separate, multiple interfaces per object supported by COM-like design pattern ('record riders'); Java, separate and multiple.

■ Circular imports: CP, illegal; Java, legal, arbitrarily across packages.

■ Statically allocated objects and arrays: CP, fully supported, safe, efficient; Java, not supported, non-basic types are always heap allocated.

■ Procedural programming: CP, fully supported, including procedure types and variables; Java, partially supported, camouflaged under static classes, static attributes, and static methods; no support of procedure types or variables; interfaces with single methods in conjunction with anonymous inner classes, since Java 1.1, are more general, but also more heavyweight than procedure types and variables.

■ Explicit support for low-level programming: CP, fully supported, safely contained; Java, none (must exit to native code implemented in different language).

■ Full language and runtime system implementation using same language: CP, yes, everything implemented in CP; language-level strict and static separation of safe and unsafe modules; Java, no, needs to rely on 'native' libraries, implemented using a different language (usually C or C++).

Component Pascal is a small language – much smaller than most other commercial languages, including Java. The features left out in Component Pascal are handled by libraries instead. Component Pascal is easy to teach and learn incrementally, whereas feature interaction in Java requires an almost complete understanding of the language before developing even small working examples. (For example, the use of checked exceptions in the interfaces of basic input libraries requires early introduction of exceptions and exception handling.) Component Pascal and Java code are about equally readable 'in the large.' The syntax for statements, typed declarations, and expressions differs significantly, following the Pascal and C heritage respectively.

Bibliography

Addresses and Web sites

The following non-exhaustive list of points of contact is meant to simplify the reader's task. No responsibility is accepted for completeness, correctness, or accuracy of the information provided.

Active Group (ActiveX standards)

Web: http://www.activex.org/

Andersen Consulting (Eagle, CBSE)

Web: http://www.ac.com/ http://www.ac.com/eagle/ http://www.ac.com/cstar/

Apple Computer, Inc. (Cyberdog, NeXT, OpenStep)

Web: http://www.apple.com/ http://www.next.com/

ComponentWare Consortium (broker for complete component solutions)

Web: http://www.componentware.com/

Corinto (ontology-based component repositories)

Web: http://corinto.interbusiness.it/

Forrester Research, Inc.

Mail: 1033 Massachusetts Avenue, Cambridge, MA 02138, USA. Tel: (+1) 617 497 7090; Fax: (+1) 617 868 0577.

Net: forrester@forrester.com
Web: http://www.forrester.com/

Gartner Group

Mail: Gartner Group Headquarters, 56 Top Gallant Road, PO Box 10212, Stamford, CT 06904, USA. Tel: (+1) 203 964 0096; Fax: (+1) 203 316 1100.
Web: http://www.gartner.com/

IBM (SOM, DSOM, Visual Age, ComponentBroker; OpenDoc sources)

Web: http://www.ibm.com/ http://www.software.ibm.com/

International Data Corporation (IDC)

Mail: Five Speen Street, Framingham, MA 01701, USA; 6 Dukes Gate, Acton Lane, London W4 5DX, UK. Tel: (+1) 508 872 8200; Fax: (+1) 508 935 4015.
Web: http://www.idcresearch.com/

IONA (Orbix)

Web: http://www.iona.com/

JavaSoft (Java, JavaBeans)

Mail: Sun Microsystems, Inc., 2550 Garcia Avenue, Mountain View, CA 94043 1100, USA. Tel: (+1) 512 434 1591, (800) JAVASOFT.
Web: http://www.javasoft.come; http://java.sun.com/; http://java.sun.com/beans/

Meta Group, Inc.

Mail: 208 Harbor Drive, PO Box 120061, Stamford, CT 06912 0061, USA. Tel: (+1) 203 973 6700, (800) 945-META; Fax: (+1) 203 359 8066.
Web: http://www.metagroup.com/

Microsoft Corporation (COM, DCOM, ActiveX, OLE)

Mail: One Microsoft Way, Redmond, WA 98052 6399, USA.
Web: http://www.microsoft.com/ http://www.microsoft.com/activex/

Oberon microsystems, Inc. (Component Pascal, BlackBox, Portos, Denia)

Mail: Technoparkstrasse 1, CH-8005 Zurich, Switzerland. Tel: (+41) 1 445 1751; Fax: (+41) 1 445 1752.

Net: oberon@oberon.ch

Web: http://www.oberon.ch/

Object Management Group (OMA, CORBA, IIOP, OpenDoc)

Mail: OMG Headquarters, 492 Old Connecticut Path, Framingham, MA 01701, USA.

Net: pubs@omg.org

Web: http://www.omg.org/

OPC Foundation (OLE for process control)

Mail: PO Box 140524, Austin, TX 76714 0524, USA. Fax: (+1) 512 834 7200.

Net: info@opcfoundation.org

Web: http://www.opcfoundation.org/

Open Application Group (business transaction APIs)

Mail: 401 North Michigan Avenue, Chicago, IL 60611, USA. Tel: (+1) 312 527 6799; Fax: (+1) 312 245 1081.

Net: oag@sba.com

Web: http://www.oag.org/

The Open Group (x/Open, OSF)

Mail: 11 Cambridge Center, Cambridge, MA 02142, USA.

Web: http://www.opengroup.org/

Ovum, Inc.

Mail: Customer Services, Ovum Ltd, 1 Mortimer Street, London, W1N 7RH, UK; 1 New England Executive Park, Burlington, MA 01803, USA. Tel: (+1) 617 272 6414, (800) 642-OVUM; Fax: (+1) 617 272 7446.

Net: webinfo@ovum.com

Web: http://www.ovum.com/

The Patricia Seybold Group

Mail: 85 Devonshire Street, 5th Floor, Boston, MA 02109-3504, USA. Tel: (+1) 617 742 5200; Fax: (+1) 617 742 1028.
Web: http://www.psgroup.com/

SAP AG (R/3 with components via COM)

Mail: SAP AG, Walldorf, Germany.
Web: http://www.sap.com/

Software AG (COM and DCOM ports)

Web: http://www.sagus.com/

Software Engineering Institute (software architecture)

Mail: 4500 Fifth Avenue, Pittsburgh, PA 15213 3890, USA. Tel: (+1) 412 268 5800.
Net: customer-relations@sei.cmu.edu
Web: http://www.sei.cmu.edu/; http://www.sei.com.edu/technology/architecture/

Strategic Focus

Mail: 500 E. Calaveras Blvd., #321, Milpitas, CA 95035, USA. Tel: (+1) 408 942 1500; Fax: (+1) 408 262 1786.
Net: jay@strategicfocus.com
Web: http://www.strategicfocus.com/

Taligent (Taligent Frameworks, HOOPS)

Web: http://www.taligent.com/

Visigenic (Visibroker)

Web: http://www.visigenic.com/

Books

Below is a non-exhaustive list of books that complement the material presented in this book. The full bibliographic details can be found in the References section.

Grady Booch, *Object-Oriented Analysis and Design* (Booch, 1994)
Classic reading. Before the arrival of today's component technology.

Don Box, *Essential COM* (Box, 1998)
Practical programming of components implemented in C++ and utilizing DCOM.

Kraig Brockschmidt, *Inside OLE* (Brockschmidt, 1995).
Thorough and in-depth coverage of OLE and COM just before DCOM.

David Chappell, *Understanding ActiveX and OLE – A Guide for Developers & Managers* (Chappel, 1996).
For those looking for overall understanding rather than endless detail, this is the best current account of Microsoft's evolving COM-based technologies with just enough technical detail to enable a thorough understanding of all essential aspects. Even for developers, this book leaves surprisingly few important questions unanswered.

Adam Denning, *ActiveX Controls Inside Out* (Denning, 1997)
Standard text on ActiveX control programming.

Erich Gamma, Richard Helm, Ralph Johnson, John Vlissides, *Design Patterns: Elements of Reusable Object-Oriented Software* (Gamma *et al.*, 1995).
A very well written and presented catalog of fundamental design patterns for object-oriented programming. Also an excellent introduction to the subject of patterns in programming.

Adele Goldberg and Keneth S. Rubin, *Succeeding with Objects – Design Frameworks for Project Management* (Goldberg and Rubin, 1995).
A high-level introduction to all aspects of object-oriented software development. Targeted at project managers, this book combines technically shallow (but informative) material with the process and market underpinning required to facilitate managerial decision making. Also a rich source of case studies and quantitative breakdowns.

Oscar Nierstrasz and Dennis Tsichritzis (eds), *Object-Oriented Software Composition* (Nierstrasz and Tsichritzis, 1995).
A collection of papers

Robert Orfali, Dan Harkey, and Jeri Edwards, *The Essential Distributed Objects Survival Guide* (Orfali *et al.*, 1996).
A detailed description of many of the major competing technologies for distributed objects and components evolving around CORBA and COM (written before the era of DCOM and Java), together with their compound document technologies, OpenDoc and OLE. The text has an explicit bias toward CORBA/OpenDoc (against COM/OLE) and unfortunately contains a number of technical inaccuracies. It also explores frameworks, including detailed presentation of Taligent's CommonPoint, NeXT's OpenStep, and the Newi Business Object approach.

Dale Rogerson, *Inside COM* (Rogerson, 1997).
An excellent introduction to COM programming. For the beginning developer.

James Rumbaugh, Michael Blaha, William Premerlani, Frederick Eddy, and William Lorenson, *Object-Oriented Modelling and Design* (Rumbaugh *et al.*, 1991).

A classic. Introduced the Object Modeling Technique (OMT) with its popular notations for class, interaction, and object diagrams. Besides Booch's method, OMT formed one of the pillars of the new unified modeling language (Rumbaugh *et al.*, 1997) which recently superseded OMT.

References and further reading

This list contains the full bibliographic detail of all publications referred to in this book. Most of the references point to articles of interest to those readers with the academic nerve and patience to follow up on some of the loose ends and unresolved problems mentioned in this book.

(OOPSLA is the ACM Conference on Object-Oriented Programming Systems, Languages, and Applications. ECOOP is the European Conference on Object-Oriented Programming.)

Abadi M. and Cardelli L. (1996) *A Theory of Objects*. Springer-Verlag, Berlin.

Accetta M., Baron R., Bolosky W., Golub D., Rashid R., Tevanlan A. and Young M. (1986) Mach: a new kernel foundation for UNIX development. In *Proceedings, Summer USENIX Conference, Atlanta, Georgia*, July 1986.

Agha G. and Hewitt C. (1987) Actors: a conceptual foundation for concurrent object-oriented programming. In Shriver B. and Wegner P. (eds) *Research Directions in Object-Oriented Programming*, pp. 49–74. MIT Press, Cambridge, MA.

Andersen Consulting (1997a) Component-based software engineering (CBSE) project. Software Engineering Laboratory, Center for Strategic Technology Research (CSTaR), Andersen Consulting (http://www.ac.com/aboutus/tech/cstar/sel/frames/au_dfrsel.html).

Andersen Consulting (1997b) Eagle – an integrated set of tools, architectures, processes, patterns and reusable components (http://www.ac.com/eagle/).

Anderson B., Shaw M., Best L. and Beck K. (1993) Software architecture: the next step for object technology (panel). In *Proceedings, OOPSLA93*, ACM SIGPLAN Notices, 28(10), pp. 356–359. ACM Press, Reading, MA, and Addison-Wesley, Reading, MA.

Apple Computer (1992) *Dylan – An Object-Oriented Dynamic Language*. Apple Computer Eastern Research and Technology Center, Cambridge.

Arnold K. and Gosling J. (1996) *The Java Programming Language*, Addison-Wesley, Reading, MA.

Astudillo H., (1996) Reorganizing split objects. In *Proceedings, OOPSLA96*, ACM SIGPLAN Notives, 31(10), pp. 138–149, ACM Press, Reading, MA, and Addison-Wesley, Reading, MA.

Back R.J.R. and Kurki-Suonio R. (1988) Distributed co-operation with action systems. *ACM Transactions on Program Languages and Systems (TOPLAS)*, **10**, 513–554.

Bardou D. and Dony C. (1996) Split objects: a disciplined use of delegation within objects. In *Proceedings, OOPSLA96*, ACM SIGPLAN Notives, 31(10), pp. 122–137. ACM Press, Reading, MA, and Addison-Wesley, Reading, MA.

Berry G. and Gonthier G. (1992) The Estrel programming language: design, semantics, and implementation. *Science of Computer Programming*, **19**(2) 87–152.

Birman K.P. (1985) Replication and fault-tolerance in the ISIS system. *Proceedings, 10th ACM Symposium on Operating System Principles (SOSP)*. *ACM Operating System Review*, **19**(5), 79–86.

Birrel A.D. and Nelson B.J. (1984) Implementing remote procedure calls. *ACM Transactions on Computer Systems (TOCS)*, **2**(1), 39–59.

Birrel A., Evers D., Nelson G., Owicki S. and Wobber E. (1993) Distributed garbage collection for network objects. *Technical Report* 116, DEC Systems Research Center, Palo Alto.

Birrel A., Nelson G. and Owicki S. (1994) Network objects. *Technical Report* 115. DEC Systems Research Center, Palo Alto.

Blaschek G. (1994) *Object-Oriented Programming with Prototypes*. Springer-Verlag, Berlin.

Booch G. (1987) *Software Components with Ada: Structures, Tools, and Subsystems*. Benjamin-Cummings, Redwood City, CA.

Booch G. (1994) *Object-Oriented Analysis and Design*, 2nd edn. Benjamin-Cummings, Redwood City, CA.

Box D. (1998) *Essential COM*. Addison-Wesley, Reading, MA.

Bracha G. and Cook W. (1990) Mixin-based inheritance. In Meyrowitz N. (ed.) *Proceedings, OOPSLA/ECOOP 90*, ACM SIGPLAN Notices, 25(10), pp. 303–311. ACM Press, Reading, MA, and Addison-Wesley, Reading, MA.

Bracha G. and Griswold D. (1993) Strongtalk: typechecking Smalltalk in a production environment. In *Proceedings, OOPSLA93*, ACM SIGPLAN Notices, 28(10), pp. 215–230. ACM Press, Reading, MA, and Addison-Wesley, Reading, MA.

Brockschmidt K. (1995) *Inside OLE*, 2nd edn. Microsoft Press, Redmond, WA.

Brodie L. (1984) *Thinking FORTH*. Prentice-Hall, Englewood Cliffs, NJ.

Brodie M.L. (1996) Putting objects to work on a massive scale. In *Proceedings, 9th International Symposium on Foundations of Intelligent Systems (ISMIS)*.

Brodie M.L. and M. Stonebreaker M. (1995) *Migrating Legacy Systems: Gateways, Interfaces, and the Incremental Approach*. Morgan Kaufmann Publishers, Palo Alto, CA.

Brown A.W. (ed.) (1996) *Component-based Software Engineering: Selected Papers from the Software Engineering Institute*. IEEE Computer Society Press, Los Alamitos, CA.

Brown C.L. (1994) NATO standard for the development of reusable software components, three documents, Public Ada Library (http://wuarchive.wustl.edu/languages/ada/docs/nato_ru/).

Bruce K.B., Fiech A. and Petersen L. (1997) Subtyping is not a good match for object-oriented languages. *Proceedings, ECOOP97* (in press; see http://www.cs.williams.edu/~kim).

Büchi M. and Weck W. (1997) A plea for gray-box components. *Technical Report No. 122*, Turku Centre for Computer Science, Turku, Finland.

Cardelli L. (1989) Typeful programming. *Technical Report* 45, DEC Systems Research Center, Palo Alto.

Cardelli L. (1994) Obliq – A language with distributed scope. *Technical Report* 122, DEC Systems Research Center, Palo Alto.

Cardelli L. (1997) Program fragments, linking, and modularization. In *Proceedings, 24th ACM SIGPLAN-SIGACT Symposium on Principles of Programming Languages* (Paris, France), pp.

266–277, January 1997 (also available as *Technical Report* 144, DEC Systems Research Center, Palo Alto).

Casais E., Taivalsaari A. and Trauter R. (organizers) (1996) *Workshop on Object-Oriented Software Evolution and Reengineering* at OOPSLA96, http://www.nokia.com/oopsla96ws18/.

Chandy K.M. and Misra J. (1988) *Parallel Program Design – A Foundation*. Addison-Wesley, Reading, MA.

Chappell D. (1996) *Understanding ActiveX and OLE – A Guide for Developers & Managers*. Microsoft Press, Redmond, WA.

Chappel D. (1997) The next wave: component software enters the mainstream. Chappel & Associates, Minneapolis, MN (available from http://www.rational.com/support/techpapers/ nextwave/index.html).

Cheung D. (1996) ATM software analysis and design. *Dr. Dobb's Journal* #252, **21**(10), 70– 76.

Clark D.D. (1985) Structuring a system using up-calls. *Proceedings, 10th ACM Symposium on Operating System Principles (SOSP)*. *ACM Operating System Review*, **19**(5), 171–180.

Coleman D., Arnold P., Bodoff S., Dollin C., Gilchrist H. (1993) *Object-Oriented Development: The Fusion Method*. Prentice-Hall, Englewood Cliffs, NJ.

Coplien J.O. and Schmidt D.C. (eds) (1995) *Pattern Languages of Program Design*. Addison-Wesley, Reading, MA.

Cox B.J. (1990) Planning the software industrial revolution. *IEEE Software*, **7**(6).

Cox B.J. (1996) *Superdistribution: Objects as Property on the Electronic Frontier*. Addison-Wesley, Reading, MA.

Crelier R. (1994) *Separate Compilation and Module Extension*, PhD Thesis No. 10650, Swiss Federal Institute of Technology Zurich.

Cutler D.N. (1993) *Inside Windows NT*. Microsoft Press, Redmond, WA.

Dahl O.-J. and Nygaard K. (1970) *Simula-67 Common Base Language*, Publication S-22, Norwegian Computing Centre, Oslo 1970, 72, 84; current version: *Data Processing – Programming Languages – SIMULA*, Swedish Standard SS.63.61.14, SIS.

DeMichiel L.G. and Gabriel R.P. (1987) The Common Lisp Object System: an overview. In Béziwin J. *et al.* (eds) *Proceedings, ECOOP87, Lecture Notes in Computer Science*, No. 276, pp. 151–170. Springer-Verlag, Berlin.

DePalma D.A., Dolberg S., Mavretic M. and Jonson J. (1996) Objects on the net. *Software Strategy Report*. Forrester Research, Inc., Cambridge, MA.

Denning A. (1997) ActiveX Controls Inside Out – Harness the power of ActiveX controls, 2nd edn, Microsoft Press, Redmond, Wash.

Deutsch P. (1989) Design reuse and frameworks in the Smalltalk-80 system. In Biggerstaff T.J. and Perlis A.J. (eds) *Software Reusability*, Vol. 2. ACM Press, New York.

Dijkstra E.W. (1968) The structure of the THE multiprogramming system. *Communications of the ACM*, **11**(5), 341–346.

Dony C., Malenfant J. and Cointe P. (1992) Prototype-based languages: From a new taxonomy to constructive proposals and their validation, *Proceedings, OOPSLA92*, ACM SIGPLAN Notices, 27(10), pp. 201–217. ACM Press, Reading, MA, and Addison-Wesley, Reading, MA.

Dutoit A., Levy S., Cunningham D. and Patrick R. (1996) The Basic object system: supporting a spectrum from prototypes to hardened code. *Proceedings, OOPSLA96*, ACM SIGPLAN Notives, 31(10), pp. 104–121. ACM Press, Reading, MA, and Addison-Wesley, Reading, MA.

Dyer M. (1992) *The Cleanroom Approach to Quality Software Development*, John Wiley & Sons, New York.

Eichner B., Kamber D. and Murer S. (1997) CORBA: Principles and practical experiences. *Informatik/Informatique*, February 1997.

Ellis A. and Stroustrup B. (1994) *The Annotated C++ Reference Manual* (corrected reprint). Addison-Wesley, Reading, MA.

FAMOOS Consortium (1996) *Framework-based Approach for Mastering Object-Oriented Software Evolution*, ESPRIT Project 21975, http://www.sema.es/projects/FAMOOS/.

Forman I.R., Conner M.H., Danforth S.H. and Raper L.K. (1995) Release-to-release binary compatibility in SOM. *Proceedings, OOPSLA95*, ACM SIGPLAN Notices, 30(10), pp. 426–438. ACM Press, Reading, MA, and Addison-Wesley, Reading, MA.

Franz M. (1994) *Code-Generation On-the-Fly: A Key to Portable Software*, PhD thesis, ETH Zurich, Verlag der Fachvereine, Zurich.

Frieder O. and Segal M.E. (1991) On dynamically updating a computer program: from concept to prototype. *Journal on Systems Software*, **14**, 111–128,.

Furber S. (1996) *ARM System Architecture*. Addison-Wesley, Reading, MA.

Gabriel R.P., White J.L. and Bobrow D.G. (1991) CLOS: integrating object-oriented and functional programming. *Communications of the ACM*, **34**, 942–960.

Gamma E. (1992) *Object-Oriented Software Development based on ET++: Design Patterns, Class Library, Tools* (in German). Springer-Verlag, Berlin.

Gamma E., Helm R., Johnson R. and Vlissides J. (1995) *Design Patterns: Elements of Reusable Object-Oriented Software*. Addison-Wesley, Reading, MA.

Goldberg A. and Robson D. (1983) *Smalltalk-80: The Language and its Implementation*. Addison-Wesley, Reading, MA

Goldberg A. and Robson D. (1989)) *Smalltalk-80: The Language*, revised edition. Addison-Wesley, Reading, MA.

Goldberg A. and Rubin K.S. (1995) *Succeeding with Objects – Design Frameworks for Project Management*, Corrected Reprint. Addison-Wesley, Reading, MA.

Gough K.J., Cifuentes C., Corney D., Hynd J. and Kolb P. (1992) An experiment in mixed compilation/interpretation. *Proceedings, 14th Australasian Computer Science Conference (Hobart, Australia)*, Australian Computer Science Communications, 15(1), January 1992.

Gosling A., Joy B. and Steele G. (1996) *The Java Language Specification*. Addison-Wesley, Reading, MA.

Griffel F. (1997) *Konzepte und Techniken eines Softwareparadigmas* (in German). dpunkt Verlag, Heidelberg.

Harrison W. and Ossher H. (1993) Subject-oriented programming (a critique of pure objects). *Proceedings, OOPSLA93*, ACM SIGPLAN Notices, 28(10), pp. 411–428. ACM Press, Reading, MA, and Addison-Wesley, Reading, MA.

Hauck F.J. (1993) Inheritance modeled with explicit bindings: an approach to typed inheritance. *Proceedings, OOPSLA93*, ACM SIGPLAN Notices, 28(10), pp. 231–239. ACM Press, Reading, MA, and Addison-Wesley, Reading, MA.

Heeb B.U. *Debora: A System for the Development of Field Programmable Hardware and its Application to a Reconfigurable Computer*, PhD Thesis No. 10049, Verlag der Fachvereine, Zurich.

Helm R., Holland I.M. and Gangopadhyay D. (1990) Contracts: specifying behavioral compositions in object-oriented systems. In Meyrowitz N. (ed.) *Proceedings, OOPSLA/ECOOP 90*, ACM SIGPLAN Notices, 25(10), pp. 169–180. ACM Press, Reading, MA, and Addison-Wesley, Reading, MA.

Holland I.M. (1992) Specifying reusable components using contracts. In Lehrmann Madsen O. (ed.) *Proceedings, ECOOP 92, Lecture Notes in Computer Science*, No. 615, pp. 287–308. Springer-Verlag, Berlin.

Hölzle U. (1995) *Adaptive optimization for Self: Reconciling High Performance with Exploratory Programming*, PhD thesis, appeared as Technical Report SMLI TR-95–35, Sun Laboratories, Mountain View, CA.

Hürsch W.L. (1994) Should superclasses be abstract? In Tokoro M. and Pareschi R. (eds.) *Proceedings, ECOOP94, Lecture Notes in Computer Science*, No. 821, pp. 12–31, Springer-Verlag, Berlin.

Hüttel H. (1991) *Decidability, Behavioural Equivalences and Infinite Transition Graphs*, PhD thesis, ECS-LFCS-91–181, Computer Science Department, University of Edinburgh.

IBM (1994) The System Object Model (SOM) and the Component Object Model (COM): A comparison of technologies from a developer's perspective. White Paper. IBM Corporation, Object Technology Products Group, Austin.

IBM (1997) NetRexx 1.0, http://www2.hurley.ibm.com/netrexx/, May 1997.

Intermetrics (1997) AppletMagic Ada 95 to Java bytecode translator, Intermetrics, http://www.appletmagic.com/, February 1997.

IONA (1996) Orbix Desktop for Windows. White Paper. IONA Technologies, http://www.iona.com, July 1996.

Jacobson I. (1993) *Object-Oriented Software Engineering*, Revised Printing. Addison-Wesley, Reading, MA.

JavaSoft (1996) *JavaBeans*, Version 1.00, http://java.sun.com/beans, October 1996. Update 1.00-A, December 1996.

JavaSoft (1997) JavaSoft, *Java Electronic Commerce Framework (JEFC)*, http://java.sun.com/products/commerce/, Version 0.6 alpha, May 1997.

Johnson R. (1992) Documenting frameworks using patterns. *Proceedings, OOPSLA92*, ACM SIGPLAN Notices, 27(10), pp. 63–76. ACM Press, Reading, MA, and Addison-Wesley, Reading, MA.

Johnson R. (1994) How to design frameworks. In: *Object-Technology at Work*, Tutorial Notes, University of Zurich, 1994.

Jordan M. and Van de Vanter M. (1997) Modular system building with Java packages, *Proceedings, 8th Conference on Software Engineering Environments (SEE97)*, April 1997.

Kernighan B.W. and Ritchie D.M. (1978) *The C Programming Language*, 2nd edn 1989. Prentice-Hall, Englewood Cliffs, NJ.

Kiczales G. (1994) Why are black boxes so hard to reuse? Toward a new model of abstraction in the engineering of software, Invited Talk, *OOPSLA94* (online version available from UVC: http://www.uvc.com/kiczales/transscript.html), 1994.

Kiczales G. and Lamping J. (1992) Issues in the design and specification of class libraries, *Proceedings, OOPSLA92*, ACM SIGPLAN Notices, 27(10), pp. 435–451. ACM Press, Reading, MA, and Addison-Wesley, Reading, MA.

Kiczales G., de Riviere J. and Bobrow D.G. (1991) *The Art of the Metaobject Protocol*. MIT Press, Cambridge, MA.

Kleindienst J., Plasil F. and Tuma P. (1996) Lessons learned from implementing the CORBA Persistent Object Service, *Proceedings, OOPSLA96*, ACM SIGPLAN Notives, 31(10), pp. 150–167. ACM Press, Reading, MA, and Addison-Wesley, Reading, MA.

Krasner G. (ed.) (1983) *Smalltalk-80 Bits of History, Words of Advice*, Addison-Wesley, Reading, MA.

Krasner G.E. and Pope S.T. (1988) A cookbook for using the Model-View-Controller user interface paradigm in Smalltalk-80. *Journal of Object-Oriented Programming*, 1(3), 26–49.

Krogdahl S. (1984) Multiple inheritance in Simula-like languages. *BIT*, **25**, 318–326.

Lakos J. (1996) *Large-Scale C++ Software Design*. Addison-Wesley, Reading, MA.

Lamping J. (1993) Typing the specialisation interface. *Proceedings, OOPSLA93*, ACM SIGPLAN Notices, 28(10), pp. 201–215. ACM Press, Reading, MA, and Addison-Wesley, Reading, MA.

Lange D.B. and Chang D.T. (1996) *IBM Aglets Workbench: Programming Mobile Agents in Java*, White Paper (http://www.tri.ibm.co.jp/aglets/whitepaper.htm), IBM Japan.

Larcie D. (1993) *Component Software: A Market Perspective on the Coming Revolution in Software Development*. In-depth report. Patricia Seybold Group, Boston.

Lau, Ch. (1994) *Object-Oriented Programming Using SOM and DSOM*. Van Nostrand Reinhold, New York.

Leach N. and Moeller M. (1997) ActiveX lags in Web race. *PC Week*, 9 June 1997.

Lehrmann Madsen O., Magnusson B. and Møller-Pedersen B. (1990) Strong typing of object-oriented languages revisited. In Meyrowitz N. (ed.) *Proceedings, OOPSLA/ECOOP 90*, ACM SIGPLAN Notices, 25(10), pp. 140–150. ACM Press, Reading, MA, and Addison-Wesley, Reading, MA.

Lehrmann Madsen O., Møller-Pedersen B. and Nygaard K. (1993) *Object-Oriented Programming in the Beta Programming Language*. Addison-Wesley, Wokingham, England.

Leveson N.G. (1995) *Safeware: System Safety and Computers*, Addison-Wesley, Reading, MA.

Lewis T.G. (1995) *Object-Oriented Application Frameworks*. Manning/Prentice-Hall, New York.

Lieberman H. (1986) Using prototypical objects to implement shared behavior in object-oriented systems. In Meyrowitz N. (ed.) *Proceedings, OOPSLA86*, ACM SIGPLAN Notices, 21(11), pp. 214–223.

Lins C. (1988) *The Modula-2 Software Component Library* (four volumes), Springer-Verlag, New York.

Liskov B. and Wing J.M. (1994) A behavioral notion of subtyping. *ACM Transactions on Programming Languages and Systems*, 16(6), 11–41.

McGraw G. and Felten E. (1997) *Java Security: Hostile Applets, Holes, and Antidotes*. John Wiley & Sons, New York.

McIlroy M.D. (1968) Mass produced software components. In (Naur *et al.*, 1969), pp. 88–98.

Magnusson B. (1991) Code reuse considered harmful (guest editorial). *Journal of Object-Oriented Programming*, **4**(3), 8.

Malenfant J. (1995) On the semantic diversity of delegation-based programming languages. *Proceedings, OOPSLA95*, ACM SIGPLAN Notices, 30(10), pp. 215–230. ACM Press, Reading, MA, and Addison-Wesley, Reading, MA.

Meyer B. (1988) *Object-Oriented Software Construction*, 2nd edn 1997, Series in Computer Science. Prentice-Hall, Englewood Cliffs, NJ.

Meyer B. (1990) *Eiffel – The Language*, Series in Computer Science, Prentice-Hall, Englewood Cliffs, NJ.

Meyer B. (1994) *Reusable Software: The Base Object-Oriented Component Libraries*. Prentice-Hall, Englewood Cliffs, NJ.

Meyer B. (1996) Static typing and other mysteries of life. *Object Currents*, 1(1), http://www.sigs.com/objectcurrents/.

Moon D.A. (1986) Object-oriented programming with flavors. In Meyrowitz N. (ed.) *Proceedings, OOPSLA86*, ACM SIGPLAN Notices, 21(11), pp. 1–8, November 1986.

Morgan C. (1990) *Programming from Specifications*. Prentice-Hall, Englewood Cliffs, NJ.

Mössenböck H. (1993) *Object-Oriented Programming in Oberon-2*. Springer-Verlag, Berlin.

Mühlhäuser M. (ed.) (1997) *Special Issues in Object-Oriented Programming – ECOOP96 Workshop Reader*. dpunkt Verlag , Heidleberg.

Musser D.R. and Saini A. (1996) *STL Tutorial and Reference Guide*. Addison-Wesley, Reading, MA.

Naur P. and Randell B. (eds) (1969) *Proceedings, NATO Conference on Software Engineering*, Garmisch, Germany, October 1968, NATO Science Committee, Brussels (published as a book in 1976.)

Nelson G. (ed.) (1991) *Systems Programming with Modula-3*. Prentice-Hall, Englewood Cliffs, NJ.

Netscape (1996) *Netscape ONE – Open Networking Environment*, White Paper Version 1.0, Netscape Communications Corp., July 1996.

NeXT (no date) *Object-Oriented Programming and the Objective-C Language*, NeXT Software, Inc. (part no. N6123.02), online version at http://www.next.com/Pubs/Documents/OPENSTEP/ObjectiveC/.

Nierstrasz O. (1991) The next 700 concurrent object-oriented languages – reflections on the future of object-based concurrency. In Tsichritzis D. (ed.) *Object Composition*. Centre Universitaire d'Informatique, University of Geneva.

Nierstrasz O. (1993) Regular types for active objects. *Proceedings, OOPSLA93*, ACM SIGPLAN Notices, 28(10), pp. 1–15. ACM Press, Reading, MA, and Addison-Wesley, Reading, MA.

Nierstrasz O. and Dami L. (1995) Component-oriented software technology. In Nierstrasz O. and Tsichritzis D. (eds) *Object-Oriented Software Composition*. Prentice-Hall, Englewood Cliffs, NJ.

Nierstrasz O. and Tsichritzis D. (eds) (1995) *Object-Oriented Software Composition*. Prentice-Hall, Englewood Cliffs, NJ.

Nierstrasz O., Gibbs S. and Tsichritzis D. (1992) Component-oriented software development. *Communications of the ACM*, **35**(9), 160–165.

Nori K.V., Amman U., Jensen K., Nägeli H.H. and Jacobi C. (1991) Pascal-P implementation notes. In Barron D.W. (ed.) *Pascal: The Language and its Implementation*. John Wiley & Sons, New York.

Oberon microsystems, Inc. (1994) *Oberon/F Users Guide*, Oberon microsystems (http://www.oberon.ch).

Oberon microsystems, Inc. (1997a) *Portos Realtime Operating System and Denia Development Environment for Portos*. Oberon microsystems (http://www.oberon.ch).

Oberon microsystems, Inc. (1997b) *BlackBox Developer and BlackBox Component Framework*. Oberon microsystems (http://www.oberon.ch).

Olafsson A. and Bryan D. (1997) On the need for required interfaces of components. In Mühlhäuser M. (ed.) *Special Issues in Object-Oriented Programming – ECOOP96 Workshop Reader*, pp. 159–171. dpunkt Verlag, Heidelberg.

OMG (1997a)*The Common Object Request Broker: Architecture and Specification*, Revision 2.0 July 1995, Update July 1996, Object Management Group, formal document 97–02–25, (http://www.omg.org).

OMG(1997b) *The Object Management Architecture Guide*. Object Management Group (http://www.omg.org).

OMG(1997c) *CORBAservices: Common Object Services Specification*, Object Management Group, formal document 97–02–04, (http://www.omg.org).

Orfali R., Harkey, D. and Edwards J. (1996) *The Essential Distributed Objects Survival Guide*. John Wiley & Sons, New York.

Omohundro S. and Stoutamire D. (1996) *Sather 1.1 Language Specification*, Technical Report, International Computer Science Institute (http://www.icsi.berkeley.edu/Sather/).

Ossher H. and Harrison W. (1992) Combination of inheritance hierarchies. *Proceedings, OOPSLA92*, ACM SIGPLAN Notices, 27(10), pp. 25–40. ACM Press, Reading, MA, and Addison-Wesley, Reading, MA.

Ossher H., Kaplan M., Harrison W., Katz A. and Kruskal V. (1995) Subject-oriented composition rules. *Proceedings, OOPSLA95*, ACM SIGPLAN Notices, 30(10), pp. 235–250. ACM Press, Reading, MA, and Addison-Wesley, Reading, MA.

Paznesh E. (1997) Gazelle: An Oberon/F based Internet development framework. *The Oberon Tribune*, **2**(1), 23–24. Oberon microsystems, Inc., Zurich (available from http://www.oberon.ch/).

Palsberg J. and Schwartzbach M.I. (1991) Object-oriented type inference. *Proceedings, OOPSLA91*, ACM SIGPLAN Notices, 26(10), pp. 146–161. ACM Press, Reading, MA, and Addison-Wesley, Reading, MA.

Pinson L.J. and Wiener R.S. (1991) *Objective-C: Object-Oriented Programming Techniques*. Addison-Wesley, Reading, MA.

Potel M. with Cotter S. (1995) *Inside Taligent Technology*. Addison-Wesley, Reading, MA.

Reiser M. and Wirth N. (1992) *Programming in Oberon*. Addison-Wesley, Reading, MA.

Ring K. and Carnelly P. (1995) *Distributed Objects – Creating the Virtual Mainframe*. Ovum, London.

Roe P. and Szyperski C. (1997) Lightweight parametric polymorphism for Oberon. In Mössenböck H. (ed.) *Proceedings, 4th Joint Modular Languages Conference (JMLC97)*, Lecture Notes in Computing Science, No. 1204, pp. 140–154. Springer-Verlag, Berlin.

Rogerson D. (1997) *Inside COM*. Microsoft Press, Redmond, WA.

Rösch M. (1997) Softwarekomponenten nicht vor 2001 (Software components not before 2001, article in German). *OBJEKTspektrum*, no. 3, May/June 1997.

Rossie Jr J.G. and Friedman D.P. (1995) An algebraic semantics of subobjects. *Proceedings, OOPSLA95*, ACM SIGPLAN Notices, 30(10), pp. 187–199. ACM Press, Reading, MA, and Addison-Wesley, Reading, MA.

Rumbaugh J. (1994) The life of an object model: How the object model changes during development. *Journal of Object-Oriented Programming*, 7(1), 24–32.

Rumbaugh J., Blaha M., Lorenson W., Eddy F. and Premerlani W. (1991) *Object-Oriented Modelling and Design*. Prentice-Hall, Englewood Cliffs, NJ.

Rumbaugh J., Jacobson I. and Booch G. (1997) *Unified Modeling Language Reference Manual*. Addison-Wesley, Reading, MA.

Sametinger J. (1997) *Software Engineering with Reusable Components*. Springer-Verlag, Town.

Schmid H.A. (1995) Creating the architecture of a manufacturing framework by design patterns. *Proceedings, OOPSLA95*, ACM SIGPLAN Notices, 30(10), pp. 370–384. ACM Press, Reading, MA, and Addison-Wesley, Reading, MA.

Shapiro M. (1989) Structure and encapsulation in distributed systems: the proxy principle. *Proceedings, 6th Intl Conf on Distributed Computer Systems (ICDCS86)*, IEEE Press, May 1986.

Shaw M. and Garlan D. (1996) *Software Architecture: Perspectives on an Emerging Discipline*. Prentice-Hall, Englewood Cliffs, NJ.

Sims O. (1994) *Business Objects: Delivering Cooperative Objects for Client–Server*. McGraw-Hill, New York.

Smith R.B. and Ungar D. (1995) Programming as an experience: the inspiration for Self. In Olthoff W. (ed.) *Proceedings, ECOOP95*, *Lecture Notes in Computer Science*, No. 952, pp. 303–330, Springer-Verlag, Berlin.

Snyder A. (1986) Encapsulation and inheritance in object-oriented programming languages. In Meyrowitz N. (ed.) *Proceedings, OOPSLA86*, ACM SIGPLAN Notices, 21(11), pp. 38–45, November 1986.

Snyder A. (1987) Inheritance and the development of encapsulated software components. In Shriver B. and Wegner P. (eds) *Research Directions in Object-Oriented Programming*, pp. 165–188. MIT Press.

Stata R. and Guttag J. (1995) Modular reasoning in the presence of subclassing. *Proceedings, OOPSLA95*, ACM SIGPLAN Notices, 30(10), pp. 200–214. ACM Press, Reading, MA, and Addison-Wesley, Reading, MA.

Steel J. (1996) *Component Technology*, IDC White Paper (part one), International Data Corporation, London.

Stein L.A. (1987) Delegation is inheritance. *Proceedings, OOPSLA87*, ACM SIGPLAN Notices, 22(12), pp. 138–146, October 1987.

Steyaert P., Lucas C., Mens K. and D'Hondt T. (1996) Reuse contracts: managing the evolution of reusable assets. *Proceedings, OOPSLA96*, ACM SIGPLAN Notices, 31(10), pp. 268–285.

Stroustrup B. (1987) Multiple inheritance for C++. *Proceedings, EUUG Spring Conference*, May 1987 (also in: *Computing Systems*, 2(4), 1989; for a discussion see Stroustrup, 1994).

Stroustrup B. (1994) *The Design and Evolution of C++* (corrected reprint 1995). Addison-Wesley, Reading, MA.

Swaine M. (1997) Some observations on Apple and Java. *Dr. Dobb's Journal*, #262, **22**(2), 91–93.

Szyperski C. (1992a) Import is not inheritance – why we need both: modules and classes. In Lehrmann Madsen O. (ed.) *Proceedings, ECOOP 92, Lecture Notes in Computer Science*, No. 615, pp. 19–32, Springer-Verlag, Berlin.

Szyperski C. (1992b) *Insight Ethos: On Object-Orientation in Operating Systems*, PhD thesis, ETH No. 9884, Informatik Dissertationen der ETH Zürich, No. 40, Verlag der Fachvereine Zurich.

Szyperski C. (1995) Component-oriented programming: a refined variation on object-oriented programming. *The Oberon Tribune*, **1**(2), Oberon microsystems, Inc., Zurich (available from http://www.oberon.ch/), December 1995.

Szyperski C. (1996) Independently extensible systems – software engineering potential and challenges. *Proceedings, 19th Australasian Computer Science Conference. Australian Computer Science Communications*, **18**(1), pp. 203–212.

Szyperski N. (1997) Component software: A market on the verge of success. *The Oberon Tribune*, **2**(1), 1–4, Oberon microsystems, Inc., Zürich (available from http://www.oberon.ch/), January 1997.

Szyperski C. and Gough J. (1995) The role of programming languages in the lifecycle of safe systems. *Proceedings, International Conference on Safety through Quality (STQ95, Kennedy Space Center, Cape Canaveral, Florida)*, pp. 99–114. Alpha Books, Bristol, UK.

Szyperski C. and Pfister C. (1997) Workshop on Component-Oriented Programming, Summary. In Mühlhäuser M. (ed.) *Special Issues in Object-Oriented Programming – ECOOP96 Workshop Reader*. dpunkt Verlag , Heidelberg.

Szyperski C., Omohundro St. and Murer St. (1994) Engineering a programming language – the type and class system of Sather. In Gutknecht J. (ed.) *Proceedings, First International Conference on Programming Languages and System Architecture, Lecture Notes in Computer Science*, No. 782. Springer-Verlag, Berlin.

Taligent (1994) *Taligent's Guide to Designing Programs: Well-Mannered Object-Oriented Design in C++*. Addison-Wesley, Reading, MA.

Udell J. (1994) ComponentWare. *BYTE Magazine*, **19**(5), 46–56.

Ungar D. (1995) Annotating objects for transport to other worlds, *Proceedings, OOPSLA95*, ACM SIGPLAN Notices, 30(10), pp. 73–87. ACM Press, Reading, MA, and Addison-Wesley, Reading, MA.

Ungar D. and Smith R.B. (1987) Self: the power of simplicity. *Proceedings, OOPSLA87*, ACM SIGPLAN Notices, 22(12), pp. 227–241, October 1987 (a revised version appeared in *Lisp and Symbolic Computation*, **4**(3), 187–205, 1991).

Valdés R. (1994) Introducing interoperable objects. *Dr. Dobb's Journal* #225, **19**(16), pp. 4–6, special issue, Winter 1994/95.

Visual Basic (1992) *Visual Basic*. Microsoft Press, Redmond, WA.

Vlissides J.M., Coplien J.O. and Kerth N.L. (1996) *Pattern Languages of Program Design 2*. Addison-Wesley, Reading, MA.

Wahbe R., Lucco S., Anderson T. and Graham S. (1993) Efficient software-based fault isolation. *Proceedings, 14th ACM Symposium on Operating System Principles (SOSP93)*, pp. 203–216, December 1993.

Wallace E. and Wallnau K.C. (1996) A situated evaluation of the Object Management Group's Object Management Architecture (OMA). *Proceedings, OOPSLA96*, ACM SIGPLAN Notives, 31(10), pp.168–178. ACM Press, Reading, MA, and Addison-Wesley, Reading, MA.

Weck W. (1996) *On Document-Centered Mathematical Component Software*, PhD Dissertation, ETH Zurich, No. 11817, 1996.

Weck W. (1997) Independently extensible component frameworks, *Proceedings, Intl. Workshop on Component-Oriented Programming (WCOP96)* at ECOOP96, Linz, Austra. In Mühlhäuser M. (ed.) *Special Issues in Object-Oriented Programming – ECOOP96 Workshop Reader*. dpunkt Verlag , Heidelberg.

Wegner P. (1987) Dimensions of object-based language design. *Proceedings, OOPSLA87*, ACM SIGPLAN Notices, 22(12), pp. 168–182, October 1987. Also appeared in *Journal of Object-Oriented Programming*, 1(1).

Wiederhold C., Wegner P. and Ceri S. (1992) Toward megaprogramming. *Communications of the ACM*, **35**(11), 89–99.

Wills A. (1991) Capsules and types in Fresco – program verification in Smalltalk. In America P. (ed.) *Proceedings, ECOOP91, Lecture Notes in Computer Science*, 512, pp. 59–76, Springer-Verlag, Berlin.

Wirth N. (1971) The programming language PASCAL. *Acta Informatica*, 1, 35–63.

Wirth N. (1982) *Programming in Modula-2*. Springer-Verlag, Berlin.

Wirth N. and Gutknecht J. (1992) *Project Oberon – The Design of an Operating System and Compiler*. Addison-Wesley, Reading, MA.

Wirthman L. (1997) SunSoft Plan: OS Modularity. *PC Week*, 21 April 1997.

Zweben S., Edwards S., Weide B. and Hollingsworth J. (1995) The effects of layering and encapsulation on software development cost and quality. *IEEE Transactions on Software Engineering*, **21**(3), 200–208 (IEEE 0098-5589/95).

Glossary

The following glossary provides a brief introduction to the terminology used in this book. More thorough definitions and comments can be found in the body of this book; please refer also to the index.

Abstract class

A *class* that cannot be instantiated, that is no object can be a direct instance of an abstract class. An abstract class can have unimplemented *methods* (abstract methods). Non-abstract classes inheriting from an abstract class have to implement all such abstract methods.

ActiveX

Microsoft standard for controls that reside in documents in the widest sense, including Web pages. Controls are visual objects ranging from push buttons to complex mini-applications, such as spreadsheets. ActiveX controls are a generalization of the older OLE custom extensions (OCXs). These again developed out of the original Visual Basic Extensions (VBXs). Unlike OCXs, ActiveX controls can be *containers* themselves, allowing for the nesting of controls. Also, unlike OCXs, ActiveX controls can have non-rectangular shape.

Adapter

A *component* that mediates between clients and providers that use different sets of *interfaces*.

Applet

Java terminology for a visual object embedded in a Web page. Applets can be compared to *ActiveX* controls, but today cannot be containers and therefore do not support nesting.

Application framework

See *Class framework*.

Architecture

Overall design of a system. An architecture integrates separate but interfering issues of a system, such as provisions for independent evolution and openness combined with overall reliability and performance requirements. An architecture defines guidelines that together help to achieve the overall targets without having to invent ad hoc compromises during system composition. An architecture must be carefully evolved to avoid deterioration as the system itself evolves and the requirements change. The right architectures and properly managed architecture evolution are probably the most important and challenging aspects of component software engineering.

Attribute
Also called field. A feature of a *class*.

Behavioral subtyping
Regular *subtyping* refers only to the availability of operations as far as their signatures are concerned. Behavioral subtyping restricts this further by also requiring behavioral consistency. An object of a subtype, if seen as a member of its base type, may only exhibit behavior (state transitions and answers to queries) that are explicable on the basis of the *specification* of the base type alone. Objects of behavioral subtypes are always *substitutable* for the base type objects.

BlackBox component framework and builder
The BlackBox family of products from Oberon microsystems focus on the construction of components for compound document and compound user interface based applications. BlackBox is available for a number of platforms and integrates with the platform's native object and compound document models. For example, the Windows version integrates with COM, OLE, and ActiveX. BlackBox is fully implemented in *Component Pascal*, and the BlackBox component builder uses Component Pascal as an all-purpose component-oriented programming language, from scripting, to component construction, to component framework construction. Direct support of standard object models enables seamless integration with components developed using other languages or tools.

Blackbox reuse
Reusing a component solely on the basis of its interfaces and their contractual specification. Reusability of a blackbox component thus fully depends on the quality of the interfaces and their specification. In contrast, glassbox reuse allows for inspection of the implementation of a component (but not its modification). The implementation thus serves as the most specific specification of the component, effectively preventing any further evolution of the component without the risk of breaking clients (*semantic fragile base class problem*). Whitebox reuse also allows modification of the implementation of a reused component. If used without restricting conventions (discipline), implementation inheritance is a technique to apply arbitrary modifications to an implementation that is inherited from. In a true component setting, such intrusive modifications cannot be allowed, as they eliminate the potential for independent evolution. Finally, graybox reuse is a term sometimes used to refer to the case where part of a component's implementation is opened for inspection and modification (via inheritance). Many blackbox abstractions in current practice are actually gray.

C++
A hybrid object-oriented programming language. C++ is typed but not *type-safe*. C++ does not have a *module* system. C++ does not have *automatic memory management*. Implementing *components* in C++ requires *hardware protection* or software *sandboxing*.

CI Labs
Component Integration Labs, dissolved in March 1997. Used to be responsible for registration and validation of *OpenDoc*-related technology and products.

Class
A static description specifying the state (fields) and behavior (methods) shared by all objects that are instances of that class. A class can use *interface inheritance* and *implementation inheritance* to inherit fields and methods from other classes, its superclasses. Also, other classes, called subclasses, may inherit from a class. The inheritance graph has to be acyclic. It may or may not have a single root. It may or may not allow for multiple superclasses of a class (multiple versus single inheritance). An object is said to be a direct instance of a class if that class is the most refined class that the object is an instance of. The object is said to be an indirect instance of all superclasses of that class. Fields introduce instance variables, unique to each instance of a class, or class variables, shared by all instances of a class. Methods introduce named operations that accept arguments and have an implementation. Class methods operate only on the shared state of that class, its class variables. Instance methods operate on the specific state of an object, its instance variables. Instance methods are invoked by dynamically determining the direct class of the object that the method is invoked on (method dispatch). This is sometimes called sending a message to an object; a method is then said to handle such a method. Classes interact with *types*.

Class framework
A framework that defines a set of classes and the part of their interaction that is common to multiple applications in the domain of the framework. Applications are created by subclassing some of the framework's classes (cf. *whitebox reuse*).

Cleanroom
A component development method based on rigorous formal methods. All provided and required interfaces of the component need to be fully specified (*contract*). Testing is not used except for final statistical quality measurement.

Cloning
Creation of a new object by copying an existing object, sometimes called a prototype (object). Depending on the system, the clone is either initialized to the state of the prototype or initialized to a normal initial state, possibly based on arguments to the clone operation.

Co/contra/invariance under subtyping
The objects of a *subtype* must accept all operations defined over their base type. However, they can refine these operations by weakening *preconditions* (expecting

less) or strengthening *postconditions* (guaranteeing more). In particular, types of input parameters can be widened to supertypes (contravariance), types of output parameters can be narrowed to subtypes (covariance), and types of inout parameters must be left unchanged (invariance). An interesting exception are those parameters that are used to select an operation's implementation. These can be modified covariantly regardless of mode (in, out, or inout). In traditional object-oriented languages, only one such dispatch parameter exists: the receiver object.

Code inheritance
See *Inheritance*.

COM
Microsoft's component object model. A binary standard for the efficient interoperation across *component* boundaries. A COM component can implement several COM classes, each uniquely identified by a class ID (CLSID). Each COM class can implement several *COM interfaces*. A COM interface provides a set of operations and is uniquely identified by an interface ID (IID). A COM object is an instance of a COM class but does not necessarily constitute a single object (*split object*). Clients use COM objects solely via the interfaces provided by that object. Each interface has a QueryInterface operation that can be used to ask for any of the other interfaces of the COM object based on IIDs.

COM interface
A *COM* interface is uniquely identified by an interface ID (IID). Once published, a COM interface is considered *immutable*. New versions of the interface or its specification require allocation of a new IID, effectively forcing the introduction of a new interface. Multiple versions can thus be supported simultaneously. Old versions can be phased out by no longer supporting them in a COM class.

Common Object Request Broker Architecture (CORBA)
See *OMA*.

Component
In the context of this book always a software component. A component is a unit of composition with contractually specified interfaces and explicit context dependencies only. Context dependencies are specified by stating the required *interfaces* and the acceptable execution platform(s). A component can be deployed independently and is subject to composition by third parties. For the purposes of independent deployment, a component needs to be a binary unit. To distinguish between the deployable unit and the instances it supports, a component is defined to have no mutable persistent state. Technically, a component is a set of atomic components, each of which is a module plus resources.

Component framework
A collection of rules and interfaces (*contracts*) that govern the interaction of *components* plugged into the framework. A component framework typically enforces some of the more vital rules of interaction by encapsulating the required interaction mechanisms.

Component instance

A simplifying notion. *Components* as such do not normally have direct *instances*. However, typical components provide a number of instantiable abstractions, such as *classes*. Where a web of instances created by a component forms a conceptual whole, this whole is sometimes called a component instance. For example, a component may provide three classes and every useful interaction with the component is an interaction with a triple of objects, one instance from each of the classes. Such an object triple would then be called a component instance.

Component-oriented programming (COP)

Programming that focuses on the design and implementation of *components*, in particular, on the concepts of encapsulation, polymorphism, late binding and safety. Contrast this with the key concepts underpinning *object-oriented programming*.

Component Pascal

A *hybrid object-oriented programming language* that is particularly suitable for *component-oriented programming*. Component Pascal is *type-safe*, *module-safe*, and provides *automatic memory management*. A bit of (incomplete) history: Component Pascal evolved out of Oberon-2, an object-oriented extension of Oberon. Oberon is the descendant of Modula-2, which itself followed Pascal. Pascal, Modula-2, Oberon, and Oberon-2 were developed at the Swiss Federal Institute of Technology (ETH Zurich). Component Pascal is a development of Oberon microsystems, Zurich. Modula-3 is an independent offspring developed at the DEC System Research Center, Palo Alto. Modula-3 evolved out of Modula-2+ (Olivetti Research), which had its roots in Modula-2. Modula-3 notably influenced the design of Java.

Component system

A composition of *components*, possibly structured into a number of *component frameworks*.

Composite

See *Composition*.

Composition

Assembly of parts (*components*) into a whole (a composite) without modifying the parts. Parts have compositional properties if the semantics of the composite can be derived from those of the components.

Container

In general, an object that contains other objects, in particular a visual object that can contain other visual objects. For example, *ActiveX* controls can be container controls.

Contract

Specification attached to an interface that mutually binds the clients and providers (implementers) of that interface. Contracts can cover functional and non-functional aspects. Functional aspects include the syntax and semantics of an interface. Non-functional aspects relate to quality-of-service guarantees.

Contravariance
See *co/contra/invariance under subtyping*.

Control
See *ActiveX*.

CORBA (Common Object Request Broker Architecture)
See *OMA*.

Covariance
See *co/contra/invariance under subtyping*.

Decomposition
See *Partitioning*.

Deployment
In the context of this book: installation of a *component* into a *component system* without modification of the component. The deployed component is typically acquired from an independent source or developed in house. The component system combines components from independent sources (principle of *independent extensibility*).

Deserialization
See *Externalization*.

Dispatch
Synonym for dynamic binding.

Dispatch interfaces
Special COM interfaces that allow for dynamic binding.

Encapsulation
Enclosure of a part of the state space of a system such that only operations enclosed together with that part can effect state changes on that part. Typical units of encapsulation are *objects*, *classes*, *modules*, and *packages*.

Ethos
An experimental operating system that supported *independent extensibility* on all levels: from device drivers over schedulers, memory management, file systems, to compound document frameworks, applications, and scripts. The conceptual root of the *BlackBox component framework and builder*.

Events
If a part of a system detects a state change that it expects other parts to be interested in, it can raise an event. Events are propagated using descriptors, called messages or event objects. These descriptors travel from the event source to the interested event sinks. The transport mechanism can be direct: sinks register with sources. Alternatively, it can be indirect and events are sent to a distribution service. Either sinks register with such a service or the service uses a multicasting or broadcasting strategy to locate potentially interested sinks.

Externalization

The mapping of an object's identity and state, including references to other objects, to a serial stream. Also called serialization. The inverse mechanism that maps a stream back to webs of objects is called internalization or deserialization. Fundamental problems of externalization and internalization are: support of evolving object implementations without breaking previously externalized files; proper re-establishment of the sharing structure occurring when multiple objects refer to the same third object; protection of an object's encapsulation barrier; partial internalization in the absence of some of the objects' classes (not installed, version clash, and so on).

Factory

An abstraction that creates instances of other abstractions. Examples are factory *methods* and factory *objects*. The *indirection* introduced by factory abstractions allows for late configuration of running systems.

Field

A feature of a *class*.

Fragile base class problem

A problem occurring when a *class* and its subclasses can evolve independently. This is a significant problem when using implementation inheritance across *component* boundaries.

Framework

A partial architecture for a system.

Function

An operation that deterministically returns results solely based on its arguments. A function does not have any effect on state.

Glassbox reuse

See *Blackbox reuse*.

Graybox reuse

See *Blackbox reuse*.

Hardware protection

Isolation of processes or other computing resources using strict hardware protection barriers.

has-a *relation*

Relation between an object and one of its conceptually contained objects. Containment is not normally directly expressible in object-oriented languages. Instead, a regular reference to the contained object is used to represent the containment relation (cf. *is-a relation*).

History

The conceptual trace of states that would be recorded when tracking all state changes effected by a system under observation. Formal specifications can be formulated in terms of permissible histories. For example, algebraic specifications describe all legal state changes given an established legal (well-formed) history. Such specifications therefore precisely describe all legal ways to reach a valid state from a valid initial state.

Hybrid object-oriented programming language

A programming language that supports other programming paradigms besides that of object-oriented programming. Typical hybrid OOPLs add procedural programming. Examples are: C++ and Component Pascal.

Identity

A property of *objects*.

IDL (interface definition language)

Used to define an *interface* according to a certain model (usually an *object* model) in a programming language-neutral form. Two prominent examples are the *OMG* IDL and the *COM* IDL. The OMG IDL is based on a traditional object model, where an object has a single interface that can be composed out of other interfaces using multiple interface *inheritance*. The methods of an OMG IDL-described interface are called operations. OMG IDL also supports a set of primitive (non-object) types, such as basic types and a selection of constructed types, including structures, arrays, and sequences. The COM IDL is based on the COM object model. It does not at all refer to objects or classes, but merely specifies interfaces. A COM object can implement any number of such interfaces. COM IDL supports single interface inheritance as a convenience feature, but in COM there is no semantic relation between an interface and its subinterfaces. In both IDLs, *polymorphism* is achieved by separating implementations from interfaces. In OMG IDL, additional polymorphism is achieved via multiple interface inheritance. In COM IDL, additional polymorphism is achieved via subsets of interface sets implemented by objects.

Indirection

'There is no problem in computer programming that cannot be solved by an added level of indirection' (Maurice Wilkes). The corollary: 'There is no performance problem that cannot be solved by eliminating a level of indirection' (Jim Gray). (As quoted in Orfali *et al.*, 1996.)

Immutability

The property that an item does not change over time.

Immutability of components

See *Component*.

Immutability of interfaces

The concept that an *interface and* its specification must no longer be changed once published.

Implementation

A software fragment that implements the operations defined in an *interface*. The implementation has to satisfy its side of the *contract* serving as the interface's specification.

Implementation inheritance
See *Inheritance*.

Inclusion polymorphism
See *Polymorphism*.

Independent extensibility
A key property of *component systems*. As *components* can be independently developed, acquired and deployed, the system is open and cannot be subjected to global analysis. Proper functioning of the whole must be derivable from the parts. Components need to be analyzed (and tested!) individually against the contracts attached as specifications to the interfaces they provide and the interfaces they require. An extreme approach to developing components is *Cleanroom*.

Inheritance
Incorporation of aspects of one abstraction into another, in particular inheritance of interfaces or implementation or both. Inheritance of interfaces under observation of certain rules (*co/contravariance*) leads to formation of *subtypes*. Typical subclassing involves interface and implementation inheritance.

Instance
Abstractions fall into three categories. They are either state-less, operate on a fixed state, or support multiple instances (copies) of the state space. *Functions* are an example in the first category, abstract data structures one in the second, and abstract data types or *classes* are an example of the third. The instances of classes are called *objects*.

Interface
Abstraction of a service that only defines the operations supported by that service (publicly accessible variables, procedures, or *methods*), but not their *implementation*.

Interface definition language
See *IDL*.

Interface inheritance
See *Inheritance*.

Internalization
See *Externalization*.

Invariant
Formal property expressed over a confined state space and guaranteed to hold at certain static points of a program that can observe (part of) the state space. Important examples are loop, class, and module invariants. A loop invariant is a property over variables modified by a loop that holds on entry into a loop and is either left intact or is re-established by every branch of the loop, and hence also holds on exit from the loop. A class invariant is a property over fields that always holds upon calls to public methods of that class. A module invariant is a property

over (part of) the state space introduced by that module, including global variables and fields of classes nested in that module.

is-a *relation*
See *Substitutability*. Compare with *has-a relation*.

Java
A *pure object-oriented programming language*. Java objects are instances of classes. A class inherits implementation from exactly one superclass; the default is class Object. Every Java class can, in addition, implement any number of interfaces. An interface is equivalent to a fully *abstract class*. Java is *type-safe*. A Java package consists of an open set of class files. As Java packages are open constructs, Java is not inherently *module-safe*. Package-level access protection can be subverted by adding a new class file to an existing package. However, module safety can be enforced by simple checks on configurations: the addition of new class files from untrusted sources to existing packages needs to be prevented.

JavaScript
A scripting language introduced by Netscape and bearing only a superficial resemblance to Java. Untyped and not capable of introducing new objects. Safety is guaranteed by the execution environment (normally an interpreter).

Juice
Technology developed at the University of California at Irvine that supports platform-independent delivery of Oberon components (*Gazelle*).

Late binding
Generally, an approach to defer decisions about the association of parts of a system. Early binding refers to a more static decision; the earliest is at compile time. Late binding refers to decisions after compile time, for example at link time, load time, or runtime. For example, late binding in the context of *method invocations* refers to the dynamic determination of the *method* implementation to be invoked. The implementation is determined based on the *class* to which the *object* that should handle the method invocation belongs. As variables are dynamically bound to objects of different classes (unless the variable has monomorphic type), the method dispatched on a variable cannot normally be statically resolved. Even later binding occurs when a call to a method of computed name is performed.

Live objects
See *OpenDoc*.

Message
Either a synonym for a *method invocation* or for an *event* object.

Meta-programming
The acting of a system on its own representation using *reflection* of its own structure and effecting changes on this structure. For example, meta-programming can be used to dynamically create new *classes*, insert them into an existing *inheritance* graph, and then instantiate them.

Method
A feature of a *class*.

Method dispatch
See *Late binding*.

Modula-2, Modula-3
See *Component Pascal*.

Module
A closed static unit that *encapsulates* embedded abstractions. Such abstractions include *types*, variables, functions, procedures, or *classes*. As a module is a closed unit, its encapsulated domain is fixed and can be fully analyzed. In a *module-safe* approach, such modules can be used to establish strong invariants that cannot be invalidated by other modules in the same system. Compare with *package*.

Module-safe
A module-safe programming language enables the programming of *modules* that can establish module *invariants* irrespective of other modules in the system. To be module-safe, a language needs to strictly enforce memory invariants and enable modules to erect static access protection barriers that limit access from external modules to certain parts of the module.

Monomorphic
Opposite of *polymorphic*. The property that a view on entities in a given context always refers to the same kind of entities. For example, a monomorphic variable can only be bound to *objects* of exactly the variable's type, but not to objects of a *subtype*.

Multiple subtyping
A term coined after *multiple inheritance*, but somewhat misnaming the important property. Creation of multiple subtypes of a type is the normal case. However, multiple subtyping is about types that can have multiple supertypes. On the basis of the definition of types as sets of values, multiple supertypes are easily explained as multiple supersets that all fully include the set defined by the common subtype.

Oberon, Oberon-2
See *Component Pascal*.

Object
An entity that combines state (*fields*) and behavior (*methods*) and has a unique identity, that is can be consistently distinguished from all other objects of overlapping lifetime and access domain, irrespective of changes to its or other objects' state.

Object linking and embedding
See *OLE*.

Object management architecture
See *OMA*.

Object modeling technique
See *OMT*.

Object Management Group
See *OMG*.

Object-oriented programming (OOP)
Programming that focuses on the design and implementation of *objects*. In particular, OOP builds on the concepts of encapsulation, polymorphism, and implementation inheritance. Contrast this with the key concepts underpinning *component-oriented programming*.

Object server
A process that executes the *component* implementing an *object*.

OCX
See *ActiveX*.

OLE
Microsoft collection of *COM* interfaces supporting compound documents. (Originally, OLE stood for object linking and embedding, but today it is used as a word rather than as an acronym.)

OLE custom extension
See *ActiveX*.

OMA
The object management architecture organizes the wide spectrum of standards that the *OMG* is working on. The heart of the OMA is CORBA, the common object request broker architecture. First and foremost, CORBA covers the specification of the interfaces of object request brokers (ORBs). An ORB accepts requests for method invocations and relays them to the addressed object, bridging platform and language gaps. An ORB also provides interface and implementation repositories that make the system fully self-describing (*reflection*). CORBA also covers the binding of programming languages to ORB-understood interfaces. Such interfaces are described in a standardized interface definition language (*IDL*). Today, bindings for Ada, C, COBOL, C++, and Smalltalk exist. A binding for *Java* is about to be finalized (although still based on Java 1.0.2). Further OMA standards are grouped into two areas: general object services (CORBAservices) and general horizontal and vertical (domain-specific) facilities (CORBAfacilities). Important general services include transaction and naming services. An example of a horizontal facility is compound document handling – the current OMA standard for this is *OpenDoc*. Domain specific standards are under preparation in many areas – banking is an example.

OMG
The Object Management Group is a large international standardization body working on a wide range of standards based on the object management architecture (*OMA*). Today, the OMG has around 700 member companies.

OMG IDL

The *IDL* used by the *OMG* specifications.

OMT

Object modeling technique, a popular technique to describe object designs graphically . Superseded by *UML*.

OpenDoc

A *compound document* architecture, originally developed by Apple and IBM, but recently dropped as a commercial product and released into the public domain. OpenDoc is a standard of the *OMG*, part of the *OMA*. OpenDoc document parts were called Live Objects.

Operation

General: collective name for *functions*, *procedures*, and *methods*. Particular use as a synonym for method, for example in *OMG IDL* terminology.

Package

A package is either closed, that is a *module* (for example Ada), or open (for example *Java*). An open package can be joined by new abstractions and implementation fragments at any time. Open packages themselves cannot establish strong invariants based on package encapsulation, as by definition new parts can join the package at any time. A package needs to be closed before it can be fully analyzed to verify that a given invariant holds. Statically closing a package creates a module. Dynamically closing a package can be used to erect protection barriers in a system with partially open access, for example a Web browser combining locally installed Java packages and remotely downloaded packages.

Parametric polymorphism

See *Polymorphism*.

Partitioning

Splitting a system into non-overlapping parts, such that the sum of the parts covers the whole system. In conjunction with *components*, the term decomposition of a composite is also used.

Pattern

A structure that occurs repeatedly in similar form. The pattern description captures the similarity and its typical variations (pattern applications). A prominent example is program design patterns.

Persistence

An object is said to have persistent state if that state survives the particular instantiation of the object. The object itself is said to be persistent if it survives the context in which it was created without losing its identity. Identity preservation requires preservation of references between persistent objects.

Polymorphism

The ability to view different kinds of entities through a common projection. For example, various objects of different classes may be compatible with a certain variable type. Then this variable is polymorphically typed, as its bindings can be of varying most specific type. Another example is a polymorphic operation: an operation that has parameters of polymorphic type. Two main forms of polymorphism are parametric and inclusion polymorphism. Parametric polymorphism assigns a fixed monomorphic type to any instance of a variable but allows for different type assignments from one instance to the next. Parametric polymorphism is particularly useful to assign the same type to instances of multiple variables, ensuring mutual compatibility of these variables. Inclusion polymorphism (also called *subtyping*) allows a polymorphic variable of a certain type to be bound to objects of any subtype of the variable's type.

Postcondition
A formal condition that is expected to hold just after completion of an *operation*.

Precondition
A formal condition that is expected to hold just before execution of an *operation*.

Procedure
A self-standing operation that can have effects, that is modify *state*. Compare with *function* and *method*.

Prototype object
See *Cloning*.

Quality of service
The non-functional aspects guaranteed under a *contract*. Examples are guaranteed levels of performance, reliability, or security.

Release-to-release binary compatibility
See *syntactic fragile base class problem*.

Resources of a component
As *components* are units of deployment, they have to come with all resources that are not listed as context dependencies. Such resources may include images or other frozen media used by the component for presentation and user interface purposes. Mutable resources are not included, as they are conceptually associated with concrete instances supported by a component. Thus, a database is not part of a database component but part of the state maintained by a database object supported by the database component. (A typical database component would contain implementations, classes, for many other objects.) This separation of mutable from immutable persistent state eliminates the management problems resulting from a proliferation of components' versions.

Safe language
A programming language is called safe if the artifacts produced using that language achieve certain *safety* levels, provided the language implementation and runtime system are correct. Safety levels include *memory safety*, *type safety*, and *module safety*. For example, Smalltalk is memory safe, Sather is also type safe, and Component Pascal is in addition module safe.

Safety
The property of a system to prevent certain failures either by statically eliminating classes of errors or by dynamically detecting errors and handling them to avoid failures.

Safety of a component system
Components are either strictly separated from each other, for example using *hardware protection*, or need to be individually safe. The principle of *independent extensibility* of component systems excludes global analysis as a means to verify that the composite is safe, while each of the components would have the potential to be unsafe.

Sandboxing
Exclusion of unwanted side-effects caused by the execution of a component's implementation. Such side-effects can occur if a component has been constructed using a language supporting unsafe access to a low-level memory model. Accidental or malicious interference with memory allocated to a different component endangers the integrity of a component system. Software sandboxing uses conservative checking of code at compile time, link time, load time, or runtime. To facilitate the last-mentioned, code may need to be interpreted or rewritten at load time to incorporate checks. Alternatives to sandboxing are *hardware protection* or the use of *type-safe* and *module-safe* languages.

Script
A program fragment that on its own does not introduce any abstractions based on persistent state (cf. *script component*).

Script component
A script component is a degenerated component that merely packages *scripts*.

Semantic fragile base class problem
The subproblem of the general *fragile base class problem* that covers the aspects of semantic incompatibility between different releases.

Serialization
See *Externalization*.

Server
See *Object server*.

SOM
IBM's system object model. Evolved out of the OS/2 Workplace Shell into a *CORBA*-compliant *object request broker*. Has currently unique support for *metaprogramming*. Establishes release-to-release binary compatibility by maintaining a release order: features are added to classes in a way that preserves offsets and indices assigned to features already present in earlier releases. Clients continue to be able to access such features, even if compiled against an old release, but then (dynamically) linked against a new release. Thus, SOM solves the *syntactic fragile base class problem*.

State
The binding of values to mutable variables at any given point in time.

Static method
See *Procedure*.

Subclassing
See *Inheritance*.

Substitutability
The property that one object can be substituted for another, normally of different type, without breaking the clients of that other object. An object can thus be substituted for another if it respects the *contract* between that other object and its clients. The relation between an object and another that it can be substituted for is called *is-a relation*.

Subtyping
Formation of subtypes of a *type*. As a type is a set of objects and a subtype is a subset of such a set, subtyping can only reduce (narrow) the set of objects. In particular, all operations valid on any object of a certain type are also valid on objects of a subtype. Subtyping is therefore also called interface inheritance. Subtyping is fundamental to inclusion polymorphism: the ability to refer to a family of types by statically referring only to the supertype of this family while dynamically retaining the precise types. In strongly typed languages, variables are for their lifetime of a certain type. With subtyping, such variables can actually refer to objects of subtypes of the variable's type *and* this fact can be discovered dynamically.

Subtyping and type matching
Type matching is a relation between types that is similar to but different from subtyping. Type matching effectively distinguishes between monomorphic contexts – when a typed variable can only refer to objects of exactly that type – and polymorphic contexts –when a variable can also refer to objects of subtypes. In monomorphic contexts, the strict co/contravariance requirements of subtyping can be relaxed. For example, if the exact type of two objects is statically know, it is safe to invoke an operation that works for two objects of this type, but not for two objects of (possibly different) subtypes.

Syntactic fragile base class problem
The subproblem of the general *fragile base class problem* that covers the aspects of binary release-to-release compatibility. For example, if method indices for the same methods are not preserved across releases, then clients compiled on the basis of such indices will break.

Trace
See *History*.

Type

A type is a set of objects. Subsets of values are characterized by *subtypes* and supersets by supertypes. Operations are said to have a signature that specifies the types of values they operate on. For example, a method specifies as part of its signature the type of the receiver (the object the method is dispatched on), the type of all parameters, the return type (if present), and the types of declared (checked) exceptions (if present). The type of an object may require the object to support a certain set of *methods* or *fields*.

Type matching

See *Subtyping*.

Type-safe

Property of a language that operations defined over certain types can only be applied to values of these or compatible types. A language is said to be strongly typed if all operations and their arguments are type-safe. It is statically typed if type-safety is fully established at compile-time. It is dynamically typed if type-safety is established on the basis of runtime checks. Modern object-oriented languages combine aspects of static and dynamic type safety. For example, invoking an operation of computed name and arguments on an arbitrary object is a powerful operation, but it cannot be statically type-checked.

UML

Universal modeling language, merger and refinement of several popular object design notations, including the *OMT*.

Units of <property>

In this book, software fragments are categorized on the basis of properties that hold for an entire fragment. Important properties include those that support: separate development, separate static analysis, separate compilability, separate delivery and deployment, and so on. A fragment that satisfies such requirements is called a unit of analysis, a unit of compilation, and so on. See Chapter 8 for a detailed discussion. *Components* are at least units of independent deployment.

Universal modeling language

See *UML*.

Whitebox reuse

See *Blackbox reuse*.

VBX

See *ActiveX*.

Visual Basic extension

See *ActiveX*.

Index